PEEP SHOWS

CULT FILM AND THE CINE-EROTIC

EDITED BY XAVIER MENDIK

WALLFLOWER PRESS
LONDON & NEW YORK

A Wallflower Press Book
Published by
Columbia University Press
Publishers Since 1893
New York · Chichester, West Sussex
cup.columbia.edu

A complete CIP record is available from the Library of Congress

ISBN 978-1-906660-35-2 (pbk. : alk. paper)
ISBN 978-0-231-50289-4 (e-book)

Design by Elsa Mathern

Columbia University Press books are printed on permanent
and durable acid-free paper.
This book is printed on paper with recycled content.
Printed in the United States of America

p 10 9 8 7 6 5 4 3 2 1

CONTENTS

ACKNOWLEDGEMENTS

The editor would like to thank all of the writers who contributed so much hard work to this volume. I would also like to offer sincere my thanks to Veronica Hart for contributing the foreword. Thanks also to Erin Brown, Mike Esterman, Christian Hallman, Christina Lindberg, Buck Naked, Magnus Paulsson and Michael L. Raso for their support and assistance with compiling the interview materials used in this book. I would also like to thank Christian Hallman, Stefan Nylén and Magnus Paulsson for allowing us to reproduce some of the exclusive interview material contained in the documentary *Desperately Seeking Seka* for the chapter on the actress. In addition, I would also like to thank Seka herself for providing further visual materials to illustrate that section of the volume.

Additionally, I would like to thank Eve Bennett for all her invaluable editorial and proof-reading assistance in the initial stages of preparing the volume. Further thanks go to Professor Julian Petley for his assistance with the completion of this book. On a personal level I would like to offer my sincere thanks to my friend and colleague Ernest Mathijs who was not able to co-edit this project with me as initially planned but who continued to guide and support its completion with integrity and commitment. Finally, I offer my sincere thanks and gratitude to Yoram Allon and all the staff at Wallflower Press for their patience and support for *Peep Shows* and the *AlterImage* series as a whole.

An earlier version of Jacob Smith's article 'Sound and Performance in Stephen Sayadian's *Night Dreams* and *Café Flesh*' appeared in *Velvet Light Trap* (vol. 59, 2007), and is reproduced here courtesy of University of Texas Press. Emily Shelton's article 'A Star is Porn: Corpulence, Comedy, and the Homosocial Cult of Adult Film Star Ron Jeremy' first appeared in *Camera Obscura* (vol. 17, no. 3; 2002) and is reproduced here courtesy of Duke University Press. An earlier version of Ian Hunter's chapter 'A Clockwork Orgy: A User's Guide' was published in Elizabeth Wells and Tamar Jeffers McDonald (eds) *Realities and Remediations: The Limits of Representation* (Newcastle upon Tyne: Cambridge Scholars Publishing, 2007).

The images used in the chapter 'Sound and Performance in Stephen Sayadian's *Nights Dreams* and *Café Flesh*' were sourced with the assistance of the director. The images of the actress used in the chapter 'Blonde Fire: An Interview with Seka' are courtesy of the actress, and are sourced from the website www.seka.com. I would like to thank Seka for her assistance in allowing us to reproduce these images here. The images used in the chapter 'That's L'Amorte: Joe D'Amato and the Sadean Art of Love' were provided by Fab Press, and I would like to thank Harvey Fenton for his assistance in sourcing these images for use in this volume. The images used in the chapters 'When Spiderman Became Spiderbabe: Appropriation and the Political Economy of the "Soft-Core Spoof" Genre' and 'The Erotic Adventures of Misty Mundae' are courtesy of Michael L. Raso and Seduction Cinema. The images used in the chapter '"I Guess They Got Past Their Fear of Porn": Women Viewing Porn Films' are from the film *Anna's Mates*, produced and directed by Anna Span, and included courtesy of Easy on the Eye Productions. The images used in the chapter '"If You Ache Beneath Your Intestines or Scream Silently in the Cavities of Your Chest, Then This Picture is For You": Curt McDowell's *Thundercrack!* are courtesy of Melinda McDowell, and I would like to thank her for allowing us to reproduce these exclusive on-set images from the making of the film. The images used in the chapter '"Let's Do Something You Won't Enjoy": Dominatrix Porn, Performance and Subjectivity' are courtesy of Dom Productions, and I would like to thank Derek Bartle for allowing us to reproduce them here. The images used in the chapter 'Neo-Liberal Avant-Garde Sexploitation in Japan: The Interplay of Collaboration and Revolution in the Pink Film' are courtesy of the author's personal collection. The images of *Thriller* (aka *They Call Her One Eye*) used in the chapter 'Flesh (Fur) and Fury: An Interview with Christina Lindberg' are courtesy of Synapse Films and I would like to thank Don May Jr for allowing us to reproduce them in this volume. Additional publicity photographs of Christina Lindberg were provided by the actress herself, for which we offer our grateful thanks. The images used in the chapter 'Semblance and the Sexual Revolution: A Critical Review of Viva' are courtesy of Nouveaux Pictures-*Cine-Excess*.

The rest of the images contained in the book are the property of the production and distribution companies concerned. They are reproduced here in the spirit of publicity and the promotion of the films in question.

This volume is dedicated with much love to Zena and Caroline.

NOTES ON CONTRIBUTORS

ELERI BUTLER is a sociologist, has an MA in Cult Film and TV, and has also produced and worked on a number of short films, including the documentaries *Fear at 400 Degrees: The Cine-Excess of Suspiria* (2010) and *The Long Road Back From Hell: Reclaiming Cannibal Holocaust* (2011). Eleri has worked professionally for several years in the prevention of violence against women, and is currently Chief Executive of a charity that supports women survivors of domestic violence and women offenders. She is also a Trustee of the UK charity Against Violence and Abuse, which supports services to improve their response to women, children and men who experience or perpetrate different forms of violence against women and girls.

JENNY BARRETT is the Programme Leader in Film Studies at Edge Hill University. She has published various work on the dominatrix and BDSM and how they are represented in popular culture. Her other research interests include American Civil War films (she is the author of *Shooting the Civil War: Cinema, History and American National Identity*, I. B. Tauris, 2009), and representations of ethnicity in the western.

CHRISTIAN HALLMAN is a writer/producer/director working through his production company Grindhouse Pictures in Sweden. Among his work is *Desperately Seeking Seka* (feature documentary) and *Cravings*, *The White Gold* and *Jann of Sweden* (all short fiction). He also works as a freelance production manager, and worked on the development of the Swedish vampire film *Frostbiten*, produced by Solid Entertainment. Christian is also member of the board and co-ordinator of the European Fantastic Film Festivals Federation and its website melies.org, the largest network of genre film festivals in the world, as well as programme co-director of Lund International Fantastic Film Festival.

KEVIN HEFFERNAN teaches media culture and history in the Division of Film and Media Arts at Southern Methodist University. *Divine Trash*, a documentary on the early career of John Waters on which Heffernan served as associate producer and co-screenwriter, won the Filmmakers' Trophy in Documentary at the 1998 Sundance Film Festival. He is the author of *Ghouls, Gimmicks and Gold: Horror Films and the American Movie Business, 1952–1968* (Duke University Press, 2004) and co-author, with Frances Milstead and Steve Yeager, of *My Son Divine* (Alyson Publications, 2001). His essays on the horror film, Asian cinema, queer filmmakers, sexploitation, and porn can be found in a number of journals and critical anthologies.

CLAIRE HINES is Senior Lecturer in Film and Television Studies at Southampton Solent University, UK. Her research and publications focus on sexuality, gender, fantasy and 007. She is the co-author of *Fantasy* (Routledge, 2011) and the co-editor, with Darren Kerr, of *Hard to Swallow: Hard-core Pornography on Screen* (Wallflower Press, 2012). She is currently writing a book that explores the relationship between James Bond and *Playboy*.

I. Q. HUNTER is Reader in Film Studies at De Montfort University, Leicester. He has published widely on cult and trash cinema, including *British Trash Cinema* (BFI/Palgrave, 2013).

BETH JOHNSON is Lecturer in Television and Film Studies at Keele University, UK. She is the author of various publications in journals such as *Angelaki* and the *Journal of Cultural Research* as well as various contributions to edited anthologies. She is also the co-editor, with James Aston and Basil Glynn, of *Television, Sex and Society: Analyzing Contemporary Representations* (Continuum Press, 2012).

XAVIER MENDIK is Director of the *Cine-Excess* International Film Festival and DVD label, and has written extensively on European and American cult and exploitation cinema traditions. Some of his books (as author, editor and co-editor) include *100 Cult Movies* (Palgrave BFI, 2011), *The Cult Film Reader* (Open University Press, 2008), *Alternative Europe: Eurotrash and Exploitation Cinema Since 1945* (Wallflower Press, 2004), *Underground USA: Filmmaking Beyond the Hollywood Canon* (Wallflower Press, 2002), *Shocking Cinema of the Seventies* (Noir Publishing, 2002), *Dario Argento's Tenebrae* (Flicks Books, 2000) and *Unruly Pleasures: The Cult Film and its Critics* (FAB Press, 2000).

GARY NEEDHAM is Senior Lecturer in Film and Television Studies at Nottingham Trent University. He is the author of *Brokeback Mountain* (Edinburgh University Press, 2010), co-editor, with Dimitris Eleftheriotis, of *Asian Cinemas: A Reader and Guide* (Edinburgh University Press, 2006) and, with Glyn Davis, *Queer TV: Histories, Theories, Politics* (Routledge, 2009).

STEFAN NYLÉN has been working as a film critic for Sweden's most prominent men's lifestyle magazines, *Café*, since the mid-1990s. He is currently working as an editor of Sweden's major movie magazine, *Cinema*, which he's been doing for several years. His main research interests are in the realms of exploitation, sexploitation, women in prison, bad action and biker films. Stefan has written profiles and appreciations on leading European female sexploitation starlets including Essy Persson, Christina Lindberg, Harriet Andersson, as well as on American porn performers including Jane Hamilton, Seka and Nina Hartley.

BILL OSGERBY is Professor of Media, Culture and Communications at London Metropolitan University. His research focuses on twentieth century British and American cultural history, and his books include *Youth in Britain Since 1945* (Blackwell, 1998), *Playboys in Paradise:*

Youth, Masculinity and Leisure-Style in Modern America (Berg/New York University Press, 2001), *Youth Media* (Routledge, 2004), and a co-edited anthology, with Anna Gough Yates, *Action TV: Tough-Guys, Smooth Operators and Foxy Chicks* (Routledge, 2001).

MAGNUS PAULSSON is a film producer at Solid Entertainment in Sweden. He is also the founder of Fantastisk Filmfestival FFF – Scandinavia's only film festival dedicated to horror, sci-fi and fantasy.

JULIAN PETLEY is Professor of Screen Media in the School of Arts, Brunel University, Chair of the Campaign for Press and Broadcasting Freedom, and a member of the board of Index on Censorship. Julian's recent books include *Censorship: A Beginner's Guide* (Oneworld 2009) and *Film and Video Censorship in Contemporary Britain* (Edinburgh University Press, 2011).

MARCELLE PERKS is a British author and journalist presently living in Germany. She has specialised in writing sexually-themed guide books and the analysis of gender in horror cinema, but also writes short stories. She is the author of *Secrets of Porn Star Sex* (Infinite Ideas, 2007), and has contributed to a wide variety of books and journals that deal with issues of horror, erotica and the fantastic, as well as writing extensively about horror films in *Fangoria*, *Shivers*, *Redeemer*, *Flesh and Blood*, *Eyeball* and *Videoworld* magazines.

SIMONE PYNE is a Film and Event Programmer. After graduating from the University of East Anglia with a BA in Film Studies and MA in Film and Film Archiving, Simone worked as an archive film researcher for Associated Press as well as on numerous freelance projects including an award-winning documentary on the artist Grayson Perry for Channel 4. She currently works for The Hospital Club, programming films and events, but has also worked for Curzon Cinemas and the BFI London Film Festival. She has presented academic papers on early colour film processes in the US and UK and visited as guest-lecturer at Brunel University. As well as being one of four producers of The Smoking Cabinet, she has also been a programmer of guest programmes for several festivals including The London Lesbian & Gay Film Festival, and is also a judge for Rushes Soho Shorts Film Festival, amongst others.

EMILY SHELTON graduated from Amherst College and received her Ph.D. in English from the University of Chicago, where she was a Whiting Fellow. Her work has appeared in *Camera Obscura*, *Chicago Review*, *Quarterly West*, *La Petite Zine* and *Another Chicago Magazine*, among other journals. Emily teaches in the College Writing Program at Harvard University, and is at work on a novel based on the West Memphis Three case.

CLARISSA SMITH is Reader in Sexual Cultures at the University of Sunderland, UK. Her research is in the areas of sexuality in contemporary culture; representations of sex and sexuality; identities and the body; pornographies, their production, consumption and regulation; taboo/

controversial media. Her publications include *One for the Girls!: The Pleasures and Practices of Women's Porn* (Intellect, 2007) and the co-editor, with Feona Attwood, of a *Sex Education* special issue on Sexualisation and Young People (2011).

IAIN ROBERT SMITH is Lecturer in Film Studies at the University of Roehampton, London. He is the author of *The Hollywood Meme: Global Adaptations of American Film and Television* (Edinburgh University Press, 2013) and editor of *Cultural Borrowings: Appropriation, Reworking, Transformation* (*Scope: An Online Journal of Film and TV Studies*, 2009). He has published articles in a range of international journals including *Velvet Light Trap* and he is currently a co-investigator on the AHRC-funded research network 'Media Across Borders'.

JACOB SMITH is Assistant Professor in the Radio-Television-Film Department at Northwestern University. In addition to writing the books *Vocal Tracks: Performance and Sound Media* (University of California Press, 2008), *Spoken Word: Postwar American Phonograph Cultures* (University of California Press, 2011) and *The Thrill Makers: Celebrity, Masculinity and Stunt Performance* (University of California Press, 2012), he has published articles on media history, sound and performance.

ALEXANDER ZAHLTEN is Assistant Professor in the Department of East Asian Languages and Civilizations, Harvard University. His research on film and audiovisual culture in East Asia and especially Japan from the 1960s onward focuses on the connection between larger economic, social and institutional structures and aesthetic modalities. Recent publications have examined the role of postcolonial fantasy in Korean 'remakes' of Japanese films, the question of categories in a media mix environment, and the history of German sexploitation cinema. Alex has also curated film programmes for institutions such as the German Film Museum and the Athenee Francais Cultural Center, Tokyo, and was Program Director for the Nippon Connection Film Festival from 2002 to 2010.

FOREWORD

PLEASURE, RESPONSIBILITY AND REFLECTION...

Veronica Hart

Peep Shows is a very interesting and diverse book that considers erotic movies at two levels. I at once see it as a fan book, as it has some wonderful new interviews with some of the women and men who were acting in the movies or making them. I also see it as a collection of intellectual dissertations on the nature of pornographic films and what their sociological and cultural implications are. So it's a book that basically mimics the same conversations I have been having with myself for over thirty years.

When you're acting and performing either in films or on stage, you have a completely different feeling about the material. Every time I walk into a strip joint, the thought goes through my mind, 'How can these girls do that? They are so comfortable placing themselves on display.' But of course, I was a stripper for years and I never thought twice about it. It was just performing, putting on a show. I think the same kinds of things when I'm on a hard-core movie set. 'How can the performers do that? How can they be so comfortable running around naked and performing in front of everyone?' Yet I performed hard-core for several years and of course I'm still acting when I get the chance. For some reason, it's always different when you're doing it, rather than reviewing it.

I know that a lot of the performers, myself included, needed to make movies in order to stay alive, to pay the rent and eat. It's very difficult to turn down roles because of the way they might portray women. I was always aware of that though, and how the movies I made could affect the way women were thought of or how they might be treated has been a subject of concern for me as both an actress and a director.

Take the subject of rape for example. The first movie I was ever in had a scene where Eric Edwards came in through the window and had me. I really didn't think anything about it. I was excited. It was my first paid acting gig – other than being an extra, a dancer or as a model. I was definitely not in any danger. I was only acting – the sex was real enough but I wasn't scared at all. But as I got to be in more and more movies, I thought more of how the audience would be affected. I had huge discussions with Lasse Braun before we made *American Desire* (1981). I didn't want to be portrayed as a woman who enjoyed being raped. Yet when I asked some women at the time what they thought of the movie, they saw it as very exciting.

It's a very strange paradox. Rape is an incredibly common female fantasy. You're being forced into sex. You're not a bad girl asking for it. It's been forced upon you, the decision to have sex has been removed from you, so if you enjoy it and orgasm, it's not your fault. You're still a good girl. But how do you portray that without getting the erroneous message across that all women secretly desire to be raped? Because women don't. We really don't. That's why it's called a fantasy.

When the Internet seemed to be the wild, wild, west and when a few people started doing things the majority of the adult business had agreed not to do – things like coerced and violent sex and then spoke of the women who were acting in these films as degenerate and psychotic bitches, I got a little upset. I got up on my very high horse and started publicly calling down some of these filmmakers. But what I in effect was doing was trying to impose my own censorship. A very slippery slope for an ex-porn-star/pornographer herself! Of course some people thought the adult material I was making was every bit as despicable as the adult material that I deplored. It finally dawned on me that I could be a pornographer and not be responsible for all of pornography.

So how do you represent that rape fantasy or forced sex without promoting rape? In *Edgeplay* (2001), when I was directing Marilyn Chambers in one of her comeback films, I made sure that women could always opt out of the scene that had been presented to them. If they didn't want it, they could refuse it. But if they did want it, then they could enjoy it and they could stop at anytime with a safe word. In *Taken* (2005), it appeared as though my heroine (Ginger Lynn) got kidnapped and ultimately fell for her kidnapper (Evan Stone) who just happened to be handsome, wealthy and very in love with her. You find out at the end of the movie that she'd actually fallen asleep and was dreaming – having her secret wishes fulfilled – to be loved and adored and paid attention to; things she definitely was not getting from her husband.

There's a story I'd like to relate about an actress who I particularly liked and had hired in some of my movies. She chose to do some very rough movies where it appeared she was being treated terribly. I asked her how she could do that. She said all the guys and her were joking around before they started filming. Then when they started, slapping her and spitting on her – when there was a cut in the action, the guys would say they hoped she was alright, they made sure she wasn't really hurt. She chose to do the scene to see if she could and to feel the intensity. She told me she had been much more abused by a director that was hired by the same person who hired me. That long hours of shooting with no consideration, no proper food and no respect given to her was a much more horrible experience. But the first movie showed brutal treatment of women and the second one did not.

When I started working for other people, one of the directors I was producing for was one of the kindest, most loving and talented men, who just liked very rough sex. He was working for a company that also wanted fairly extreme movies. Ultimately I had to stop working for him, even though he had the most fun, relaxed sets and was a favorite person of mine, because of the content of the films we were making.

There have been other directors who make beautiful movies where the sex is lovely and the women are glorified, but I've stopped working for them, because I didn't like the way they treated the crew or the talent.

As I got older I was able to understand a lot more about very intense, extreme sex. A summer relationship with an S/M master showed me how it could be very addictive. If someone is grabbing you, is taking you right on the spot and happens to have an incredible erection, it's very flattering. There's no question of 'Am I turning this person on?' Because of the intensity, it makes you feel desired and very alive. So although I'm much more at ease in beautiful depictions of sex, I understand raw passion which sometimes can leave you a little bruised and sore and to the observer might appear to be abuse! Not good as a steady diet, at least for me, but a very interesting experience.

I've spent most of my life trying to make sense of all this. How misogynists can make gorgeous movies; how beautiful people can either be in, or make, violent or tasteless movies! While reading this book, I'm sure you'll be surprised by the interviews with the actresses and enlightened and educated as to the place of these movies in our society. Believe me, most of us never thought that the fun, sexy and rebellious movies we were making would one day be studied and commented on as part of cinematic history! Please keep in mind that not all appears as it really is. After all, it's only the movies…

Veronica Hart, Director
June 2012

INTRODUCTION
PERVASIVE PEEPING:
NEW WAYS TO SURVEY THE CINE-EROTIC

Xavier Mendik

> Where once it seemed necessary to argue vehemently against pro-censorship, anti-pornography feminism for the value and importance of studying pornography … today porn studies addresses a veritable explosion of sexually explicit materials that cry out for a better understanding. Feminist debates about whether pornography should exist at all have paled before the simple fact that still and moving image pornographies have become fully recognizable fixtures of popular culture.[1]

As Linda Williams' opening quotation indicates, recent years have witnessed an explosion of critical interest in the pervasive influences of the erotic image. From mediations on the structure of explicit narratives and star-studies of prominent porn performers, to discussions of national traditions of titillation and their links to new technology, the study of the 'cine-erotic' has emerged as one of the most significant and subversive aspects of film and cultural studies in recent years. Given *AlterImage*'s aim to explore trends and traditions of cult and underground cinema, it seems more than appropriate that the third edition of this series focuses on representations of sexuality in these often marginal texts. Therefore, the contributions to this volume use the term cine-erotic (rather than just pornography) to refer to the extent to which taboo sexual imagery is often rearticulated by a wide range of cult cycles that transcend soft and hard-core pornographic divisions. The cine-erotic ranges from 1950s American burlesque dramas and 1960s 'sin as social problem' exposes, to the explosion of 1970s full-length explicit epics and their replacement by a plethora of contemporary direct to video genres and cycles, which often parody and reflect current trends in mainstream film and TV production. As Williams herself has noted:

> Hollywood makes approximately 400 films a year, while the porn industry now makes from 10,000 to 11,000. Seven hundred million porn videos are rented each year... Pornography revenues – which can broadly be construed to include magazines, internet websites, magazines, cable, in-room hotel movies, and sex toys – total between 10 and 14 billion dollars annually. This figure, as *New York Times* critic Frank Rich has noted, is not only bigger than movie revenues; it is bigger than professional football, basketball, and baseball put together.[2]

As the data from the author's account indicates, the proliferation of these differing formats of cine-erotic activity points to a plurality of genres, trends and national traditions, all with very differing and complex modes of audience appeal. Alongside these new cycles of the sexually explicit have come revised accounts of how to comprehend the carnal (and controversial) image.

Although the study of both soft-core erotica (which integrates sexual relations into a wider narrative frame) and hard-core pornography (in which explicit sexual relations *are* the narrative) have circulated in academic discourses of cinema since the mid-1970s, these debates have often been framed via wider feminist and gender-based accounts around ideology, 'harm' and regressive representation (as Williams' opening commentary would attest). Whilst the cine-erotic has traditionally been defined through official and governmental attempts to censure and control, the late 1970s and early 1980s saw the publication of a number of landmark studies that situated the subject of the sexually explicit through wider discourses of gender difference. Most notably, classic accounts such as Andrea Dworkin's *Pornography: Men Possessing Women*[3] and Susan Griffin's *Pornography and Silence*[4] forcibly made the connection between the male-centered production of pornography and wider ideological repressions being enacted against women during this era. It was this powerful and politicised perception of pornography that led critics such as Dworkin to define pornographers in the following terms:

> Most of them are small-time pimps or big time pimps. They sell women; the real flesh and blood women in the pictures. They like the excitement of domination; they are greedy for profit; they are sadistic in their exploitation of women; they hate women and the pornography they make is a distillation of that hate'[5]

Adding to these discourses of discontent, connections between the treatment of women engaged in pornography and wider regimes of gender exploitation were seemingly and sensationally confirmed by volumes such as *Ordeal* (1980), in which Linda Lovelace (aka Linda Marchiano) famously rejected her iconic sex star status to reveal a catalogue of abuse she endured at the hands of former husband/manager Chuck Traynor.[6] It was such jaded porn-star biographies which seemed to indicate the link between the creators of erotica and wider systems of oppression. As Dianna E. H. Russell concluded, despite its appearance as a feel-good porn narrative, the Lovelace vehicle *Deep Throat* (Gerard Damiano, 1972) could actually be viewed 'as a documentary of rape from beginning to end'.[7]

While such accounts sought to uncover the abusive link between carnal creators and their ideological systems of sexual representation, it was presumed that the characteristically male consumer similarly functioned as an off-screen designate of abuse and oppression. As Catherine MacKinnon famously commented 'Pornography is masturbation material. It is used for sex. It is therefore sex. Men know this… With pornography, men masturbate to women being exposed, humiliated, violated, degraded, mutilated, dismembered, bound, gagged, tortured and killed. In the visual materials, they experience this *being done* by watching it *being done*.'[8]

Whilst acknowledging that any cinema of sex could not easily be divorced from the wider principles of power and distinction which underpinned them, it was the 1989 publication of Linda Williams' landmark volume *Hard Core: Power, Pleasure and the 'Frenzy of the Visible'* which began to revise existing accounts of the sexually explicit, focusing on the narrative structures, gender configurations and presumed modes of audience appeal within a range of cinematic case-studies. By considering a variety of 1970s and 1980s hard-core porn productions, Williams noted that the explicit image often conveyed narrative tendencies which operated in subversive opposition to the modes of identification and control frequently displayed by mainstream film. These narrative and thematic particularities offer up the potential for a more utopian reading of gender and sexuality in the case-studies that the author considers. Williams does concede that 'attentive viewers who have read the Lovelace-Marchiano story can look for the bruises on her body – bruises that become evidence of that off-camera coercion'.[9] However, what is significant about the *Hard Core* account is that it moves beyond presumed biography (and the problematic modes of interpretation this often entails), to consider the proliferation of pleasure(s) and power dynamics at play in erotic material, which often function to privilege the depicted female (rather than male) protagonist. For instance, as well as considering Damiano's controversial classic, the author also assesses other noted works such as the Mitchell Bros.' 1972 hit *Behind the Green Door*. Although the film (which features a heroine abducted to perform group sex acts at an avant-garde swingers club), would appear to fit existing models linking the pornographic image to depictions of female suffering, Williams explores the often complex construction of female desire within the narrative, which exceeds any simple equation between womanhood and victimisation. Equally, Williams also notes that films such as *Behind the Green Door* often function to favour the sexually endowed heroines over the phallically challenged males that appear to populate these works.

Since the publication of Williams' volume, a number of recent significant studies have expanded the range and scope of the cine-erotic to consider a wide variety of topics that convey dual cult and erotic appeal. From studies exploring potential female spaces of subjectivity in lesbian erotic dramas[10] and queer readings of the male body in direct to video erotica,[11] to depictions of the white body in hard-core imagery[12] and cross-cultural representations of subversive sex practices,[13] these accounts have undoubtedly expanded a critical understanding of the genres and potential audiences of the cine-erotic. Equally, other important accounts by theorists such as Brian McNair and Feona Attwood[14] have also charted the extension of explicit representations into wider everyday elements of visual culture: from MTV pop programming and post-watershed dramas to the steamier aspects of reality TV, on-line culture and beyond. It is in light of these emergent lines of enquiry into the cine-erotic, the third edition of the *AlterImage* series also extends a range of approaches to the study of differing traditions and cultures of cult erotica.

Peep Shows thus takes as its starting point the long history of debates around 'representation', 'taste' and 'affect' that have marked these previous gender and cultural studies interventions in this arena.[15] *Peep Shows* expands these debates to indicate the ways in which a wide variety of soft and hard-core formats mediate images of desire and sexuality that reproduce national, cultural and historical trends and tensions, as well as reflecting on more 'legitimate' realms of cinematic activity. As part of this book's aim to provide novel ways to survey the cine-erotic, the volume provides new readings on previously untheorised national trends and tendencies of the sexually explicit, as well as addressing the complex nature of spectatorship that these powerful and problematic works often provoke. Whilst acknowledging the increased theoretical interest in star studies and porn profiles, *Peep Shows* also seeks to provide new accounts of leading icons in this arena by combining theoretical accounts with exclusive interview material prepared for the volume.

Peep Shows' commitment to re-evaluating some of the leading icons of cult erotica is confirmed by Bill Osgerby's opening essay to the volume, which profiles one of cinema's most enigmatic and endearing pin-up icons: Bettie Page. In the chapter 'Pages of Sin: Bettie Page – From "Cheesecake" Tease to Bondage Queen', Osgerby charts the turbulent career of this post-World War II erotic icon, while contextualising her cultural rise and fall against the wider social and sexual contradictions of 1950s American society. In an incisive analysis, Osgerby connects Cold War paranoia surrounding the suppression of communism to an ideological project of 'domestic containment', which saw women primarily (re)constructed as role-models of familial bliss. If this project of post-war gender realignment wrestled with conflicting ideals of prescribed feminine passivity and the far more active (but unacknowledged) female sex drive, then these contradictions clearly circulated around the differing personas that Page 'performed'. As Osgerby notes, the model's pervasive persona was divided between 'cheesecake' photo-spreads which traded on her semi-clad status as 'passive' object before a presumed male consumer, and a far more infamous set of salacious S/M vignettes that earned her the moniker of 'Dark Angel'.

Although these images often featured elaborate bondage sessions with Page characteristically gagged and bound in a number of different sexual poses, the author argues that these spreads functioned to introduce an element of 'polysemic ambiguity' into the model's modes of display, rather than confirm any overarching concept of misogyny. This interesting division in Page's work developed from early cheesecake pin-up sessions for established 'lifestyle' auteur Robert Harrison (which were published in glamour magazines such as *Eyeful*, *Wink* and *Whisper*), to the more daring and sexually subversive S/M shoots she pioneered with the movie stills and pin-up impresario Irving Klaw during the mid-to-late 1950s. Underlying both images of Bettie Page are elements of 'playful satire', which Osgerby analyses in relation to burlesque theory *and* filmic example (derived from commercial films such as *Varietese* (1954) and *Teaserama* (1955), which featured Page alongside other established strip-acts such as Lili St. Cyr and Tempest Storm). As the author argues, within these 'highly ritualised' modes of sexual performance, Page portrayed a 'mixture of impertinent humour and provocative displays', which clearly strained against 'oppressive and objectifying' structures present within American society at the time. And in this respect, Osgerby's analysis of Page's work with the female pin-up photographer Bunny Yaeger is of particular importance for discussing the mechanisms through which the pair re-appropriated the masculine vocabulary of female sexual display via a definite knowing irony. If, as Osgerby concludes, Page's work highlighted the 'continuously contested and contradictory' arena of sexuality within 1950s America, then this is confirmed by the official senate investigation which abruptly ended her career and brought down Irving Klaw's subversive S/M empire. Having been cited by puritanical Democrat senator Estes Kefauver's moral campaign against juvenile delinquency, Klaw closed down his business in 1957, and Page disappeared into obscurity, lending to later rumours that she had first succumbed to the bottle before finding God. Despite her sudden disappearance, Osgerby charts the subsequent sub-cultural fascination that has revived cult interest in the Dark Angel. Ranging from restorations of her 1950s Klaw photo-shoots, to fanzines dedicated to her work and distinctive visual look, to biopics and even comic strip adaptations of her adventures, these cultural re-appropriations point to the continued fascination that audiences have with both the model, and the confused 1950s sexual landscape from which she emerged.

While Bill Osgerby profiles one of the most prolific post-1945 female cine-erotic performers, Jacob Smith reviews the influential oeuvre of postmodern porn auteur Stephen Sayadian (aka 'Rinse Dream'). In his chapter 'Sound and Performance in Stephen Sayadian's *Night Dreams* and *Café Flesh*', Smith makes a convincing case for viewing the director as able to adapt an avant-garde aesthetic into the otherwise uninspiring American direct-to-video hard-core landscape of the 1980s. In particular, the author points to potentially subversive soundscapes, performative strategies and self-reflexive modes of audience address derived from Sayadian's satirical comic-book background, which he explores through pertinent biographical and formal textual analysis. In terms of the director's biography, Smith considers Sayadian's background as a satirist (in publications such as *Mad* magazine, Marvel comics and *National Lampoon*), as providing the impetus for the unorthodox nature of his output, while his longstanding collaborations with writer Jerry Stahl and cinematographer Frank Delia (whom he met while working on *Hustler* magazine in Ohio) evidence a clear authorial intention running through his output. Indeed, from his earliest ad parody contributions to *Hustler* in 1977, Sayadian revealed a subversive sexploitation agenda. These included caption features such as 'What Sort of Man Reads Slayboy?', complete with a Hugh Hefner-like male model surrounded by bunny-girl body bits. From these earliest porn mediations then, Sayadian's presentation of the body was 'at once dark, playful, and anxious'. As Smith notes 'this is certainly not the upscale air-brushed fantasy of Hugh Hefner's *Playboy*', and it was this particularly dark and often macabre vision of sexual desire that the director began to pursue more fully in his post-*Hustler* film career. Drawing on Joan Hawkins' work on the American 'downtown' avant-garde, Smith argues that Sayadian's work expresses a similar body aesthetic to artists and filmmakers such as Nick Zedd, Richard Kern and Kathy Acker, who often drew on low genre products (such as horror, science-fiction and porn) to recode human sexual relations as zones of social and political struggle. For Smith, these atypical porno parables are evidenced in productions such as *Night Dreams* (1981) and *Café Flesh* (1982), which failed to make a commercial dent on the hard-core circuit, but were critically acclaimed in terms of their wider receptions. For Smith, the reason such films had a wider impact outside the traditional erotic grindhouse arena is centrally derived from the experimental qualities which Sayadian infused into these unsettling and often confrontational narratives. Some of the strategies that the director employed in *Night Dreams* included subverting the presumed power (and invisibility) of the male porn spectator via the inclusion of an intrusive direct-to-camera address by the central female lead (Dorothy Le May), as well as an experimental use of 'erotic sonotopes' which often disrupt erotic fantasy with abrasive industrial sounds. These stylistic deviations were exaggerated by a fluid cross-generic construction in the later *Café Flesh*. Here, porn pleasures become defused by a post-apocalyptic scenario dealing with the frustrated desires of 'impotent Sex Negatives' who constitute the bulk of the infected post-nuclear population. By rendering the assembled fictional audience of the film, (and the wider male porn spectator) as 'chronically-passive observers', Smith concludes Sayadian is offering uncomfortable critiques of dominant systems of pleasure which circulate within the cine-erotic.

It is a similar appeal to disruptive avant-garde strategies which dominates Eleri Butler's analysis of the French extreme cinema icon Catherine Breillat. In her chapter 'Catherine Breillat: Anatomy of a Hard-Core Agitator', Butler argues that the director fuses challenging images of female desire with a subversive stylistic address, which evidences a concern with 'dismantling the peep show aesthetic', rather than affording any simplistic 'aid to masturbation'. In so doing, Butler's analysis offers a new way of reading this so-called 'porn auteur' in line with anti-porn feminist perspectives, whilst also examining her work in light of existing experimental film traditions. The author supports this thesis by offering an account of both Breillat's literary and political roots (against the tumultuous but ultimately unsatisfying backdrop of female expectations that surrounded the May 1968 uprisings), as well as profiling the director's key titles. These include the suppressed 1975 first feature *A Real Young Girl* (which juxtaposed an adolescent's sexual awakening to abject images of corpses, animal entrails and waste matter), as well as the later international breakthrough hits of *Romance* (1999) and the controversial *Anatomy of Hell* (2004). Importantly, Butler situates these works in terms of their dual adaptation *and* subversion of porn tactics (most notably evidenced by Breillat's anti-traditional casting of Italian porn stud Rocco Siffredi), which can be linked to a wider political agenda that explores repressed aspects of the female sexual experience. For instance, her analysis of *Romance* acknowledges that while the film gained notoriety for ushering shots of erect penises into mainstream cinema, porn conventions of 'ejaculation, penetration and spread labia are suitably subverted'. Importantly, this is achieved by conflating imagery of anticipatory sexual excess, with abject representations of the female body and its secretions (a feature which is controversially extended in *Anatomy of Hell*'s fantasy vignettes depicting the sexual activity of heavily pregnant women). If these abrasive scenes indicate Breillat's commentary on the essential incompatibility between male-oriented erotica and the distinct vocabulary of female sexual expression, then it is echoed by the avant-garde strategies that the director applies to her most unsettling scenes. As Butler notes, these sequences come to be dominated by 'slow pace, minimal set-ups, tight framing and long takes … to convey an almost unbearable proximity, scrutiny and duration'. If these structures facilitate a disorienting process of distanciation at pertinent points of porn narration, then they are also coupled with re-mediations of the soundtrack, which employ voice-overs as interior monologues (often recorded by Breillat herself) to convey the female experience during these periods of erotic intensity. At the levels of both soundtrack and image then, Breillat's cinema does not 'enhance the potential for erotic pleasure but focuses on the sexual discontents of women'. Through such mechanisms, Breillat's cinema both advances startling sexual imagery into mainstream film, while also using anti-porn agendas to dismantle the presumptions that underpin such sexual representations.

Whereas various aspects of the experimental erotic image dominate debates around European auteurs such as Breillat, it is the subject of the porn soundscape, rather than its image, which is the focus of Gary Needham's contribution. In the chapter 'Disco Sucks!: Pornography and Disco in the 1970s', he links the late 1970s backlash against disco to a conservative ideology linking the roots of this musical phenomenon to both explicit queer desire and politicised female emancipation. Whilst disco has long held connections to a camp aesthetic, Needham notes that the mainstreaming of this phenomenon was achieved by a 'de-gaying' of the music, which effectively rendered it as 'kitschy and self-depreciating'. As the author comments, from its very subterranean late 1960s outset, disco was intrinsically connected to subcultural sexual politics, with clubs emerging against a backdrop of countercultural revolt and catering to those groups who were deemed both sexually and racially disenfranchised. Moreover, by the mid-to-late 1970s, the disco had become as significant a venue as the bathhouse as a locale of 'gay sexual activity and socialisation'. Needham further connects disco to 1970s porn by identifying a number of pivotal narratives (such as *The Boys of Venice* (1978) and *A Night at Adonis* (1978)), which link disco soundtracks to explicit representations of queer sexuality. Moreover, these frequent fusions of disco with desire exhibit an 'aural spatialisation' within the 1970s gay porn, which function to displace the cine-erotic conventions onto the accompanying disco soundtrack. In such texts, the sexual encounter is often organised and orchestrated around the climax of a disco number, with the performer's articulations of orgasm being achieved by aural accompaniments, rather than porn's preferred visual methods. Not only does Needham's analysis find a number of key examples of porn depictions being edited to fit the rhythm of an accompanying disco beat, but the lyrics of tracks such as 'Two Hot For Love' are listed and ordered as an erotic suite with demarcated track sections for 'excitement', 'climax' and 'resolution.' While the author's cross-media analysis of porn and disco affords some fascinating insights on 1970s queer popular culture, it also raises some significant questions about the role of women in these dual musical and erotic subcultures. Although disco is often associated with a marginalisation of female sexuality, Needham argues that both the music and the pornoscapes it spawned point to erotically defuse concepts of gender and sexuality. Indeed, for all their emphasis on exploring the boundaries of same sex couplings, it is women who dominate 'aurally rather than visually' on the disco soundtracks of gay porn movies. If the absence of male vocalisations of desire within the soundtrack 'affords an agency to the female voice in a world visually dominated by men', it seems confirmed by the frequency with which female porn stars went on to be disco divas (as the author's closing account of Andrea True attests). In arguing that porn and disco point to a brief period where the cine-erotic was governed by a 'democracy of eroticisation', Needham's account also offers a fascinating study of the point where pop/subcultures and the cine-erotic meet.

Whereas Gary Needham considers the sights and sounds of 1970s porn, Stefan Nylén, Christian Hallman and Magnus Paulsson interview one of the most colourful and controversial figures from the decade when porn was born: Seka. The American actress (born Dorothea Hundley Patton in 1954), shot to fame as the platinum blonde pin-up girl of the *Swedish Erotica* stag series, in which she worked with a number of iconic figures including John Holmes, John Leslie, Jamie Gillis, Veronica Hart and Ron Jeremy. Her prolific output in this area resulted in her starring in over 180 films (including compilations), the key titles of which Nylén, Hallman and Paulsson profile in this probing piece. The authors also consider the extensive fan-base that was constructed around Seka's star persona by porn barons at the time, with many of her productions being titled or re-titled as star vehicles (such as *Seka for Christmas* (1979), *Princess Seka* (Leonard Kirtman, 1980) and *Confessions of Seka* (Leonard Kirtman, 1980)). The Seka interview also discusses some of the actress's other creative interventions into the cine-erotic, such as the full-length porn productions she co-directed and wrote. Here, Seka also talks candidly about her recollections of working with porn legends such as John Holmes, as well as discussing the sexual and cultural backdrops to 1970s hard-core production (and importantly, their links to the mainstream cinema of the decade). As well as reflecting on her iconic status as a 1970s porn legend, Seka also discusses her sensational decision to quit the industry at the height of her career in the early 1980s as well as offering some well-judged concluding comments on contemporary porn practices and the ways in which these impact on the female erotic performer.

In direct contrast to the 1970s 'feel good' porn narratives of Seka, Xavier Mendik's chapter profiles one of Italy's most controversial bad-boys of cult cinema: Joe D'Amato (AKA Aristide Massaccesi). In the essay 'That's L'Amorte: Joe D'Amato and the Sadean Art of Love', he explores the unpalatable representations of sexuality and death that dominated the late filmmaker's entire catalogue, as well as the disturbing hard-core epics he directed with male porn pin-ups such as Rocco Siffredi. As Mendik notes, despite working in a variety of genres from horror to pornography, post-apocalypse science fiction to neo-noir erotic thriller, an unsettling eroticisation of death and decay remains the consistent theme throughout D'Amato's output. At his most controversial, D'Amato pioneered a series of bizarre 'sex and death' genre-hybrids such as *Le Notti Erotiche Dei Morti Viventi* (*Erotic Nights of the Living Dead* (1979)) and *Holocausto Porno* (*Porno Holocaust* (1980)), in which a European woman is forced to have anal sex with a third-world zombie. Although Joe D'Amato's later hard-core productions of the late 1980s and 1990s (such as *X-Hamlet* (1994), *Barone Von Masoch* (1994) and *Tarzan-X: Shame Of Jane* (1994)), seem to share little connection with the director's earlier, controversial output, Mendik uncovers similarly horrific regimes of punishment, suffering and male sexual exhibitionism, which he analyses using contemporary readings of Sade (by authors such as Maurice Charney and John Phillips). As the chapter argues, it is not merely the fact that D'Amato films such as *120 Days of the Anal* and *The Marquis De Sade* (both 1995) draw on libertine ideas for their subject matter, but rather the style and repetitive structure of these works retain a Sadean emphasis that also draws parity with the director's earlier controversial output. For instance, Mendik argues that both *120 Days of the Anal* and *The Marquis De Sade* use D'Amato's favoured technique of extended flashback structures to explore 'a basis of sexual trauma upon which the narrative continually returns', effectively impeding fictional progression in a manner comparable to Sade's epic narrative deviations. As with Sade's work, both D'Amato films discussed also exploit the disturbance of privatised desire via concealed voyeurs and the recodification of intense emotion as a theatrical 'communal affair'. Adapting recent re-readings of the politics of sexual difference depicted in Sade's work, Mendik argues that D'Amato's movies also disrupt totalised and empowered visions of masculinity. As the author notes, the director either degrades his porn actor's body to a series of 'genital vignettes' which rob them of corporeal unity, or else induces a high degree of sexual ambiguity into their porn performances. As a result, D'Amato's films can be seen as unsettling many of the conventions associated with male-centred porn.

Unlike the textual emphasis offered by Mendik's account, Iain Robert Smith calls attention to the corporate and marketing strategies exhibited by contemporary soft-core 'parody' cycles such as *Spiderbabe* (Johnny Crash, 2003), as well as their wider associations with the mainstream blockbusters they are derived from. In his essay 'When *Spiderman* Became *Spiderbabe*: Pornographic Appropriation and the Political Economy of the "Soft-Core Spoof" Genre', Smith discusses the prolific growth of 'disreputable, subterranean films', whose erotic parodies feed off a 'web of intertextual associations and consumer awareness' of mainstream blockbusters. The focus of Smith's analysis is Michael L. Raso's company 'ei Independent

9

cinema', whose Seduction cinema label specialises in parasitic sexploitation versions of mainstream Hollywood blockbusters including *The Erotic Witch Project* (John Bacchus, 2001), *Playmate of the Apes* (John Bacchus, 2001) and *Lord of the G-Strings* (Terry West, 2003). As well as considering the parodic connections between these films and the Hollywood templates from which they are derived, Smith also affords crucial consideration to the business and marketing strategies that have seen ei evolve from a micro-budgeted organisation to a corporate-friendly production house, whose products have been ensured distribution via mainstream franchises such as Blockbusters and Borders. As Smith notes, given the increasingly corporate orientation of the adult industry, ei's business model and clearly conceived constructions of audience demographics are by no means unique. However, the author argues that the company is distinguished from other soft-core distributors by their explicit attempts to appeal to both mainstream and cult consumers, with the latter market being targeted via on-campus events, fan conventions and fanzine articles. If, as Smith argues, 'the company propagates the development of a cult fan community', then a central element of this targeted appeal revolves around the star personas developed by their central female leads. For instance, Smith offers a revealing case-study of noted Seduction starlet Misty Mundae (Erin Brown) to indicate how the brand 'relies on a female star system reminiscent both of the classical Hollywood system of contract players and the more recent cultish conception of "scream queens"'. Indeed, it is interesting to note that the Seduction remakes often give more narrative prominence to female agency than the Hollywood blockbusters they parody, leading Smith to question whether the company is pioneering a more 'female-friendly model of soft-core sex'. Although the author offers some intriguing conclusions on whether ei's distinct female emphasis and orientation towards same-sex encounters challenges or confirms hetero-normative porn conventions, what cannot be denied is the significance that Raso's company and Mundae's performances have had across the contemporary erotic landscape.

As an addendum to Smith's analysis of porn parodies, we are delighted to publish an exclusive interview with Seduction's most iconic star, which has been especially commissioned for this volume. In 'The Erotic Adventures of Misty Mundae: An Interview with Actress Erin Brown', Smith discusses a number of pertinent topics with the articulate and attuned performer, who already boasts over eighty screen credits in a variety of film and TV productions, as well as directing, editing and music composition credits on ei films including *Confessions of a Natural Beauty* (2003), *Lustful Addiction* (2003) and *Voodoun Blues* (2004). Whilst commenting on Brown's ability to shift between performative and production duties, the interview also expands on the unique cult following that the actress has secured across her roles. As Smith notes, despite her distinctly anti-traditional porn looks 'Erin has developed a devoted fan following and a level of consumer awareness unmatched by almost any other soft-core star'. The actress also accounts for her 'accidental' career as a porn pin-up, whilst distinguishing the creative aspirations of Erin Brown the horror film fan, from 'Misty Mundae … the indelible actress'. As Brown, comments, her introduction to the industry came not through sexploitation but subculture: namely an alternative music label which lead to her early appearances in slacker horror flicks such as *International Necktie Strangler* (Billy Hellfire, 2000) and the controversial and much censored *Duck!: The Carbine High Massacre* (Billy Hellfire, 1999). When discussing the latter, Brown concludes that while the film 'was way too offensive and socially distasteful for anyone to want to put it out for the masses', the production also offered 'total creative freedom via socio-political commentary'. It is this quest to retain an independent spirit that appears central to the loyal fan-base that Brown has garnered in the subsequent Seduction period, which she discusses in the closing sections of the interview. Here, she also reveals her planned move back to horror-oriented products following the critical acclaim she received for her role in Lucky McKee's *Masters of Horror* entry *Sick Girl* (2006), indicating that the actress will be diversifying into a range of related cult directions in the future.

The topic of porn parodies pioneered by companies such as ei is one of the subjects discussed by I. Q. Hunter's contribution '*A Clockwork Orgy*: A User's Guide'. This chapter uses Nic Cramer's 1995 hard-core rendition of Stanley Kubrick's classic dystopian vision to consider links between the contemporary cine-erotic and the art of adaptation. As Hunter argues, rather than being 'mere parasites upon their originals', hard-core porn parodies often use an unruly fusion of flesh and gags to make 'subversive commentaries' upon mainstream cinema's ideological and sexual subtexts. Via his incisive analysis, Hunter offers an account of both Cramer's movie, and the development of parodic hard-core as a format. Here, he notes that while these porno-comic productions were largely confined to vampire and folktale renditions during the 1970s, the subgenre rapidly evolved during the increasingly corporatised Hollywood blockbuster years of the 1980s and 1990s. However, while other inventively titled hard-core rip-offs such as *Charlie's Anals* (2001) and *Edward Penishands* (Paul Norman, 1991), only play on key iconographic details before departing towards stylised sex scenes, *A Clockwork Orgy* remains interesting for its attempts to offer a frame by frame parody of all of the elements from *A Clockwork Orange* (1971), resulting in some interesting genre and gender deviations. In Cramer's rendition, the rebellious central lead is a libidinous heroine named Alexandra (Kaitlyn Ashley), who roams the dystopian city space with a gang of female droogs, in an endless quest for 'ultra-sex'. As Hunter notes, these subtle gender modifications facilitate and sanitise some of the implied and actualised violence of Kubrick's original, by having Alexandra's droogs target men as potential victims of sexual intimidation. Despite pinpointing some of the sexual contradictions that the film (and mainstream heterosexual porn) contains, Hunter still defines *A Clockwork Orgy* as 'porn with a mission', which offers the potential for a progressive reading of unabated female desire within the post-AIDS/pro-celibacy environments which were gaining ground at the time of the film's release. Indeed, this seems underscored by one of the novel departures from Kubrick's original template, in which Alexandra's enforced 're-education' (at the hands of a government keen to limit the spread of sexual promiscuity), involve her being forced to watch hard-core porn loops until she feels repelled. This sets up a curiously complex and self-reflexive position whereby *A Clockwork Orgy* seems to be 'warning against watching films like itself'. Via his close reading of the film (as well as the possible porno connections he raises in Kubrick's original text), Hunter points to the intricate processes of adaptation and intertexual play which differentiate *A Clockwork Orgy* from the 'largely pre-classical, non narrative' reality cycles of porn performance which continue to dominate the market. In this respect, he argues that Cramer's text remains 'distinctive (and classy) in a market otherwise flooded with interchangeable products, as well as potentially lending it some cult appeal'.

Given that the topic of porn parody is so central to contemporary representations of the cine-erotic and debates around their representations, it is more than appropriate that we profile one of the most influential producers of parodic porn. In his chapter 'King of the Porn Spoofs: An Interview with Michael L. Raso', Iain Robert Smith talks to the prolific head of ei cinema, who has produced over a hundred feature films with an erotic and parodic twist. Some of Raso's most celebrated titles include *The Erotic Witch Project*, *Playmate of the Apes*, *Spiderbabe* and *Kinky Kong* (2006). Although initially formed to produce low-budget horror and comedy flicks for the home video market, ei exploded into the pop-porn consciousness with a whole range of erotic parodies which exploited Raso's philosophy that 'the spoof becomes a perfect marketing tool'. Whilst discussing the rapid evolution of ei and the Seduction range for which they have become synonymous, the producer also describes the specific strategies that he has utilised to maintain ei's foundational cult fan-base, while also being able to negotiate the more corporate structures in which ei's product now circulates. As Raso notes, this cult fan-base has been central to the continued success of the company, to the extent that they have been producing up to eight features per year to meet this audience demand since 1997. As Raso also explains, active fan participation in the Seduction circuit is ensured not only through a regularisation of product (i.e. a definable cast and crew), but also through the star personas created for the label's iconic female peformers. Central to the cult appeal of the Seduction brand is the star status that the company has created for Misty Mundae, whose popularity Raso links to her status as 'the perfect anti-sex symbol'. Raso's concluding comments on the atypical construction of this pivotal starlet, as well as his observations on the role of men in his erotic epics who he sees as 'strictly on the screen for gags', casts some illuminating comments on how indie cult sensibilities are increasingly being fused with erotic material to increase an appeal to both mainstream and alternative fan communities.

Although critical studies of female erotic icons (such as Seka and Misty Mundae) have become crucial springboards to wider examinations of ideology, representation and resistance within the cine-erotic image, there remain relatively few studies of the male performers operating within these contexts. In her chapter 'A Star is Porn: Corpulence, Comedy and the Homosocial Cult of Adult Film Star Ron Jeremy', Emily Shelton examines the cult status of one of adult cinema's (literally) larger-than-life male stars. As she notes, Ron Jeremy remains an anomaly in the current porn industry for several reasons. Not only is he one of the few adult stars from the golden age of the 1970s to remain active in the industry (boasting over a thousand screen credits and directing titles to his name), but he has even escaped the hard-core ghetto to appear in both indie cult shockers such as *Terror Firmer* (Lloyd Kaufman, 1999) and *Citizen Toxie: Toxic Avenger IV* (Lloyd Kaufman, 2000), as well as more mainstream movies such as *Killing*

Zoe (Roger Avary, 1993). Ron Jeremy's stature is such that he is also celebrated in a diverse range of pop culture products from bio-pic documentaries such as *Porn Star: The Legend of Ron Jeremy* (Scott J. Gill, 2001) and MTV satires such as *Beavis and Butthead* (1993–97) to rap videos, and even comic books. What makes this mass marketing of Jeremy's image even more spectacular is that it is based on a physicality that Emily Shelton shrewdly gauges as 'overweight … with a disobedient tangle of curly brown hair and scraggly moustache'. Given Jeremy's manifest status as 'the anti-aesthetic of the inferred pornographic fantasy', this chapter seeks to explain his continued popularity in an era of photo-shopped, porno-sheened perfection, as well as exploring the possible contradictions inherent in his appeal to 'heterosexual' male audiences. In an interesting deviation from Jeremy's perceived status as a porn performer, Shelton links the actor's style and appearance to 'a long tradition of corpulent and physically reckless male comics, from Fatty Arbuckle to John Belushi to Chris Farley'. It is these comic mediations which also offer important ways for gender and film theorists to reconsider the presumed patterns of identification and appeal for the actor's presumed male audience. By defining Jeremy's output within the sexually and socially subversive realms of 'pornedy', Shelton draws on Bakhtinian accounts to consider the ways in which the actor's physical excess and comic gestures evoke the lower bodily comic traditions discussed in classical accounts of the carnivalesque. By parodying the presumed conventions of heterosexual performance, she also argues that Jeremy's texts mark out a 'hysterical index of homosocial pleasure', evidenced by an emphasis on anality (in both the act and the titles that Jeremy appears in), as well as productions which bring him into close proximity with other groups of men (such as 'gang bang' narratives). The sexual tensions reproduced in Jeremy's narratives are confirmed in their modes of male consumption, which tend to be public (such as porn theatres, frat parties and all-male social environments), rather than the privatised arenas associated with hard-core viewing. Shelton uses the actor's appearance in the 1987 film *Never Say Good-Bi*, to show how these tensions circulate via a principle of 'compulsory homosociality'. Here, the actor's comic presence functions to 'police' the same-sex sexual activity in the film (with Jeremy appearing as a pizza-guzzling spectator to the frequent male-on-male encounters), as well as the viewer's reaction to it. Equally, the author concludes that Jeremy's comic performances in such texts facilitate a process of sexual disavowal, which mediates more fluid processes of desire through a comforting comic lens. In so doing, it can be argued that his films raise interesting questions about the nature of sexual identification within the comic hard-core canon.

While Emily Shelton profiles the matrix of sexual associations that circulate around the untheorised male porn performer, Clarissa Smith offers a crucial insight into the often overlooked female audience for erotic material. In her essay '"I Guess They Got Past Their Fear of Porn": Women Viewing Porn Films', Smith argues that the crucial area of research into the female audience reception of pornography has often been hampered by the 'need for some kind of limit on its consumption'. Despite the continued taboos around female consumption of pornography meaning that 'it can be very difficult to find willing participants for a research project … about the place of pornography in an individual's life', Smith offers a fascinating

13

and challenging oversight of the female erotic respondent, derived from a sample study of heterosexual women aged 25–48. Importantly, the author notes that while quantitative data suggests the marked increase in the female use of porn, wider cultural constructions about these participants as 'bad consumers' of porn have resulted in the belief that they constitute a 'coarsening of a natural and properly feminine sensibility towards the sexually explicit'. However, rather than just being 'tied up with the structural inequalities of heteronormative, patriarchal society', the active voices of Smith's female respondents indicate 'the very individual personal histories that are entwined with the sense-making and pleasures of pornography'. As a result, the author's sample cast some illuminating comments on the value that pornography has in their lives, which radically undercut presumptions of the gratification involved with the consumption of such material. For instance, some female respondents cited the use of such material not as a primary aid to masturbation, but rather as a trigger for heightening body perceptions that assisted with the other social and domestic tasks they undertook. As Smith concludes, these important commentaries confirm the often reductive presumption that all porn is constructed in the same manner, and will impact on their consumers in identical ways. By advocating the concept of the 'discriminating' female porn consumer, the author notes that her respondents repeatedly returned to the concept of 'authenticity' to make distinctions between their own desires and the way these may deviate from the male-oriented images they frequently surveyed. Not only did this lead to the sample frequently seeking out elements of emotional intensity and bodily performance in their search for the sexually authentic, but some respondents even highlighted ancillary elements (such as costume design and décor), which were found to be as appealing as the erotic acts that they were supposed to be focusing on. As Smith's important study indicates, although female consumers of pornography are often 'dogged by questions of harm, subordination, objectification', theoretical attention should now focus on 'good' viewers of pornographic material, whose quest for an active and authentic engagement with the text provide important new ways of understanding our relationship to the cine-erotic.

Whereas Clarissa Smith studies the real-life activities of female porn consumers, Kevin Heffernan explores the larger-than-life production history of an art-house cult porn classic: *Thundercrack!* With its images of bisexual experimentation, hard-core ecstasy and cross-generic excess, the film provoked outrage at the time of its 1976 release, even failing to secure a stable audience in the 'underground' movie crowd. While examining the film's 'slow-burn' cult status, Heffernan also analyses the backgrounds of *Thundercrack!*'s key creators, screenwriter George Kuchar and director Curt McDowell. Whereas Kuchar's status as one of the leading directors on the 1960s New York underground film scene has already been well documented, Heffernan employs exclusive access to unpublished diaries and personal production notes to profile Kuchar's former student and lover, McDowell. While providing a fascinating overview of *Thundercrack!* in light of the director's other sexually explicit shorts, Heffernan also teases out the specific family dynamics that influenced the film and its creator. In particular, the author highlights a unique creative synergy that existed between McDowell and his younger sister Melinda. As well as functioning as the director's muse (and a key focal point of the *Thundercrack!* narrative), Heffernan explores the extent to which the film represented a fictional expansion of the siblings' quest to upend all that represented the 'safe world of monogamous heterosexual desire'. It was this consistent attempt to queer the heteronormative dynamic of porn which made *Thundercrack!* such a *cause celebre* and ensured its uneven and unsympathetic reception during the 1970s. As Heffernan notes in the closing sections of his chapter, negative reviews ranged from critiques of the film's style, plot, pacing and running time, to critical uproar at its uneasy conflation of horror and porn tropes. Underpinning the hostile reception of *Thundercrack!* was the film's pansexual approach to transgression, which appeared too bisexual for the mainstream porno-chic crowd as well as falling short of the 'queer' tag pivotal to legitimisation in the American alternative film scene of the period. If these atypical traits ensured *Thundercrack!*'s resistance to established methods of distribution (even for the backers of John Waters' back-catalogue), it also ensured a cult erotic status that circulated on the cinematic and sexual subcultures of the 1970s film scene. Whilst Heffernan concludes that *Thundercrack!* remains a movie of 'delirious incoherence', its mystique has survived the untimely demise of Curt McDowell from AIDS-related illnesses to become a central influence for a new generation of attuned erotic performers and creators.

Whilst Kevin Heffernan considers *Thundercrack!*'s sustained status as an underground cult skin-flick, Jenny Barrett considers the gradual transition of the female dominatrix figure from underground to mainstream sexual representations. In her essay 'Let's Do Something You Won't Enjoy': Dominatrix Porn, Performance and Subjectivity', Barrett considers this most intriguing of female porn figures from a specifically British perspective. Noting that discussions of American sadomasochism imagery have become normalised via theorisations of texts such as *The Punishment of Anne* (Radley Metzger, 1979), Barrett turns her attention to the interesting national configurations which dominate British versions of the dominatrix. As she comments, in direct contrast to the highly stylised 'aesthetic sadomasochism' and 'apparent glamour of American S/M porn', British depictions of the figure emphasise the apparent ordinariness of the 'dominatrix-next-door', with their activities often depicted in a documentary/realist manner through companies such as Dom Productions, whose output forms a central case-study in her account. As Barrett notes, while American representations of the figure emphasise 'female porn performers who are youthful, attractive, with perfectly applied make-up, coiffed hair, false nails and false breasts', British versions of this figure draw on the far more challenging figure of 'the tough and violent' women in popular culture, as personified by dom icons such as 'Mistress Beverly'. As the author notes, this female figure (and associated characters such as 'Mistress Smoke') point to the plurality of performances undertaken by the British dom, whose costumes and modes of display function to highlight the 'theatrical' nature of gender arrangements she portrays. Drawing on Judith Butler's work around gender performativity, Barrett views the British dominatrix as functioning to exaggerate codes of femininity (through aspects of her dress), whilst also revealing a far more aggressive and masculine mode (particularly through her treatment of the often passive males depicted in the Dom films). Importantly, she also draws on Barbara Creed's psychoanalytic account of *The Monstrous Feminine* (1993) to explore the extent to which such depictions also draw out 'tough' representations of the maternal agent as both a nurturing and chastising figure. Noting a repeated pattern of infantilisation of the male submissive by the female dominatrix, Barrett argues that with the 'kind of language used in dominatrix porn, "little girl", "bad body" and so forth, the power relationship that is performed is close to that of mother and child'. This familial matrix is further confirmed by 'enforced' thumb-sucking, spanking and other regressive activities that Dom narratives focus on, leading Barrett to conclude that the female dominatrix reproduces the figure of the phallically empowered pre-Oedipal mother, who is able to oscillate between the figures of 'gentle mummy, then cruel matriarch'. Although she does concede that depictions of the female dominatrix are often orchestrated by male creators, an element of camp and aesthetic distanciation often accompanies these productions, which further complicates the power relations they evoke. In so doing, Barrett's analysis offers a novel interpretation of the performative strategies evidenced in this most intriguing of British porn subcultures.

As with Jenny Barrett's contribution, Alexander Zahlten also considers the national dynamics that underpin cycles of the cine-erotic, through his consideration of Japan's 'pink' porn phenomenon of the 1960s. Although the films (which often combine female nudity with violence, social deviation and a strong revenge motif) have already been the subject of several significant textual studies, Zahlten offers a fascinating overview of the industrial factors behind the series in light of their links to wider social upheavals occurring in Japan during the 1960s. In 'Neo-Liberal Avant-Garde Sexploitation in Japan: The Interplay of Collaboration and Revolution in the Pink Film', he notes that the peak period of the pink production was in the early-to-mid-1960s, with more than two hundred titles associated with the template being produced between the years of 1962–65. As Zahlten notes, through their emphasis on 'the literature of the flesh', the pink movie became associated with independent and leftist cinema of the decade, which 'used the body as the starting point for re-establishing a sense of personal subjectivity'. As well as being marked by an often experimental style, the cycle initially boasted strong political content (and union connections), which stood in direct opposition to the authoritarian ideologies represented by Japan's six leading film studios of the period. Indeed, Zahlten goes as far as to state that the pink directors viewed themselves as 'a blue collar lot', whose role was to expose some of the social and sexual contradictions underpinning Japanese society during this period. This led to a number of populist Japanese works being acclaimed at overseas festivals, while (in the case of titles such as *Black Snow* (Takeschi Tetsuji, 1965)) being the subject of censure and obscenity prosecutions in the domestic sphere. Indeed, as Zahlten notes, pink directors were even able to integrate the controversy of the series into their fictional narratives to create satirical and socially attuned commentaries. This seems confirmed by the discussion of Yamamoto Shinya's *Molester 365* (1972) 'which responded to an official warning issued by the metropolitan police that sexploitation films were becoming too daring', by featuring a concealed abuser later revealed to be a 'perverted policeman'. Whilst discussing the political dynamics which accompanied the peak period of pink production, Zahlten also explores some economic contradictions underpinning the production of the cycle, whose popularity was partly ensured by a slow-down in production by the major studios. As he notes, this degree of unofficial overlap between sexploitation and the studios is further evidenced by the fact that the majors later co-opted some of the pink cycle's more sexually explicit traits and even adopted its production practices and leading stars. As well as studying some of these overlaps, Zahlten profiles some of the pink films' leading producers, including Okura Mitsugi, who pioneered a brand of erotic-grotesque narratives that was to become synonymous with the cycle. Charting Mitsugi's rise from a narrator of silent Japanese films to an exhibition chain owner and studio head, it is interesting to note that this leading movie mogul first used pink product to supplement the more mainstream productions he was overseeing. However, when mainstream audiences began to decline, Mitsugi became synonymous with films 'spliced heavily ... with horror, violence and eroticism'. Although these films were initially controversial upon the time of their release, the author charts the extent to which Mitsugi's model of pink production and exhibition provided a model of standardisation which was to become attractive to the very studios they were meant to oppose. As Zahlten concludes, the pink movie remains Japan's own contribution to the celluloid culture of the cine-erotic. And while the cycle can be seen as displaying socially driven and experimentally-oriented roots, the format's gradual co-option by major studios of the period offer an interesting case-study to examine the points where sexploitation and wider social requirements intersect.

Following on from Alexander Zahlten's analysis of classic cult erotica, Claire Hines also considers the influence of early sexploitation titles on non-heterosexual viewers in her article '"How Far Will a Girl Go to Satisfy Her Needs?": From Dykesploitation to Lesbian Hard-Core'. As with other entries in this volume, Hines notes the ability for cult erotica to be read against the grain by those marginal audiences not originally intended as the target consumer of these titillating cycles. For instance, by using the term 'dykesploitation', she evokes a certain class of 1960s soft-core entertainment which used daring themes of teenage lesbianism and scenes of same-sex couplings to directly appeal to heterosexual male audiences. However, as Hines notes, it is these very same sexual stereotypes employed by exploitation cycles that have subsequently been re-read by a new generation of lesbian viewers able to respond to the camp aesthetic and (often unintentional) heterosexual cynicism engrained within these productions. Thus, by focusing on the 'queering of dykesploitation' by non-heterosexual viewers, Hines offers an incisive reading of one of the most significant entries to the cycle, *Chained Girls* (1965). The film was directed by noted sexploitation auteur Joseph P. Mawra, who incorporated a number of documentary-style techniques into the narrative (such as inserted pseudo-scientific data, *verité* camerawork and guiding male narration), to the extent that the film reads the theme of lesbian desire as more social problem than sexploitation topic. By structuring the narrative of *Chained Girls* around the theme of 'preventative education', Hines argues that Mawra's film established a series of *exposé*-style tropes adopted by later dykesploitation entries. These scientific elements (and the masculine assumptions they belie), often jarred with the excessively melodramatic modes of female delivery and marketing that dominated the dykesploitation fiction and its exhibition. For Hines, this facilitates a crucial and 'ironic gap' between the original text, its promotional material and the reception of these texts by contemporary lesbian audiences, who now read these works as offering a crucial index of cult lesbian visibility during the 1960s. It is the continued influence of these early dykesploitation classics on contemporary modes of lesbian erotica which dominate the closing sections of Hines' account. Here, she profiles the output of lesbian production company SIR, as well as their key titles including *Sugar High Glitter City* (Shar Rednour and Jackie Strano (2001)), which are notable for their adaption of classic dykesploitation conventions for contemporary lesbian audiences. From shifting authorial voice-over narration from male to female agency and updating documentary and photography to include a dominating lesbian gaze, as well as expanding the repertoire of same-sex scenarios beyond the 1960s cycle, Hines reads these films as very much co-opting rather than rejecting the limitations of the heterosexually defined soft-core films of the 1960s. If the contemporary SIR titles are putting the 'dyke into dykesploitation', as the author suggests, then its points to the complex ways in which the such imagery can be recoded and reclaimed by the divergent cine-erotic consumer.

Whilst Claire Hines focuses on reclaiming previously marginal images of lesbian erotica, Xavier Mendik reassesses one of Sweden's most influential female sexploitation icons: Christina Lindberg. In 'Flesh (Fur) and Fury: An Interview With Christina Lindberg', he profiles the infamous performer, who emerged from Sweden's golden era of porn. Having evolved from model to actress, Lindberg appeared in eighteen significant soft-core productions between 1970 and 1974, which confirmed her iconic status as both a domestic and export signifier of sexual liberation. As the actress explains, although promoted for their daring images of teenage abandon, these narratives often fused sex with commentary on the changing Swedish society of the period. For instance, *Exposed* (1971) questions the male-dominated drives of the 1960s counterculture, while *Anita: Swedish Nymphet* (1973) functioned as a Swedish social problem film rather than sexploitation potboiler, depicting how a young woman's uncontrollable sex drives lead to her gradual isolation from the more conformist settings of 1970s society. Whilst discussing the significance of these productions, Lindberg also considers the continued influence of her most controversial and celebrated cult title, *Thriller* (Bo Arne Vibenius, 1974). This influential shocker cast Lindberg as the lethal, mute female vigilante Madeleine, who takes revenge on the pimp and his clients who ensnared her into a brutal world of enforced prostitution, drug addiction and violence. It was the infamous image of Madeleine being blinded in one eye with a scalpel for resisting the advances that led to the film being instantly banned in Sweden. This scene, and subsequent images of Lindberg toting a shotgun whilst wearing a single black eyepatch also gave *Thriller* an enduring cult iconography and in part explains the genesis of the similarly disabled but potent female character of Ellie Driver initially seen in Tarantino's *Kill Bill: Vol. 1* (2003). As well as considering the influence of *Thriller* on Tarantino's later film, Lindberg also offers a fascinating oversight into the performative strategies she employed to convey the mute heroine's emotional turmoil and resistance. The actress also discusses how her more recent activities as a journalist and animal rights campaigner should be considered as an expansion of her previous acting roles, in this interview exclusively commissioned for this volume.

Although the recent proliferation of erotic material on film, DVD and download has also spawned a number of significant film festivals devoted to considering contemporary trends of the sexually 'permissive', it is the silent cinematic roots of the cine-erotic which Simone Pyne explores in her essay 'Black & White Frills/Silent Thrills'. Here, she offers an industrial account of the Smoking Cabinet Festival of Burlesque and Cabaret Cinema, which tours a number of leading independent UK cinemas on an annual basis. While offering a crucial account of the marketing and funding structures underpinning the event, Pyne also offers an interesting index of the kinds of consumer attracted to the event (stratified along several cinematic subcultures that include cross-over neo-burlesque fans, early cinema fanatics, London gay community members and burlesque performers). The varied participants to this cross-media event evidence the recent surge of interest in burlesque culture (particularly in metropolitan areas), which Pyne accounts for in her engaging exhibition study. As she notes, although neo-burlesque culture has now been mainstreamed, what is often overlooked are the connections between these forms of expressive and suggestive movement, and their long and important connections to early silent film traditions, which the Smoking Cabinet festival seeks to foreground. As indicated in the essay, the earliest forms of pornographic material began to appear largely in France in the 1920s, often as black market shorts simply known as 'risqué films'. These stag scenarios often traded on explicit representations of lesbianism and heterosexual couplings, thus providing a porno-blueprint of the sound and colour productions that would evolve in later decades. These films were supplemented by less explicit (but still controversial) shorts, which often combined female strip routines within burlesque and exotic dance routines. Often underscoring their original exhibition in carnival and circus environments, a number of early arousing shorts such as *Fatima's Coochie-Coochie Dance* (1896) and *Trapeze Disrobing Act* (1902) used the trope of female circus performers who disrobe as part of their public performances. While such scenarios indicate the existence of a male-dominated ideology within early burlesque traditions, Pyne's analysis provides plenty of evidence to suggest these early examples of the cine-suggestive, also recognised women 'as agents of change in dominant roles, negotiating situations on their own terms'. For instance, her account offers a profile of a number of burlesque performers, including 'Peerless Annabelle' Whitford, who used her popularity as an erotic dancing spectacle able to guide and manipulate the desiring male gaze. As Pyne notes, central to the Smoking Cabinet's exhibition remit is not only to foreground the silent cinematic culture of burlesque, but also to provide a critical mediation of its images through related panel debates and lectures on topics of gender representation and non-classical film structures contained within the movement. In this respect, the festival offers an interesting site to study some of the earliest forms of the cine-erotic, whose images evoke both an appeal to the outwardly daring that draws parity with later pornographic traditions, while also often using more subtle form of allusion to create an impact. As Pyne concludes, the event evokes both the traditions and spirit of burlesque culture by combining live musical interludes and dance routines alongside silent screened material. It is through this critical conjoining of screening material and with related seminars and mixed media matter that the Smoking Cabinet explores the fascinating intersection between cinema, dance and suggestive sexual spectacle that emerged between the period of 1895–1933.

Alongside star-studies of noted erotic performers such as Bettie Page, Seka, Ron Jeremy and Christina Lindberg, *Peep Shows* is delighted to profile one of erotica's most original and pioneering performers: Buck Angel. The actor's output is surveyed in Marcelle Perks' chapter 'The Adventures of Buck Naked: The Thrill of the Transgendered Peep Show', which contains both an overview and interview with this significant porn performer. As Perks notes, in recent years transgendered porn has moved from a marginal sex subgenre to become one of the most debated aspects of cine-erotic activity, often through an alignment with wider 'queer' and psychoanalytic approaches. However, these accounts largely revolve around male-to-female depictions of sexual desire and the fluid notions of gender they detail. As one of the few female-to-male porn performers currently operating in commercial erotica, Buck Angel has become a significant corrective to current transgender conventions and their theorisation. As Perks comments, 'the transgendered porn subject is typically presented as someone abnormal who fails to pass successfully as male or female, and thus becomes reduced to being only a sexual curiosity or a joke'. In actively seeking to displace the transgendered body as a site of freakish spectacle, Buck Angel has both starred in and directed a series of parodic and experimental porn narratives that draw attention to the wider range of sexual performativity at play within the cine-erotic canon. Perks notes that Angel's transgendered status has resulted in a wide and divergent fan-base, including a large gay male following, as well as female and sexual subculture supporters. In part, his varied appeal lies in the fact that the performer upturns many of the conventions of heterosexual porn by emphasising intense pleasure (without visualised climax), whilst parodying the phallic obsessions of mainstream erotica through the extended use of an obviously fake penis. This semi-comic undercutting of the prized signifier of porn pleasure confirms the fact that 'the point of the Angel film is to privilege the fake, to endow it with a hyperrealism so that Angel's artificial penis becomes better than a biologically functioning one'. If Angel's noticeably altered body does indeed defy existing gender binaries, this sexually subversive element carries over to the climactic scenes of each encounter, which once again function to defy the primacy of the phallus in porno representation. As Perks notes, 'in the FTM porn film we learn that transmen prefer to handle their clitoris differently, they "jill off" exactly as if they were handling a miniature penis'. Through these scenes, as well as a range of vignettes in which Buck Angel is represented as both 'penetrator and penetrated', the performer's works point to the plurality of subjectivity positions at play within his narratives. In an important expansion of these debates, Perks draws on psychoanalytic notions such as the archaic mother to explore pre-Oedipal alignments between Angel's character and the 'Black Queen' depicted in Richard Kimmel's avant-garde *Schwarzwald* (2007), which both the author and the star discuss in the accompanying interview. This narrative which combines frenzied hard-core interactions with musical inserts and masculinist mythology represents a new way of depicting the cine-erotic, confirming Perks' view that 'Angel is very much a pioneer at the cutting edge of porn, and it's important to remember that his sexual transgressions are our gain'.

As already discussed, the long history of debates around the cine-erotic cannot be divorced from wider strategies of policing and control which have marked the most significant periods of pornographic production. It is precisely these mechanisms of official state censure which Julian Petley discusses in his essay 'Punishing the Peep Show: Carnality and the Dangerous Images Act'. Here, he discusses the extent to which erotic materials and the freedoms of its users are directly challenged by recent governmental attempts to revise the terms and conditions of the 1964 Obscene Publications Act. The original act targeted materials deemed to 'deprave and corrupt persons who are likely, in all circumstances, to read, see or hear matter contained and embodied in it'. As Petley notes, given the broad nature of the frames of reference contained within the original act, it is unsurprising that a varied range of materials from literary classics such as D. H. Lawrence's *Lady Chatterley's Lover* (1960) and Hubert Selby Jr's *Last Exit to Brooklyn* (1964) to porn tie-in adaptations such as *Inside Linda Lovelace* (1974) have all been 'subject to failed prosecution' under its terms. However, using a fascinating mix of historical account and individual case-study, Petley reveals how the cine-erotic is increasingly being censured by new and more pernicious regulations embodied in the Dangerous Images Act of 2008. As he notes, this newest legislation (as with previous acts such as the Video Recordings Act of 1984 and the Criminal Justice Act of 1988), must be contextualised against wider social fears surrounding the consumption of new technologies and the (re-)mediations of desire they contain. As Petley concludes, the legislation has its origins in the fact that 'thanks to the increasingly global nature of communication, and not least the development of the Internet, British subjects are now able to access material which the OPA would have made it extremely difficult to distribute in former times'. With its emphasis on the containment of the 'extreme pornographic image', the Dangerous Images Act for the first time criminalises the possession (rather than distribution) of images which are deemed not merely 'pornographic' but also 'extreme'. Namely, the act targets images defined as 'grossly offensive, disgusting, or otherwise of an obscene character', and importantly is no longer dependant on the realism of the image, but rather its *apparent* realism. In this respect, Petley argues that a wide range of pornographic material which gives the *appearance* of inducing pain and suffering (such as fictional BDSM material) now falls into the same prosecuting framework as actual images of bodily pain and mutilation. With the installation of these new methods of sexual policing, 'the possession of certain entirely fictional feature films is now set to become a criminal offence'. As he concludes, this new legislation now means that many cult film classics which previously fused 'both real sex and simulated violence' are now liable to prosecution. These include Joe D'Amato's more extreme entries to the *Black Emanuelle* series (titles such as *Emanuelle in America* and *Emanuelle Around the World* (both 1977)), as well as many 'women in prison' movies including Oswaldo de Oliveria's *Bare Behind Bars* (1980). Petley's findings reveal the extent to which fictional configurations of the cine-erotic now fall within shifting new legal criteria, thus producing a study of significance to future consumers *and* researchers of pornographic material.

Whilst the volume opens with a contemporary re-reading of the vintage erotica of Bettie Page, it closes with an overview of *Viva* (2009), Anna Biller's recent feature which subverts the processes of vintage erotica from an attuned and politically engaged perspective. In her chapter 'Semblance and the Sexual Revolution: A Critical Review of *Viva*', Beth Johnson offers an account of the movie and the future of feminist-inspired mediations of sexploitation tropes. *Viva* details the story of Barbie (played by Biller herself), a bored 1960s housewife whose search for sexual thrills leads to an odyssey of swinging liaisons, orgies and kinky countercultural kicks. By revisiting 'classic' sexploitation through a cool, contemporary and cerebral feminist lens, Biller's film provides both a seductive 1960s scenario, as well as a self-reflexive and savvy commentary on the so-called sexual revolution of the psychedelic decade. In this respect, Johnson argues that *Viva* offers a striking and complex structure which seeks not only to 'visually seduce the contemporary viewer, but significantly, to mentally stimulate them'.

To this end, Johnson notes Biller's self-conscious use of a series of narrative tropes designed to facilitate critical reflection on the heroine's thwarted desire for sexual liberation. From the overtly flat delivery of Viva's monologues about the positive aspects of her sexual journey to the structuring of these adventures as a series of self-contained vignettes which often end with a direct-to-camera address, a critical commentary on the female representation within sexploitation aesthetics cuts across a number of differing levels within the movie. As Johnson notes, it is used to convey the fact that 'like the audience, Barbie is repeatedly disappointed; left unfulfilled'. In this respect, she notes the 'obnoxious laughter' that often accompanies various characters' involvement with Barbie's sex quest, clearly exceeding narrative requirement, and used 'as a political comment on, and direct response to, some audience members who have one-dimensional expectations of *Viva*'. If Biller's formal strategies indicate a willingness to use classic sexploitation mythology in order to account for the failings of sexual liberation, then this is further achieved by overloading Barbie's encounters at nudist camps, free-wheeling orgies and pin-up sessions with an overtly melodramatic drive, which adds yet an another level of commentary upon the sexual proceedings depicted. This is achieved not only through the strongly expressive colour coding that the director infuses into scenes of sexual desire, but also the frequent musical moments where characters break into song and directly address the spectator as if seeking commentary on their wider sense of sexual angst. Even the film's climactic orgy scene (which paradoxically features a drugged and unconscious heroine effectively sleeping through her long-desired quest for liberation) are interrupted by elaborate moments of animation in which apples transform into leering mouths, as if to mock Barbie's sexual naivety. Commenting on the uneven reception that *Viva* received on the international festival market, Johnson concludes that the film is purposely situated between classic sexploitation traditions and more knowing feminist re-appropriations of such tropes. In this respect, the movie 'sits oddly between the pulp porn of Gerard Damiano and the avant-garde anger of Breillat. The film is neither solely a dreamy exploration of female sexuality nor a hard-core confrontation of abuse.' In so doing, Biller's work combines *Playboy* chic with postmodern commentary, feminism with freak-out retro spectacle, thus pointing to a significant new trend of the self-conscious cine-erotic.

The chapters contained within this volume thus explore various traditions of the cine-erotic, as well as integrating performer interviews and industrial accounts alongside more 'traditional' academic approaches. In this respect, the reach and remit of the volume can be seen as part of a wider examination of global cult film cultures that the *AlterImage* book series is engaged in through its base at the Cult Film Archive. Since the publication of the last entry to the series,[16] a number of significant research advances have occurred in the study of cult cinema. As well as the proliferation of a number of important conferences and publications in this area, the Cult Film Archive has also launched *Cine-Excess*, its own international cult film conference and festival which acts as a focus for international cult film scholars and critics working in the field (for more information visit www.cine-excess.co.uk).

The annual *Cine-Excess* event follows the established *AlterImage* philosophy of integrating academic and industrial approaches to the cult image, by offering a unique forum for leading international filmmakers, scholars, critics and distributors to meet and discuss a range of global cult and underground film traditions. In terms of filmmaker participation, *Cine-Excess* has hosted visits from a wide range of leading cult directors including John Landis (*An American Werewolf in London* (1981), *Trading Places* (1983)), Roger Corman (*Masque of the Red Death* (1964), *Wild Angels* (1966), *The Trip* (1967)) Stuart Gordon (*Re-Animator* (1985), *King of the Ants* (2003)), Dario Argento (*Deep Red* (1975), *Suspiria* (1977), *Tenebrae* (1982)), Joe Dante (*Piranha* (1978), *The Howling* (1982)), Franco Nero (*Django* (1966), *Keoma* (1976), *Die Hard II* (1992)) and Ruggero Deodato (*Cannibal Holocaust* (1979), *The House on the Edge of the Park* (1980)). The event also hosts around forty talks and plenary discussions by a wide variety of international scholars, as well as hosting UK upcoming cult releases.

The annual *Cine-Excess* event actively encompasses the Cult Film Archive's philosophy of 'taking trash seriously' and this statement also underpins the related *Cine-Excess* DVD label, which was launched in May 2009 in conjunction with Nouveaux Pictures. The label aims to further expand connections between academic and industrial discourses of cult cinema by providing the UK's first dual commercial and educational cult film DVD label, which releases a wide range of classic and contemporary cult titles with extras created by academics as ancillary teaching tools. To date, three titles have been released on the *Cine-Excess* label, including Anna Biller's *Viva*, Dick Maas's influential Dutch thriller *Amsterdamned* (1988), as well as the newly restored Blu-ray version of Dario Argento's supernatural classic *Suspiria* (1977).

Through these conference and DVD activities, the Cult Film Archive is participating in a dramatic increase of academic interest in cult cinema genres that has occurred since the publication of the last *AlterImage* volume. This has been evidenced by the number of significant international events dedicated to the topic. There is also an increased emphasis on cult debate in campus curricula, academic departments and on-line research communities (such as the

North American research portal cult media studies (http://cultmediastudies.ning.com/)). More recently, the formation of the AHRC-funded Onscenity network is studying the increased proliferation of the cine-erotic and its commercialisation through both cinema, subculture and new technology (see www.onscenity.org for more information). The intention of the network is to use critical debate to create a crucial dialogue between academics and policy makers working in this area, as well as expanding the intellectual and industrial comprehensions of these challenging images. It is intended that *Peep Shows* will contribute to these significant and on-going debates around cult cinema's more explicit traditions and codes of representations. It is also envisaged that that this new international and increased interest in what is increasingly coming to be termed as 'cult film studies' will also provide further debate and discussion for future issues of the *AlterImage* series.

CHAPTER 1
PAGES OF SIN:
BETTIE PAGE – FROM 'CHEESECAKE' TEASE TO BONDAGE QUEEN

Bill Osgerby

INTRODUCTION: THE 'DARK ANGEL' OF THE 1950S

In *Bettie Being Bad*, his comic-book homage to Bettie Page, the 1950s pin-up queen, American artist John Workman celebrates the icon's cult cachet. For Workman, Bettie Page offered a walk on the wild side. Against a tide of bland conventionality, he argues, Page lined up in an army of cultural outlaws who refused to toe the conformist line and instead cocked a defiant snook at the compliant, conservative world of 'the squares'. Or, as Workman puts it:

> In the 1950s, they had Ozzie and Harriet, Davy Crockett and Doris Day. We had Lenny Bruce, E.C. comics and BETTIE PAGE![1]

During the 1950s the image of Bettie Page graced the covers of myriad American men's magazines. Starting her career as a model for amateur camera clubs, Page found fame amid

BP-328

FIGURE 1.1 Bettie Page: the 'Dark Angel' of 1950s America

the mid-century boom in pin-up magazine publishing, her trademark raven black hairstyle and beguiling smile captivating a legion of admirers. Tame by modern-day standards, Page's pin-ups were what the publishing industry called 'cheesecake' – photo-spreads of seductively posed (often semi-nude) pretty girls who delighted readers through their winning looks and buxom charms. By the mid-1950s Page had cornered the 'cheesecake' market and was omnipresent across the gamut of American men's magazines, appearing especially regularly in Robert Harrison's stable of pin-up titles, as well as innumerable film loops and photo-sessions produced by the New York 'Pin-up King', Irving Klaw.

But Bettie Page's other work with Klaw also helped establish her more infamous reputation as the 'Dark Angel' of the 1950s. Page appeared in scores of Klaw's short films featuring fetish vignettes (depicting 'cat-fights', spanking and elaborate bondage sessions), as well as sado-masochistic photo-shoots where Page posed in improbably high-heeled stiletto boots, leather corsets and long-sleeved leather gloves, sometimes brandishing a whip or trussed-up in ropes, chains and a ball-gag.

The sexual dynamics of this facet to Page's career, however, were always shot-through with polysemic ambiguity. As Maria Buszek argues, rather than being simple exercises in misogyny, the sheer theatricality of Page's bondage routines can be read as a pantomime of transgressive parody that roguishly revealed the constructed, performative nature of sexual roles and identities:

> Even in the … more extreme, intricately constructed bondage scenarios, Page's participation and performativity shine through as she manages absolutely comical body language through ominous looking binding and ball-gags. Not only does such imagery expose the control and playfulness that Page exerted in her pin-ups, to this day such imagery is held up by many S-M [Sado-Masochism] and B-D [Bondage-Domination] practitioners as exemplary of their belief in role-playing and consent.[2]

Part of Bettie Page's cult appeal, therefore, lies in the way her bondage scenes were characterised by a complex plurality that encompassed elements of frisk theatricality. But the way Page oscillated between her 'good girl' and 'bad girl' imagery is also important. The two sides to Bettie Page's modelling career make her an enthralling character who has become symbolic of the processes of flux and fragmentation endemic to American public and private life throughout the postwar era. While Page's 'cheesecake' photo-features connoted a bold and buoyant age of playful open-mindedness, her bondage and fetish work was both darker and more mischievous – pointing a sardonic finger at the insecurities and fears lurking behind the confident façade of 1950s America. And it is this plurality and wealth of contradictions that have sustained Bettie Page's cult status. Indeed, since the 1980s a Bettie Page 'revival' has seen the pin-up star enshrined as a popular cultural icon in two biopic movies (*Bettie Page: Dark Angel* (2004) and *The Notorious Bettie Page* (2006)), as well as a host of DVD re-releases, comics, fanzines and all manner of popular kitsch. This continuing fascination is indebted to the way Bettie Page

FIGURE 1.2 Bettie Page as pin-up icon

functions as a signifier for the tensions of 1950s America, her image combining both the public face of upbeat sparkle and the more private world of guilty secrets.

BURLESQUE BETTIE

Born in Nashville, Tennessee in 1923, Bettie Page (many 1950s magazines misspelled her name as 'Betty') grew up in itinerant poverty. Her father, a womanising drunkard, wandered the Depression-hit South in search of work and, after her parents divorced, Bettie spent some time living in an orphanage before settling with her five brothers and sisters and disciplinarian mother. Despite a tough childhood, Page was a hardworking student and, with hopes of becoming a teacher, won a college scholarship and graduated with a degree in Education. Marrying a sailor in 1943, she got a job as a secretary but, after divorcing four years later, she moved to California with the dream of becoming an actress. Modelling work came her way but, despite a handful of screen tests with major studios, a Hollywood career never materialised. Disappointed, Page moved to New York in 1950 and picked up more modelling and secretarial work.[3] But things were soon to change.

Wandering along Coney Island beach in autumn 1950, Page got talking with Jerry Tibbs, a black Brooklyn cop and keen amateur photographer. Struck by Page's looks, Tibbs offered to make her up a portfolio of photographs to hawk around studios and photographers if she agreed to pose for him. The two struck up a friendship, and it was Tibbs who persuaded Page to adopt her trademark hairstyle, suggesting she swap her run-of-the-mill ponytail for a curved fringe (known as 'bangs' in America) that would became famous as the classic Bettie Page 'look'. Through Tibbs and other photographer contacts, Page quickly found work posing on the amateur and semi-professional camera club circuit that had sprung up in America during the 1940s. Ostensibly existing to promote 'artistic' photography, many 'camera clubs' served as a means of circumventing legal restrictions on the production of nude photos, and Page regularly posed for local clubs on weekend photo jaunts to upstate New York and rural New Jersey.

Page also attracted the attention of pin-up mogul Robert Harrison. During World War II, American pin-up magazines had prospered, partly as a consequence of a general loosening of sexual morality and partly as a result of a burgeoning market among libidinous servicemen.[4] Harrison had quickly capitalised on the opportunity, launching his first pin-up title, *Beauty Parade*, in 1941 and repeating its success with a series of clones – *Eyeful* (launched in 1942), *Wink* (1945), *Whisper* (1946), *Titter* (1946) and *Flirt* (1947)

During the early 1950s the pin-up boom continued. Harrison's attentions, however, were increasingly focusing on the runaway success of his muckraking scandal sheet, *Confidential* (launched in 1952), but his pin-up titles were still a big earner and in 1951 Bettie Page began gracing their covers and photo-spreads on a regular basis.

In many respects it is easy to see the covers and pictorials of magazines such as *Beauty Parade* and *Eyeful* as the embodiment of an oppressive and objectifying 'male gaze'. But, as Stuart Hall has famously argued, popular culture is invariably an arena characterised by 'the double movement of containment and resistance'.[5] And, in these terms, it is possible to situate Harrison's pin-up magazines in the long, seditious heritage of American burlesque.

As Robert Allen shows, during the mid-nineteenth century a tradition of theatrical burlesque won popular success through its mixture of impertinent humour and provocative displays of female sensuality. For Allen, burlesque was culturally subversive because it was 'a physical and ideological inversion of the Victorian ideal of femininity'.[6] The scantily-clad burlesque performer, Allen suggests, was a rebellious and self-aware 'sexual other' who transgressed norms of 'proper' feminine behaviour and appearance by 'revel[ing] in the display of the female body as a sexed and sensuous object'.[7] But, Allen argues, while burlesque initially played to a respectable, middle-class audience, it was quickly relegated to the shadow-world of working-class male leisure. And, in the process, the burlesque performer steadily 'lost' her voice. As burlesque increasingly revolved around the display of the performer's body, Allen contends, 'her transgressive power was circumscribed by her construction as an exotic other removed from the world of ordinary women'.[8]

Allen's account, however, is too hasty in announcing the demise of burlesque's subversive potential. During the 1950s, for example, echoes of burlesque's tradition of transgression still reverberated through American popular culture. For instance, while Robert Harrison's pin-up magazines certainly presented pin-up models as sexual objects, they also featured marked elements of camp humour and playful satire. Many of Harrison's photo-spreads, for example, featured models acting out spoof scenarios in elaborate 'comic book'-style photo stories whose tongue-in-cheek silliness effectively elaborated a self-parody of the whole pin-up genre. 'Gal and a Gorilla', for instance, saw Bettie Page zipping around New York with her 'constant escort', the scooter-riding Gus – a man dressed in a ludicrous gorilla costume.[9]

And the burlesque resonated through many other aspects of Bettie Page's career. Her work with photographer Bunny Yaeger, for instance, undoubtedly traded on Page's knockout looks, but it was also marked by a knowing sense of irony. Yaeger had, herself, been a successful pin-up model and was trying to get her foot in the door as a photographer when she teamed up with Page in 1954. In Florida the pair spent a month working on some of Page's most successful photo-shoots. One of the most famous was the 'Jungle Bettie' session that took place at the USA Africa Wildlife Park. Clad in a spectacular leopard-skin outfit (that, like most of her costumes, she had made herself), Page posed with a pair of leashed cheetahs, swung like Tarzan from lush mango trees and was captured by a tribe of cannibals in a series of photographs that at once both celebrated *and* playfully lampooned stock stereotypes of the 'exotic Amazon'.

Another light-hearted Yaeger shoot saw Bettie posing nude, aside from a jolly Santa Claus hat and a cheeky wink given to the camera – an image that was quickly snapped up by Hugh Hefner and used as the centrefold to the January 1955 edition of his flourishing *Playboy* magazine.

Burlesque traits also surfaced in Page's work with Irving Klaw. It was through her work with Robert Harrison that Page first got to know Klaw and his sister Paula. The Klaws had started in business during the 1930s, running a second-hand bookstore in Manhattan, with a sideline in mail order magic tricks. Neither trade was exactly a money-spinner. But in 1941 they struck lucky when Irving noticed his customers' annoying habit of ripping-out pictures of movie stars from his magazine stock. Spotting a market opportunity, the Klaws went into

FIGURE 1.3 'Jungle Bettie': stereotypes of sexuality and race are parodied in Page's work with Bunny Yaeger

business selling movie posters and publicity stills. Abandoning the magic tricks, they set up a new company – Movie Star News – and did a brisk trade in mail order sales of movie material. During the war the Klaws enjoyed a lucrative turnover selling pictures of Rita Hayworth and

FIGURE 1.4 Burlesque goes celluloid: Bettie Page in the influential *Teaserama*

Betty Grable to GIs posted overseas, but during the 1950s they moved into producing their own pin-ups of hired models, working with Bettie Page for the first time in 1952.[10] But, as well as the photo-shoots, Irving Klaw also had big screen ambitions.

Klaw, however, was beaten to the post by Martin Lewis. A New York cinema owner and part-time film producer, Lewis hired Page to act in his black-and-white 'B'-movie burlesque review, *Striporama* (1952). The movie's loose plot saw three hapless comics convince the 'New York Council for Culture' that burlesque was a national institution by staging a show whose acts included Bettie Page in a bubble-bath scene staged in a Sheik's harem, alongside a routine (billed as 'Rosetta and Her Well-Trained Pigeons') where a talented flock of birds make off with a performer's clothes. Despite its threadbare production values, *Striporama* was a hit, making around $80,000 within nine weeks of its release, a success that spurred Irving Klaw to sign Page up for movies of his own.

Klaw had already shot Page in a few 8mm and 16mm film shorts, but he began thinking bigger and soon included her in two feature-length films, *Varitease* (1954) and *Teaserama* (1955). Shot in Eastman Color, both abandoned conventional narrative, and instead comprised sequences of various burlesque routines. The main attraction of *Varitease* was the established burlesque star Lili St. Cyr, but Bettie Page also got high billing for her appearance as a sequined harem girl performing an over-the-top version of the 'Dance of the Seven Veils'. *Teaserama* saw Page in a more central role, wearing a variety of campy costumes to introduce the acts and appearing in a black, silk maid's outfit in a routine alongside burlesque luminary Tempest Storm.

According to Allen, the wave of 1950s burlesque films of which *Varitease* and *Teaserama* were a part can be seen as exemplifying a sexist scopic regime of the kind identified by Laura Mulvey in her renowned 1975 essay 'Visual Pleasure and Narrative Cinema'.[11] In these terms, texts are seen as constructing women as the sexual objects of masculine pleasure. And, indeed, burlesque performers such as Bettie Page, Lili St. Cyr and Tempest Storm were certainly 'objects' of a gaze. But, as Eric Schaefer points out, the burlesque genre is open to a much broader range of readings than simply that offered by Mulvey's notion of male visual pleasure.[12] According to Schaefer, the burlesque striptease films of the 1950s had the potential to be socially transgressive in much the same way as the nineteenth-century shows championed by Allen. As he explains, by removing her clothing in a highly ritualised and stylised way, the 1950s burlesque performer not only became a potential object of erotic desire, but in making a spectacle of herself

> she simultaneously made a spectacle of gender identity. As performers, strippers were not merely the bearers of meaning in films, but active makers of meaning, calling attention to the performative aspect of gender.[13]

And these elements of burlesque transgression, inherent in many facets of Bettie Page's career, raise interesting questions about the way 1950s America should be understood. According to many historians, American society during the Cold War was characterised by a deep suspicion of dissension and stern pressures to conform. From this perspective, US foreign policies geared to the 'containment' of communist influence abroad found their parallel at home. Alan Nadel, for example, argues that America's cultural agenda during the 1950s was infused by paradigms of containment, with literature, cinema and the spectrum of popular culture deploying narratives that 'functioned to foreclose dissent, pre-empt dialogue and preclude contradiction'.[14]

At the heart of these ideologies of containment stood archetypal images of straight-laced, suburban domesticity. As Elaine Tyler May shows, family life was configured as a vision of reassuring certainty in an unpredictable and threatening world. As the superpowers squared up, pressures for social stability intensified and nonconformity – whether configured in political, cultural or sexual terms – was increasingly perceived as a threat to American security. Amid this ambience of anxiety and distrust, May argues, strategies of 'domestic containment' promoted domesticity and 'normal' family life as fundamental to the strength and vitality of the nation – and any deviation from these norms risked charges of abnormality and deviance.[15]

Certainly, there is a lot of truth to this depiction of 1950s America. The McCarthyite witch-hunts, for example, may have been geared to ferreting out 'reds under the bed', but John D'Emilio[16] and David Johnson[17] both show how they were also a 'lavender scare' that conflated red-baiting with rabid homophobia. Representations of contented family life, meanwhile, were undoubtedly ubiquitous in American culture throughout the 1950s. Academics, politicians and the mass media all championed the family as both the cornerstone of American liberty and as a panacea to the perceived social and sexual dangers of the day. In magazines like *Life*, depictions of the middle-class family embodied a confident sense of national identity,[18] while television series such as *Ozzie and Harriet* (1952–66), *Father Knows Best* (1954–63) and *Leave It to Beaver* (1957–63) all presented an idealised family life of cheerful tranquillity.

Nevertheless, just as American foreign policy failed to 'contain' communist influence abroad, 'domestic containment' failed to exercise an iron grip over cultural life at home. Indeed, the sheer amount of effort invested in pressing down the lid of 'containment' suggests that many people were embracing cultural values sharply at odds with traditional gender roles and dominant ideals of family-oriented domesticity. Indeed, contrary to popular perceptions of the 1950s as a time of relative tranquillity and consensus, historians have increasingly shown the decade to be 'an era of conflict and contradiction, an era in which a complex set of ideologies contended for public allegiance'.[19] Authors such as Larry May[20] and Joel Foreman,[21] for instance, have highlighted the dimensions of disruption and dissent that distinguished the decade. From this perspective, the attention accorded to the authoritarian discourses of the 1950s has enriched our understanding of the era, but it has also

> contributed to an imbalanced view that so amplifies the effect of socio-political coercions that the substantial manifestations of dissent and resistance disappear into an easily overlooked background. To one degree or another, most studies of the 1950s are affected by this disposition and thus appear as histories of victimization rather than histories of nascent rebellion and liberation.[22]

This is especially true with regard to constructions of femininity. Betty Friedan's 1963 bestseller, *The Feminine Mystique*,[23] has left an enduring image of women in 1950s America as the suffocated victims of a 'comfortable concentration camp', with the claustrophobia of suburban drudgery generating feelings of confusion, self-doubt and despair. Yet Joanne Meyerowitz[24] incisively shows how femininity and its cultural representations were much more diverse than allowed for in accounts such as Friedan's. Alongside conservative visions of submissive domesticity, Meyerowitz demonstrates how there *also* existed many representations of women as independent, creative and non-conformist. And, while it is folly to cast Bettie Page as any kind of figurehead for 1950s feminism, the prevalence of her image across the panoply of American popular culture certainly flipped an irreverent middle-finger to the nation's puritanical moral guardians. More importantly, Page's traits of burlesque parody and pastiche served to reveal the artificiality and performativity of gender identities. And, while these elements were always a significant facet to her 'Good Bettie' cheesecake pin-ups, they were even more pronounced in her 'Bad Bettie' bondage work.

THE DELIGHTS OF DISCIPLINE

Irving and Paula Klaw's movie stills and pin-up business thrived, but they found some customers, especially those from the higher end of the social scale – doctors, lawyers, businessmen – often asked for more specialised 'Damsel in Distress' photos, where models were bound, gagged and roundly spanked by a leather-clad dominatrix.

Never ones to miss a market opportunity, the Klaws were happy to oblige. With hired models and a stockpile of lingerie, fetish costumes and props, the Klaws began producing photos and short film loops featuring elaborate scenarios of bondage and domination, with Irving directing and Paula taking many of the photos.[25] The images dealt with the *outré*, the taboo and the outright kinky but, because the Klaws were desperate to avoid charges of peddling pornography, nudity was strictly *verboten*. Indeed, it was not uncommon for Irving to insist that models wore two pairs of knickers, lest an unruly tuft of pubic hair creep into shot.

Throughout the early 1950s Bettie Page was one of the Klaws' most popular bondage models. Alongside her camera club and men's magazine modeling, she regularly worked with the Klaws on short bondage films and photo-shoots. *Jungle Girl Tied to Trees*, for example, saw Page dressed in a leopard-skin bikini and roped between two trees, being menaced by a woman wearing a leather skirt and high heels and wielding a huge bull-whip. *Betty Gets Bound and Kidnapped*, meanwhile, found Page drugged, abducted and trussed up in her underwear by two wicked dominatrices. Some customer requests were particularly bizarre. As Page recalled with a chuckle in one of her rare interviews, 'the wildest request' she ever had was

> when this guy sent in a pony outfit with a hood, covered in black leather. And I had to get down on my feet and hands like a pony, and Paula put this costume over me. You couldn't even see my face, but that's what this guy wanted.[26]

FIGURE 1.5 Creating a bondage icon: Irving Klaw and Bettie Page

For the customer, these convoluted bondage scenarios were obviously a source of illicit sexual thrills. But there were also other, possibly more renegade, meanings at stake. Like the burlesque qualities inherent in Page's pin-ups, her bondage work can be seen as highlighting the perfomativity of gender roles and sexual identities. According to the influential work of Judith Butler, gender is not a stable entity or an 'agency from which various acts follow', rather it is 'an identity tenuously constituted in time, instituted in an exterior space through a stylized repetition of acts'.[27] In these terms, gender can be understood as a shifting set of 'performances' – a 'corporeal style' that is fabricated and sustained through a set of performative acts and 'a ritualized repetition of conventions'.[28] For Maria Buszek, Bettie Page's bondage work with the Klaws is a case in point. Oscillating between the virgin and the vamp, she argues, Page helped 'maintain the presence of the complex, pluralistic pin-up in an era that vigorously sought to use the genre to communicate far more binary – and therefore stable – constructions of female sexuality'.[29] Particularly significant is the plurality of roles Page assumes in the bondage shots. Rather than being exclusively dominant or solely submissive, she switches between the two, taking on each theatrical performance with an over-the-top gusto – whether snarling with cartoonish menace as the 'spanker', or wincing with indignation as the helpless 'spankee'.

THE DARK ANGEL'S DOWNFALL

Throughout the 1950s the terrain of sexual politics was continuously contested and contradictory. But authoritarian 'containment' was always a force to be reckoned with. By 1955 Joseph McCarthy's political witch-hunts had run out of steam, but Estes Kefauver's cultural crusade was just getting in its stride. In 1951 Kefauver, the Democratic Senator for Tennessee, made his mark as head of a Senate investigation into organised crime. Four years later he set his sights on another spectre that ostensibly menaced postwar America – juvenile delinquency. Appointed in 1953, the Senate Subcommittee to Investigate Juvenile Delinquency had already been underway for two years when Kefauver assumed its chairmanship, but under his direction the proceedings gained energy and gravitas.

Televised from gavel-to-gavel, the Subcommittee considered a range of potential causes of juvenile crime, but they were preoccupied with the possible influence of the media. Throughout the mid-1950s the Senators heard testimony from a parade of experts and moral crusaders such as the psychologist Frederic Wertham, who cited the media's proclivity for violence as having a woeful impact on the nation's youth. While the clamour for tighter federal censorship was resisted, the Subcommittee demanded that the media exercise stricter self-regulation – a call that prompted the Comics Magazine Association to pass its infamous Comics Code in 1954, effectively outlawing the horror and crime comics beloved by rebellious youngsters. Having smashed horror comics, Kefauver turned his attention to pornography. In 1955 he came to New York looking for scalps, and Irving Klaw was high on his hit-list.

Though he struggled hard, Kefauver could never prove a link between pornography and juvenile delinquency. But the Klaws and Page were subpoenaed to appear before his Subcommittee. Ultimately, Page was not called to testify, but Irving Klaw was hauled-up for a fierce grilling. Kefauver bent over backwards to paint Klaw as a kingpin of American porn and an arch-corruptor of the nation's youth, but Klaw resolutely denied that he dealt in obscene material (his films, after all, featured no nudity) and he defiantly 'took the fifth', refusing to co-operate with the investigation.

FIGURE 1.6 Bettie as 'Spanker' and 'Spankee': modes of gender performance in her work with Irving Klaw

At the end of the day, Kefauver got nowhere. His Subcommittee's work finally sputtered out in a 1960 report, *Control of Obscene Material*, which was largely ignored by federal and state legislators alike.[30] But the hearings effectively broke the Klaws. In the face of bad publicity

and FBI harassment, Irving feared prosecution and closed down his business in 1957. Burning most of his pin-up and bondage negatives (though some were luckily saved by Paula), he retired to Florida. The Kefauver hearings also had a traumatic impact on Bettie Page. In 1957 she quit New York and never returned to the big city or her modelling career. As her personal life became increasingly unstable, she drifted through a series of failed relationships and succumbed to the ravages of alcoholism, mental illness and, perhaps even worse, evangelical Christianity.

BETTIE PAGE REBORN

Vanishing from the public eye enhanced Bettie Page's aura of mystique, and by the late 1970s a cult interest in the model had begun to cohere. During the 1970s and 1980s a series of books appeared featuring assorted photos of Page from the 1950s, presenting them as a 'nostalgic' look at the erotica of days gone by. In 1976, for example, Eros published *A Nostalgic Look at Bettie Page*, while Belier Press launched four volumes of *Betty Page: Private Peeks* between 1978 and 1980; and in 1983 London Enterprises released *In Praise of Bettie Page: A Nostalgic Collector's Item*, reprinting a series of camera club photos and a 'cat-fight' photo-shoot. In 1987, meanwhile, Greg Theakstone started the fanzine *The Betty Pages*, recounting tales of Page's life and adventures during the camera club days. Two biopics, Nico B's *Bettie Page: Dark Angel* (featuring fetish model Paige Richards as Page) and Mary Harron's *The Notorious Bettie Page* (with Gretchen Mol as the eponymous lead) were also bathed in wistful nostalgia, presenting Page as a *risqué* heroine in an age of uptight repression.

But Page was also revived and innovatively reconceived by a host of artists and comic-book writers. During the early 1980s, for example, talented illustrator Dave Stevens used Page as the basis for a leading character in his comic series, *The Rocketeer*, while the 1990s saw Dark Horse Comics release a comic-book series based on Page's fictional adventures and Eros Comics followed suit with a number of tongue-in-cheek Bettie Page titles. And Page has also been the inspiration for many of artist Olivia De Berardinis's critically acclaimed erotic paintings. Page, moreover, has been a powerful influence in the world of fashion and subcultural style, with many female rockabillies, punks and goths dying their hair and cutting it into 'bangs' to emulate the striking Bettie Page 'look'.

A postmodern theorist such as Fredric Jameson might see the recycling of Bettie Page's image in a condescending light, viewing the Page revival as part of a more general cultural malaise. In the late twentieth century, Jameson argues, original cultural production gave way to a new world of pastiche, a world where cultural innovation was no longer possible and people had 'nowhere to turn but to the past'[31] and a retreat into the 'complacent play of historical allusion'.[32]

But John Storey has taken issue with Jameson's postmodern pessimism. For Storey, Jameson's account fails to grasp the new meanings actively generated through processes of cultural recycling. Rather than being a random, and uniquely 'postmodern', cannibalisation of the past, Storey suggests, the plundering of historical style is part of a tradition of appropriation, *bricolage* and intertextuality that has always characterised popular culture.[33] Moreover, Storey argues, contemporary expressions of retro-styling and historical allusion – of which the Bettie Page revival is indicative – do not represent a depthless 'imitation of dead styles',[34] but are practices of active cultural enterprise in which cultural symbols from the past are commandeered and mobilised in meaningful ways in the lived cultures of the present. From this perspective, then, the cult revival of Bettie Page can be seen as an active appropriation and reanimation of a cultural icon whose complex, pluralistic performances of 1950s femininity offer enticing opportunities for parodying and destabilising dominant gender archetypes.

CHAPTER 2

SOUND AND PERFORMANCE IN STEPHEN SAYADIAN'S
NIGHT DREAMS AND *CAFÉ FLESH*

Jacob Smith

In 1982, a television news crew from the Midwest arrived in Los Angeles to document the making of a pornographic film. The adult videotape market was just beginning to surge, inspiring these savvy TV journalists to take a behind-the-scenes look at a typical porn production. The news crew's presence on the set only added to a general atmosphere of controlled chaos: the entire film had to be shot over eleven days in a small studio in the heart of downtown LA; electricity was being illegally patched-in to power the equipment; and extras were recruited from a nearby blood bank and methadone clinic. After three days on the set, the news crew went home, titillated and satisfied that they had gotten their story. It was not however, exactly the story they thought they were getting. Though they were unaware of it at the time, they were not so much witnessing the making of a typical porno as the making of a cult film. While featuring hard-core sex, the film that they saw being made departed from many of the conventions of adult films, and would find its greatest success not in porn theatres, but on the midnight movie circuit. That film was director Stephen Sayadian's second adult feature, *Café Flesh*.

The works of Stephen Sayadian (aka 'Rinse Dream') stand out as some of the most interesting and complicated in the adult genre. Sayadian made *Night Dreams* (1981) and *Café Flesh* (1982) in collaboration with writer Jerry Stahl and cinematographer Frank Delia, and both films are notable for their novel approaches to sound and performance, as well as their complicated relationship with the audience. In reviews of Sayadian's films, one often finds phrases such as 'the thinking-person's porn film', suggesting their uncertain relationship to the porn genre.[1] Indeed, both films feature idiosyncratic stylistic choices that were intended by the filmmakers to confound the generic expectations of the porn audience. Sayadian's distinctive soundscapes complicate the meaning of onscreen hard-core action, and demonstrate the importance of sound in the cinematic depiction of sexual fantasy. Performance is one of Sayadian's central themes, and his films feature styles of acting that are typically associated with the avant-garde. Paradoxically, provocative stylistic techniques such as these provided their own powerful eroticism, and helped the films to flourish in contexts of reception outside of porn. The style of *Night Dreams* and *Café Flesh* is best understood when placed in dialogue with a historical account of the production and reception of these films. Sayadian's career provides a lens onto a pivotal time in the history of the porn industry, and can allow us to explore connections between porn and other forms of cultural production, such as the magazine industry of the 1970s, cultures of avant-garde and midnight movies in the 1980s, and the rise of the home video market.

FROM *HUSTLER* TO HOLLYWOOD

Before turning to Sayadian's film work in the 1980s, it will be useful to begin by considering his earlier career in the magazine industry. Indeed, the team that produced *Night Dreams* and *Café Flesh* – Sayadian, Stahl and Delia – met in the mid-1970s while working at Larry Flynt's *Hustler* magazine. Sayadian had come to the magazine as a satirist, having previously submitted work to *Mad Magazine*, Marvel Comics and *National Lampoon* in the early 1970s. In the fall of 1976, Sayadian – then twenty years old – took his portfolio to Larry Flynt in Columbus, Ohio, who hired him on the spot as *Hustler*'s creative director in charge of humour and advertising. This position entailed making the advertisements for Flynt's novelty sex products: 'There were no advertisers,' Sayadian recalls, 'we made our own advertising.' In fact, Sayadian asserts that Flynt made more money from sex products than from sales of the magazine.[2]

Flynt and Sayadian's goal was to make the advertising share 'the same sensibility as the rest of the magazine', to imbue every aspect of *Hustler* with their nervy sense of satire so that, as Sayadian says, 'when you looked at the advertising, you wouldn't know if it was a parody or if it was real.'[3] Consider Sayadian's contributions to the January 1977 issue of *Hustler* (vol. 3, no. 7). This is, in fact, Sayadian's debut, and the editors welcome him to the team in the front-matter of the issue: 'Steve is now a member of *Hustler*'s advertising staff, where he can apply his distaste for ridiculous sales pitches to ensure honesty and a clever approach to our ads.' One such ad, entitled 'Love Doll', features a bizarre photo of a cartoonish prison inmate chomping on a cigar. His cell is a minimalist blank set, with bars that represent a window, a toilet, and a few photos suggesting a wall. He cradles in his arms an inflatable doll – in actuality a living nude model – who it appears he has just removed from the box. 'Leisure Time's inflatable Love Dolls have countless uses', the ad copy asserts, 'traveling companion, gag gift, conversation piece, bunk mate…' The description of the 'Susie' doll is as follows: 'No moving parts, but a certain quiet charm. Easy to beat at poker. Washable.'

Ads such as this feature a visual style and twisted sense of humour that make them blend in with ad parodies found in the same issue. In a feature called 'Hustler Takes a Look at Madison Avenue', Sayadian presents a gory send-up of Playboy's famous ad campaign. Above the caption 'What Sort of Man Reads Slayboy?' we see a gruesome photo of a dapper man in smoking jacket and pipe, surrounded by the bodies of three Playboy bunnies he has apparently killed. A similarly gory parody of a Curtail chainsaw ad depicts Sayadian himself, reclining in an elegant white suit, chainsaw in hand, surrounded by bloody severed limbs. The themes of violence and dismemberment continue in the 'STUDential Life' ad parody, wherein a woman, seated at an elegant dinner table, smiles while preparing to slice into the large severed penis on her plate.

Though certainly crass, Sayadian's work at Hustler has a media-savvy, confrontational edge that makes it similar to the aesthetics both of Mad Magazine and National Lampoon. Such ad parodies were a central part of Hustler's style, and subsequent issues would take aim at the cigarette industry as well as the Rev. Jerry Falwell in the famous 1983 Campari ad campaign parody, 'Jerry Falwell Talks About His First Time'. It is not surprising then, that Michael O'Donaghue – influential writer for the National Lampoon and Saturday Night Live – wrote the Hustler staff a fan letter, declaring it to be his favourite magazine.[4] Nor is it surprising that Laura Kipnis would observe that Hustler was like a 'Mad magazine cartoon come to life'.[5] As we have seen, much of the credit for the development of that style goes to Sayadian, as well as a larger creative team at Hustler that included photographer Delia and writer Stahl.

When Sayadian's approach to satire was combined with hard-core sexual images, the result was a presentation of the body that was at once erotic, dark, playful and anxious. This is certainly not the upscale, air-brushed fantasy of Hugh Hefner's Playboy. Consider that in the issue of Hustler described above, one cannot only see pornographic images of naked women and men, but also gory ad parodies with severed penises, and a graphic feature on war atrocities entitled 'The Real Obscenity: War.' Indeed, Hustler succeeded in part because its vulgarity and political edge appealed to the same college audience that was consuming the twisted satire of National Lampoon. While it would be ridiculous to assert that the magazine's notoriously explicit nude photos played only a small role in its success, Sayadian and Stahl's twisted black humour were nevertheless important factors in the magazine's style and can help to contextualise both Flynt's magazine and their subsequent film work.

Regardless of the source of its appeal, it is undeniable that Flynt's magazine experienced phenomenal growth in the late 1970s. Sayadian recalls that, when he came to Columbus, the magazine was selling about 200,000 a month, but within a year and a half that figure was three million, and it was only 'a handful' of people doing it.[6] In the wake of such growth, Flynt moved his corporate headquarters from Columbus to Los Angeles: 'We went from this funky building [in Columbus] to the top floors at Century City. I mean the growth was ridiculous.'[7] Flynt and company had plans to expand into other media, specifically film. 'We had such plans,' Sayadian remembers, 'we were going to start our own film company. We were going to make horror films, off-beat films.'[8] All these plans had to be put on hold, however, when Flynt was shot in Lawrenceville, Georgia on 6 March 1978. While Flynt began his long, painful recovery, he lost control of much of his media empire, including the film company.

Stahl, Sayadian and Delia had moved to LA with *Hustler*, where the latter two men opened an art design studio. They continued to work on a contract basis with *Hustler*, but also began making posters and one-sheets for Hollywood films such as *The Fog* (John Carpenter, 1980), *Dressed to Kill* (Brian De Palma, 1980) and *Escape From New York* (John Carpenter, 1981). Their studio was located in the Cherokee Building in downtown LA, which also provided practice space for local punk rock bands such as the Germs and Wall of Voodoo, and office space for Brendan Mullen, the owner of LA's premier punk rock club, The Masque. This overlap with the LA punk scene was to have an influence on Sayadian's subsequent film work: 'there was a sub-genre of punk which sort of crossed into the movies I was making, and that had more to do with geography than anything else.'[9]

This geographical influence on Sayadian's work suggests a connection to what Joan Hawkins describes as a 'late twentieth-century avant-garde' that emerged in the 1980s when artists and filmmakers began moving downtown – to the East Village in Manhattan, the warehouse district in Chicago, and the South Market area (SOMA) in San Francisco.[10] These depressed areas had yet to be gentrified and contained cheap studio space for artists, filmmakers and musicians. Hawkins argues that diverse downtown artists and filmmakers such as David Lynch, Nick Zedd, Richard Kern, Larry Fessenden, Todd Haynes, Kathy Acker and Tom Palazzolo were united by a 'common urban lifestyle' and 'roots in the punk underground' as well as 'a shared commitment to formal and narrative experimentation, a view of the human body as a site of social and political struggle, an interest in radical identity politics and a mistrust of institutionalized mechanisms of wealth and power'.[11] Importantly, many of these downtown filmmakers borrowed heavily from 'low' cultural forms such as 'erotic thrillers, horror, sci-fi and porn'.[12] The films made by Sayadian, Stahl and Delia in the early 1980s fit the general outlines of the downtown avant-garde. However, where many downtown filmmakers were incorporating aspects of pornography into avant-garde film, Sayadian made the opposite move, bringing techniques associated with art films to his first adult feature: *Night Dreams*.

NIGHT DREAMS

The opening credits of *Night Dreams* list Stahl as writer, Delia as director and Sayadian as producer. Stahl and Sayadian wrote the script together, and Sayadian oversaw the shooting: 'Jerry was never on the sets. We worked really well together because I was sort of in charge with the visuals and he was in charge with the dialogue.'[13] I say that Sayadian, Stahl and Delia are credited in the film, but in fact, the names that appear are aliases. Delia became F. X. Pope, Stahl became Herbert W. Day (the name of a high school principal he wanted to saddle with the title of pornographer), and Sayadian became Rinse Dream: 'Jerry started calling me that, and then everybody followed.'[14] These aliases were used in part to avoid the LA Vice Squad.

At the time, working in porn required the acceptance of a certain level of risk, though it also meant the possibility of financial backing. *Night Dreams* was made for a budget of $65,000, supplied by what Sayadian calls 'traditional porno people', though the final film itself was anything but traditional. In fact, Sayadian stated that 'it took a lot of charm and boyish enthusiasm' to convince his financial backers not to break his arms: 'but they liked me, and that goes a long way'.[15] Indeed, neither *Night Dreams* nor *Café Flesh* were successful on the porn exhibition circuit. Yet it was the very stylistic techniques that prevented these films from working in porn theatres that allowed them to succeed in other reception contexts. Thus, in order to understand the cultural life of Sayadian's films, we will need to consider the idiosyncratic ways in which sound, performance and narrative function within them.

The narrative of *Night Dreams* is structured around sessions in a surreal sex therapy clinic. The first image we see is an extreme close-up of Mrs. Van Houton (Dorothy Le May), kneeling in a stark white clinical observation room, electrodes connected to her forehead. She looks directly at the camera and says, 'I know you're watching me. I feel your eyes like fingers touching me in certain places.' The camera cuts to a shot of a male and female doctor (Andy Nichols and Jennifer West) observing Mrs. Van Houton on the other side of one-way glass. For the rest of the film Mrs. Van Houton delivers direct-address stream-of-consciousness monologues to the camera that segue into stylised sex sequences while, on the other side of the glass, the exasperated doctors try to make sense of her behaviour. This structure distances the sex scenes from the film's larger narrative, creating a certain ambiguity as to whether the fantasies are those of Mrs. Van Houton or the doctors.

The role of the therapists in *Night Dreams* differs from male sexologists in adult films such as *Deep Throat* (Gerard Damiano, 1972) and *The Opening of Misty Beethoven* (Radley Metzger, 1975). For Linda Williams, such figures occupied the position once held in literary pornography by the libertine, whose 'scientific knowledge of the pleasure of sexuality' leads to the variety of sexual numbers.[16] In *Night Dreams* we find a different dynamic: the sexual numbers are presented as arising from the fantasies of the female client, not the male sexologist. In fact, not only is the male doctor subordinate to the female doctor ('don't forget who's assisting who', she tells him at one point), but neither of the therapists are found to be in control of the situation. That is, the film ends with a surprise role reversal: the doctors are revealed to be the clients/patients when Mrs. Van Houton emerges from the observation room and asks, 'Will I see you next week?' In robotic unison, the two doctors turn to each other and reply, 'Do we have a choice?'

Thus the use of the therapy motif in *Night Dreams* does not work so much to anchor the sex to a male authority figure, but instead to motivate the film's surrealist stylistic excess. Stahl wrote in an email interview that 'therapy is the perfect way into the surreal. Not to mention

FIGURE 2.1 'Avant-garde weirdness' as sexual thrill in *Night Dreams*

that its inherent power structure invites sexual parallels.'[17] Indeed, the film is peppered with moments of flat-out, avant-garde weirdness similar in tone to David Lynch's *Eraserhead* (1976). In one scene, Mrs. Van Houton pulls a fetus from a man's trousers, in another she relaxes and shares a cigarette in what seems like post-coital bliss with a large fish. Set designs are minimalist and stylised, at times resembling the *Hustler* advertisements described above.

While the narrative and imagery set *Night Dreams* apart from most adult films, we should also note how Sayadian's film sounds. For one thing, *Night Dreams* features the use of recorded music to make critical and satiric comments on the accompanying images: in one sequence, Mrs. Van Houton performs oral sex on an African American man wearing a cardboard Cream of Wheat box – literally the corporate trademark come to life – as the soundtrack plays the Ink Spots' light jazz version of 'Old Man River'; later Sayadian make ironic use of Eric Satie's 'Trois Gymnopedies' and we hear a recording of Johnny Cash's 'Ring of Fire' as performed by Cherokee Building denizens Wall of Voodoo. Sayadian stated that simply hearing 'a cutting edge band' like Wall of Voodoo on an adult soundtrack at this time was 'unique'. In fact, one of the most distinctive aspects of *Night Dreams* is the use of sound.[18]

SOUNDSCAPES OF DESIRE

The generic conventions of the porn soundtrack call for what Rich Cante and Angelo Restivo call porno-performativity: post-synced moans and asides that function to authenticate the pleasure of the (typically female) performers.[19] Such vocalisations are often accompanied by slick, trance-inducing dance music (disco, funk, or more recently techno) played by anonymous session musicians. That kind of clichéd porn music is completely absent from *Night Dreams*, and while the film does contain porno-perfomativity, it is overshadowed by stunning *musique concrete*-style multitrack soundscapes. In order to get a sense of how these soundscapes function in the film, it will be necessary to consider them in relation to theoretical writings on film sound, pornography and sexual fantasy.

Returning to the opening moments of the film, we hear the sounds of amplified heartbeats and breathing over a black screen, and then cut to the close-up of Mrs. Van Houton in an observation room. After the initial dialogue, fast cuts of the oversized faces of dolls mark a transition to a fantasy sequence that takes place in a dimly-lit children's playroom where a huge jack in the box pops open to reveal a sinister-looking clown, his penis exposed through his garish costume. As Mrs. Van Houton and the clown engage in oral sex, we hear loops of high-pitched laughter, a distant rhythmic chanting, and sounds that resemble the squeaking of plastic toys. The distant laughter and chanting in this scene contrast with the 'too close' quality of over-dubbed porno-performativity. Linda Williams describes how post-sync 'sounds of pleasure' have a certain clarity that makes them seem to come from very close up. Not only does this lend a certain ambiguity as to the performer's position in space (a sense of 'spacelessness'), but porno-performativity also provides an index of intimacy.[20] The loops of laughter and distant chanting in the scene described above frame the onscreen sexual action in a different kind of space.

In fact, there is an intimate relationship between sound and space, which might be encapsulated in the term 'sonotope', which designates the sonic representation of a particular space.[21] Sound always contains messages about the space through which it has passed. Consider for example, a sound that is 'wet' with reverberation. That 'wetness' is actually a perceptual image of the source of the sound combined with the influence of the large reverberant space through which the sound has travelled. Sonotopes can shape how we understand the performances given within them and the images that accompany them. Sonotope can be a useful concept for considering the genre of film pornography when one considers arguments that sexual fantasy is best understood not as a linear narrative with a fixed subject position, but as a certain setting, atmosphere or ambiance capable of sustaining a set of interconnected relationships and points of view.[22] If fantasy is best understood as the setting of a scene, and sound is uniquely able to convey the experience of space, then sound design emerges as a central aspect of the representation of sexual fantasy in adult film. Sound is a powerful – perhaps *the most* powerful – index of setting, and the choice of sonotope employed in a particular scene will profoundly shape the subsequent experience of fantasy.

Because of its novel approaches to sound design in a hard-core context, *Night Dreams* provides a rich text for the consideration of what might be called erotic sonotopes. I have already mentioned how the over-dubbed moans of porno-performativity suggest a certain sound-space: the closeness of intimacy. Sayadian's use of sound in the sex scenes described above frames the on-screen sex as occurring within a larger space, at the margins of some other off-screen activity. That is, the distant laughter, chanting and murmured speech, frame the sex as somewhat obscure or secret, thus subtly heightening its erotic affect. We might identify another sonotope in a sequence in which Mrs. Van Houton masturbates in front of a bathroom mirror before being attacked by a masked stranger who has been watching her from an open door. The soundtrack during this scene features a dripping faucet saturated with reverb, as well as atonal electronic music in the style of Morten Subotnick's 1967 composition, 'Silver Apples of the Moon'. The reverberant dripping faucet places the listener within a wide, open space with hard surfaces: not so much a bathroom as a concrete parking garage or empty industrial warehouse. A similar kind of space is suggested in a later sequence in *Night Dreams*, when Mrs. Van Houton finds herself in 'hell', involved in a *ménage a trois* with a devil prone to bizarre *non-sequiturs* and one of his female slaves. The soundtrack features blistering sheets of white noise as well as loops of clanging industrial machinery and the distant cries of the damned.

The 'industrial' sonotope heard here is indicative of a setting quite prevalent in film pornography. Perhaps part of its appeal is the way in which it suggests an exhibitionistic fantasy of sex in open, public spaces. But such a frame for sexual imagery also establishes a contrast in terms of texture: the cold, hard industrial spaces suggested by the soundtrack clash with the soft, warm wetness of sexual intimacy, thus creating an arresting dissonance. What becomes clear is that Sayadian's use of pre-recorded music, tape loops and sonic collages creates a range

48

FIGURE 2.2 Sadism and sonotope: aural and visual landscapes in *Night Dreams*

FIGURE 2.3 Complicating carnality: the self-reflexive thrills of *Café Flesh*

of evocative sonotopes that in turn frame the film's hard-core sequences with a distinctive emotional tone. In the end, Sayadian's approach to sound has less to do with the conventions of porn than it does with the soundtracks of 'downtown' filmmakers such as David Lynch. Hawkins points out that the work of avant-garde downtown artists frequently attempted to 'directly challenge the viewer.'[23] The desire to challenge both generic conventions and the expectations of the porn audience were key factors in the next film made by the Sayadian, Stahl, Delia partnership: *Café Flesh*.

CAFÉ FLESH

This time, Sayadian's budget was $100,000, all of which came in bags of change since its financial backers were in the coin-operated peep show business. As noted above, the film was shot in eleven days in Sayadian's studio on one of the busiest street corners in Hollywood, the crew in constant fear of being busted by the Vice Squad while bumping elbows with a leering network news crew. At one point, Sayadian's landlord demanded to know why there were so many people – including half-clad women – on the premises. Sayadian recalls telling him that he was 'doing rehearsals without the skates for the Ice Capades. He bought that'.[24]

If *Night Dreams* was a generic hybrid of porn and downtown art film, *Café Flesh* combined the adult genre with both the movie musical and post-apocalyptic science fiction. Stahl wrote that their goal was 'to perpetrate a World War III musical. We had in mind a kind of high-rad *Cabaret* in which trendy mutants and atomic mobsters held sway over survivors bombed beyond all normal pleasures. Lots of people made movies about the end of the world, but how many showed what the night life would be like?'[25] The plot hinged on the idea that after a nuclear apocalypse 99 per cent of the survivors would be 'D.O.A. between the legs':

> These were the Sex Negatives. Unable to relieve their lust – they got nauseated when they tried – the Negs nevertheless craved the sight of others who could still pull off the act. These others, the functioning one per cent, were called Sex Positives. By rigidly enforced edict, Pozzies were required to perform for Neggies. And the 'in' spot where all the lame and denatured went to slaver? Café Flesh, post-nuke Copacabana.[26]

The presentation of a world in which sex is cast in terms of paranoia, anxiety and mysterious dysfunction has often been seen as a prescient parable for the dawning AIDS era – in fact, the disease was first named in 1982, the year of the film's release. 'When we did *Café Flesh*, the whole thing with the positives and negatives', Sayadian stated, 'that was six months before AIDS, and everyone has always seen the parallel.'[27]

The plot of *Café Flesh* – like *Night Dreams* – separates narrative and sexual numbers quite starkly. Again, this allows for stylistic excess: where therapy allowed avant-garde imagery in *Night Dreams*, a Busby Berkeley-style floorshow is an excuse for surreal costumes and sets in

FIGURE 2.4 Pornoscapes and the postmodern musical number: modes of performativity in *Café Flesh*

FIGURE 2.5 Tears from the 'chronically passive audience': erotic viewing as trauma in *Café Flesh*

Café Flesh. The separation of narrative and number also has implications for the film's relationship with the audience. Joan Hawkins notes that *Café Flesh* is 'a self-reflexive porn film, one that is not at all easy about the circumstances (mandated spectacularized sex) of its own production'.[28] Indeed, as with *Night Dreams*, the viewer is forced to identify in an uncomfortable and unflattering way with an onscreen surrogate audience: in this case, the impotent Sex Negatives.

Consider the opening titles of the film: 'After the nuclear kiss, the Positives remain to love, to perform ... And the others, well, we Negatives can only watch ... can only come ... to ... CAFÉ FLESH.' From the beginning of the film the audience is explicitly placed in the position of the dysfunctional Negatives. Further, throughout the film, shots of sex are intercut with images of the gawking audience, presented in a grotesque style akin to the photographs of Diane Arbus. In one particularly startling juxtaposition, an on-stage money shot is immediately followed by the image of a male audience member with a tear rolling down his face. In this jarring moment we move from the 'pornotopia' of the money shot to the depiction of both the audience in the film and by extension ourselves as pathetic, chronically-passive observers. We might observe that while the film separates narrative and number – a kind of porn narrative that Linda Williams argues tends to be 'particularly regressive and misogynist' – it still contains a self-reflexive genre critique on the level of narrative and style.[29]

It should be noted that the sex number that inspired the audience member's tear was anything but typical porno fare. While on the soundtrack we hear loops of industrial machinery,

FIGURE 2.6 A hard(core) day at the office: cliché as erotic distanciation in *Café Flesh*

behind the stage at Café Flesh we see an impressionistic backdrop of oil rigs. Meanwhile, a naked secretary blankly pokes at a typewriter while another woman in lingerie reclines on an office desk. A man wearing a suit and enormous pencil mask emerges, stiffly dancing to music on the soundtrack. The pencil-man proceeds to engage in fairly robotic sex with the woman on the desk, while the secretary repeatedly addresses the camera, intoning, 'Do you want me to type a memo?'

MAGNITUDES OF PORNO PERFORMANCE

Thus far I have been focusing on the use of sound in Sayadian's films. But the secretary's performance in the sex scene described above is illustrative of Sayadian's equally distinctive approach to acting. In fact, Sayadian stated that the decision to shoot *Café Flesh* was largely based on questions of acting. That is, the plot allowed him to work with better actors than were typically found in the adult industry: 'I was trying to say, "How can I make a porno film where I can use some decent Off-Broadway-style actors that don't have to have sex, and yet I need sex. How can I do that?" And I said, "Well, if I did a club, where they watch people have sex, then I don't need everybody to have sex."'[30] Similarly, Stahl wrote that the 'best part' of the plot was that most of the 'Chucks and Suzies' who had to 'lock femurs onscreen never had to utter a word – a definite plus.' As he continued, 'Your solid porno pro, as gifted as he may be at expressive rooting, generally lacks dramatic verve when it comes to mouthing dialogue. But the way *Café Flesh* was remolded, just about all the snappy patter could be handled by "real" actors (out-of-work Strasberg grads and sitcom hopefuls). And the sex, pesky business, ended up in a series of choreographed side shows – stagy diversions, I like to think, in the gala tradition of the June Taylor dance segments on the old *Jackie Gleason Show*.'[31] The separation of club performers and audience, of Positives and Negatives, thus allowed for a division of labour in terms of acting. Some of the 'sitcom hopefuls' who appeared in the film but didn't have sex were Paul McGibboney (Nick, the romantic lead), Andy Nichols (the male doctor from *Night Dreams*, here the emcee of Café Flesh, Max Melodramatic), and even an uncredited cameo by comedian Richard Belzer as a loud-mouthed patron.

If the narrative allowed for more professional acting performances from some of the cast, the actors who did 'lock femurs onscreen' were given unusual direction from Sayadian:

> Most of the people that make their living having sex, it was true back then and I'm sure its true now, they enjoy it. That's why they're in the business. Every time they began to enjoy the lovemaking and the sex during the filming I would call cut. I would say, 'You look like you're enjoying it, I want you to think of the worst memory of your life while you're doing this. I want it very unpleasant. Not that you're being raped, that's not the point. But I want it to be as mundane as if you were a clerk typing or filing, I want you to approach it like that.'[32]

In addition to making the audience aware of itself as passive, even dysfunctional voyeurs, the film therefore also calls attention to the perfunctory, and (most damning of all), routine quality of the performance of sex in film pornography. Typically, porn performers utilise techniques designed to ostentatiously externalise feelings of sexual pleasure. In *Café Flesh* however, sex performers wear the blank expression of the avant-garde. More specifically, these performances resemble those made by what James Naremore refers to as the 'antirealistic Brechtian player', who is 'concerned less with emotional truth than with critical awareness; instead of expressing an essential self, she or he examines the relation between roles on the stage and roles in society, deliberately calling attention to the artificiality of performance, foregrounding the staginess of spectacle, and addressing the audience in didactic fashion'.[33]

I have already noted the use of direct address in *Night Dreams*. This technique is also found in *Café Flesh*, particularly when Max the emcee speaks directly to the camera as he addresses the audience at Café Flesh. Sayadian also tends to have characters chant lines of dialogue in unison, preventing the audience from losing itself in the world of the story. In a hard-core context, such Brechtian techniques can serve to further objectify the performer as a sexual object, what Naremore calls 'pure biological performance'.[34] That is, antirealist techniques allow the audience to see through the role being played by the actor, allowing the performer to be perceived in social terms or as pure bodily presence. But in Sayadian's films, this performance style also works to short-circuit the belief that the performance of

FIGURE 2.7 Masking the self: concealment as porno performativity in *Café Flesh*

intimate sexual acts somehow reveals a privileged or essential expression of the actors' selves. By foregoing attempts to naturalise the sex, the audience is encouraged to see it as spectacle, one that is just as much a constructed performance as the delivery of ostentatiously scripted lines.

Given this foregrounding of performance, it is interesting to note how frequently masks appear as a motif in Sayadian's films: the jack in the box and the male attacker in the 'Dressed to Kill' sequence in *Night Dreams*; anonymous figures in white masks and a milkman who wears a rat mask in *Café Flesh*. Masks of course, are a 'classic prop in pornographic representation' because they allow the wearer an anonymity and resulting sense of sexual license, but as theorists such as Mikhail Bakhtin have argued, the mask is also a powerful emblem of metamorphosis, as well as the performative nature and fluidity of the self.[35] The presence of all these masks is one more indication of how Sayadian's films thematise performance, rejecting a presentation of sex as a utopian route to the self.

MIDNIGHT DREAMS

Such a depiction of sex was bound to frustrate much of the porn audience – which in fact, was one of the goals of the filmmakers. Jerry Stahl wrote in an email interview that 'we wanted [the audience] to be repelled – it's not like we wanted to be making porn.'[36] In another interview, Stahl stated that they had intentionally 'stuck in the most objectionable, repulsive kind of sex we could imagine. Really cold and chilly and weird.'[37] However, as the avant-garde use of sound in *Night Dreams* had paradoxically made the film even more erotically potent, the style of *Café Flesh* led not only to the film's failure on the traditional porn theatre circuit, but also to its remarkable second act as a midnight movie cult film. Sayadian explains that when *Café Flesh* was released in adult film houses, 'it did nothing': 'It played at a couple of porn theatres. There was literally a riot in one theatre, people demanding their money back.'[38] The film was pulled out of distribution, and sold to another company where it sat on the shelf. According to Sayadian, a young marketing executive at that company came across the print, and decided to re-release it not as a porno, but as a cult film. To this end, the film was shown at the NuArt theatre in LA: the home for midnight movie classics including John Waters' *Pink Flamingos* (1972), *The Rocky Horror Picture Show* (Jim Sharman, 1975) and *Eraserhead*. The NuArt put up money for an ad campaign, and on its first night the film broke the house record. *Café Flesh* proceeded to break the house record for six consecutive weeks, and played there for over a year.[39] From this beginning at the NuArt, word of mouth about the film began to spread. Soon Sayadian was fielding calls from college campuses and art theatres, and booking the film in both the US and Europe.

J. Hoberman and Jonathan Rosenbaum have written that successful midnight movies tended to offer relevant social metaphors that usually had to do both with transgressing taboos and 'articulating a potent, new fantasy'. *The Rocky Horror Picture Show*, in their view, became a midnight blockbuster in part because it recapitulated 1960s sexual politics while also creating 'a kind of adolescent initiation'.[40] What relevant social metaphor did *Café Flesh* offer the midnight audience?

The first thing to point out is that Sayadian's films, with their stylised sets and performances, and bizarre, kitschy humour, certainly had camp appeal. In fact, Sayadian has noted that based on his interaction with fans, a large proportion of his audience were gay men.[41] In fact, while they do not depict any gay male sex scenes, the clearest 'social metaphor' that *Café Flesh* offers has to do with sexual politics in the wake of AIDS. But also consider that *Café Flesh*'s success at the NuArt, and later on the cult circuit was due in part to the film's resonance with punk subculture. The extras who played the Negatives watching sex acts at Café Flesh were taken, according to Sayadian, 'right from the blood bank and the methadone clinic', and tended to be part of the LA punk scene.[42] As a result, Sayadian states that screenings of the film became a popular punk hang out. In Stahl's words, the film's 'synthesis of punk fashion and 1950s dialogue' gave it a particular appeal to 'youthful art victims': 'In Los Angeles, at least, part of what fueled its 18-month run was that half the town's underground avant actually appeared in the movie. This bestowed on us a built-in cachet among local Nuevo-ettes, a breed of heavily mascaraed existential gals who smoked Gitanes and kept tattered copies of *Naked Lunch* in the glove compartments of their Karmann-Ghias.'[43]

Sayadian's film is thus 'post-apocalyptic' on two levels – in the literal sense of being set after a nuclear holocaust, but following Jonathan Rosenbaum, it is also post-apocalyptic in the sense that *Eraserhead* is: 'if we take the "apocalypse" to be the dissolution of the counterculture'.[44] Sayadian's stylistic choices regarding performance – in large part pragmatic responses to the logistical imperatives of porn production – ended up shaping an aesthetic that ran parallel to a punk subculture that took an unsentimental, jaded view of sex, and rejected the 1960s countercultural assertion of the liberating potential of free love. *Café Flesh* offers a metaphoric depiction of changing sexual mores in the Reagan era, when AIDS, punk and a conservative cultural backlash would drive a stake through the heart of the free love ideal of the counterculture.

Indeed, the film's *blasé* presentation of hard-core sex stands as a fitting reflection of the porn industry in the early 1980s. Driven from mainstream theatres, porn was nevertheless rapidly becoming a ubiquitous commodity on videotape. *Café Flesh*'s crossover success from porn to midnight movie came at a time when both were feeling the effects of the emerging home VCR market. Home video was an important factor in the demise of the midnight movie circuit, another being the Reagan administration's encouragement of entertainment industry monopolies, which subsequently forced small exhibitors out of business.[45] Meanwhile, the market for porn was opening up to a wider couples audience watching on home VCRs, who were perhaps more interested in the kind of overt stylisation found in *Night Dreams* and *Café Flesh*. In trying to account for his film's surprising success, Sayadian stated that *Café Flesh* 'allowed people that normally didn't want to watch porno because it was so bad cinematically, to say, "I can watch this one because it's kinda got a hip sensibility." So that while you're watching, you don't have to feel self-conscious that I'm watching some really bad smut. I'm watching something kind of interesting. And lo and behold, it's a bit of a turn on.'[46]

Sayadian's films have a complex relationship to the adult genre – the men who made them had mixed feelings about working in porn, helping to fuel a desire to play with its conventions and to challenge its audience. The paradox is that, in pushing those boundaries, these films have become seminal and much-imitated texts in the adult industry. This is not surprising, considering that Sayadian's provocative use of sound and performance in the service of hard-core erotica stand as some of the most original and evocative explorations of the spaces of sexual fantasy. But the cultural life of these films demonstrates that the genre of film pornography cannot be seen in isolation. That is, Sayadian's work is best understood as a complex intertextual hybrid that overlaps with cultures of magazine satire, subcultures of popular music, avant-garde film and adult film, and midnight movies. As such, these films illustrate the need to consider film pornography in connection with adjacent media forms, and to avoid sweeping generalisations about porn production.

Author's note

I would like to thank Stephen Sayadian and Randi Fiat for being so generous with their time. Also thanks to Jerry Stahl and Frank Delia for taking time to answer my questions; to Brad Stevens for helping me track people down; and to Glenn Gass for help with obtaining images. Finally, many thanks to Prof. Joan Hawkins for reading an early draft and offering suggestions, encouragement and inspiration.

CHAPTER 3
CATHERINE BREILLAT: ANATOMY OF A HARD-CORE AGITATOR

Eleri Butler

> There is just one point of view about sex, and it is pornographic ... what I must do is show images that are not showable.[1]
>
> — Catherine Breillat

From outrageous images of vaginas, erections, ejaculation and bloody secretions to provocative scenes that involve masturbation, masochism and bondage, Catherine Breillat's cinema is obsessed with sex. In that respect, her work would seem perfectly suited to a volume exploring cult traditions of the erotic. However, rather than conforming to any existing notion of a porno aesthetic, Breillat's visceral creations are concerned with dismantling the peep show aesthetic to reveal the 'truth' about women's bodies, sexuality and desire; that which is 'not showable'. By profiling Breillat's controversial career and taking a closer look at two of her most explicit productions, *Romance* (1999) and *Anatomie de l'Enfer* (*Anatomy of Hell* (2004)), I aim to show that her filmmaking presents a greater challenge to the viewer than the usual approach to watching sex, shock and gore. Breillat documents women's dissatisfaction and discontent with sex and in doing so provides a welcome intervention into the flurry of critical enquiry into sex on screen

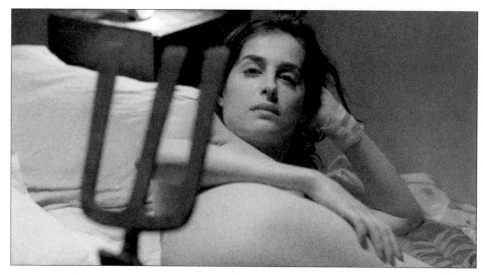

FIGURE 3.1 Confrontational carnality: Breillat's cinema of agitation

and the recent academic trend for 'porn studies'. Furthermore, her challenge to the dominant discourse on sex, sexuality and desire resurrects and re-visions feminist debates on pornography, in a manner reminiscent of Adrienne Rich's call to re-vision, to adopt the revolutionary potential of 'the act of looking back … of entering an old text from a new critical direction'.[2]

CATHERINE BREILLAT: THE OTHER FRENCH REVOLUTION

By way of introduction, a brief overview of Breillat and her body of work proves useful to any discussion of her as a hard-core agitator. Born in France in 1948, Catherine Breillat began her career as a writer, and wrote *L'Homme Facile* (1968) at the age of seventeen (although it was not published until three years later); she would not have been legally permitted to buy her first novel because of its explicitness. This irony was not lost on Breillat who, when questioned about her provocative work and feminist influence, said:

> It is a discourse that should make men run away but the purpose is the opposite: to retain him … It's a feminist cinema because it is from the point of view of women since there are certain things that are forbidden for women. I want to show these things, explore them beyond their limits … Is the provocation in my films intentional? … I started writing when I was 17. I wrote a book that was prohibited for people of less than 18 years. I was forbidden to read the same book I had written. If you consider that this is a provocation, this is what I do.[3]

Breillat's film career spans three decades, originating in the 1970s when a re-emerging women's movement questioned the representation of women's sexuality and subjectivity, and challenged patriarchal norms and modes of representation. This was also a time when the social and political popular discourse of post-1968 France called for the disturbance or destruction of hierarchy and redistribution of power, the regaining of power and control of language by those traditionally without access to the power of speech, and the recognition that the dominant structures of political and economic systems extend into cultural and sexual relations, the home and the workplace.[4] As Breillat has since recalled however, filmmakers, critics and theorists at the time were mostly gender blind in their approach:

> Women were totally excluded from the '68 revolution, just as we were excluded from the French Revolution itself … 'Liberté, Egalité, Fraternité' … the term 'brotherhood' explicitly highlights the collusion of men in subordinating women. So if nothing else, May '68 made it clear to women that in this revolution, as in the first, they had been cheated.[5]

Breillat's response was to launch her own literary and cinematic revolution. After writing several novels and screenplays, and briefly pursuing acting – she played a supporting role in Bernardo Bertolucci's *Last Tango in Paris* (1972) – Breillat made her feature directorial debut with *Une Vraie Jeune Fille* (*A Real Young Girl*, 1976), an adaptation of her fourth novel, *Le Soupirail* (1974). The film explores the sexual awakening and desires of fourteen-year-old Alice, played by Charlotte Alexandra (who in 1974 had starred in Walerian Borowczyk's *Immoral Tales*, and went on to appear in *Goodbye Emmanuelle* in 1977). Breillat's transformative vision is presented through confrontation with the abject, which indicates the pending rupture in Alice's sexual identity. Corpses, animal entrails, flies buzzing around waste and refuse, smashed egg yolks and bodily fluids – blood, urine, vomit, earwax, semen – dominate the *mise-en-scène* as Alice becomes fascinated not only with her bodily excretions but also with the slimy, smelly debris she discovers in nature.

The film was culturally prohibited, considered visually illicit and suppressed on its completion, which was surprising given that it was a product of the same cultural time that produced and distributed *Last Tango in Paris, Salo* (Pier Paolo Pasolini, 1975), *Histoire d' O* (Just Jaeckin, 1975) and *Ai No Corrida* (Nagisa Oshima, 1976). Evidently the world was not ready for a film made by a woman that pushed the boundaries of the adolescent coming-of-age genre, and that simultaneously exposed the confines of patriarchal oppression. It was only after the relative critical success of *Romance* that *Une Vraie Jeune Fille* was eventually given a limited theatrical and DVD release in 2000.

I have chosen *Romance* as one focus of my analysis, as it was with this vision of hardcore agitation that Breillat received significant international exposure. The film follows Marie's (Caroline Ducey) journey in search of her sexual self, involving oral sex, intercourse, rape and bondage with a series of men, after being rejected by her lover Paul (Sagamore Stévenin). *Romance* was quickly followed by *À Ma Soeur!* (*Fat Girl*, 2000), a film renowned for its shocking and violent climax, about the relationship between two sisters, twelve-year-old Anaïs

(Anaïs Reboux), and her flirtatious fifteen-year-old sister Elena (Roxane Mesquida), whose virginity is under siege by Italian law student Fernando (Libero de Rienzo). *Sex is Comedy* (2002), a semi-fictional film about filmmaking, was based on the experience of shooting the long sex scene central to the narrative of *À Ma Soeur* in which Fernando tries out various seduction techniques to force Elena to lose her virginity. The film exposes the sexual and power dynamics in relationships on- and offscreen as director Jeanne (Anne Parillaud) struggles to capture the sex scene between the Actor (Grégoire Colin) and the Actress (Roxane Mesquida). *Anatomie de L'Enfer*, a two-character film in which we see a Woman (Amira Casar) pay a Man (Rocco Siffredi) to 'look' at her over the course of four nights, is Breillat's most controversial and graphic exploration of misogyny. *Anatomie de L'Enfer* concludes her decalogue – which includes *Tapage Nocturne* (*Nocturnal Uproar*, 1979), *36 Fillette* (*Virgin*, 1988), *Sale Comme Un Ange* (*Dirty Like An Angel*, 1991), *Parfait Amour!* (*Perfect Love!*, 1996) and *Brève Traversée* (*Brief Crossing*, 2001) – because, Breillat states, she 'couldn't go any further, that the tenth would be the conclusion of a decalogue. The X of X-rated film.'[6]

Breillat's subsequent production, *Une Vieille Maîtresse* (*The Last Mistress*, 2007), provides the deaprture she forewarned, although the production was delayed after the director suffered a severe stroke in 2004 and was hospitalised for five months. This is her first costume drama, in which Asia Argento plays Spanish courtesan La Vellini who entices young libertine Ryno de Marigny (Fu'ad Aït Aattou) from his virginal bride, the French aristocrat Hermangarde (Roxane Mesquida). This is also Breillat's first adaptation of another author's work; that she chose this 1865 novel is unsurprising however, given that the eighteenth-century French author Jules-Amédée Barbey d'Aurevilly is best known for his themes of violent sexuality.

DIRECTING SEX: ART IS THE THEORY, PORN IS THE PRACTICE?

Breillat's work forms part of a well-documented trend in recent French 'extreme' cinema for explicit sex and violence, including Patrice Chéreau's *Intimacy* (2001), Léos Carax's *Pola X* (1999), and Virginie Despentes and Coralie Trinh Thi's *Baise-Moi* (2000). Whilst the representation of sex in her films is important to their characterisation and visual style, Breillat insists she does not cross over into pornography. Her assertion that she takes sexuality 'as the subject, not as the object' of her work is where some of the controversy and challenge in Breillat's work lies.[7] Some might say she has deliberately courted this controversy by using explicit hard-core conventions and casting pornographic actor and producer Rocco Siffredi, infamous for his anal, and sometimes violent, porn films.

Siffredi, who appeared first in *Romance* and later in *Anatomie de L'Enfer* was cast because, Breillat said, 'mainstream actors have refused to act in my films … he had the physical qualities I needed for the role' and he was 'something of a cult star of the porn industry'.[8]

Breillat's use of a 'meat merchant' such as Siffredi in an arthouse production on the extreme limits of female desire pushes many of the buttons associated with the cult film text, both for its fusion of high/low cultural registers, as well as its problematic and challenging depictions of

FIGURE 3.2 Cult casting: Breillat's use of the infamous porn performer Rocco Siffredi

female sexuality. Breillat did not underestimate the impact casting Siffredi would have when shooting *Romance*, and reputedly withheld this information from cast and crew for as long as possible in order to keep them on board. Caroline Ducey was reportedly disturbed when she found out on the day of the shoot that she would be filming sex scenes with Siffredi. As Breillat recollects:

61

> I felt that had I told anyone I was going to cast Rocco for the role, there would have been an uncontrollable reaction … It was very, very difficult … for Rocco, because there are so many biting tongues on the set [and] for Caroline … she bore it for hours … At 3 o'clock in the morning she couldn't stand it anymore, it's true. How could she be the only one to find it normal to film with Rocco when everybody else was appalled? … There was terror on the set when he arrived.[9]

Similarly Breillat recalls that the shoot for *Anatomie de L'Enfer* was also very difficult for cast and crew, and the relationship between Amira Casar and Siffredi was reportedly tense. Casar insisted a body double be used for intimate close-ups: the film's laborious opening titles deliver Casar's contractual disclaimer, stating 'A film is an illusion, not reality-fiction or a happening: it is a true work of fiction. For the actress's most intimate scenes, a body double was used. It's not her body, it's an extension of a fictional character.' Siffredi recalls her first words to him were 'Stay away two metres from me with your dick [sic.]' although less widely reported was Siffredi's objection to a scene involving him receiving a blowjob from another man, stating: 'Catherine is much more liberal than me sexually … I'm supposed to receive a blow job from a boy, and I said – 'What?' She says 'Rocco Siffredi gives me censorship on sex now? Get a blowjob from a man or girl, I don't see the difference.'[10]

Despite such onset revelations, Breillat deliberately exploits her medium to show provocative sex, to reinforce the abjection seen on screen, to minimise the conventional entertainment value of the film and to shock the spectator. Since *Romance* Breillat has worked with cinematographer Yorgos Arvanitis to achieve her characteristic slow pace, minimal set-ups, tight framing and long takes that rely on a gently panning or slow circular tracking camera, to convey an almost unbearable proximity, scrutiny and duration. This is often accompanied by deliberately choreographed performances, sometimes by nonprofessional actors, to hinder the spectator's identification with the protagonist and to limit the voyeur's space for the fantasy and pleasure traditionally available in hard-core porn.

Although labelled a 'porn auteur' because of her use of unsimulated sex, Breillat has vehemently refuted this characterisation of her work. Indeed her stated aim, in recognition that historically and culturally 'pornography is written on every woman's body', is to explore 'the nature of sex ... to transcend the usual, horrible images that form the basis of the porno films'.[11] Critics question, however, how liberating and challenging is it really to expose women's flesh and to display explicit sex on screen to challenge porn and highlight women's inequality?

SEX AND ITS DISCONTENTS

Linda Williams' account of the history and generic features of pornography in *Hard Core* (1999) paved the way for the emergence of 'porn studies' as an academic discipline.[12] Williams argued that the genre has moved away from its marginal and deviant origins being consumed exclusively by men, and that pornography offers women oscillating sexual identities with which to identify and enjoy. This position is expanded in Williams' later anthology, *Porn Studies* (2004), which includes textual analyses of a diverse range of contemporary and historical 'pornographies', and explicitly calls for a shift from feminist debates that divided feminisms along the lines of sexist oppression versus sexual repression, to move beyond the 'agonizing over sexual politics that characterised an earlier era in the study of pornography'.[13]

In her review of *Porn Studies*, Karen Boyle criticises its selective boundaries and focus on the 'soft' or the 'marginal'; its lack of attention to mainstream heterosexual and violent pornography, and its analysis of texts that are not specifically produced, distributed or consumed as pornography.[14] This blurring of the boundaries of pornography, and proliferation of pornographic images and practices being embraced in mainstream texts, has led to what Boyle calls the 'birth of a new genre: a pornography-documentary hybrid – or 'docuporn' ... a reality-based entertainment genre that takes pornography as its subject and offers sexual display and sexual talk as its key attractions'. This genre is not made and sold as pornography, but offers 'a commentary on commercial sex' in the mainstream, and facilitates its future consumption by focussing on the supply side, the 'inside-view' of women who sell sex.[15]

Similarly, Breillat's work takes the representation of sex as its subject whilst using explicit sexual display and hard-core conventions in the process; it aims to expose the 'truth' about sex from women's point of view; and is not made and sold as pornography. However, while the women interviewed naked in docuporn 'talk repeatedly of their love of sex; and their bodily functions and responses are described in detail',[16] Breillat's agitation is founded on her challenge to this postmodern pro-porn sensibility: her protagonists portray sex under patriarchy as particularly joyless and punitive. The stories they tell have more in common with anti-pornography feminism than critics have acknowledged, probably because to do so would assume an association with an anti-sex pro-censorship position, which Breillat's reputation as a controversial filmmaker and anti-censorship campaigner evidently does not support.

In this respect Breillat's films have proved difficult to categorise. Whilst their themes are not inherently shocking – for example they explore the violence and deceit of seduction and romantic love and the impact this has on women's subjectivity, and the search for an autonomous female sexuality – it is the way Breillat's female characters breach culturally prohibited feminine ways of looking and behaving that is transgressive. It is also easy to assume, after a cursory glance, that she presents masculinity and femininity as monolithic fixed identities. Yet gender as masquerade is a recurring Breillat motif, as is the doubling of characters to expose the construction of femininity and masculinity under patriarchy, of women being comprised of fractured parts of an incomplete whole; the dichotomy between the virginal 'inaccessible woman up on a pedestal' and the promiscuous other 'in a brothel'.[17] It is this complex and contradictory construction of her heroines that makes movies like *Romance* both memorable and misunderstood.

63

NOT A LOVE STORY?: BREILLAT'S ROMANCE

Romance will be greeted [with] a wall of hate, proportionate to this hell on earth that has been created for women.[18]

In *Romance*, Marie's boyfriend Paul refuses to have sex with her, which instigates her exploratory sex with Paolo (Rocco Siffredi), a man she meets in a bar; masochistic performance with head-teacher Robert (François Berléand); and a street encounter with a man (Reza Habouhossein) who first pays to 'eat' her cunt before anally raping her. Following inconclusive sex with Paul she becomes pregnant; he takes her to a nightclub and humiliates her, and the film concludes with Marie's graphic (re)birth and murder of Paul – described by Breillat as 'the birth of a woman into a whole being ... she no longer needs a man and a romance with a man to be complete ... she's the one who gives meaning to her life, by herself.'[19]

Romance is renowned for showing an erect penis and its ejaculate to mainstream audiences and for its scenes of female masochism. Yet, as Lisa Downing argues, it is not a pornographic film, more a 'documentary account of ... the quest of a heterosexual woman for self-discovery'. Whilst this nevertheless sounds like a typical premise for a porn narrative, what destabilises it are the techniques of 'subtle de-eroticization' that are common to Breillat's films.[20]

In *Romance*, the staple pornographic shots of ejaculation, penetration and spread labia are suitably subverted. It is in Robert's apartment, shot in an earthy red palette in contrast to the clinically white space most of the film inhabits, that we first evidence Marie's sticky desire dripping from her vagina; the reimagined male cum shot. The image of a woman's body as always accessible, always penetrable by men's pricks is replaced by the pregnant Marie being violated by a team of medical students, who line up to take turns to thrust their fingers into her vagina. *Romance* culminates with a series of supposed fantasy sequences, including a controversial hard-core scene in which we see the upper bodies of pregnant women, Marie included, occupy a clinical space lying on hospital beds, comforted by hand-holding male partners; whilst a circular wall, like a guillotine, separates them from their lower bodies which lie, legs spread, in a cavernous brothel through which masturbating men roam and line up to penetrate these accessible yet anonymous vaginas. This sequence ends with a man ejaculating on a woman's stomach, which is juxtaposed with ultrasound liquid being squirted on Marie's pregnant stomach (the hard-core and ejaculation shot was cut for the Region 2 DVD release). Later, pornography's typical 'split beaver' shot is replaced with an extreme close-up of a baby's head emerging from an extended vagina. In these scenes, Breillat exposes the duality of the feminine in film, typified by 'two extremes of [its] deformation … in pornography, on the one hand, and Hollywood on the other – ass and romance. Each in its own way caricatures, fetishises and exploits women.'[21]

Another stylistic feature that reinforces the concern with fractured women is the female protagonist's interior monologue that is spoken as voiceover throughout most of her films. This doesn't enhance the potential for erotic pleasure but focuses on the sexual discontents of women. Breillat's voiceovers reinforce her intent to distance the spectator from any sense of erotic pleasure with their 'meandering stream of consciousness, mingling clichés with contradictory assessments [just as the] close-up images … do not yield the investigative, unveiling thrust that characterises the pornographic image.'[22]

Romance is an important prequel to *Anatomie de L'Enfer*. The former sets up stereotypes only to challenge and change their meaning, for example Marie's performance of masochism with schoolteacher Robert is just that, whilst the film's real masochism is located in her emotionally abusive relationship with partner Paul.

Normative heterosexual discourses of masculinity and femininity are also established as

FIGURE 3.3 Performing masochism: gender boundaries and binaries blurred in *Romance*

masquerade: in the opening scene Paul is being made-up as a matador for a photo shoot, the white powder invoking a feminised mask, as the photographer coaxes him to 'stand like a man'. Later Paul's phallic performance is again exposed when he fails to get an erection in bed with Marie. This challenge to the very nature of female masochism and gendered performance lays the groundwork for The Woman in *Anatomie de L'Enfer* to expose The Man to the truth about women, sex and desire.

I filmed a hairy horrifying/horrified vulva, like the face of the Medusa. It was not about a real sexual organ, but about this world-wide fantasy of the vulva as a horrifying thing.[23]

Anatomie de L'Enfer, based on Breillat's novel *Pornocratie* (published in France in 2001 and translated into English as *Pornocracy* in 2006), was received with critical condemnation on its release, exemplified by Manohla Dargis's review in the *New York Times* who called it 'painfully foolish … a brutal self-parody of a filmmaker [with] nothing left to show'.[24] The film opens in a nightclub full of men, uninterested in the solitary woman watching them. Breillat's stated aim was to establish a separation between an autonomous male homosociality and the solitude and isolation of the female; the club is 'an allegory', she explains, a place where 'men come together, men who don't like the company of women … more than for desire, she is looking for her sexual identity, for her "self".'[25] The Woman's isolation and self-loathing leads her to attempt suicide by cutting her wrists; the reason, she explains to The Man who finds her, is 'because I am a woman'. The Woman then enters into a contract with The Man, paying him to sit with her over four nights to watch her where she is 'unwatchable'.

The bedroom that provides the backdrop for the sacrificial sex and shameful secretions that follow is meticulously staged for inspection: a light hangs over a bed in the middle of a sparsely decorated room, behind which hangs a crucifix on the wall, which together with the bars on the imposing bedstead, symbolise confinement and the oppressive role of religion and the phallus in the subjugation of women. Although The Woman has set up the contractual relationship between them by paying him to watch her, the complexity of the gendered power dynamics involved when men or women buy access to the others' body is exposed: this is The Man's journey and it is his body that has feelings and who retains power and agency throughout the film; The Woman pays financially and with her life to enable his initiation. The Man, having determined that The Woman will 'pay, for everything', watches her undress and lie naked on the bed.

Breillat proceeds to tear down the patriarchal pillars of female beauty; constructing the narrative around those mechanisms – hair removal, cosmetics, tampons – that are commonly used to prohibit women from being who they really are. The Man criticises the woman's unshaved body hair as contributing to her obscenity; 'even if you removed the hair from your crack, you wouldn't be rid of your obscene nature'. Fingering her vaginal secretion, he compares her genitals – the source of her impurity - to 'pestilence' and to a frog, noting 'the sloppy shapeless aspects' of her 'hidden lips'. While The Woman sleeps, he outlines her labia, anus and mouth with dark red lipstick before penetrating her with his penis. This is a scene reminiscent of many described by Andrea Dworkin, in which women are dehumanised and turned into a target: 'vaginal lips are painted purple for the consumer to clue him in as to where to focus his attention … our rectum are highlighted so that he knows where to push. Our mouths are used and our throats are used for deep penetration … red marks the spot where he's supposed to get you.'[26]

The woman's secretions are alien, slimy and the subject of curiosity combined with revulsion: when the man encounters them – he studies, touches, smells then tastes – he remarks that 'the fragility of female flesh inspires disgust or brutality'; which forewarns his later ceremonious penetration of her anus with a three-pronged garden rake whilst she sleeps.

Her exposure of the revulsion that women's bodies can incite is a characteristic shared with pornography and docuporn. According to Boyle, when women in docuporn films relay how often they have sex against a checklist of sexual performances (ranging from girl-on-girl, double and triple penetration, bukkake, BDSM, humiliation, strangulation and so on) this is not for the purpose of arousal but disgust, rendering women's bodies and by implication their desire as increasingly freakish.[27] As Breillat notes, commenting on the imagery in *Anatomie de L'Enfer*, male dominance is a political system, the more there is deliberate attribution of 'obscenity and disgust with women's bodies, the fewer rights they'll have … it's a tool used to dominate and subjugate women'.[28] Her observation echoes Dworkin's view of the practice of pornography: 'its what men want us to be, think we are, make us into; how men use us, not because biologically they are men but because this is how their social power is organised'.[29]

Behind the woman's seductive, passive façade lies the goriest of all taboos, one that invokes women's impurity and threat to stable borders and rules. Menstruation – that signifier of monstrosity in religion, the sex industry and horror films – and female blood is a recurring motif in the film and also a motif that recurs throughout Breillat's work.

The Man's probing fingers, tongue and penis provide a commentary on the mystery of woman and how her blood stains everything she touches. The Woman offers him a drink of bloody water in which her used tampon is soaking, in an act of symbolic ritual – 'don't

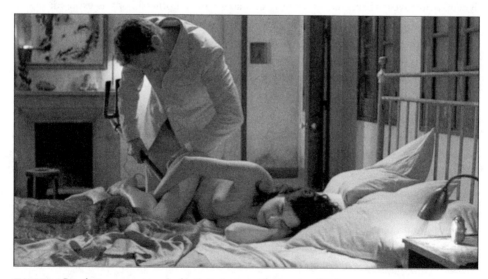

FIGURE 3.4 Ritualistic examinations: the female body exposed in *Anatomy of Hell*

FIGURE 3.5 Anatomies of disgust: fears around female body fluids exposed

we drink the blood of our enemies?'– before she scorns the male preoccupation with vaginal orgasm by inserting a tampon, which occupies 'the same space as most human penises' and can be inserted 'without feeling anything, no sensation of pleasure at all'. Later, in a scene reminiscent of Marie's childbirth in *Romance*, she proceeds to expel a stone dildo from her bloody vagina, shot in extreme close-up. The image of a post-coital Rocco stroking his blood-drenched penis contrasts starkly with the expected eroticism of the image, and intertextually evokes the underlying normalised violence of heterosexual sex and seduction, which Breillat explores in earlier films.

Inevitably The Man's journey ends in The Woman's death, during a fantasy sequence in which he pushes her off a cliff into the womb-like feminine space of the ocean. This is the price she pays for exposing herself, for showing him he cannot humiliate her, and for initiating him into a new way of seeing women's bodies. Yet he cannot deal with this knowledge and in a bar full of men resorts to mundanely recounting his conquest, dehumanising The Woman in the process:

> She was a queen of sluts … I reamed her pussy so hard, no one will want her again! … I made her crap her shit and wallow in her piss. That slut! She was a pigsty by the time I left. A human being wouldn't let anyone use her as I did. But she always wanted more. I should have ripped her guts out and made her eat them! … I don't even know her name.

Siffredi's speech, above, not only illustrates the pornographic fantasy of the anonymous fuck, of women's perpetual sexual availability, but also reveals the language and abusive homosociality often associated with pornography in which 'the sharing of women among men … reinforce[es] the power of the male group *vis-à-vis* the degraded female "other".[30] As Breillat says, 'he describes sex in the ugly way it is presented in pornography – he says he fucked her, and then he turned her over and fucked her up the ass – with no emotion … it's the way all men talk about sex, and also all the censors and religious creeds that teach us it's an abominable act'.[31]

HARD-CORE AGITATION

> There is no masculine psychology in my cinema. There is only the resentments and desires of women.[32]

Of all Breillat's films, *Romance* and *Anatomie de L'Enfer* evidently provide a cinematic intervention into debates about pornography. And, at a time when 'porn studies' has effectively usurped feminist analyses of pornography, what Breillat contributes is significant. Linda Williams contends that Breillat has found 'new ways of presenting and visually experiencing cinematic sex acts'; that with *Romance*, for example, the point was 'never simply to show pleasure but, rather, to show how short-lived and difficult such "pure" desire is'.[33] However, Breillat's work is not necessarily a re-vision of the pornography Williams advocates in *Hard Core*, when she cites Candida Royalle's Femme Productions as an early example of women reframing porn as entertainment for women.

Whilst Breillat's work has been aligned with pornography and with third-wave feminist appropriation of female masochism and submission as 'empowering',[34] Breillat denies her work is pornographic, and also refutes claims that she explores masochism as pleasurable for women. Talking about *Romance* for example, Breillat states:

> On the contrary, the relationship that Marie has with her boyfriend is based on masochism and self-depreciation. On her journey she goes through scenes of masochism and learns to free herself – exactly the opposite of *The Story of O*, which posits the norm is pleasure through masochism and through being dominated. The headmaster in *Romance* doesn't initiate her through masochism: on the contrary, he uses her masochism to take her to the other side and free her from masochism. He uses the fact that she is used to masochism, through her relationship with Paul, to take her somewhere else.[35]

It would seem that pain and pleasure co-exist in Breillat's films only as a transformative stage for women and men to transcend, 'a passage … once she's reached that stage, it does not mean she'll remain addicted … Quite the opposite – she'll have left behind all her masochism … masochism is something that women have learned rather than were born with … so its pretty hard to get rid of.'[36]

Whilst Boyle and other anti-pornography feminists might disagree with Breillat's means, their transformative vision is closer than it would initially seem. Breillat challenges the current trend towards 'a peep show chic', in which pornography's codes and conventions become aligned with a sophisticated sex-positive sensibility. Breillat does not deny – as is currently fashionable – that feminism has no place in explorations of sexual relations and identity; nor does she ignore how a particular construction of women's sexuality and sexualised violence has historically been deployed to reinforce social hierarchies of gender, class and race under patriarchy.

Breillat's hard-core agitation is founded on showing what is *really* 'not showable' within an ever-expanding pornographic lens that frames popular culture. She exposes women's dissatisfaction and discontent with the sex on offer and reminds us of the misogynistic roots of the dominant structures of patriarchy and religion, as she peels back the layers of hatred that men have held for women for centuries. By focusing on women's subjectivity and discontents, Breillat provides a much-needed re-vision of, and update to, anti-pornography feminism, combining an anti-porn aesthetic with an anti-censorship sensibility to expose the gender inequality and exploitation, which typically structures the depiction of sex. Her position is clear: whilst she is against censorship – 'one cannot forbid an image. If the image is masturbatory, then the film is an X-rated film because sex becomes an object rather than the subject'[37] – Breillat also challenges the system of representation that associates women's sexuality with shame and subordination, and attributes women's bodies with obscenity and disgust, because 'we're shown things that are allowed in porn movies and we're told that that's the way we ought to behave. Girls are raised for that purpose, which induces a behaviour where you can find pleasure in shame.'[38]

At a time when mainstream pornography threatens to become increasingly more degrading, humiliating and violent, and when much popular feminist critique has become depoliticised and less able to resist it, Breillat's deconstruction of how women are represented in relation to men is timely, and demands nothing less than the transcendence of dominant religious, cultural and patriarchal norms that reinforce women's oppression, so that a new discourse of sex, sexuality and desire can begin.

CHAPTER 4
DISCO SUCKS!: PORNOGRAPHY AND DISCO IN THE 1970s

Gary Needham

The backlash against disco music occurred in July 1979 when a Chicago baseball park was witness to an anti-disco riot fuelled by the blowing-up of a pile of twelve-inch disco singles. This event was billed as Disco Demolition Night and was the culmination of a phobia hystericised by the slogan 'Disco Sucks!'. The anti-disco sentiments of 'Disco Sucks' has two meanings here; on the one hand the music sucks because it's considered rubbish and on the other hand disco fans suck, as in they suck cock. In other words, 'Disco Sucks!' is a rather thinly veiled homophobic and anti-women agenda.[1]

I want to open my chapter with this reminder because it suggests such strong links between music and sex, or rather disco and fellatio, consumption and cultural identity, and in the context of this volume the overlap between a music genre and the genre of pornography. Therefore, I will be exploring the different connections and mutually reflecting discourses relating disco and pornography during the 1970s, in terms of the general erotic underpinnings of disco music, how it sounds, the associated images, discotheque spaces, and the enmeshment of disco in gay culture and the sexual culture of the 1970s.

FIGURE 4.1 Sensual revolutions and the sexual backlash: music and marginal sexuality conflated

The everyday use of the word 'disco' today is a catch-all term for danceable music from the 1970s but rarely does contemporary usage reflect the complexity and historicity of disco, what it truly meant, what the experience was like, and how it sounded. Disco is certainly not associated with cultures of gay sex, pornography and female orgasms. This is because the de-historicisation and de-politicisation of the genre and culture, including its links to gay liberation and women's liberation, has turned disco into merely the mainstream fodder of an inauthentic nostalgia for the 1970s. For those of us who do know and love real disco, and I mean here expert knowledge about disco music, history and culture, will bemoan the distortion of its legacy in which ABBA and The Village People rather than Suzi Lane, Theo Vaness and Taana Gardner take on the ambassadorial function. In the popular imagination disco mainly survives and is inculcated through songs that were big chart hits during the 1970s rather than the actual music that was heard as part of the disco experience. One only has to refer to deejay charts, sets and mixes from the period to see this major difference between what was experienced as disco and what now gets passed off as disco. This lack of continuity and authenticity is obvious in films like *The Last Days of Disco* (Whit Stillman, 1998) and *54* (Mark Christopher, 1998) in which every well-known chart-topping disco song can be heard during the disco scenes. The music in *The Last Days of Disco* is too wide-ranging with tracks spanning several years in a period constructed as the end of 1980; the music is chosen because it is well known rather than an authenticating reflection of a disco's music policy in 1980. The logic here of course is to sell a soundtrack, thus historical accuracy has to be dispensed with but this also defines the general mainstreaming of disco post-1970s.

The effect of this posthumous re-organisation of the meaning of disco, the selective hearing process of cinema and the mainstream disco compilation of top-ten hits, are bound to a de-gaying and de-sexing of disco. Although the mainstreaming of disco is contemporaneously understood to be essentially a camp phenomenon, this version of camp has nothing to do with gay culture and more to do with a kitschy and trashy self-depreciating sense of the popular as solipsistic fun. Certainly, contemporaneously, disco has long been divorced from its relationship to cultural sexual experimentation and dissent, pornography, orgasms and gay abandon. Furthermore, disco always had a very different relationship to heterosexuality than it did to homosexuality; for example, disco's queer relation never ended in 1980 with the same resonance of embarrassment that quickly ushered its straight fans into the disco closet.

Here I want to restore the relationship between disco and sexual culture, an epistemological mapping as it were, through the following salient features of interconnectedness between a music genre, cultural identity and a pornographic milieu. However, it should be noted, not all disco culture was related to sexuality and pornography; for example, the *Sesame Street Fever* (1978) album from the popular children's television show, and one would be hard pushed to find anything erotic in relation to *The Ethel Merman Disco Album* (1979).

CRUISING THE BEATS: SPATIALISING DISCO AND PORNOGRAPHY

The origins of the disco scene begins in the late 1960s and early 1970s; the emergence of a dance music culture almost immediately following the Stonewall riot of July 1969 and the ushering in of gay liberation. These discos were private parties like The Loft and clubs like The Sanctuary, the latter described as 'the cathedral of Sodom and Gomorrah',[2] spaces inhabited by a large gay clientele but also including those Americans marginalised and disenfranchised by race as well as sexuality. While the *discotheque* as a concept of leisure was in vogue throughout the 1960s as part of the 'Swinging Sixties' it quickly went into decline by the end of that decade. The decline of this earlier straight version of the *discotheque* was superseded by a different version of disco that privileged the role of the deejay in providing a danceable experience out of pre-recorded music, mixed and extended in near-seamless fashion without interruption, with the addition of drug-use and non-stop dancing, the experience was ecstatic and transcendental; when matched with gay liberation politics this was also tremendously affective. It was in these spaces of dancing with the music skilfully shaped by the deejay that the sound, the people and the venue merged into the concept of disco; the term comes to describe both the music and the space. Although the initial discos were about dancing, partying and meeting people they eventually, although not exclusively, transformed in to places that also accommodated sexual activity often sensationally described as such: 'Put fifteen hundred gay boys in a private club, feed them every drug in the pharmacopoeia, turn up the music loud, and pour the drinks like soda pop – presto! You've got an orgy.'[3] While the early discos were certainly not this way inclined, the notion of a public space for sex often informed the idea that the smaller gay dance clubs were also sex clubs, or at the very least had spaces that accommodated both sex and dancing, bodily activities not entirely unrelated.

Contemporary representations of the disco in film and retro fashion trends try their hardest to make disco appear erotically charged but ultimately fail to convey the complexity of its sexual dynamic. However, a number of articles from the period in *The Village Voice*,[4] books like Albert Goldman's *Disco* (1978) and Andrew Holleran's gay literary classic *The Dancer from the Dance* (1978)[5] appear during the latter part of the 1970s and through their immediacy offer a more attuned and nuanced description of the spaces, pleasures and identities of disco culture, offering a very different account from more recent popular conceptions. Goldman, the controversial music biographer and American Professor, wrote a widely-read book on disco, albeit from the point of view of his identity as a white heterosexual academic; the book tends to read like an anthropological discovery of a newly discovered tribe and treads a fine line between objectivity and sensation. What fascinates me about Goldman's book, from which I have already quoted, is the lengthy passages given over to describing the spaces of the disco in sexual terms especially as he ventures into the darkest depths of the New York gay scene of the 1970s. Goldman's narrative is akin to the structure of Dante's *Inferno*; the author descends the circles of a disco hell looking on in a shocked awe, offering the reader licentious descriptions of sinners and sodomites. Take for example his description of the legendary disco Paradise Garage:

> The Paradise Garage, the hottest gay disco, is an immense cast-concrete truck garage down on the docks (the gay's happy hunting ground). As you climb its steeply angled ramp to the second floor, which is illuminated only by rows of sinister little red eyes, you feel like a character in a Kafka novel. From overhead comes the heavy pounding of the disco beat like a fearful migraine. When you reach the 'bar', a huge bare parking area, you are astonished to see immense pornographic murals of Greek and Trojan warriors locked in sado-masochistic combat running from floor to ceiling.[6]

As the book continues Goldman gets more feverish in this obsession with the gay sex unfolding in the discos that culminates in his description of the 'discos with the orgy back rooms, where you stick your cock through a hole in the wall and hope for the best … where a hard-muscled hairy arm with a big fist plunges first into a can of Crisco and then so far up some guy's asshole that his eyes bulge'.[7] Goldman attempts to shock his reader with such descriptions of glory holes and fisting, and I admire his refusal to sanitise disco since his publication followed the commercial de-gaying and mainstream ascendancy of disco – those countless disco dancing instruction books that centralise complementary heterosexual pairings and of course the film *Saturday Night Fever* (1977). According to Goldman then, all manner of kinky practices unfold not just in the spaces of the disco but also because of disco.

The discos, along with the bathhouses, were important locations of gay sexual activity and socialisation in the 1970s, particularly in the way the spaces of the disco were organised to furnish areas for dancing and areas for sex although these were not mutually exclusive in terms of what happened and where. It's important to stress that having sex and listening to disco could be simultaneous experiences. The discos described and documented no longer exist except in memory, the sexual escapades curtailed by the onset of AIDS in the early 1980s, the histories intertwined with personal recollection, most passionately written about in detail in disco pioneer Mel Cheren's biography *Keep on Dancin'* (2000)[8] and in the documentary *Gay Sex and the 1970s* (Joseph Lovett, 2005). There is surviving footage of Paradise Garage, for example, in the house music documentary *Maestro* (Josell Ramos, 2003), and the continual over-exposure of Studio 54 on television and in pop culture, but there are so many spaces of disco life (nightclubs, bars, bathhouses, cinemas) once celebrated yet mostly undocumented, and certainly central to the formation of gay identity and sexual culture through the interlocking of sound and space as a collective experience. However, a number of these spaces of historical significance for disco dancing and music have found their preservation in the domain of gay adult cinema especially in those films which nominate the spaces for inclusion through a sort of ethnographic mapping and accompanying disco soundtrack. I am thinking here of *Boys of Venice* (William Higgins, 1978) which documents the East Coast gay disco and roller-skating scene in L.A., *A Night at the Adonis* (Jack Deveau, 1978) set in New York's Adonis theatre, the soft-core comedy *Saturday Night at the Baths* (David Buckley, 1975) filmed in the Continental Baths, and *Boots and Saddles* (Francis Ellie, 1978) filmed in the once strictly-dress-code-policed 'denim and plaid' gay bar of the same name.[9]

The ethno-documentary impulse of gay pornography is also noted by Richard Cante and Angelo Restivo in their remarks that 'feature length all-male filmic porn was deeply invested in narratologically and imagistically "gaying" such itineraries of everyday life' of which I would suggest disco is one such location of meaning for a gay 1970s ontology.[10]

The mapping of gay life through film goes further back than this; the textual exchange between experimental film and documentary in films like *Gay San Francisco* (1965–70) forms a point of discussion in the underground cinema section of Richard Dyer's *Now You See It* (1990).[11] The commitment to filming on location in gay pornography, like in *Boots and Saddles*, is a testament to the way in which pornography is understood to be intrinsic to rather than separate from gay life during the 1970s. Films like *Fire Island Fever* (Jack Deveau, 1979) taught gay men how to cruise and pick-up, where they could hang out, and go on holiday to places like Fire Island. Bob Alvarez, the producer and editor of Hand in Hand's *A Night at the Adonis* and *Fire Island Fever* has said 'we tried to show as much as possible what the true scene was'.[12] The ability to make pornography, and to exhibit it legally, to perform in it and consume it, these were not expressions of exploitation and abuse but a means through which to represent gay life. It is worth remembering that gay liberation is also sexual liberation, freedom from the shame and guilt of being gay and porn once represented an act of self-affirmation and defiance in ways which seem impossible to argue for in the context of heterosexual pornography and subsequently in the industrial development of gay video pornography from the 1980s onwards. Early examples of feature-length gay pornography such as Wakefield Poole's *Bijou* (1972) and

Fred Halsted's *L.A. Plays Itself* (1972) are in fact closer in spirit to underground cinema, like Kenneth Anger's *Scorpio Rising* (1964) and Andy Warhol's *My Hustler* (1965), especially in their homoerotic visuals, experimental and avant-garde film techniques. Activist and writer Patrick Moore even suggests that we understand early gay pornography and sexual practice as a form of gay art, discos being the theatres of sexual experimentation, and that as gay men we ought to re-contextualise our sexual cultures as sources of artistic creativity and heritage.[13] While I agree with Moore and fully align myself with his radical politics of anti-shame, I would caution against fully equating gayness in sexual terms; yet, it must be noted that one of the most potent strategies of gay politics was to make gay sex and sexual culture visible, the antidote to shameful, hidden and closeted versions of gayness.

The construction of filmic space is an essential difference between gay and straight porn; the spaces of gay pornography are not solely within the realm of fantasy as they often are in heterosexual porn. In *A Night at the Adonis* one could actually be in New York's Adonis theatre watching the very film in the space of the film itself; a sort of spectatorial *mise-en-abyme*. The hetero-spatial tropes of the doctor's office, the college dorm, the school classroom, the roller rink, are straight porn fantasies that transform mundane public spaces into carnal localities and stand in contradistinction to the very quotidian spaces of gay life and leisure which are self-reflexively documented and self-affirmative in nature.

FIGURE 4.2 Soundtracks to the sexual subculture: recreating the disco scene in *A Night at the Adonis*

Cante and Restivo refer to a 'mandate toward spatiality'[14] in gay porn and I would add that, importantly, the soundtrack and disco also give equal meaning to porn not just as a visual spatialisation of place and pleasure but an aural spatialisation too. The soundtrack that accompanies the visualising of space and the representation of sex in *A Night at the Adonis* is pure disco heaven; discophiles will recognise Tuxedo Junction's version of 'Moonlight Serenade' (1978) and THP's 'Two Hot for Love' (1978).

There are three points worth teasing out here in relation to the disco soundtrack and the way it represents some conventions of sound practice in gay films from the period. Firstly, the structure of the music often determines the organisation of the sex scene and the climax sometimes comes through the music rather than the image of ejaculation, that is, the climax is heard rather than seen. Secondly, this often means that the sequential logic of the sex is displaced on to the formal structures of the music rather than performance, determined not by the conventional linear logic of straight pornography: foreplay; oral sex; penetration; the definitive use of ejaculation as scene closure. Thirdly, in *A Night at the Adonis* there is more of a montage structure to the sex scenes; they are fragmented, often unfinished or begun *in media res*, they are subject to parallel editing with lengthy non-sex scenes, and one can observe how continuity tends to be maintained not through the ordering of sex and bodies (since gender is not the disparity here) but rather sex gets ordered through the structure of the music heard; a seamless filmic experience is constructed through sound rather than image.

In a reversal of this cinematic convention in which sound proffers continuity on the image, the organisation of disco music in 'Two Hot for Love' turns out to be structured as a linear sexual encounter; the music is ready made for porno. The A-side of 'Two Hot for Love' heard in *A Night at the Adonis* is a blissful fifteen minutes that is listed on the record label as follows:

A1. Two Hot For Love
Four-Play / 3:05
Excitement Part 1 / 5:11
Excitement Part 2 / 2:50
Climax / 2:10
Resolution / 2:35

The efficacy of disco to fashion itself through sexual tropes cannot be overstated here. The classical music convention of organising the music as a suite is rendered wholly in sexual terms, a sexualisation of the classical, thus making audible and legible relations between sex and music or rather disco and pornography.

FEELING MIGHTY REAL: SOUNDS, LYRICS AND PORNO CROSSOVERS

Two Hot For Love is just one of hundreds of disco songs which use sexual language, metaphors, kinky allusions and straightforward smut. Disco constantly employs the word funk as a synonym for fuck that in disco-style singing allows the two terms to sound almost homophonous. For example, Sylvester's 'Do You Wanna Funk' (1982) or Giorgio Moroder's 'I Wanna Funk With You Tonight' (1976) make no claim to be anything but songs about the invitation to fuck. In Moroder's track we have a typical call and response situation when the male voice sings 'I wanna funk with you tonight' and the susurrus tones of the female voice returns with 'yeah baby, lets funk tonight'. Obviously these moments have to be heard for their full effects. It is also worth reminding the reader that the original African-American vernacular term funk once referred to the smell of sex on the body. Along with stimulating lyrics there is a good deal of (predominantly) female performers oohing and aahing in disco music as concrete vocalisations of sexual pleasure. These 'bird calls' are often identical to the vocalisations you can hear in the post-dubbed porno soundtrack that Linda Williams suggests are the 'prominent signifier of female pleasure, in the absence of other, more visual assurances'.[15]

Patriarchal and anti-feminist anxieties around disco music were often couched in concerns that disco music was obscene in its sexual suggestiveness. Clearly an attack on female sexuality *qua* independence expressed in terms of a pleasure without men. Disco was central in reifying the female orgasm through a popular music form. Donna Summer's 'Love to Love You Baby' (1975) was a seventeen-minute orgasmic musical journey with the formal structure and texture of the music, stopping and starting, taking it slow, taking it fast, echoing the rhythm of a sensuous masturbation session. The B-side of Summer's breakthrough hit was evocatively called 'Need a Man Blues' and the photographic cover of the 12" single showed the singer lying back in her feathered nightdress perhaps leaving us in no doubt about the 'baby' she was loving outside the frame. 'Love to Love You Baby' is the benchmark in disco ecstasy and the vocalisations of pleasure and climax were copied in countless other disco releases, some even more obviously pornographic such as Poussez's orgasm workout 'Come On and Do It!' (1979).

The structure of the music in 'Love to Love You Baby', and in disco and dance music more generally, is firstly related to being taken on a affective musical journey, of getting taken somewhere by the music which is, secondly, understood in sexual terms as you lose yourself in the pleasure of the beat; we submit ourselves to the beat, becomes slaves to the rhythm. The crescendos and whooshing noises central to Summer's disco sound created by Giorgio Moroder and the extensive pitch of her vocal range mean the music is full of intensity and upward movement; in fact, you really feel you are taking off, it gives a *frisson*, a tingle on the back of the neck. The effect of Summer's disco is structurally equivalent to orgasmic tension and release, only the music here gives us multiple climaxes over and over again. The arrangement of intensity and upward movement of Summer's 'No More Tears (Enough is Enough)' (1979), a duet with Barbara Streisand, when the vocals soar and the beats kick in, is as close to ecstasy as one might ever get through music. The transcendence associated with disco offers such an experience; according to John Gill in *Queer Noises* (1995)[16] dance music in general is one that closely corresponds to Roland Barthes' concept of *jouissance*.[17] Through *jouissance* we surrender and give our body over to unconscious experience as a deeply-felt restorative bliss takes over and returns us to pre-subjective rapture. The aesthetics of disco, letting the body be overcome with music, the hot and sweaty dark space of the disco itself, indicates those moments at which *jouissance* takes hold in the upward scales of movement, the crescendos, the soaring vocals, the whooshing sounds and synthesizer pops, disco's musical textures producing rapture and bliss. Disco tells us what *jouissance* might sound like as if orgasms could be musical rendered. One is reminded here of the 'Excessive Machine' in *Barbarella* (Roger Vadim, 1968), a huge organ-like instrument whose effect is death by orgasm as music is played on the body. Andrew Kopkind writing in *The Village Voice* in 1979 writes that 'a "hot" disco mix in a dance club is a sexual metaphor; the dejaay plays with the audience's emotions, pleasing and teasing in a crescendo of feeling'.[18] The 'disco mix' itself, often a remixed and reworked extension of the three-minute pop song, is imagined in sexual terms to be stretched out into a sensuous experience. The conventional musical form of pop is extended, manipulated and transformed from a radio-friendly ditty into a raunchy beat-throbbing crescendo-driven workout that asks us to feel the beat and ride the rhythm. Kopkind's quotes one disco dancer who tells the deejay that 'you were fucking me with your music! Do me a favour and fuck me again.'[19]

A number of erotically conceived disco songs also include raunchy dialogue and spoken sexual scenarios. The original thirteen-minute 'Cruisin' the Streets' by Boy's Town Gang, works both as a form of gay tutelage and an aural porn experience; the track tells you how to cruise and where to cruise. This is an important song released in 1981 by the San Francisco record label Moby Dick Records who along with the Megatone label shaped the synthesizer-led HI-NRG 'gay sound' central to the transition from 1970s disco music into 1980s dance music. 'Cruisin' the Streets' is sung by Cynthia Manley, in the role of a sassy street walker, who tells the listener:

> You can find anything you might be lookin' for
> You might find a big boy nine inches or more
> Listen I promise you it might make you sore
> Absolutely guaranteed it won't be a bore

Following such licentious rhymes, about seven minutes in, we are treated to a rather cinematic moment. The sounds of the night, high heels clacking and cars passing, allows us to visualise through the music a pornographic scenario; two butch men's voices exchange dialogue and pick each other up, while Manley asks to watch as the two men get off. Again lots of oohing and aahing, what Cante and Restivo refer to in film as 'pornoperformative vocalizations',[20] for example, 'oh yeah' and 'suck it'. The three-way is interrupted by a police officer ('what are you fags up to?') who is in turn accosted ('up against the wall, you cunt!') and sexually assaulted as the moaning of all four characters take over the music, mapping the orgiastic vocals to the structural crescendo.

The presence of a woman who sings instructions for the listener on how to cruise and also becomes an observer and finally a participant in the gay sex action described above; nothing out of the ordinary in the 1970s. If we link this female presence back to films like *A Night at the Adonis* or any number of disco-scored gay films one can observe that women are continually present only aurally rather visually. The sex scenes scored to disco mentioned in the previous films are often dominated by disembodied female voices; not only does sound confer continuity on the image through disco music but it also affords an agency to the female voice in a world visually dominated by men. Women are everywhere in gay porn albeit through the presence of disco music gesturing to a debate to be argued elsewhere on the sound politics of gay male/straight female relations.

The male singing voice is largely absent from gay pornography in the 1970s except in the few odd cases where the singer is known to be gay, queer and/or popular with gay audiences. For example, *Boots and Saddles* includes music by male diva Sylvester and the moustachioed Dennis Parker. As another point of connection between disco and pornography I should briefly recount Parker's story here. He had one disco album with the biggest label, Casablanca, called *Like an Eagle* (1978), however, prior to his recording career Parker's *nom de plum* was Wade Nichols and he featured in a number of gay porn loops. He also worked briefly in straight porn (for example Radley Metzger's *Barbara Broadcast* (1977)), but Parker is better known for his roles in gay classics like Hand in Hand's *Boynapped* (Jack Devau, 1975). His inclusion in the soundtrack to *Boots and Saddles* is clearly an homage.

The porno/disco crossover was not unique to gay culture although it was certainly forged there. One of the most commercially successful disco songs of all time is Andrea True Connection's 'More, More, More' (1976). Andrea True was a porn star with Avon Films but unlike Parker she did not hide the fact, even singing about it. The lyrics of 'More, More, More' include the lines 'get the camera's rolling, get the action going' and explicitly quote her adult film career. More shockingly, Andrea True was part of the Avon film company along with Annie Sprinkle in films that were notorious as the nastiest, roughest and most horrific of all commercially released straight pornography. They also made a few 'vanilla' films, *Sex Rink* (Ray Dennis Steckler, 1976) and *Plato's Retreat* (Ray Dennis Steckler, 1979), set in a disco-related roller-skating contexts, no doubt an inspiration for Heather Graham's roller girl in *Boogie Nights* (Paul Thomas Anderson, 1997). Avon films were used as the most heinous examples of the porn industry, the benchmark of depravity during the federal investigation of pornography in the US known as the Meese Commission. 'More, More, More' is quintessential disco, originally remixed by Tom Moulton, but the song's longevity has allowed it to survive as a classic played by mobile deejays, heard at office parties, in pub discos, stuck on cheap compilation CDs; versions of the song have been used for shampoo adverts, and its been covered by pop acts Bananarama and Rachel Stevens, all with little knowledge of its seedy origins.

Sex still sells dance music but with one caveat; women are being exploited rather than celebrated in a cultural context that is imagined through sexism rather than liberation. The commercial end of dance music has become the locus for a laddish pornographic imaginary as any number of worthless compilations, mix-CDs and cheap videos feel it necessary to package the music through soft-porn images of the female body; it's even sold to female consumers this way. I find it depressing that the origins of dance music in disco have been visually co-opted upon such unequal terms, so much so that the work of woman and gays as consumers, producers and artists is erased and hidden behind the solicitation of male fantasy.

Disco was a democracy of eroticism that favoured both sexes and sexualities in equal measure. Richard Dyer famously defended disco in 1979 referring to it's 'whole body eroticism'[21] in contrast to the cock-centred logic of rock with its hip thrusting and phallic iconography. For Dyer 'disco restores eroticism to the whole body'[22] but with the contemporary mainstreaming of dance music we are witnessing a reversal of this politics in which the apparent sexiness of the music becomes dependent on a commercial imperative that only objectifies the female body. The marketing images and artwork of disco in the 1970s conveyed a very different set of sexual politics. Images of the female body, the male body and obvious gay iconography were

FIGURE 4.3 Looks between men: creating the homoerotic gaze in disco marketing

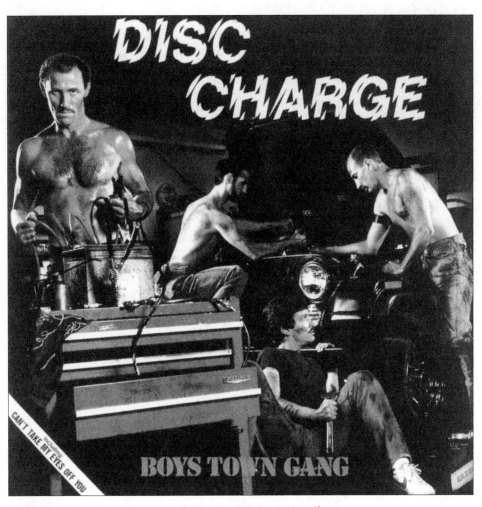

FIGURE 4.4 Pornographic *mise-en-scenes* and music: the 1981 cover to *Disc Charge*

everywhere. Already mentioned, the sleeve of Donna Summer's 'Love to Love You Baby' shows the singer lying back and, we assume, pleasuring herself. There is no solicitation of the gaze here; this is an introspective scene of desire between self and music.

The *Playboy* come-hither look emanating from the eyes of models, the standard of a need to legitimise the look by invitation, adorns a great deal of the marketing of contemporary dance music as I have suggested. However, in classic disco iconography, the structures of looking were often organised between men. The sleeve of Macho's *I'm a Man* (1978) is a classic in terms of gay iconography (leather jackets, white t-shirts, aviator sunglasses) and the looking relay of cruising. The sunglasses of the man facing us, reflect both the man in the black leather jacket, with the album title chalked on his back, but upon a closer look we can also see in the details the reflection of a naked torso, a man waiting outside the frame for some three-way action.

The reverse side of the sleeve is an intimate close-up of a hairy chest with the credits overlaying the image. The sleeves of both Revanche's *Music Man* (1979) and the Boy's Town Gang's *Disc Charge* (1981) also present us with pornographic *mise-en-scènes*; the settings here are a garage and a pier. The imagery includes half-naked motor mechanics, greased up and ready for action; *Music Man* features sailors and military men waiting for sex, and in true democratic fashion a woman is joining in on the action.

In conclusion, the legacies of disco and gay pornography as tenets of 1970s culture need to be properly contextualised in terms of their impact on the formation of sexual identities through the pleasures of popular culture. Certainly, from the perspective of queer studies and gay history, the original disco culture has to be continually reclaimed, rediscovered, canonised, for its inspirational models of life that remain benchmarks of a 1970s gay ontology. Disco and pornography were the nexus of a liberating experience for queers and, to echo Patrick Moore here, 'as a gay man who missed those years, I refuse to abandon their memory'.[23] Furthermore, examining the relationship between disco as a popular form of music and leisure in the 1970s and its salient connections to pornography and gay culture hopefully reconstructs the period in ways which challenge the contemporary solipsistic and pejorative definitions of disco, in other words, bringing sexy back.

CHAPTER 5

BLONDE FIRE: AN INTERVIEW WITH SEKA

Interview by Stefan Nylén (with Christian Hallman and Magnus Paulsson)
Introduction by Xavier Mendik

INTRODUCTION

Since the publication of Linda Williams landmark volume *Hard Core: Power, Pleasure and the Frenzy of the Visible*, critics and theorists have begun to reassess the key productions and performers associated with the American porn industry of the 1970s. From mediations on the mixed merits of Gerard Damiano's *Deep Throat* (and the controversial treatment of its star Linda Lovelace), to considerations of the comedic potential of iconic porn performers such as Ron Jeremy, this decade of porno-chic has become *the* blueprint for theorising the blue movie.

However, while many actors associated with the decade when big-screen porn was born are now subject to critical consideration, one 1970s sensual icon has remained legendary but largely elusive: Seka. The American actress (born Dorothea Hundley Patton in 1954), shot to fame as the platinum blonde pin-up girl of the 1970s *Swedish Erotica* stag series. Through this

FIGURE 5.1 Blonde fire: Seka as the lost icon of 1970s porno-chic

cycle, Seka worked with many leading performers in the American adult industry, including John Holmes, John Leslie, Jamie Gillis, Veronica Hart and Ron Jeremy. She also established a firm fan-base for her work, which resulted in her often being cited as one of the world's leading porn stars by the early 1980s.

Even by the marathon standards of American pornographic production, Seka's exhaustive output and chronology remains startling. She has starred in over 180 films (including compilations),[1] with her output rocketing from two productions in 1978 to 24 movies in 1980, with a further thirty films being completed in 1981. Indeed, Seka's ascension to porno-chic superstardom is indicated by the fact that from 1979 onwards many of her productions were titled or re-titled as star vehicles (with examples being *Seka for Christmas* (1979), *Princess Seka* (Leonard Kirtman, 1980) and *Confessions of Seka* (Leonard Kirtman, 1980)).

Although much of this rapid output consisted of *Swedish Erotica* short sexual interludes, Seka's work during the late 1970s and mid-1980s also encompassed the emergent trend for feature-length, 35 mm productions, indicative of the industry's maturation from the 'perverse' margins to the porno-chic mainstream. For instance, Seka starred in many hard-core features that are now viewed as carnal classics. Not only did the actress work on *Dracula Sucks* (Phillip Marshak, 1979), which pre-empted the parodic nature of many contemporary erotic/horror hybrids, but she also starred alongside John Holmes in *Blonde Fire* (Bob Chinn, 1978), one of the more accomplished porno-pulp entries to the 'Johnny Wadd' series that director Bob Chinn prepared as a salacious star vehicle for the oversized male icon. Seka also headlined as the alien heroine in *Ultra Flesh* (Svetlana, 1980), a deliriously ambitious SFX and sleaze science fiction extravaganza that took porn production values to a new level. As well as appearing in a number of pivotal porn productions, Seka also directed two erotic features: *Inside Seka* (with Ken Yontz, 1980) and *Careful, He May Be Watching* (Seka/Richard Pacheco, 1987), in which she played a frustrated housewife masquerading as a porn star.

At the height of her career, Seka suddenly quit the adult film business, only briefly returning to the erotic cinema in a 1993 comeback movie *American Garter* (Henri Pachard/Gloria Leonard). Until 2002, even the former sex starlet's whereabouts remained a mystery before Swedish filmmakers Magnus Paulsson, Christian Hallman and journalist Stefan Nylén mounted an elaborate filmed journey to track her down. Their resultant documentary was entitled *Desperately Seeking Seka* (Magnus Paulsson and Christian Hallman, 2002) and combined exclusive interviews with the actress alongside other commentaries from leading voices associated with the 1970s American porn industry.

We are delighted to have been given exclusive access to all of the original materials from the *Desperately Seeking Seka* documentary and wish to thank the filmmakers, Grindhouse Pictures and Planet X for allowing excerpts from these transcripts to be exclusively reproduced in this volume.

DESPERATELY SEEKING SEKA: THE INTERVIEW

Stefan Nylén: *You were one of the true icons of the American porn industry, how did you get into the business?*

Seka: Well, let's see. During the seventies I owned adult bookstores, and I would go to a place in Baltimore, Maryland to buy the supplies for the stores. Everything that I saw in these movies I was like, 'I can do this, and I can do this better.' One of the distributors said they were shooting a movie and asked if I wanted to be in it – I said 'Sure', so I did. I don't remember the name of the movie, it was a short loop. I don't know what name they used for me on it? I know they did still pictures with it and it came out as a magazine first. So I had it in all my stores, and it flew of the shelves! That's when I went to Los Angeles. I said to myself 'Maybe I should give this a try!'

FIGURE 5.2 Playing the European as 'exotic': Hutton recast as a Swedish nymphet

You were very closely associated with the Swedish Erotica *label, which was in fact an American series.*

Yes. I have no idea why these guys used the name *Swedish Erotica*! I know that when the company started, they began with the magazine. Their basic logo was that you could tell that a girl was a *Swedish Erotica* girl was they had a scarf around their neck. That was always the clue that the films came from that company. I guess at that particular time, Sweden and that part of Europe was thought of being very open and free sexually, so I guess it was more appealing.

Tell me about the name Seka? Who came up with that idea?

The name Seka? When I was living in Las Vegas there was a girl that I met, she was blonde, had blue eyes, she was Swedish, and that was her name. They first asked me what name I wanted to use I said 'I don't know, use Seka', and I did; it stuck and it worked really well for a long time!

What was the hardest part of those movies, having sex or acting?

Acting – I've never claimed to be an actress, I'm not an actress. A sex performer – yes, someone who enjoys sex very much – yes, but an actress – never.

But just like acting, women can fake an orgasm during sex on film…

Oh, yes if they want to be stupid they can fake it! I can honestly say that I didn't fake it most of the time, maybe only three to four times ever. I figured if I am going to do this I might as well have fun with it! I mean why waste a good orgasm? It would be very stupid, a very silly thing to do. Meg Ryan did it in a coffee shop in Seattle! But what fun is that?

What was it like being such a porn celebrity?

Unreal! I remember going to see *Inside Seka* at the premiere in New York. That was in the days when they were doing adult movie premieres in a big theatre house. They would advertise it, and the stars would be there signing autographs. It was like a big Hollywood opening for a film. That was kind of fun. I took my aunt, my mother and my cousin to see the premiere of *Inside Seka*. My mother and my aunt had to leave; because when I was doing the oral sex scene with the guy they were like, 'Oh, that is disgusting!' They got up and said, 'We would never do something like that!' I said, 'Ok that's your loss.' But they got up and left and I went out to them and told them that they could come back in when the scene had finished. So they were kind of funny…

Many of those porno films were shot hard and fast like many exploitation films. Did you have time for script revisions and rehearsals?

No, we never had rehearsals! We were lucky if we got the lines out as it was. I mean that part was pretty easy for me. I can read something and remember it pretty much line for line. We didn't have to stick that closely to a script, unless it was something that was relevant to what was supposed to be happening on screen. You have to remember, these were X-rated movies, it wasn't *Gone With the Wind*, you know. It wasn't anything earth shattering. So as long as you got the gist of the beginning, the middle, and the end that was mainly what they were concerned about.

Yet many of these films had a creativity about them. One of my favourites being Ultra Flesh, *the science fiction porno movie.*

Ultra Flesh, that was fun, because Jamie Gillis was in that one. He played Mr. Sugarman or something, so it was fun in that respect. It was not real pleasant having on that plastic alien costume during the shoot though. We shot that part of that movie in the same place as we shot *Dracula Sucks* and in order to get that main scene, from a distance where I'm standing on a mountain, they took me in a helicopter and dropped me off on the top of this mountain, in the snow, in the cold, in a plastic costume! At first I was sweating so the costume was fogging up, and then once I got up there I couldn't move because it started cracking, it started to actually crumble, like shattering into glass. I said to them 'You'd better get me out off this thing because I'm going to cut myself to death', because it was that cold up there. That was kind of fun. Then once we got back to Los Angeles to do the other stuff it was like a 130 degrees [54°C] because we were in the Valley in the summer time, so we went from extreme cold to extreme heat and people were actually passing out. The outerspace women with the bald heads couldn't keep the bald caps on them because it was so hot it was melting; the make-up was melting that was how hot it was with all the lights and the temperature at the same time. These poor girls were passing out, and we had people in plastic in 130 degree weather, with bald caps on so that no sweat was coming out so they were just passing out and falling into the pool.

Are there any other productions which you are proud of?

Yes. I wrote one film called *Careful He May Be Watching* and I directed parts of it. It did pretty well; I think we won an award for it. I don't remember because it has been so long. Also there is one film, which was produced but never released, that I wished I could get my hands on because it was a really good film. *Careful He May Be Watching* was pretty interesting because I played dual parts in the film. I played Molly Fling the redhead porn star, and I played Jane Smith the housewife. The husband was a pilot and he didn't know what his wife was doing during the day while he was up flying the plane. In fact, she was doing porno films, and Molly Fling was his favourite porno actress, except he didn't know it was his wife. So it was pretty cute.

You worked with some of the legends of the seventies porn industry, including John Holmes.

Yes, the first full-length feature movie I did I worked with John Holmes, which was scary obviously, but he was a very nice man, and he was very nice to me. A lot of women didn't get along with John, but I did.

Do you remember when John Holmes died, and how his life ended?

Well, John Holmes was a pretty fucked up guy. I mean he wasn't to me. He was a heavy

FIGURE 5.3 Careful, she may be watching: the 1970s porn performer as auteur

cocaine user, and when you couldn't find John on the set you would probably find him in a closet somewhere hiding because he was so high, he was paranoid. Drugs were John's downfall. The whole thing with the Wonderland Murders and everything that happened to him was all over drugs. At the time of his death, everybody was asking me if I was afraid of contracting AIDS because I had worked with him. But if you think about it logically, all of a sudden John

FIGURE 5.4 Surviving the 1970s: Seka on working with John Holmes

Holmes had AIDS and three months later he was dead. You don't get AIDS and then die in three months. It lasts a lot longer than that. I personally think that John's death was a hit, perhaps by an active AIDS needle in prison because he had a wife and a child and they are both living. Neither one of them are sick. So think about it; it is kind of strange. He was a dead man whether he went to prison or not, because of the people he was dealing with. It is a pretty messed up world you get into when you carry a briefcase of cocaine around with you.

Do you have any great stories of working with guys like Jamie Gillis?

Well, yes. I actually have one great memory of working with Jamie. We were doing this scene, and Jamie was supposed to be the dominant person. It was two girls and Jamie, and I think I had on a black satin cape with red satin inside and really high black leather pumps. I don't know what happened to me that day, or why I felt like this, but I started dominating Jamie, and he just like freaked out. Jamie went, 'I like this!' The directors didn't understand what was going on and Jamie was like, 'No this is cool, I like this.' So I got to dominate Jamie Gillis, which I really liked!

What about working with someone like Ron Jeremy?

God, Ron Jeremy! There was a scene I did in a movie with him that sums Ron Jeremy up. In the scene, I think there were eight guys in a circle, and I was doing all of them. For some reason the character that Ron Jeremy was playing was annoying, which Ron is. He is an annoying little hairy fat man, but I love him to death! He sort of like weaseled his way into the group act, even though he wasn't supposed to be one of the guys in the circle. So I told him 'Why don't you go blow yourself', and he did! I had to stop and watch because I couldn't believe someone could do that, but evidently if they are Ron Jeremy, they can!

Did you ever think of a career in mainstream movies after you were done with porno films?

God, no. I never thought of a career in mainstream movies. Maybe if I hadn't made adult films first I could have, but like I said I'm not an actress, I don't think that I could ever be an actress, and once you have done adult films it is not that easy to cross over to mainstream, at least not in the United States. After I finished doing hard-core I did the *Electric Blue* stuff, which was a club magazine out of London. But that wasn't hard-core stuff, it was R-rated stuff. I didn't do any other movies at that time.

How did you adjust from hard-core to R-rated movie?

Actually doing an R-rated movie is really strange. When you are used to doing X-rated movies, to go and do an R-rated movie is like thinking, 'OK, I'm ready now, where is the sex? Oh there is no sex!' So that was a little strange for me; having to fake having sex.

Then you had a comeback movie in 1993, called American Garter.

Yes, I did have a comeback film, or I guess that is what they called it. I said, 'Let me see if this is something I still want to do?' as I wasn't sure if I wanted to do another film or not. I did that movie for VCA, and found out that I really didn't want to do any more movies! It was a lot more stressful and difficult than I had remembered. I don't regret doing it. I had a good time.

During the late seventies and early 1980s, you had a very established fan-base. Did you ever have any problems with them?

You mean fans that thought that just because you made X-rated films you'd go to bed with

FIGURE 5.5 The Comeback Kid: Seka re-branded as contemporary adult icon

anyone! Of course there were people like that and still there are. I don't pay any attention to it, because you expect people to do that sometimes. Most of the time, the fans were very nice.

Did you have any death threats?

I have had quite a few. There was one psycho in particular. He would start off his letters very grateful and praising. They were really long letters, and as they went on it would go to the point of how he was going to bash my head in, and how bloody it was going to be. He would always send rusty fishhooks inside the letters. I don't know, some people are very strange! It was pretty scary to me because I was getting two or three letters a day from this guy, and it was every day. They got more intense as time went on and I turned it over to the FBI because I was really afraid. But then he made the big mistake of copying his driver's license with his picture and address on it and sending it to me. So I think he is spending a little time in jail for stalking.

Porn fans can be scary then!

Not just porn fans, but porn partners! When I first started doing X-rated stuff, I was living with someone and he wanted me to do these movies, as did I. He went on to become very controlling. He had to be on the set when I was working, or be in the movie that I was in, and it got to the point where I had to get away from him because he was making me nuts.

Was it nervous to have him on the set when you were having sex with other men?

It was very nerve-wracking to have him on the set whether I was having sex or just doing a regular scene! I felt like I wasn't going to do it right or to the perfection he thought I should, which made me very uncomfortable. Plus he was controlling the money at the time. So I never had any money in my pocket and I knew that this wasn't very good. If I needed to get away and something happened I didn't have any way to escape, which was basically pretty much what happened. He got very violent, and I ended up calling *Swedish Erotica* to help me get away from this guy. They came in to the house where I was living in California to help me get my belongings out and put me in a safe house underground basically for six to seven months. So they helped me a lot that way. It was kind of hard to get away from him because he was around the business and people were afraid of him. When I was working they were afraid that he would find out and come around to cause a scene.

You were at the height of your popularity when you quit the industry. Why did you leave so suddenly?

Why did I stop doing films? I got too old. You know there comes a time when you want to do other things. For instance, eat! I love to eat. Doing those films you have to stay thin, and in shape and I would go to the gym for four and a half hours a day, seven days a week. I never ate anything fattening. I never went out and partied or drank. I was tired of it. I wanted to have some fun. I am comfortable the way I am. My boyfriend likes me the way I am. I didn't want to work that hard at looking good and feeling miserable!

Finally, American porn production is now much bigger, more established and even accepted than when you were working. How do you feel about the industry and the stars today?

Yes bigger, but better? All the girls look alike. They look like they come out of a cookie

93

cutter. They are all blonde, they all have big tits, they all wear these big platform shoes and nobody has any individuality left anymore it seems to me. They all even sound alike to me. They have these little tiny voices. I am sure they are very nice girls, I don't know them, but they all seem to look alike, and either they are very prissy or they are very slutty. When I was doing films there was Marilyn Chambers, there was me, Vanessa Del Rio, Veronica Hart, Annette Haven and we all looked different. I mean that our bodies were different, our faces were different, our hair was different, and today it looks like all these girls go to the same plastic surgeon to get their faces and bodies done, and the same hairdresser to dye their hair. There is not enough spice anymore!

As a result of the resurgence of interest in her films and career, Seka has started the website www.seka.com.

CHAPTER 6
THAT'S L'AMORTE:
JOE D'AMATO AND THE SADEAN ART OF LOVE

Xavier Mendik

With a bizarre back catalogue which repeatedly fused elements of sexual excess with punishment and humiliation, the late Italian exploitation director Joe D'Amato (real name Aristade Massachessi) can also rightly claim the label of being a 'Sadean' filmmaker. This definition is applicable not merely because much of D'Amato's output circulated within the domain of the 'pornographic'. Rather, it is the fact that his narratives were marked by a type of cross-generic overload, which combined outrageous doses of sex and horror in an appeal to different 'grindhouse' audiences. The extreme nature of many of D'Amato's crossover productions can be inferred by a brief consideration of some of his most notorious titles. These centred on macabre depictions of sex which saw zombies attacking Westerners with monstrous phalluses (*Porno Holocaust* (1979)), as well as voodoo priestesses castrating their lovers at the point of orgasm (*Erotic Nights of the Living Dead* (1980)). Other outrageous scenes of sexual trauma that D'Amato concocted included those featuring repressed taxidermists seducing young women in the same bed as their dead brides (*Beyond the Darkness* (1979)), as well as sexually charged couples who copulate before images of filmed female mutilation (*Emanuelle in America* (1976)).

What united all of these productions was D'Amato's unflinching fusion of sex and gore. This clearly drew on Sade's favoured combination of eroticism and violence, to the extent that the boundaries of sexual desire and displeasure were dissolved. For instance, writing in *Sade: The Libertine Novels*, John Phillips has defined works such as *120 Days of Sodom* as dominated by 'a criminal orgy of sexual deviance protracted well beyond the normal limits of human endurance'.[1]

At the level of film form, D'Amato's fusion of disparate generic elements also affected the logical structure of his works. These were marked by a repetitious, meandering and often illogical structure that frequently outraged many of the director's detractors. However, these strategies also recall the contradictory nature of narrative excess and deviation found in Sade's work. As Maurice Charney has noted, 'Sade's gargantuan sexual imagination is not intended to provoke or inflame desire; rather the vast repetition has a numbing effect'.[2] It is precisely such a numbing effect which accompanied the erotic and macabre crossover imagery in Joe D'Amato's cinema.

While the Sadean influences can be found in both the form and content of D'Amato's delirious 1970s productions, little comment has been made on the 35mm hard-core films with which he became involved from 1994 until his death in 1999. For many, these glossy, 'feel good' porn productions (whose titles included *X-Hamlet* (1994), *Barone Von Masoch* (1994) and *Tarzan-X Shame of Jane* (1994)), seem to share little connection with the director's earlier, controversial output.

However, by considering two of D'Amato's later porn titles: *120 Days of the Anal* and *The Marquis De Sade* (both 1995), I wish to show an essential Sadean continuity between these texts and the director's earlier infamous output. It is not merely the fact that these two films take the figure of Sade and his philosophy as their focus, rather they retain the director's interest in emphasising the horrific nature of sexuality, while also presenting these images in a convoluted and repetitive narrative form. In order to identify these features, I want to firstly offer a case study drawn from D'Amato's 1970s output before considering its links to his later hard-core productions.

SADEAN SEX IN THE 1970s

Several of the Sadean thematic and stylistic structures for which Joe D'Amato first gained international exposure (and notoriety) are evident in his 1976 film *Emanuelle and Françoise*. This production recounts the (literally) fatal coupling between a manipulative womaniser named Carlo (played by D'Amato's scriptwriter/acting regular George Eastman), and two sisters: Françoise and Emanuelle. The narrative is organised around a number of disorientating flashbacks that detail the catalogue of sexual humiliations forced upon the virginal Françoise (Patrizia Gori) by Carlo, resulting in her eventual suicide. These fatal actions are later revealed to the more sexually liberated Emanuelle (Rosemarie Lindt), in the form of a suicide note penned by Françoise before she jumped to her death under a speeding train. The document reveals that Carlo forced his lover to appear in pornographic movies against her will (as well as coercing her into sexual encounters with a number of his business associates). It thus becomes the trigger upon which Emanuelle plots a violent revenge against the male protagonist.

After orchestrating a meeting with Carlo, the heroine manipulates his sexual interest in her, inviting the protagonist to her home with the promises of seduction. Emanuelle then drugs Carlo and when the protagonist awakens, he is revealed as being imprisoned behind a two-way mirror. From this position of incarceration, Carlo is forced to watch Emanuelle engage in a number of sexual liaisons with male and female partners (including his current girlfriend Mira).

FIGURE 6.1 The anguish of voyeurism: Carlo as the incarcerated viewer of Emanuelle's revenge

Via the heroine's revenge plot, *Emanuelle and Françoise* renders the thrill of sexual excess and display as a source of humiliation and trauma. Not only does Emanuelle proceed to starve, torture, threaten to kill and castrate her captive, but she also uses drugs to further disorientate and terrorise him. For instance, one hallucinogenic scene features Carlo imagining that he is witnessing a refined dinner party that ends in a bizarre cannibalistic orgy with the diners feasting on severed human limbs.

In its theme and arrangement, *Emanuelle and Françoise* embodies many of the traits of Sadean fiction as described by critics such as Maurice Charney. For instance, its separation of female protagonists into virginal and sexual types clearly recalls Sade's classic division of virtue and vice in the duel female figures of Justine and Juliette, with the distinction between regimes of sexual power (and powerlessness) that this implies. Indeed, Carlo's exploitation of the emotionally scarred and vulnerable Françoise is juxtaposed and contrasted with his own manipulation by the erotically charged Emanuelle. This division between virgin and vamp draws parity with the distinction that Charney makes between 'Justine's virginal passivity and Juliette's sexual terror'.[3]

D'Amato even manipulates the film's convoluted narrative structure as a way of drawing distinctions between his two heroines. For instance, the opening credit scene of the film reveals Françoise stripping confidently before a cameraman in what appears to be a consensual 'glamour' photography shoot. It is only the later discovery of the heroine's suicide note that reveals Carlo's coercion of the protagonist into these pornographic scenarios against her will. Carlo's treatment of Françoise indicates in the words of Maurice Charney that 'all sex in Sade is a form of tyranny, by which the dominant partner imposes his will on the subservient sex object'.[4] This serves to distinguish the fate of the heroine from the subsequent actions of Emanuelle, who by subverting Carlo's control over the sexual scenario places him in the very masochistic position previously enforced on her sister. Within the realm of Sadean aesthetics,

97

the film's constantly changing set of power dynamics indicates that all sexual relations 'are sadomasochistic ones, with the possibility that roles can be temporarily changed for the purposes of experimentation'.[5]

However, it is not merely the oscillation between states of power and oppression that underlie the Sadean impetus in *Emanuelle and Françoise*. Rather, it is the film's very obsession with *seeing* its protagonists *perform* the sexual act that translates its erotic acts into scenarios of theatrical display. Here, sex is relocated from a private into a public act, echoing what John Phillips has termed the essentially 'public and theatrical' nature of Sade's writing.[6] As with novels like *The 120 Days of Sodom*,[7] D'Amato's film produces sexual activity staged before an audience, the outcome of which is liable to evoke a number of contradictory and uncomfortable emotions.

This capacity for erotic satisfaction to be transmuted into a scenario of suffering is indicated in the film's opening segment. Here, a montage sequence offers the illusion of a content Françoise shopping for a variety of gifts for Carlo on her way home from the glamour photography shoot. Although these scenes establish an up-beat theme to the proceedings, they are suddenly disrupted when she arrives home to discover Carlo making love to another woman. Watching the erotic encounter through an open door, Françoise adopts the position of the classic D'Amato voyeur: a protagonist whose obsession with looking overrides the traumatic potential for what is actually viewed. During the scene, the camera pans between Françoise's horrified gaze, Carlo's erotic coupling and a small statue that adorns a bedside cabinet. This monument, with distorted features and oversized, leering eyes in many respects echoes the near-monstrous status that D'Amato gives his voyeurs in the film. Indeed, if it is the case that D'Amato's 'lookers' assume a fatalistic and masochistic position, then this structure finds its logical conclusion in Carlo's positioning as the bound/tortured voyeur in the final stages of the film.

While this rendering of sexual activity as a site of public spectacle provides a motivating principle for *Emanuelle and Françoise*, it also constructs a point of traumatic repetition around which the narrative revolves. Although the heroine dies within the first five minutes of the film, her suicide note effectively keeps her alive, as well as prolonging her past-tense suffering via a series of extended flashbacks. These shifts in filmic time add to the narrative's already convoluted structure, much to the confusion of many of the film's contemporary reviewers. For instance, David Badder derided the structure of the narrative as 'deadly dull'; concluding that it was guaranteed to send the bulk of its 'frustrated audience into a deep sleep long before its predictable dénouement'.[8]

It is precisely because of these criticisms, that the structure of D'Amato's film can be viewed within the Sadean tradition. Here, narrative structure is used as a form of experimentation, duplication and deviation that frequently works at odds to the erotic impact that the content attempts to create. Writing in *Sade: The Libertine Novels*, John Phillips has noted that the repetitive and self-referential comments about how the libertine orgies of *The 120 Days of Sodom* are being staged and executed produces a diminishing of 'erotic impact on the reader'.[9] As Phillips comments:

Overall... *Les 120 Journées* functions inefficiently as a work of pornography since, as we have seen, the reader's interest is constantly displaced from any erotic effect to the ways in which sexuality is represented through linguistic, arithmetical and other formal structures.[10]

While the unsettling combination of titillation and trauma packaged in a monotonous, alienating form link D'Amato's 1970s work to the effect that Phillips describes, these features are also present in the director's later hard-core productions which deal explicitly with the figure of Sade and his ideas.

LUST IN A LOOP: THE ROLE OF REPETITION IN *120 DAYS OF THE ANAL*

An Italian/American co-production, *120 Days of the Anal* appears as the more 'restrained' of the two Sadean films that D'Amato completed in 1995. The film translates Sade's victimised heroine Justine into the figure of Martine, who is imprisoned and molested by a group of lusty servants in the opening scene. Her fate is secured by the sudden intervention of an unnamed libertine (played by porn icon Marc Davis). The hero persuades the assembled males that their erotic satisfaction will be heightened through their victim's compliance, arguing that he will be able to 'seduce' her into submission with tales of the libertine orgies he has organised. At first, Davis's plan is greeted with derision, with one of the assembled males sneering that one 'cannot fuck with your eyes', after being asked to assume the position of voyeur.

While Martine's gradual and increasingly sexualised writhing convinces the crowd of the libertine's scheme, it also underscores the fact that any subsequent erotic 'adventures' will be premised upon the unpalatable outcome of her impending abuse. While the more disturbing aspects of the libertine's plan are softened by the 'consensual' nature of the film's pornographic motifs, it also functions as a basis of sexual trauma upon which the narrative continually returns. Equally, in Davis's re-organisation of the male crowd into a gathering of sexual gazers, the film demonstrates the centrality of voyeurism and exhibitionistic display within the Sadean setting. For Maurice Charney, in these scenarios, 'sex is theatricalised in Sade, and the orgy is his most natural form of sexual experience'.[11] This point is demonstrated through the several flashback scenes through which Davis recounts his debauched past.

Here, at least two of the four extended sex scenes play upon vision (and indeed a lack of sight) as being a precursor to erotic excitement. For instance, the second flashback scene features a group of masked men who have to guess the identity of their female sexual partners by the smell of their body fluids, before an orgy ensues. Equally, the third flashback sequence features a hooded female who is at first offered to the assembled male libertines before being ravished by the group's well-endowed black servant. During the sequence, D'Amato's camera appears as if concealed behind plants and bushes (before focusing more fully on the sexual acts depicted), a strategy that once again underscores the voyeuristic potential inherent in the libertine regime.

FIGURE 6.2 Titillating and traumatic repetitions: sexual 'looping' in *120 Days of the Anal*

Even when the film is not shifting its male and female protagonists through regimes of voyeurism/concealed sight, the impetus to *look* is central to the staging of the sex scenes as a sight of public spectacle. For instance, one of the final flashbacks from *120 Days of the Anal* features a female engaged in an act of masturbation before the libertine crowd organised in a circular pattern around her. As the scene unfolds, Davis and his black servant join her in an act of vaginal and anal intercourse. Rather than enter the coupling, the rest of the assembled group find gratification in their roles as voyeurs, leading to several shots of male and female self-pleasuring. Through these scenes, *120 Days of the Anal* confirms Sade's view of the erotic act as a communal affair. As Phillips has noted, for Sade 'debauchery here is above all a shared activity in which to be seen is as important as to see'.[12]

In its use of features such as the traumatic basis of sexual activity, as well as a voyeuristic obsession with erotic events, *120 Days of the Anal* draws clear connections with not only the philosophy of Sade, but also the earlier output of Joe D'Amato. The film's connection with both of these sources is also confirmed through the repetitive shifting between the flashback and present-tense scenes that make up the structure of the film. *120 Days of the Anal* is constructed around four key flashback scenes, which are alternated with shots of Martine's increasing sexual frenzy as Davis recounts the tales. What is noticeable about this structuring process is the way in which duration alters to mirror the heroine's increasing sexual excitement. While the first two flashbacks are of similar length, the final ones occupy a much shorter time-span, being fragmented by D'Amato's brief return to Martine's approaching sexual climax.

However, if the structure of the film is constructed around the frenzied drive towards orgasm, this does not necessarily guarantee the sexual release and satisfaction that the term may imply. Rather, it condemns the viewer to a type of formal alienation, similar to the effect that Phillips has identified in Sade's writings. Here, the constant alternation between differing cinematic tenses robs the spectator of the necessary temporal (and frequently visual) anchors from which to secure a position of gratification. If this is a result of the repetitive and convoluted form in which sexual activity takes place, then its disengaging effect is heightened by the way in which D'Amato frames the sexual activity of the libertine's recollections. Whereas Martine's sexual excitement is shot from an overhead position (allowing the viewer access to the whole of her body), the libertine encounters are framed in such extreme close-up that a 'genital vignette' replaces total, human interaction.

Via this method, the camera gazes in extreme proximity on a succession of penis, vagina and anus shots, which prove more alienating than arousing to the viewing eye. This is particularly marked in the 'group' encounters that dominate the first two flashbacks. Here, the camera frequently switches between differing sets of sex organs without identifying their respective owners. In so doing, D'Amato's film provokes a curious barrier between the audience and the sexual excesses it depicts. This provides a visual equivalent of the 'de-realising' effect that Phillips has identified in Sade's literary works. Here, textual complexity and ambiguity 'focuses attention on process rather than erotic content'.[13]

TITILLATION AND TORTURE: ROCCO AND HIS BROTHER

With *120 Days of the Anal*, Joe D'Amato gestures towards the repetition of traumatic/sexual encounters that were evident in his 1970s productions. His 1995 companion piece *The Marquis De Sade* makes these links even more explicit, by taking Sade's own incarceration as its central subject matter. In many respects, the film shares the complicated formal structure of the director's earlier works such as *Emanuelle and Françoise*. Here, Donatien's fall from grace is depicted within a series of extended flashbacks that are fragmented by sudden (and often unmotivated) shifts in filmic tense.

From the outset, D'Amato makes good use of a doubling motif to initiate the flashback sequences. Here, the imprisoned Marquis finds his past actions challenged by an imaginary incarnation of himself. Both Sade and his chastising double are played by the famed Italian porn stud (and D'Amato regular) Rocco Siffredi.

This iconic male performer gained exposure on the adult circuit for not only the excessive size of his penis (as well as its ejaculating capacities), but also his well toned, body-building physique. However, in contrast to his usually fine-tuned appearance, D'Amato casts him here as a gaunt figure who is wracked by the demons of his past.

As with D'Amato's earlier incarnation of the voyeuristic Carlo from *Emanuelle and Françoise*, this is a figure whose reflections and sexual obsessions are a source of displeasure rather than guaranteed sexual satisfaction. The traumatic basis to the protagonist's malaise is indicated in the film's first flashback, when the Marquis' double asks him to recollect 'his first discovery of the female sex'. The flashback that follows features the camera adopting a point of view style, whilst concealed within a closet. From this position, a subjective perspective is given watching a young maid disrobe. When the illicit gazer (revealed as a childhood Sade) is discovered, it is interesting to note that it is the camera lens itself that is directly reprimanded, being beaten and shaken by the semi-naked woman. Thus it can be argued that it is not only the protagonist, but also the viewer (beyond the limits of the film frame), who come to share Sade's humiliation. Such images confirm that in the Sadean universe, sexuality is linked to despair and mistreatment rather than physical liberation. According to Charney:

> Sade is a spokesman for hard and difficult sex, violent, cruel and energetic. Orgasm unites man with the animal creation and is a kind of epileptic fit or temporary seizure by which we abandon all pretensions to reason and false enlightenment. Against a benevolent and optimistic romanticism, Sade opposes a negative, primitive, chaotic and destructive view of the sexual relationship.[14]

Although the later flashback scenes recounting the activities of the adult Sade show him in a dominating position over his varied female partners, they must be premised upon the initial scene of violence and humiliation enacted against the protagonist (as well as the character's torment from his imaginary divided self in the present-tense scenes punctuating these sexual

FIGURE 6.3 Rocco and His Body: the male porn star as phallic icon?

encounters). Indeed, the lyrics of the film's theme tune 'Love and Pain' that accompany each of Sade's adult sexual encounters reiterates the connection between eroticism and displeasure that the film is trying to create. Equally, even those scenes which feature Sade orchestrating the sexual humiliation of others feature an act of voyeurism on the part of an aroused on-looker, thereby connecting them with the perils of voyeurism identified in D'Amato's earlier work.

An example of such a scenario can be found in the second flashback scene featuring the adult Sade. Here, Renee (the Marquis' future bride), conceals herself and watches with a mixture of passion and disgust as the libertine coerces a prostitute into a series of couplings that are intended to degrade. Firstly, Sade attempts to placate his new conquest with promises of gold coins, before making her crouch down and urinate over the reward on offer. When her bladder skills are revealed as too inadequate to arouse the libertine, he gestures the prostitute towards an act of oral sex before urinating over her face and hair.

The anal sex scene between the pair that follows retains these overtones of violence and sexual oppression. Firstly, Sade enters his partner roughly from behind before threatening to 'rip your guts out'. The extended scenes of anality that follow are similarly coded within a vocabulary of disgust. Here, the libertine claims that he will slice his partner's 'ass open' as well as 'pull the shit out of her'. (The violent language of eroticism demonstrated in this scene is evident in an earlier coupling between Sade and two women, where the protagonist derides his partners with terms such as 'bitch', 'whore' and 'pig'). The sex scene ends when Sade reaches a sexual climax while attempting to use his penis to choke this partner at the point of orgasm. In many respects, this body fluid-dominated sex scene draws comparison with some of the more extreme orgies enacted in *120 Days of Sodom*, including:

> other transgressive acts … promptly enacted by the libertines include urine-drinking, armpit smelling, saliva swallowing, fart swallowing, nostril licking, the drinking of menstrual blood, and of course, fucking.[15]

Arguably, the power behind these otherwise offensive scenarios lies in the ability to use the body (and its waste products) as a way of introducing an element of displeasure into an otherwise titillating scenario. As already noted, this feature is a long established trait in D'Amato's films. In *The Marquis De Sade*, the strategy of rendering pornographic 'thrills' distasteful is most marked in the sequence where two women are blindfolded before being required to arouse an unidentified suitor. Although Sade informs his sightless assistants that they are 'licking the body of a young athlete from head to foot', when their vision is restored they are as disgusted to find that they have been cavorting with an overweight, deformed, middle-aged servant. Although the women verbalise their displeasure upon this discovery, and even struggle against nausea at the sight of the servant's dwarfish genitals, Sade coerces them to a climax with this unlikely partner. Here, the pleasure of sexual release is overburdened by a sense of decay and disgust. This once again mirrors the literary source material upon which D'Amato draws. As Phillips has noted, rather than just offend the senses, Sade uses such repulsive imagery to invert 'aesthetic norms, replacing the sweet fragrances of youth and beauty with the foul smelling and ugly as a basis of sexual attraction'.[16]

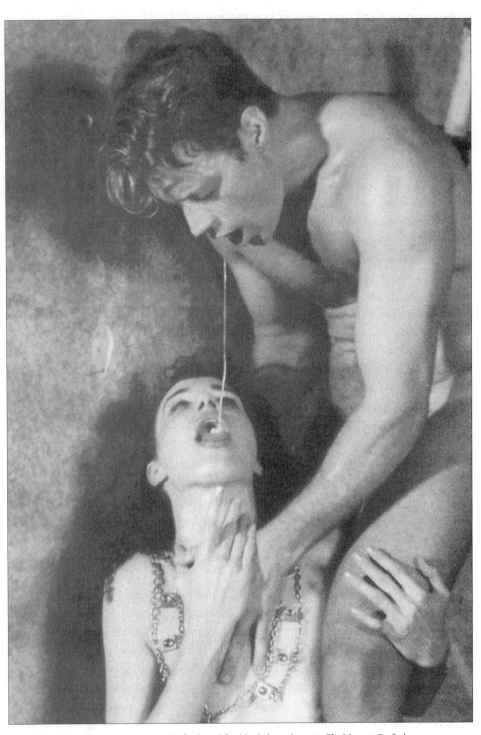

FIGURE 6.4 Abjection and eroticism: body fluids and fluid body boundaries in *The Marquis De Sade*

TITILLATION AND TRAUMA: ROCCO AND HIS BODY

Through their traumatic rendering of sex with violence, degradation or implied threat, the later films of Joe D'Amato can be aligned with the Sadean impetus that defined his most infamous output of the 1970s. These texts also display the Sadean obsessions with voyeurism and erotic exhibitionism that defined works such as *120 Days of Sodom*. Equally, the formal structure of D'Amato's works, with their emphasis on repetition and deviation can be seen as similar to the narrative experiments that critics such as Phillips and Charney have identified in Sade's fiction.

It is also worth considering the extent to which this overlap between titillation and trauma might affect depictions of masculinity within a format that has traditionally been seen as gratifying male desires. Writing in the volume *Running Scared: Masculinity and Representations of the Male Body*, Peter Lehman has noted that the conventions, motifs and modes of depiction within mainstream heterosexual pornography function to distinguish between the genders, while attributing erotic power to the male.[17] This is seen in the frequency with which male characters function as unchecked voyeurs: they have visual access to the naked female body by watching from a secret location. Equally, as Lehman notes, by focusing on the male orgasm (or 'money shot') as a guarantor of sexual satisfaction, such genre conventions confirm that

> Male sexuality lies at the centre of the porn genre. Everything turns on affirming and satisfying male desires and the hard-core scene typically ends immediately after the visual proof that this has occurred. Women's pleasure becomes merely a sign of their dependence on the phallus.[18]

By fusing sex with violence, threat and disgust, both Sade and D'Amato's work can be seen as reversing many of the male-centred conventions of pornography. From Carlo's status as impotent, imprisoned gazer in *Emanuelle and Françoise*, to the beating attributed to the visually curious youngster (and viewer) in the opening of *The Marquis De Sade*, these works introduce a generically uncharacteristic degree of punishment associated with male voyeurism. Alongside this denigration of gendered looking, D'Amato reverses the 'invisibility' often associated with modes of male display in such formats.

While it is true that women still occupy a position of visual spectacle in both his early and later erotic dramas, it is noticeable that their exhibitionistic role is in fact superseded by an obsessive focus on the male body. An example of this strategy can be seen in the first flashback featuring Rocco Siffredi as the adult Sade. Here, the protagonist is depicted as bathing while being secretly watched by two giggling chambermaids. When the females are discovered, they are invited to join the bather and an orgy ensues. What is interesting about the sexual acts that unfold here is the way in which the camera glides over the images of the females undressing (traditionally the focus of such porno explorations), coming to rest instead on shots of Sade's penis and buttocks. The scene echoes a similar focus on male exhibitionism found in *120 Days of the Anal*. For instance, during the libertine's first flashback recollection, the camera retards its focus on disrobing females in favour of extended shots of the muscular body of the black servant who comes to visually dominate the scene.

Rather than representing an isolated example, it can be argued that a visual obsession with Siffredi's body dominates both this sex scene as well as the other erotic encounters in *The Marquis De Sade*. While it is not uncommon for such iconic (and well-endowed) male porn performers to attract a high degree of visual interest, these strategies of display work in opposition to the normal conventions of masculine display within pornography. As Lehman has noted, when reduced to a site of naked spectacle, images of masculinity evoke a number of contradictory (and potentially threatening) emotions in the heterosexual male. As a result, these have to be minimised by anchoring such scenes of exhibitionism to the primary goal of servicing the depicted females. Here, as 'women desire the visibility of male ejaculation, they frequently express their desire for large penises'.[19]

In contrast to these 'traditional' uses of the male body in porn, D'Amato's depiction of Siffredi connotes a high degree of sexual ambiguity that denies the male viewer a stable point of masculine identification. These sexual tensions are evidenced in the scene where an experienced

FIGURE 6.5 Rocco and his body: the emphasis on male exhibitionism in *The Marquis De Sade*

lesbian inducts a younger woman into the pleasures of same-sex copulation, which she claims requires a rejection of 'the strong, muscular arms of a male'. After informing the sexual novice that Sade's new maid will be joining them, an unidentified 'woman' appears and is initiated into the coupling. However, as the pair begins to disrobe the dress of their new partner, they are surprised to find that is in fact Sade, who has disguised himself as a woman in order to join in the encounter. He then proceeds to initiate intercourse while still wearing his 'female' wig, earrings, corset and heavily rouged face. This scene indicates just one way in which D'Amato parodies the machismo associated with male porn stars. Another scene features a cameo by famed porn regular Christoph Clark, who is here cast as Sade's camp cousin who leaves one of his host's orgies after complaining that he can never get 'himself any cock'.

Rather than being isolated to one specific production, these atypical masculine representations dominate all of D'Amato's supposedly heterosexual hard-core works. For instance, a similar degree of feminisation happens to Marc Davis in the second flashback scene of *120 Days of the Anal*. Here, D'Amato arranges the libertine in front of his (semi-naked) black servant during an encounter with an unidentified female. This close proximity between the two men gives the appearance of a scene of homoerotic coitus, normally shunned by mainstream heterosexual porn. While this degree of feminising the male 'erotic icon' is uncommon within the boundaries heterosexual pornography, it is characteristic of Sadean sexual ambiguity from which D'Amato draws his source material. As Phllips has noted, although novels like *120 Days of the Sodom* abound with phallic imagery, these depictions of masculinity are frequently accompanied by a degree of sexual fluidity. For instance, he discusses the figure of the financier Durcet whom Sade has depicted as possessing 'an incredibly small penis and the breasts and buttocks of a woman'.[20]

The degree of sexual ambiguity found in Sade and D'Amato's work functions at the level of the iconic, whilst also affecting the way in which soundtrack connotes sexual pleasure. For critics like Lehman, although the soundtracks in porn productions are geared towards the vocalisation of female pleasure, they function merely as a response to the genre's focus on dominant male desires. Here, 'soundtrack editing further structures these moans to build with these visuals in a pattern geared to male sexual climax.'[21] In contrast to these unambiguous anchors of male heterosexual activity, the soundtrack to works such as *The Marquis De Sade* is dominated by a type of male *aural* exhibitionism. This is exemplified by the high pitched screeching of Siffredi at the point of orgasm, or the effeminate squealing of his overweight, middle-aged assistant as he nears a sexual climax. These vocal gestures find parity with the construction of the Sadean heroes that John Phillips has studied. As evidenced in novels such as *120 Days of Sodom*, these are libertines, who while gendered male, are seen to 'shriek like banshees when reaching orgasm'.[22] The evidence of these codes in the later films of Joe D'Amato, once again point to the way in which the filmmaker utilised the ideas and imagery of the Marquis de Sade to upset the patterns and presumptions within the pornographic text.

CHAPTER 7
WHEN *SPIDERMAN* BECAME *SPIDERBABE*: PORNOGRAPHIC APPROPRIATION AND THE POLITICAL ECONOMY OF THE 'SOFT-CORE SPOOF' GENRE

Iain Robert Smith

> I made Seduction Cinema a top priority in the early years with the goal of establishing a 'brand' name. When you think of cola, you think of Coca-Cola. If a fan hears about a soft-core erotic film, I wanted them to think... Seduction Cinema.
> – Michael L. Raso[1]

In this age of media conglomeratisation, some recent accounts of contemporary cinema have attempted to supplement the more traditional concerns of textual analysis with an examination of the multifaceted network of intertexts which surround a blockbuster release. From the licensing of merchandising such as fast food tie-ins, to the promotional tools of trailers and TV spots, the modern blockbuster produces a supersystem of multimedia marketing and commercial exploitation around the movie franchise.

As Eileen R Meehan has argued, in relation to one of the first major franchise blockbusters,

Batman (Tim Burton, 1989), 'the film *per se* becomes only one component in a product line that extends beyond the theatre, even beyond our contact with mass media, to penetrate the markets for toys, bedding, trinkets, cups and other minutiae comprising one's everyday life inside a commoditised, consumerised culture'.[2]

To fully understand, then, the nature of contemporary blockbuster cinema, Meehan argues that we need to look at how the blockbuster fits within wider corporate structures and market strategies. Yet while this is a valuable intervention, these elements are only part of the picture. What are rarely examined are those rather disreputable, subterranean films which feed off that very same web of intertextual associations and consumer awareness. When *Spiderman* (Sam Raimi, 2002) was released in May 2002, it was accompanied by a marketing spend of approximately $50 million, with a plethora of tie-in promotions, including a new ride at Universal Studios entitled 'Spiderman Rocks', a Spiderman video game produced by Activision, and the release of the film's theme song 'Hero' performed by Nickelback.

There was one tie-in release, however, that was not part of this corporate strategy. That was *Spiderbabe* (Johnny Crash, 2003), a soft-core spoof of the Hollywood blockbuster, which drew on the plot and characters of *Spiderman* in order to narrativise its soft-core sex scenes. By associating itself with the release of a tentpole blockbuster, this ultra low-budget film was able to capitalise on the attendant consumer interest to distinguish itself among the plethora of soft-core material available and achieve worldwide distribution. Indeed, this was one of a number of soft-core spoofs which production company ei Independent Cinema have produced since 1999, including *The Erotic Witch Project* (John Bacchus, 1999), *Gladiator Eroticvs: The Lesbian Warriors* (John Bacchus, 2001), *Play-mate of the Apes* (John Bacchus, 2002) and *Lord of the G-Strings* (Terry West, 2003). This chapter will interrogate these instances of subterranean appropriation, mapping out how ei Independent Cinema[3] capitalises on the surrounding web of intertexts and associations around a blockbuster title to distinguish their soft-core product in an economic market which does not allow for large marketing budgets or expensive promotion. It will then pay attention to the manner in which *Spiderbabe* works textually; showing how the narrative emphasis on spoof and parody – which is so central to the film's strategy of distinction – actually works in tension with the generic requirement for lengthy scenes of soft-core sexual activity. Ultimately, this will offer a privileged insight into the often-obscured symbiotic relationship between independent and studio filmmaking in the contemporary media landscape. But first, let us turn to ei Independent Cinema, the production company behind these 'soft-core spoofs'.

SEX, LIES AND VIDEOTAPES

ei Independent Cinema was founded in 1994 by Michael L. Raso to serve as a 'grass roots distribution outlet for low/no budget moviemakers and their films'.[4] Initially focused on distributing genre pictures and developing a slate of comedy/horror pictures, they gradually came to realise that they would need to diversify to guarantee the continued viability of their

FIGURE 7.1 'Sexploiting' the spoof: the poster for the 'soft-core spoof' *Spiderbabe*

studio. As Raso explains, 'My fellow colleagues and I were concentrating on horror and comedy. We never intended to shoot erotica. The market demanded erotica, so we produced it.'[5]

Adapting to the traditional commercial pressures of supply and demand, Raso set up an erotica-themed label, Seduction Cinema, which soon brought some moderate success with titles such as *Vampire Seduction* (John Bacchus, 1998) and *International Necktie Strangler*

(William Hellfire, 1998) although it wasn't until the release of *The Erotic Witch Project* in 1999 that ei Independent Cinema hit upon a strategy that would achieve substantial returns and bring their micro-budget cinema to a much larger audience.

By taking the basic premise of *The Blair Witch Project* (Daniel Myrick and Eduardo Sánchez, 1999) and altering the narrative to allow for lengthy scenes of soft-core lesbian sex, Raso and his team fashioned a surprise underground hit that went on to gain international distribution in the home video and cable markets. As this came to serve as the template for the subsequent 'soft-core spoofs', it is worth considering for a moment the intertextual strategies through which *The Erotic Witch Project* and other Seduction Cinema titles were able to distinguish themselves in the marketplace.

Firstly, the titles of these soft-core spoofs are generally based around a sexually suggestive pun such as *Planet of the Apes* (Tim Burton, 2001) becoming *Play-mate of the Apes*, or, as in this case, they simply add the prefix 'erotic' or 'sexy' to the title, hence *The Erotic Witch Project*, *The Erotic Time Machine* (John Bacchus, 2002) or *The Sexy Adventures of Van Helsing* (Max Von Diesel, 2004). These playful titles help to associate the spoof with a recognised commercial property and siphon off some of the attendant consumer interest. This works in tandem with the box art which is designed to imitate the poster of the antecedent property, in this case featuring the following tagline overlaid over some eerie woodland images:

> In November 1999, three college coeds disappeared in the woods of Bacchusville NJ, while searching for the mythical Erotic Witch. Two weeks later their home video was found.

As should be clear, the Seduction Cinema parodies work by capitalising on existing consumer knowledge of the mainstream hit they are spoofing. By creating associations with the product, through title, box art and tagline, this serves to distinguish the product from the other soft-core pornography on the market. Of course, it could be said that the choice of *The Blair Witch Project* as the object of their spoofing turned out to be a rather canny business move as the production values necessitated by their ultra-low budget – shooting on digital video, amateur actors, shaky camera work – could be excused by the similarly debased stylings of *The Blair Witch Project* itself (an excuse that could not be used when they went on to spoof a multimillion dollar franchise like *Lord of the Rings*).

In the years following the success of *The Erotic Witch Project*, ei Independent Cinema developed this model by offering soft-core spoofs of almost every major Hollywood blockbuster that was released. According to Paige Kay Davis, the company's Corporate Communications Director,

> We begin pre-production on a spoof after learning, frequently through trade magazines, of a Hollywood production that seems a good match. The timing of the release of the spoof to the Hollywood film, in conjunction with production values, is the criteria the

buyer uses when deciding to pick up a title.[6]

As we can see in the following table, this means that ei Independent Cinema would often shoot, edit and release a film in a matter of months to capitalise on the release of the latest hit:

BLOCKBUSTER RELEASE	SEDUCTION SPOOF
Gladiator 21 Nov 2000	*Gladiator Eroticvs* 6 Mar 2001
Tomb Raider 13 Nov 2001	*Mummy Raider* 8 Jan 2002
Planet of the Apes 21 Mar 2002	*Play-mate of the Apes* 26 Feb 2002
Time Machine 23 Jul 2002	*Erotic Time Machine* 27 Aug 2002
Lord of the Rings 12 Nov 2002	*Lord of the G-Strings* 25 Mar 2003
Spiderman 1 Nov 2002	*Spiderbabe* 14 Oct 2003
Van Helsing 19 Oct 2004	*Sexy Adventures of Van Helsing* 12 Oct 2004
King Kong 28 Mar 2006	*Kinky Kong* 05 Sept 2006
Ironman 30 Sept 2008	*Ironbabe* 18 Nov 2008

Table of DVD release dates in the US (Source: http://videoeta.com)

The associative promotional strategies utilised by ei Independent Cinema are made explicit in the 8x10 publicity glossies they use to sell their films at film markets. These are aimed specifically at the film buyers who are considering whether to purchase Seduction titles for distribution. As we can see in the following list of 'selling points' indicated on the glossy for *Kinky Kong* (John Bacchus, 2006), there is a distinct emphasis on the commercial potential of spoofing a successful blockbuster:

i) MPAA R-Rated

ii) Heavily promoted on top web sites (including Mr Skin with over 6 million hits per month)

iii) Full page ads in national publications including *Femme Fatales*

iv) Spoof of *King Kong* which made over $200 million at the box office[7]

With budgets under $100,000, and some even less than $10,000, it is, of course, very rare for a film at this budget level to even secure a legitimate release. Yet these Seduction films were able to capitalise on their association with a blockbuster release to gain worldwide exposure.

Indeed, through an exclusive home video deal with Ventura Distribution, ei Independent Cinema would secure releases for their films in mainstream outlets such as Blockbuster Video, Hollywood Video, Best Buy, Borders and Tower Video.

So, with recent studies of contemporary Hollywood laying emphasis on the ways in which media conglomerates privilege corporate synergy to exploit properties across various media outlets and thereby cross-promote their products through recognisable franchises and official tie-ins, it is significant to note that these cross-promotional activities also laid the way open for unofficial tie-ins which feed off those very same intertextual relationships. Imitating the will-to-brand in Hollywood, Michael Raso created his own brand identity for Seduction Cinema which would rest upon associative techniques aimed at capitalising upon the wider consumer interest surrounding these major releases.

The intertextual properties discussed above were not the only ways, however, in which the label developed its audience. A number of promotional methods were devised to draw attention to their products and build a devoted 'cult' audience. Reflecting David Andrew's observation that, 'unlike corporate soft-core, which does not stress promotion and has largely ignored its fans, cult soft-core evinces its classical lineage through vigorous, interactive publicity'[8]; ei Independent Cinema actively cultivated fandom around their releases. This was undertaken through presence at fan conventions, such as the *Fangoria*-sponsored Chiller Theatre; the publishing of an in-house fanzine *Alternative Cinema* which couples features on Seduction Cinema releases with broader cult-related articles; a variety of promotions at college/university events and, most importantly, the upkeep of affiliated websites which have brought Seduction Cinema the kind of media spotlight which is rare for a low-budget company to achieve.

They have further attempted to distance themselves from the business model of corporate soft-core through a move towards what I. Q. Hunter terms 'intentional commercial trash'[9]: the celebration of a calculatedly inept brand of high camp and low humour exemplified by companies such as Troma and Full Moon. We can see this too in the DVDs which are closer to the cult collectible than the usual anonymous soft-porn release, complete with behind-the-scenes documentaries, outtakes/bloopers, music videos, deleted scenes and trailers for other releases in the Seduction Cinema oeuvre.

Crucially, the Seduction label relies on a female star system reminiscent both of the classical Hollywood system of contract players, and the more recent cultish conception of 'scream queens' such as Brinke Stevens and Linnea Quigley. In fact, star Misty Mundae (real name Erin Brown) has come to be something of a figurehead for Seduction Cinema, having appeared in over thirty features for the company. As director Michael Raso attests, Mundae's popularity with fans was key to the success of the Seduction model:

Her normality deviates from the classic soft-core image as portrayed by late-night cable programmers. She's not bleached blonde, her hair isn't teased, she doesn't have fake breasts. She's natural. The folks at *Penthouse* and *Playboy* would not see her as acceptable, but that would be missing the point. She's wildly popular because we're

FIGURE 7.2 A 'knowing' imitation of blockbuster appeal in *Spiderbabe*

presenting her as she really is.[10]

This emphasis on cultivating fandom around their releases through vigorous publicity strategies, an evocation of a trash sensibility, and promotion of a distinctly 'natural' star illustrate the ways in which Seduction Cinema attempted to distinguish their product from other soft-core films on the market. To explore these strategies of distinction further, I will now turn to Mundae's two most prominent star vehicles, *Lord of the G-Strings* and *Spiderbabe*.

SEXY SUPERHEROES AND VOLUPTUOUS VILLAINS

Although these films are soft-core, they do share an affinity with the notorious hard-core take-offs of mainstream cinema such as *The Sperminator* (Allen Stuart, 1985) and *Shaving Ryan's Privates* (Christopher Hull, 1999). They are using a 'witty' play on the title of a blockbuster film to promote their product in the marketplace. Yet the difference, as I. Q. Hunter has observed, is that 'whereas hard-core quickly abandons narrative for lengthy depictions of sex', the Seduction spoof, 'pads out its length with story, dialogue and other erotically redundant business'.[11] So whereas a hard-core title like *The Sperminator* spends little time evoking the narrative or iconography of *The Terminator* (James Cameron, 1984), both *Lord of the G-Strings* and *Spiderbabe* spend a considerable proportion of their running time playfully spoofing their respective blockbuster properties, relying on both recreations and inversions of recognisable scenarios.

In the case of *Spiderbabe*, Misty Mundae plays Patricia Porker (Peter Parker in the original), a shy college girl in love with Mark Jeremy (MJ). She is bitten by a genetically engineered spider which transforms her into Spiderbabe, a 'wall-climbing, building-bounding beauty with superhuman strength and an erotic appetite to match'.[12] Throughout the film, subtle – and not so subtle – allusions are made to the parodied text, from the wrestling bout in which Spiderbabe proves her strength, to the infamous upside-down kiss which predictably moves further down the body. With most of the plotline from *Spiderman* being recreated – albeit at a much lower budget and with the female central characters in various states of undress – the key alteration is that one of the side effects from the spider's bite is that he/she is said to 'become more prone towards procreation'.

Hence, the plot abounds with scenes of soft-core lovemaking in which Misty Mundae and other starlets shed their clothes, halting the narrative while they indulge their supposed carnal desires. This creates a tension within the film between the narrative emphasis on spoof and parody in which recognisable plot points are recreated, and the generic requirement of soft-core pornography which requires lengthy scenes of sexual activity. As Craig Fischer has noted, 'the moments that define pornography as a genre are descriptive moments, independent of plot

116

FIGURE 7.3 Seduction scream queen: cult star Misty Mundae as *Spiderbabe*

[which render] the human body, for voyeuristic purposes'.[13] The problem, however, is that this often acts in tension with the forward momentum of the narrative.

This dichotomy is most clear in the differences between the R-Rated and Unrated cuts of *Spiderbabe*. By producing both R-Rated and Unrated versions of their films, ei Independent Cinema cater both for the high street retailer which will only stock MPAA-rated product, and the devoted fans who seek out the uncut version of the release. The primary difference between the two versions is that the Unrated edition contains longer and more explicit sex scenes, while the R-Rated edition substitutes the deleted material with more comedy and plot development. This development was in response to changes in the marketplace; as regular Seduction Cinema director Terry West attests, 'the executive producers were looking for a really meaty story and wanted something where you could cut the stronger sexual content out and still have a movie'.[14]

While this was primarily a business decision, this development towards a more prominent narrative also led to some rather significant creative choices. While the Unrated edit offers quite explicit scenes of lesbian sex, often bearing little or no relation to the plot of the film, the R-Rated edit focuses much more specifically on scenes which actually reflect the character development. This move towards a more integrated, 'motivated' form of pornography forms part of ei Independent Cinema's desire to offer a more saleable product which can appeal beyond the traditional porn consumer and widen the available market. Nevertheless, a byproduct of this strategy is that the films themselves start to appear less and less like pornography.

Ultimately, this move reflects the underlying strategic motivation for ei Independent Cinema in which producing 'erotic' cinema was not an initial goal for the company but rather a means to an end. Again, as Raso explains, 'I originally started my company to produce independent horror films. Seduction Cinema was an unintentional detour.'[15] In recent years, therefore, production focus has shifted back to horror cinema with ei Independent Cinema (now titled POP Cinema) producing titles such as *Shock-O-Rama* (Brett Piper, 2005) and *Skin Crawl* (Justin Wingenfield, 2007) while star Misty Mundae has also attempted to capitalise on the popularity attained from her soft-core titles to move into more 'legitimate' projects (under her own name, Erin Brown) such as the horror comedy *Shadow: Dead Riot* (Erik Wan, 2006) with Tony Todd, and the Lucky McKee-directed *Masters of Horror* episode 'Sick Girl' (2006). While these respective moves into more mainstream productions have yet to pay off – with Seduction Cinema continuing to release 'soft-core spoofs' such as *An Erotic Werewolf in London* (William Hellfire, 2006) and *Iron Babe* (John Bacchus, 2008) – there has been a decisive shift of emphasis in which the soft-core spoofs are just one part of a much wider release slate.

CONCLUSION

In his book *Brand Hollywood: Selling Entertainment in a Global Media Age*, Paul Grainge has argued that:

The meaning of a brand is not simply determined by those who circulate and coordinate mass media representations but is also forged in cultural instances where texts, symbols and images are used by social agents, interpreted by audiences and taken up by fan groups in potentially unforeseen ways.[16]

This reflects the work of scholars like Rosemary Coombe and Henry Jenkins who have drawn attention to the ways in which audiences and consumers can appropriate and transform elements of the media landscape around them in unexpected ways. What I have shown, however, is that this process of negotiation with branded media is not something engaged in only by audiences and fans but rather is also a tactic used by *other* media companies intending to feed off the consumer interest surrounding these well-known franchises.

In this way, Seduction Cinema offers an instructive case-study of a group of independent filmmakers working in symbiosis with Hollywood. Unlike other micro-budget film companies such as Wicked Pixel or Sub Rosa Extreme which are often positioned in opposition to the Hollywood 'mainstream' within critical and analytical writings, ei Independent Cinema instead celebrate and feed off the popularity of franchise releases in order to draw attention to their own products. This fits within a long tradition in exploitation cinema in which appropriated plotpoints and iconography from Hollywood features can function as exploitable elements to sell low-budget features – from Roger Corman films like *Piranha* (Joe Dante, 1978) and *Battle Beyond the Stars* (Jimmy T. Murakami, 1980) through to the more recent feature output of companies like The Asylum such as *Snakes on a Train* (Peter Mervis, 2006) and *Transmorphers* (Leigh Scott, 2007).

The problem for these 'soft-core spoofs', however, is that the commercial tactic of imitative spoofing works in tension with the generic requirement for extended scenes of soft-core porn. It is the catch-22 of the soft-core spoof genre: you need the spoofing to distinguish your pornography in the marketplace, but you find that, within the film itself, the spoofing actually gets in the way of the pornography. Nevertheless, as *Spiderbabe* illustrates, you don't need a credible script, three-dimensional characterisation, or convincing performances to get your low-budget film worldwide distribution. What you need are Spiderman costumes…

CHAPTER 8
THE EROTIC ADVENTURES OF MISTY MUNDAE: AN INTERVIEW WITH ACTRESS ERIN BROWN

Interview by Iain Robert Smith

One of the most prominent stars in contemporary erotic cinema, Erin Brown – better known under her pseudonym 'Misty Mundae' – has forged a career at the very forefront of the soft-core industry. From her beginnings with the underground film company Factory 2000, acting in no-budget fetish titles like *The Bizarre Case of the Electric Cord Strangler* (William Hellfire, 1999) through to her more high-profile work in Seduction Cinema titles such as *Lord of the G-Strings* (Terry West, 2003), Erin Brown has managed to develop a hugely successful career in the independent film world.

Far away from the traditional stereotype of a porn starlet, with neither bleached blonde hair nor silicone implants, Erin has been celebrated widely for her naturalistic looks and a devil-may-care attitude that has set her apart from her contemporaries. With leading roles in a series of soft-core spoofs, from *Play-mate of the Apes* (John Bacchus, 2002) and *Mummy Raider* (Brian Paulin, 2002) through to *An Erotic Werewolf in London* (William Hellfire, 2006), Erin has developed a devoted fan following and a level of consumer awareness unmatched by almost

FIGURE 8.1 Not your typical soft-core girl: Misty Mundae

any other soft-core star.

In the following interview, Erin discusses her 'accidental' career in the porn industry, the underlying gender politics involved in the genre, her move into more mainstream projects in recent years, and her thoughts on the possibility for socio-political commentary in the world of micro-budget cinema. It was a pleasure to discuss these issues with Erin and I would like to express my gratitude to her for agreeing to do this interview with me. Special thanks also to Paige Kay Davis and Seduction Cinema for coordinating the interview.

Iain Robert Smith: *To begin the interview I'd like to ask about the early years of your career with Factory 2000. You started acting in no-budget fetish films at a relatively young age working with William Hellfire on titles like* International Necktie Strangler *and* Peeping in a Girl's Dormitory *(both William Hellfire, 2000). Can you tell us a little about how you came to be working on these films?*

Erin Brown (Misty Mundae): I initially found myself working in the fetish genre of the indie-film world as a total fluke. I never had any expectations of becoming an underground film icon, or soft-core porn star (as I'm more commonly referred to) whatsoever. I grew up in a sleepy little bumblefuck town in North Jersey, where my local entourage and I felt as though there wasn't much to do with ourselves. Some friends of mine started a tiny little record label to promote some local bands. The mastermind behind this project, William Hellfire, got the bright idea to produce some no-budget, shot-on-video sexploitation films to help in financing and recording these musical endeavours. Really quickly the films developed a huge cult following, and thus the Factory films took over as the focus of our creative outlet. The rest is history. Before I knew it, I was starring in dozens of soft-core and horror-esque movies every year. It's just something I kind of fell into; and at the time, I was really just fucking off and having fun. I never imagined a decade later that I would be reflecting back on those films as something significant or pivotal for my life experience, let alone, a respectable career.

William Hellfire has talked about how Factory 2000 was modelled on the Andy Warhol Factory. Did you see yourself as part of a counter-cultural artistic collective? If not, how would you characterise the group making those films?

Counter-cultural, perhaps; artistic, mmm, not so much! All along I think that we had the intention of doing something controversial. But because the films were, more often than not, something that we farted out in an evening or two, they were often rather lacking in any artistic integrity. In reality, any douche bag with a camcorder can make a 'movie', so, in order to make our movies stand out as something different or worth acknowledging within the underground cinema movement, we felt as though we really kind of had to push the envelope in a lot of ways. And oddly enough, the sheer audacity of creating such raunchy and offensive exploitation, for reasons beyond my comprehension, becomes perceived as artistic. Art is so subjective anyway, and it's often such a fine line between what's construed as pornographic versus artistic; who's to say? I'm pretty certain that, for a group of kids with nothing better to do, we succeeded in shocking and offending people; and if the purpose of art is to evoke emotion, then I suppose it was mission accomplished…

Many of these early films were also deliberately provocative and controversial – from the notorious fetish films through to the Columbine satire Duck!: The Carbine High Massacre *(William Hellfire, 1999). Do you feel there is an extra freedom for political commentary in low-budget independent cinema?*

Oh, absolutely. Working on these totally independent films allows for almost total creative freedom via socio-political commentary and whatnot. In fact, it was literally years before anyone was even willing to distribute *Duck!*, for just such reasons. But if your motive is to create political satire, or to facilitate some political commentary regardless of how commercially viable it renders your film, then, well, isn't that sort of what it's all about? The fact that *Duck!* was way too offensive and socially distasteful for anyone to want to put it out for the masses is, in essence, what made it that much more provocative and compelling for public consumption. And as they say, any publicity is good publicity; so, all of the hullabaloo surrounding that project ultimately worked in its favour. Despite it being the antithesis of what any studio would deem an audience friendly, marketable film, that crappy little movie has permanently staked its place in underground cult cinema, and folks will probably be watching it and talking about it for years. So, ha!

Under the pseudonym Misty Mundae, you then became the figurehead for Seduction Cinema – starring in the films, serving as the public face of the company at conventions, and becoming contracted to the company in a way reminiscent of the classic Hollywood stars. How did you deal with the move from acting with a group of friends to becoming contracted as a star?

Well, the Seduction crew was always somewhat incestuous with the Factory label. That is how I initially got involved with Seduction Cinema; because we had actually all already been working together for years, anyway. So, the transition was not really that intense; I was working with compadres all along. And I really wouldn't have it any other way. Somewhere along the line I got somewhat jaded and money became my main focus in filmmaking, but for the most part, I endured in the industry because I was mostly working with close friends whom I instilled (perhaps too much) trust, and still just attempting to have fun.

Also, if this isn't too abstract a question, how did you distinguish between you as an actress and 'Misty Mundae' the character? Did you see 'Misty' as a character you were playing?

Misty Mundae is the indelible actress. Whether appearing in a film as Misty, or making a public appearance as the persona, it was always playing a part entirely separate from my true identity. My own reality is vastly different from the actress and her unhinged world; and so, for my own sanity, they have always remained mutually exclusive. I was always playing a character that was playing a character, twice removed. I'm a very private and extremely modest person, so anyone that knows me well knows that I am certainly a far cry from the alter ego that I maintained for so many years.

Many of the more successful Seduction releases were spoofs of Hollywood blockbusters and other forms of US popular culture. How would you prepare for these roles? Would you watch the films/TV shows beforehand?

Nah! I never did my homework. Often I'd have every intention of watching the films we were spoofing, to get ideas for my character and whatnot; but then I'd like, fall asleep or something halfway through *Spider-Man* [Sam Raimi, 2000]. I'd be lucky if I even read the script before showing up to set, let alone doing any sort of research for my character or anything along those lines.

You also had a chance to direct some films for Seduction Cinema such as Lustful Addiction *(2003) and* Confessions of a Natural Beauty *(2003). Do you think it affects things to have a fellow actress directing rather than one of the male directors?*

I was just sort of cutting my teeth by endeavouring to direct those movies, so I had my perpetually all-male crew to help me out throughout, anyway. So it probably wasn't so much a matter of a female director, versus the notion of a newbie director attempting to produce something coherent and hopefully somewhat captivating. But, from my memory and perception of those events, I doubt that gender played a role in the whole experience of making those films; but I could be wrong!

FIGURE 8.2 Pin-ups meet the primal: the poster for *Play-mate of the Apes*

Time for a more 'academic' question… Recently, some studies of erotic cinema have argued that these soft-core films are 'post-feminist' in that they use depoliticised elements of second-wave feminism, such as female agency, freedom and self-respect, to present their female central characters. Do you yourself think of these films as 'female friendly'?

It all depends on the context of the situation. I mean, it is called 'exploitation' for a reason, ya know? So, do I feel as though I was at times exploited during my career as a soft-core actress? Yes. Hell yes! Do I also feel as though many of the experiences and opportunities were entirely empowering? Also, hell yes! So, if you're going to get all academic on me, then I'll just say, 'Well hey, the chicks dig it, man!'

Much of the discussion of your popularity focuses on your perceived 'normality' – that you aren't the clichéd 'bleached blonde hair and silicone implants' type of starlet. Did you ever find it strange to find yourself being hailed as one of the great stars of erotic cinema?

Yes, I find it completely bizarre. In fact, just last evening my boyfriend and I were watching some cable soft-core, and I was wondering aloud how I ever became so popular in a genre of which I feel so very far removed from. I perceive myself to be the antithesis of every woman in the random porno movie that we happened upon whilst flipping through channels. And while most of the acting performances were utterly horrible yet still completely comical, especially in their pathetic attempts to be genuine, I felt that their sexual scenes were probably far more convincing than any performances I've ever turned out. So, even though I've been told that it's my 'unexpected' qualities, and the fact that I'm so drastically different than the typical soft-core gal, which makes me stand out and thus, lends some popularity or credibility, or whatever… Yeah, it's still fuckin' weird to me!

How did you cope with all the attention this brought you?

I cope with all of the attention relatively well because, in the huge scope of everything, I'm still fairly anonymous. I still get recognised fairly often, but it's infrequent enough that I don't make a total spectacle of myself every time that I leave my house. And it also depends on the context of the situation. If I'm out at a bar and someone recognises me and makes some big obnoxious scene, I'll usually be cordial and take some stupid picture with them on their camera phone and laugh it off. But when I'm out to lunch with my mother and our waiter won't shut up about how awesome *Lord of the G-Strings* [Terry West, 2003] is … that's a little annoying, bordering on humiliating. It is what it is; and if you catch me in a good mood, I'm usually pretty fuckin' cool with it!

You have often said in interviews that you are quite a fan of cult cinema, namechecking everything from Alejandro Jodorowsky through to Damon Packard. I wondered if you had an interest in other forms of cult 'erotic' cinema?

Nope. Erotica is not really my cup of tea. Something along the lines of *Vampyros Lesbos* [Jess Franco, 1971] is probably as kinky as I get. But, hey, if you could turn me on to some

124

good stuff, I am certainly open to the idea.

From interviewing Michael Raso, it seems that the production of 'erotica' wasn't his initial intention for the company but rather something that the market dictated. Did you see these films as a similar means to an end – by allowing you to move later into horror/cult cinema?

Definitely. Like I said earlier, I never had any intention of becoming any sort of erotica/soft-core starlet; it's just something I fell into. But once I recognised that I was, to a certain extent, taken seriously as an actress, and able to acquire roles that were not contingent upon me getting naked and grinding on those bleach-blonde silicone-implant gals we spoke of earlier, naturally I seized that opportunity to work in my preferred genre of horror/thriller cinema. It was only partially pre-meditated, considering that I was never entirely confident that I would ever be able to break out of the erotic film genre, after tarnishing the 'Mundae' name with all sorts of crazy titles and fetish films. However, the industry has been surprisingly forgiving, and all of those crazy fetish films that might have otherwise destroyed any potential mainstream career, have actually helped catapult me into landing a bunch of really cool roles that I would have never even been considered for, had it not been for my 'B-movie Queen' status.

In the last few years, you've dropped the name 'Misty Mundae' and acted in various other forms of cinema – from Lucky McKee's Masters of Horror *episode 'Sick Girl' through to the comedy* All Along. *Was this a conscious attempt to move away from working in 'erotic' cinema?*

Yes. I made the conscious decision to get out of the 'sex' industry and attempt to cut my teeth in other genres for a shit-ton of reasons. Mostly, the whole soft-core thing was wearing me out. It really takes a toll on your personal relationships; like, with my boyfriend, and my family, and blah blah blah! But more so, I wanted to prove to myself and to others that there was more to my abilities than just humping and moaning, ya know! I don't really feel like *Spiderbabe* [Johnny Crash, 2003] is the most flattering showcase for all my talents and attributes. And it was all beginning to feel pretty static; like every soft-core spoof was an instant replay of the film I had just previously shot. So, I decided that a challenge and some progression was long past-due.

Finally, could you tell us how the filmmaking process compares working on these different types of film?

It's surprisingly not that different. All of the soft-core films are done so professionally, it's pretty similar to working on other types of independent film. Naturally, some of the more mainstream stuff, like *Masters of Horror*, is inevitably way bigger budget and so, flying first class and staying in some fancy-shmancy hotel is a bit different than what I'm accustomed to. But, I could totally get used to that!

As could we all… Thank you very much for your time.

CHAPTER 9
A CLOCKWORK ORGY: A USER'S GUIDE

I. Q. Hunter

INTRODUCTION: WHY BOTHER TO READ A PORN FILM?

Since the 1980s academic work on pornographic film has moved on from regarding it primarily as a social problem, conduit for noxious ideologies and source of intolerable boredom. Open-minded critics such as Linda Williams, Feona Attwood and Clarissa Smith have sidelined essentialist definitions of porn and its 'effects' in order to tackle 'ordinary' film studies issues such as genre, form and authorship.[1] Yet analysing a porn film for its own sake as a meaningful aesthetic object remains fairly unusual, except in the case of art house 'erotica' like *Romance* (Catherine Breillat, 1999) and *9 Songs* (Michael Winterbottom, 2005). Given the repetition and monomaniac banality of most porn films, singling one out for thematic interpretation is likely to seem both counter-intuitive and a pretentious waste of time. Nevertheless, that is the intention of this essay, which offers an interpretation of *A Clockwork Orgy* (Nic Cramer, 1995), a 'hard-core version' of Stanley Kubrick's classic science fiction fable, *A Clockwork Orange* (1971), and something of a personal cult film.[2]

I shall approach *A Clockwork Orgy* from three directions: first, as a characteristic example of the hard-core version, one of the most significant sub-genres in contemporary porn production; second, as an adaptation and parody of *A Clockwork Orange*; and, third, generalising from my own experience, as an incitement to erotic reverie and action. My purpose is to argue that hard-core versions, in spite of their low cultural status, represent a distinctive mode of adaptation. Rather than mere parasites upon their originals, they, like exploitation films generally, are often subversive commentaries on the mainstream's erotic and ideological subtexts.

HARD-CORE ADAPTATION

Adult film versions of fairy tales, classic literature and well-known movies were first popular in the 1970s, when porn was mostly shown in cinemas. While some porn films drew on the conventions of other genres in a spirit of hybridisation – for example science fiction sex films such as *Sex World* (Anthony Spinelli, 1978) and *The Satisfiers of Alpha Blue* (Gerard Damiano, 1981) – others ripped-off one specific film or identifiable group of films. *Alice in Wonderland* (Bud Townsend, 1976) was 'an X-rated musical comedy' version of the classic children's book; *The Opening of Misty Beethoven* (Radley Metzger, 1976) was a hard-core take-off of *My Fair Lady* (George Cukor, 1964), while *The Bite* (Jerry Denby, 1975) parodied *The Sting* (George Roy Hill, 1973) and *Talk Dirty to Me* (Anthony Spinelli, 1980), *Of Mice and Men* (Lewis Milestone, 1939). The vampire film has probably inspired the most rip-offs, from *Dracula Sucks* (Phillip Marshak, 1979) to *Intercourse with the Vampire* (Paul Norman, 1994), but there exists too a significant body of what Richard Burt has dubbed 'Shakes-porn'.[3]

Since the 1980s, hard-core versions of mainstream films have flourished on video, with titles including *Ally McFeal* (David Brett, Harold Merkin, 2000), *Charlie's Anals* (n.d., 2001), and *The Ozporns* (Anthony R. Lovett, 2002). Unlike their 1970s forerunners, they rarely do more than pun on the titles and lift the basic situations of the original films. A few attempt a measure of fidelity and shoehorn the obligatory bouts of sex into recognisable imitations of their sources' plots, imagery and themes. The result can be a genuine cross-generic adaptation, in which the original film's erotic subtexts are seized upon and satirised. *Edward Penishands* (Paul Norman, 1991), for instance, a take-off of Tim Burton's *Edward Scissorhands* (1991), substitutes the hero's scissorshands with enormous prosthetic penises, and so wittily literalises the Freudian subtext of the original. With most hard-core versions, however, detailed attention to the precursor text is less important than introducing explicit sex where it is either alluded to or disavowed altogether. *Cathula* (Phil Barry, 2002), for example, one of the many sex vampire films, represents vampires as sexual predators living it up in polymorphously perverse orgies – not a bad summary, in fact, of the hidden erotic dynamic of the vampire genre itself.

In *A Clockwork Orgy* considerable effort is made to imitate Kubrick's film, unearth its sexual subtexts, and echo its themes of free will and political control. It is set in a dystopian anti-sex future (a common science fiction scenario, from Orwell's *Nineteen Eighty-Four* (1949) to the porn film *Café Flesh* (Rinse Dream, 1982)), in which Alexandra (Kaitlyn Ashley) and

FIGURE 9.1 From Alex to Alexandra:
the opening scene from *A Clockwork Orgy*

her female droogs, Dum (Rebecca Lord), Georgina (Isis Nile) and Patty (Olivia), roam the streets and force themselves on men. Alexandra is arrested, and put through a course of behaviourist retraining that involves being forced to watch sex films. Key scenes from *A Clockwork Orange* are restaged on the cheap and more or less in the same narrative order, though there are many significant omissions; for example, the murder of the Cat Lady is dropped, there is no equivalent to the fight between Alex's gang and Billy Boy's, and the droogs' assault on F. Alexander (Jon Dough) involves sex only with him and not the rape of his wife. The droogs speak a version of Nadsat, the Russianised teen-lingo of the original film, to which are added some appropriate neologisms ('gashy-washy' for vagina, for instance).

A Clockwork Orgy also reproduces some memorable camera moves and compositions. The film opens with Alexandra in close-up before pulling back, precisely as in *A Clockwork Orange*, to a wide shot of all the droogs; Alexandra's voiceover is a reworked version of Alex's first monologue, the final word of which, 'ultraviolence', has been replaced with 'ultrasex'. In the

FIGURE 9.2 From aggression to arousal: porn reframes the tramp's 'assault' in *A Clockwork Orgy*

next scene the droogs terrorise a tramp (Dick Nasty); but whereas in *A Clockwork Orange* he is beaten up, here he is subjected to extended and pleasurable sex. Throughout the film 'ultrasex' takes the place of 'ultraviolence' and the droogs' attentions are, on the whole, more to be welcomed than feared.

A key change, of course, is that in *A Clockwork Orgy* the male droogs of the original are turned into women. This gender switch is common in hard-core versions (for example, in *Whore of the Rings II* (Jim Powers, 2003), the randy hobbit stand-ins are female) because making the protagonists sexually voracious women legitimises the central fantasy of porn – that the sexes' needs and desires are harmonious and interchangeable. In *A Clockwork Orgy* it also helps defuse one of the more troubling givens of the film – the fact that the female droogs essentially rape men throughout. While men raping women is pretty much taboo in mainstream porn, generic convention insists that men cannot be forced unwillingly into sex; Alexandra's droogs are therefore not so much rapists as liberators of their victims' inner porn star. Changing the gender of the droogs corrects, too, the sexual politics of *A Clockwork Orange*, in which women are mostly big-breasted sexual playthings and marginal to the film's key themes of male violence and homoerotic power-play. In *A Clockwork Orgy* the women are still big-breasted, but at least they drive what little narrative there is. The homoeroticism of *A Clockwork Orange*, which is often overlooked, is also highlighted by Alex's becoming Alexandra.[4] In the original Alex is persistently fawned on, pawed over and molested by other men, as when Deltoid, his parole officer, slaps his hand on the 'luscious young malchick's' crotch. In the equivalent scene in *A Clockwork Orgy*, Alexandra and her (now female) parole officer engage in a full-on sex session; this lesbian sequence, while completely standard in straight porn, makes explicit the homoerotic potential of the original scene.

The relation between the latter film and its source differs sharply from that between *Whore of the Rings II* and *The Lord of the Rings: The Two Towers* (Peter Jackson, 2002), to which clings a thrill of tasteless violation.[5] Tolkien's world so furiously excludes sexual reference that 'pornogrifying' it is less erotic sabotage than a salutary corrective and breath of fresh air. *A Clockwork Orange*, on the other hand, is already imaginatively and generically halfway towards porn; Pauline Kael, for example, called it a porno violent sci-fi comedy, as if made by a strict German professor.[6] Gratuitous erotic material and images of the commodification of sex are scattered throughout *A Clockwork Orange*, confounding the distinction between high art, trash and porn. Teenage girls suck phallic ice-lollies before engaging in high-speed sex with Alex (the result is a mini porn loop in itself); the camera lingers with icy voyeurism as the Cat Woman spreads her legs during yoga; there is an aimless shot of a topless nurse when Alex is in hospital; and, in the film's most outrageous comment on the creative overlap between porn and great art, Alex commandeers Beethoven and the Bible as masturbation fodder. As Janet Staiger has pointed out, *A Clockwork Orange* is in many ways a big-budget exploitation film.[7] A troubling combination of high style and low content, it foregrounds the exploitative elements and unsettles the boundaries between art as pure form (aesthetically redeeming violent content) and art as incitement (Alex jerking off to 'Ode to Joy').[8]

Linda Ruth Williams noted that Kubrick 'long played with genre, emulating and exemplifying the pinnacles of trash genres through meticulously rendered works of cinema art'.[9] One approach to *A Clockwork Orgy* is therefore to read it – as a heuristic thought experiment – as the shadowy Other of Kubrick's film, at once an adaptation of its pornographic subtexts and a commentary on its themes and aesthetic strategies. Analogies exist, for example, between the formal and emotional distancing in both films of sex and violence. In *A Clockwork Orgy* the tension, inherent in all porn, between documentary and fiction, the recording of pro-filmic real sex and its non-spontaneous staging for the camera, echoes the masque-like performance of violence in *A Clockwork Orange*. Robert Kolker's comment on this aspect of *A Clockwork Orange* applies equally well to *A Clockwork Orgy*: 'the bodies in the film are mechanical, by definition unreal, because this is a film, not the world, and because everyone in it acts as if driven by some monomaniacal or inexplicable external force'.[10] This is underscored because both films are futuristic science fiction exempt from the usual conventions of film realism. In the case of *A Clockwork Orgy*, the science fiction setting and imagery are exceptionally appropriate. Pornography is itself a species of utopian science fiction, in whose imaginary 'pornotopia' the sexes converge, feminism did not take place, and women want what men want to do to them.[11]

Alex's therapy essentially consists of watching porn films that combine violence, sex and Nazi propaganda. The films are designed first to excite and then repel him, so that the films are identified with *A Clockwork Orange* itself. That film is meant alternately to arouse and disgust us so that we, like Alex, undergo subliminal conditioning. For example, just as the films Alex sees contaminate innocent material by associating it with violence (the treatment accidentally makes him allergic to Beethoven's Ninth Symphony), so *A Clockwork Orange*, quite deliberately, contaminates 'Singin' in the Rain' by using it to accompany rape and sadism. *A Clockwork Orgy* is similarly reflexive about itself as a porn film.

FIGURE 9.3 Erotic punishments: 'treating' the heroine of *A Clockwork Orgy*

When Alexandra is imprisoned, her treatment involves watching sex videos of the Warden (Jonathan Morgan) and a female guard intended to turn her off sex and transform a 'nasty little tramp, filthy little whore' into, as the Warden puts it, a 'lady you could meet in church on a Sunday morn'.

The reasons, again as in the original film, are political: 'our party has promised to restore decency and morality to make the streets safer for ordinary celibate citizens'; 'from today sex and promiscuity has become a thing of the past'. But whereas in *A Clockwork Orange* Alex is reconditioned by a combination of drugs and aversion therapy, there is no mention of drugs in *A Clockwork Orgy*, and Alexandra, whose eyes are not pinned open, seems merely incapable of looking away from the porn. As she gags and writhes in disgust in front of 'lovely lovely lovely flesh', it appears that what is conditioning her against sex is pornography itself. 'You feel ill,' the Warden tells her, borrowing lines from the original film, 'because you are getting better. Sex and violence are horrible things. When we are healthy, we respond to sex and promiscuity with fear, anxiety, shallowness, condemnation and even nausea.' Bizarrely, rather as in David Cronenberg's *Videodrome* (1983), *A Clockwork Orgy* seems to be warning us against watching films like itself. Porn films – even though Alexandra says she has happily watched them before – eliminate her desire and make repulsive even the thought of sex. Yet one assumes this is not how viewers are expected to respond to the explicit sex in the film.

But the film is not too bothered with this kind of narrative consistency. Take, for example, the scene towards the end of the film in which Alexandra, who is now supposedly incapable of erotic feelings, is raped by tramps. She initially chooses to be entirely passive in order not to feel nauseous ('Better to be nailed by winos than feel that horrible sickness'), but she is soon crying 'Fuck me harder!' and 'It feels good!' even though, at this point in the story, she ought to be made ill by sex rather than clamour for more of it. The generic requirements of porn override those of coherent storytelling. Women must always respond to fucking and even compulsory sex is unambiguously good.

One last comparison between the two films: both are 'about' liberation. The Ludovico

Treatment robs Alex of his free will and the moral of the film is that it is better for him freely to choose evil than to have no choice at all. It is far from clear, however, whether Alex can ever truly be free; his initial thuggery was a product of his social environment, while at the end of the film, once surgery has restored his old violent self, he has become the puppet of a fascist government. There is a similar cluster of ironies in *A Clockwork Orgy*. Alexandra and her droogs represent sex as 'natural'. Unlike Alex, whose adventures in rape and murder are obviously criminal, they are role models of sexual liberation, heroic propagandists of the erotic deed. Yet they seem clockwork mechanisms from the start: shaved, buffed and silicon-enhanced porn robots driven by insatiable sexual compulsion. At the end of the film Alexandra is returned to her 'natural' state of addictive hyper-sexuality, and the government promises to provide her with lovers and other necessities. The final scene is the orgy of the film's title in which Alexandra, her droogs and the Warden himself get it on in the junkyard. At the end Alexandra turns to the audience and says, 'I was treated [Alex in the original says, 'cured'] all right.' This carries the same ironic implication as in *A Clockwork Orange* – that her excesses (sexual rather than violent) can be co-opted and exploited by the government.

The film's celebration of (enforced) sexual promiscuity comes across as mildly progressive in the era of AIDS. All porn is progressive in the narrow sense that it stages the virtues of non-monogamous sex, but in the 1990s, a time when the celibacy movement and religious attacks against porn were gaining ground, *A Clockwork Orgy* was making a pro-1960s and anti-family values point. (Seeing Bill Clinton on the cover of *Spy* magazine, Alexandra says she'll teach him to inhale – she is willing to uphold the counterculture values in which he wouldn't fully indulge.) As the F. Alexander character says to his comrades on the phone, 'There are great traditions of sexual freedom to be defended,' and oversexed Alexandra – like the film itself – is a weapon against a sexually oppressive government. Seen in this light, *A Clockwork Orgy* is porn with a mission: a historically located intervention in sexual politics and a self-serving but passionately felt argument for permissiveness and anonymous sex.

PORN NARRATIVE

The formal structure of a porn film is easy enough to analyse, because porn's stark, algebraic quality is such that one film appears to exhaust the formal possibilities of the whole genre – 'If you've seen one, you've seen them all.' Expressive content tends to boil down to allegorical recombinations of gender archetypes. As Joseph W. Slade remarks, 'porn draws on vast reservoirs of myth, legend, belief, customs, and mores that work both for and against establishing norms of behavior. Obscene folklore … serves as the fountainhead of pornography, a collective cultural id.'[12] As to deeper intentional significance, thematic interpretation is less obviously relevant than psychoanalytic and ideological diagnosis (as, for example, by Tanya Krzywinska in an article on Cicciolina).[13] Symptom rather than expression, a porn film may indeed add up to a semiotically rich index of cultural representations, but no more so, perhaps, and to no more aesthetically compelling effect, than any other product of low popular culture. This is not to say that films like *A Clockwork Orgy* do not lend themselves to interpretation in the standard meaning-truffling sense; all films do in proportion to the energy, competence and cultural capital of the interpreter. But it is, first and last, a *porn film* and, while it is not irrelevant to consider it as an adaptation, its relation to *A Clockwork Orange* is opportunistic rather than decisive. Parodying this simply made it distinctive (and 'classy') in a market otherwise flooded with interchangeable product, as well as potentially lending it some cult appeal.

A Clockwork Orgy certainly has elements of what Gerard Genette called 'metatextuality', in that intertextual relations with its source involve a certain reworking and criticism of it.[14] But it is likely that many viewers had neither seen *A Clockwork Orange* nor, if they had, would care very much about whether *A Clockwork Orgy* was faithful to its style and themes. Parodies usually rely on audiences picking up references, but this one is post-hermeneutic; everything except the sex is disposable. I suspect many viewers' primary investment would be in whether *A Clockwork Orgy* fulfilled the generic expectations of contemporary porn; they might even resent the homage to Kubrick using up time available for uninterrupted sexual display – in porn films, story usually gets fast-forwarded.

But it is important to note that *A Clockwork Orgy*, like *Edward Penishands* and *Cathula* and virtually all contemporary hard-core versions, ends up as a series of fairly anonymous sexual numbers. Only in soft-core films, such as those produced by Seduction Cinema, is there much interest in detailed parody.[15] Hard-core versions invariably jettison narrative after a while, along with plot, humour and parody, and concentrate on uninterrupted depictions of sex. Although porn experimented with full-length, complexly narrated features during hard-core's Golden Age in the 1970s, this trend was arrested by the introduction of domestic video. Straight hard-core today is dominated by 'gonzo' (first-person documentary-style sex scenes, pioneered by John Stagliano in *The Adventures of Buttman* (1989)) and other largely pre-classical, non-narrative stagings of raw sexual performance, all of which tenaciously adhere to what Linda Williams called hard-core's 'principle of maximum visibility'.[16] Within specific categories (teen, oral, anal, mature, ebony, etc.), they tend to advertise exotic activities and fetishes that 'push the envelope' towards freakish spectacle, such as DVDA (double vaginal, double anal), bukkake (multiple ejaculations on one actress), spitting and gagging, cream pies (showing the results of internal ejaculation), and A2M (ass to mouth: sucking a penis after its withdrawal from an anus, which must be depicted in one continuous shot). The disintegration of narrative is even more pronounced on websites such as Tube8, RedTube, YouPorn and Pornotube which offer free access to amateur and pirated porn video bites, many of them reminiscent of the gross out 'body comedy' stunts of the *Jackass* TV series and movies (2000–2007).

Moreover, there are aspects of porn which resist integration into the taxonomy of film genres, and defeat conventional textual explication. Appraising porn by the standards of mainstream cinema is highly problematic, not so much because of porn's transgressive content, as because its prioritising of structure and duration over narrative makes it closer to avant-garde films (Warhol is the obvious comparison, for he was influenced by and contributed to porn filmmaking; *Vinyl*, his 1965 adaptation of the novel of *A Clockwork Orange*, draws significantly on the imagery of gay S&M porn). Porn can also usefully be compared with both pre-classical cinema and the alleged 'regression' to plotless blank spectacle in contemporary post-classical film. Furthermore, porn has elements of CCTV footage, amateur film, reality TV, found footage, and wildlife and medical documentaries, in which narrative possibilities co-exist with fugitive glimpses of 'unmediated' actuality. Associating porn with narrative film may simply be a category mistake, rather like the assumption that video games aspire to the cinematic, when they are an entirely different, visceral and experiential form of textuality. Porn, like video games, might in fact be more usefully aligned with conceptual and performance art, as predicted by the work of Annie Sprinkle and Jeff Koons.

THE PHENOMENOLOGY OF MASTURBATION

This brings me to my final point, which concerns the way that viewers make sense of a film such as *A Clockwork Orgy*. What is striking about pornography is that it so comprehensively exceeds the usual limits of what is represented that *interpretation* seems an inadequate trope for readerly response (as opposed to shock, outrage, arousal, laughter…). We do not habitually think of porn viewers as interpreting porn; that activity is associated with opponents of porn, who interpret it primarily to gauge the depth of its corruption. Porn viewers, on the other hand, are said to *use* it – a loaded word (we do not speak of 'science fiction' users or '*Lord of the Rings*' users) which suggests mindless compulsion rather than self-aware erotic arousal and engagement. At this point, however, we must move beyond issues of representation and its limits and consider porn-viewing as lived experience.

To consider porn without mentioning masturbation is rather like discussing comedy and not worrying about humour. Yet the real-life context of porn consumption is rarely discussed. There are many objections to pornography – concern for the sleaze and exploitation endured by the participants, the overlap between porn and prostitution, the desacralisation of sex, the misogyny of far too much of it – but the disquiet it arouses has much to do with residual ambivalence about masturbation, and the fear that masturbation acts as a kind of mental fixative, reinforcing associations between pleasure and sexual domination.[17] Anxieties cluster around porn viewers in ways they rarely do around viewers of westerns and romances; the nearest analogy is perhaps to the similarly 'sad' and 'addicted' users of violent horror films and video games. The fear is sharpest when the masturbating 'porn zombies' (the term used in *8MM* (Joel Schumacher, 1999)) are working class.[18]

Yet a phenomenology of masturbation is precisely what is missing from porn studies, and providing that will require surreally detailed and reflexive accounts of the erotic pleasures of active viewing. For example, discussion of porn often turns on its aesthetic poverty and in particular on its being *boring*. Peter Bradshaw has called this the 'acceptable unshockable-sophisticate alternative to condemnation on moral grounds'.[19] Nevertheless porn is self-evidently *not* boring to its millions of happy consumers; this makes sense only when porn's supposedly 'boring' descriptive moments are related to the experience of viewers primarily engaged *not* in comprehending the narrative of a film but rather in the co-ordinated physical and cognitive task of masturbating to it. The otherwise intolerable sameness of porn is wholly transformed by the act of masturbation; the initial mood of boredom (to take a Heideggerian view on it) proceeds via curiosity and fascination to one of relaxed but focused arousal. Once again the apt comparison is with avant-garde films like Andy Warhol's, which seem empty and interminable until one invests sufficient mental and physical effort to cope with and acclimatise to their unforgiving stasis and banality. As soon as this frame of mind is achieved, boredom is soon overcome by masturbation's hypnotic rhythms; and the viewer's aroused body is, in Linda Williams' words, 'caught up in an almost involuntary mimicry of the emotion or sensation of the body on the screen' – a sort of corporeal karaoke.[20] Absorbed in the zone of porn description, the stroking viewer watches (or rather witnesses) the film with rapt Zen-like attention, as s/he endeavours to align sexual pleasure with on-screen action. This intense experiential involvement is analogous to the autotelic creative state which the psychologist Mihaly Csikszentmihalyi calls 'flow', in which 'there is little distinction between self and environment, between stimulus and response, or between past, present and future'.[21] (Admittedly, this is an imperfect, albeit suggestive, analogy. Unlike the absorbing activities that produce 'flow', masturbation is often an easy pleasure requiring minimal effort and skill and no real challenges to overcome.[22]) Instead of interpreting porn along the same lines as other film genres, we can reconceptualise it as the textual focus of a meditative optimal experience.[23]

It is true that porn is not always watched in so focused a manner, and that it is also watched in company; played as TV wallpaper while one is doing something else; collected, shelved and catalogued; switched off in horror and disgust. Nor is porn always used for masturbation. Understanding a film like *A Clockwork Orgy* requires more than complacently 'seeing through' and pathologising both the film and its unusually active viewers; but, equally, it requires much more than formal analysis and textual interpretation. We must also reflect on the *experiences* of watching it as a porn film.[24] This means bracketing off consideration of *A Clockwork Orgy* as parody and adaptation and exploring instead how viewers like me integrate the film into their erotic lives.

CHAPTER 10
KING OF THE PORN SPOOFS:
AN INTERVIEW WITH MICHAEL L. RASO

Interview by Iain Robert Smith

With the rise of new media technologies and the increasing availability of DV & HD cameras, there has been a concomitant rise in micro-budget feature filmmakers that find themselves competing for attention in an already saturated marketplace. With hundreds of shot-on-digital feature films being released each year, not to mention the many thousands destined never to see the light of day, it is becoming increasingly difficult to distinguish one product from another. One producer, however, has come up with a successful strategy to draw attention to his micro-budget feature films and get them distributed around the world: (i) start an 'erotica' themed label to subsidise the rest of the production slate, then, (ii) produce 'soft-core spoofs' of all the latest Hollywood blockbusters.

Using this strategy, the founder and head of POP Cinema (formerly ei Independent Cinema), Michael L. Raso has executive produced over a hundred feature films including *The Erotic Witch Project* (John Bacchus, 1999), *Gladiator Eroticvs* (John Bacchus, 2001), *Play-mate of the Apes* (John Bacchus, 2002), *Lord of the G-Strings* (Terry West, 2003), *Spiderbabe* (Johnny

FIGURE 10.1 Parodying blockbuster appeal: the poster art for *Gladiator Eroticvs*

Crash, 2003) and *Kinky Kong* (John Bacchus, 2006).

In the following interview, Michael L. Raso takes us through the unassuming beginnings of his company in a converted fax closet in Bloomfield, NJ, his strategy to create a 'Seduction Cinema' brand identity, his struggles to pursue his 'first love' of horror cinema, as well as discussing the production context and gender politics of his slate of 'erotic' features.

Iain Robert Smith: *You began your career in the media making skit comedy as part of the* Meadowlands Showcase. *What were your main motivations in setting up ei Independent Cinema and moving into the soft-core market with your label Seduction?*

Michael L. Raso: I spent six years producing Commercial TV spots for cable television. It was during those years that I produced *Meadowlands Showcase* (for the Cable Television Network) with John Fedele and a few other college filmmaking friends. By late 1994 I felt that I had done all that I could do with both my current job and the show. I was anxious to get back to filmmaking. I discovered that my friend J. R. Bookwalter was publishing a magazine called *Alternative Cinema* in Akron, Ohio. The magazine featured DIY filmmakers from all over the country. I quit my job, put *Meadowlands Showcase* on the shelf and soon started ei Independent Cinema. I immediately began producing, acquiring and distributing indie horror features to independent video stores. No easy task. Factory 2000 filmmaker William Hellfire (real name Billy Apriceno) was my first employee. He handled phone sales out of a converted broom closet in my first office!

I started the erotic film label Seduction Cinema in 1997 when ei released *Caress of the Vampire* (Frank Terranova), to much unexpected success on VHS. There was a demand and soon a follow-up film went into production. Seduction Cinema has been producing up to eight productions per year ever since. So, demand dictated the growth of Seduction Cinema. My fellow colleagues and I were concentrating on horror and comedy. We never intended to shoot erotica. The market demanded erotica, so we produced it. As you can see by the Seduction Cinema catalogue, most of it is horror-themed erotica, comedy-themed erotica or a combination of the two.

The Seduction titles have consistently gained international distribution, a rare feat for a low-budget film company. To what do you attribute the labels' continued success?

I decided early on that I wanted to focus my energies on 'branding' movies produced by my studio. Seduction Cinema literally exploded onto the scene in 1999 with the release of our first two erotic parodies, *Titanic 2000* (John Paul Fedele) and *Erotic Witch Project*. The films were released on VHS, DVD, US cable television and international markets. I made Seduction Cinema a top priority in the early years with the goal of establishing a 'brand' name. When you think of cola, you think of Coca-Cola. If a fan hears about a soft-core erotic film, I wanted them to think... Seduction Cinema. I also believe that the 'ensemble' studio system helped our early success. Think of the Seduction Cinema cast and crew as a musical group. The same cast and crew worked on over fifty films together between 1997 and 2004 and developed quite a

FIGURE 10.2 Tolkien meets titillation: the poster art for *Lord of the G-Strings* (2003)

fan following. Movies were available in every major video chain in the US and fans could meet the cast and crew at fan conventions all over the country.

In many ways, the spoof becomes a perfect marketing tool – a way to distinguish your product in a soft-core marketplace which doesn't allow for huge marketing campaigns. How significant a role do you feel the 'spoof' elements play in getting your films' distribution?

I feel that our 'spoof' titles helped Seduction Cinema break into both the television and international markets. The fans have always supported the films on VHS and DVD, but TV and international markets eluded us because of their mainstream sensibilities. TV and international corporate buyers and fans want something that they are familiar with. The market is not as kind to small independents, so we started to develop erotic spoofs of mainstream blockbusters. How funny when you see a title like *Lord of the G-Strings*! So popular were our spoofs, that *Lord of the G-Strings* was mentioned on *The Tonight Show with Jay Leno*! With the success of the Seduction parodies, we became known in the industry as 'the spoof guys'.

One thing that marks out Seduction Cinema from its competitors are the collectible DVDs which are packed with extras. What made you decide to start offering directors' commentaries, behind the scenes footage, outtakes etc?

I grew up as a fan of cinema. I know what it is like to be a fan, so I try to make every single release very special. Extras on a DVD are very important. It allows our fans to take a peek behind the curtain and see the real people making the movie. Our fans are the most important thing and we try not to forget that.

What was the intention behind offering both R-rated and Unrated releases of some titles?

We started shooting R-rated versions of our erotic films in 2003. We felt that we could reach a much broader audience if we trimmed down the sexual content and expanded the story and character development. It worked as demonstrated when Blockbuster stocked their shelves with *SSI: Sex Squad Investigation* (Thomas J. Moose, 2006). If you told me a few years ago that a Seduction Cinema film would be available for hire in the USA's top rental chain, I would have laughed myself off of my chair! Really, who would have thought!

Over time the 'soft-core spoofs' have become much more elaborate with larger budgets and a greater emphasis on dialogue and narrative (especially in Lord of the G-Strings *and* Spiderbabe). *Did you ever worry that the story would 'get in the way' of the porn?*

No way. Story can only help develop the characters and therefore, make the film sexier. This is my opinion as I think that you would get very different answers depending on which of our directors you spoke to.

In many ways, star Misty Mundae came to be seen as the figurehead of Seduction Cinema. Why do you feel she was so popular in these titles?

Pop Cinema owns the character Misty Mundae, which is why she has become the figurehead. Erin Brown, who plays the Misty character, is the perfect 'anti-sex symbol'. She doesn't look like a typical California sex star. She is unique and has a very special screen presence. The camera loves Misty Mundae.

The female characters often take the dominant roles in your spoofs. Was this a conscious attempt to appeal to female viewers?

Not really. Early on, the Seduction films were all-girl films. We found that most of the women we hired preferred to work with other women. So, from the get-go we focused on female characters. The male characters, who did not participate in the on-screen sex, were strictly on screen for the gags.

More recently POP Cinema have moved into the cult/horror market with titles such as Shock-O-Rama *[Brett Piper, 2005] and* Skin Crawl *[Justin Wingenfeld, 2007]. How have these titles performed in comparison with the Seduction titles? What changes did they necessitate in terms of promotion/distribution?*

I originally started my company to produce independent horror films. Seduction Cinema was an unintentional detour. The films sold well and justified 'green-lighting' more. Once Seduction became branded, I was able to allow others to handle the 'hands on' while I concentrated on my first love, horror film production and launching a horror film label. I launched Shock-O-Rama Cinema in 2004 with our newly produced *Screaming Dead, Skin Crawl, Bite Me* (Brett Piper, 2004) and other films. Unfortunately, the titles did not perform as compared to Seduction Cinema titles. Our biggest and most expensive horror film, Brett Piper's *Shock-O-Rama*, has been critically acclaimed but was commercially a flop. Our newest Seduction Cinema films are *Kinky Kong* and *SSI: Sex Squad Investigation*. Their combined budgets are not even close to what we spent on our film *Shock-O-Rama*, yet they are achieving much more commercial success. The world is glutted with horror films. It is a very, very difficult market. Discouraging, but we're pressing on with our Shock-O-Rama Studio titles.

POP Cinema have often been compared with other low-budget film companies such as Troma and Full Moon. Do you see similarities/differences with these companies?

I know very little about Troma and almost nothing about Full Moon. I certainly can see the comparison to Troma because of all the comedy in our films. Most of my inspiration came from UHF TV's *The Uncle Floyd Show*, Second City Television, SNL and classic Universal horror films. I have seen clips or scenes but have never seen an entire Troma or Full Moon movie.

Independent studios often work in a symbiotic relationship with Hollywood – offering what the major studios refuse to deal with. Do you see yourself as outside the Hollywood system? If so, what advantages does this offer?

We are so far outside of the Hollywood system that we're on another planet! Hollywood doesn't even consider our movies 'actual' feature films! We work in a parallel universe. Hollywood may be an influence but never do the two worlds collide, except of course on the DVD shelf in stores. Producer Sam Sherman was thrilled when he saw our release of his *Blazing Stewardesses* {Al Adamson, 1975] next to Mel Brooks' *Blazing Saddles* [1974] in a Best Buy store!

CHAPTER 11

A STAR IS PORN: CORPULENCE, COMEDY AND THE HOMOSOCIAL CULT OF ADULT FILM STAR RON JEREMY

Emily Shelton

In a 1995 episode of MTV's *Beavis and Butthead* (Mike Judge) the flatulent, nose-picking adolescent duo take their usual spot on the couch and watch a music video by an alternative rock band called The Meices, providing their usual derisive commentary. The video stars an overweight, forty-something man with a disobedient tangle of curly brown hair and scraggly moustache smearing food all over himself in a convenience store. Beavis and Butthead snigger and guffaw at the man's unsightly body, his sagging paunch, his drooping jowls. Then Beavis remarks, 'Hey, that's the guy in the naked movie at your uncle's house!' And Butthead replies, 'You were watching the guy?'

'The guy' in the movie is Ron Jeremy, and he is a very famous man: a thirty-year veteran of the 'adult' film industry and arguably its most recognisable male icon. He has either directed or starred in over a thousand pornographic features, and made a series of tongue-in-cheek cameo appearances in a number of mainstream studio films (*52 Pick-Up* (John Frankenheimer, 1986), *Killing Zoe* (Roger Avary, 1994)) and television shows (*Nash Bridges*; *Just Shoot Me*). Jeremy also served as 'consultant' for *Boogie Nights* (Paul Thomas Anderson, 1998), the documentary *Porn Star: The Legend of Ron Jeremy* (Scott J. Gill, 2001), and is the recipient of numerous Internet fansites that register every allusion and cultural reference to the porn star that its custodian finds.

During an interview with Susan Faludi for a *New Yorker* article on male porn actors, Jeremy shows Faludi a videotape of the *Beavis and Butthead* segment where the pair ridicule his flabby body and, while consuming a plate of lox and bagels, enthuses, 'Isn't this great? I don't care what people say about me as long as they spell my name right.'[1] While other male performers in the adult film industry certainly achieve fame, theirs is a celebrity entirely confined within the limits of that industry's own tireless productivity, churning out one performer after another. The young actors get older or less attractive or less reliably erect, and there are always more fresh young men waiting to take their place. Ron Jeremy, on the other hand, seems not to change much over the years, either in popularity, physique or persona, and the nuances of this consistency afford him a unique intertextual presence in contemporary popular culture. Consequently, the fact of Jeremy's stardom – however marginal as compared to celebrities who consort less with 'low' culture – and, more specifically, the apparent incongruity of his physical appearance in the pornographic archive pose critical challenges to the dominant discourse on pornography in film and image studies, in particular the assumption that pornography is generically motivated by the desire to arouse male viewers by the objectification of the woman's body.

Like Hollywood, the adult film industry promotes 'stars', but the icons it generates are mainly either the female performers of 'straight' porn or the male stars of 'gay' porn, and the bodies they exhibit directly conform to normative models of sexual attractiveness. Ron Jeremy, on the other hand, stands as the obverse of these ideological constructions: overweight, unkempt, the anti-aesthetic of the inferred pornographic fantasy, an atypical erotic hyperbole that translates into none of the customary stereotypes. It is important to consider Jeremy not as the exception to the rule, as some marginal figure that really has nothing to do with the real circuit of viewer desire, but in fact part of a substantial tendency of visual culture to provide its perversities with scapegoats, and scapegoats whom we can, in fact, love, and by whom we love to be disgusted.[2]

With his disorderly body and boisterous lack of 'taste', Ron Jeremy bears an affinity to a long tradition of corpulent and physically reckless male comics, from Fatty Arbuckle to John Belushi to Chris Farley.[3] (Somehow it comes as little surprise to discover that Jeremy was a failed Catskills stand-up comedian before he started acting in porn.) His insalubrious comic style, replete with potty-mouth verbiage and the broad winks of old vaudeville, adheres to the 'lower stratum' humour of the bawdy joke, the limerick, the saucy comic strips of *Hustler* magazine and the dirty jokes of popularly-denigrated 'gross-out' films such as *Porky's* (Bob Clark, 1981).[4] The merry, degenerate Falstaff of porn, Jeremy's very attendance at the porn spectacle simultaneously parodies and epitomises the outrageous bodily gymnastics and physical implausibilities of the genre, which by its very nature must frame itself cinematically in order to do two things at the same time: to reveal to plain sight and, less obviously, to obfuscate from view the 'fact' of pleasure.

Its use of laughter is not so much disruptive as ambivalent; as in Mikhail Bakhtin's analysis of the rituals of carnival, laughter functions in porn as a permissible rupture of hegemony in order to signify crisis, and to prod structures of authority into renewing themselves. Its transgressive potential is always carefully circumscribed, and adheres to a strict economic structure; as Patricia Mellencamp describes in her study of television comedy, 'in contrast to the supposedly "liberating" function of jokes, humorous pleasure "saves" feeling because the reality of the situation is too painful' – or too dangerous.[5] Ron Jeremy is important to porn, I contend, because he is both big enough for his viewers to hide behind, and small enough to fit into the tiny fissures of their fantasies – or, as Angela Carter puts it with inimitable directness in her description of the pornographic text, 'a gap left in it on purpose … just the right size for the reader to insert his prick into'.[6]

In this essay I would like to pose a series of questions about Ron Jeremy, as a way of coming to terms with the question of pornography's solicitation of viewer desire. How can we account for Jeremy's presence in films where his physical like is nowhere else to be seen?

We have already heard from many critics how violence plays a role in pornographic representation, but what about how *comedy* operates within pornography, and for what purpose? And how does a consideration of comedy and Jeremy's visually and extra-textually highlighted presence complicate an understanding of porn and the viewer's presumed desire, especially when we recognise Jeremy's primary fan base as young heterosexually-identified males? Here I argue that he functions as pornography's most beloved symptom: an inflated personification of disavowal, a hysterical index of homosocial pleasure and libidinal panic that can only be soothed by overfeeding. It is my contention that pornography has a far more complex relationship to displeasure than is commonly acknowledged, and that its investment in laughter, as a neutered re-direction of pleasure, delivers rich spectatorial rewards for what I will argue is its most preferred consumer: not the male viewer, but male *viewers*.

RON COM: REDEFINING THE BOUNDARIES OF SEXUAL PLEASURE

Pornography – like that other culturally-disparaged institution of egregiously popular smut, the tabloid – cannibalises the culture industry, subsisting on its detritus and throwing a kind of iconographic Jungian shadow across Hollywood glamour. In presenting itself as a fantasy entirely besotted with the pleasure of the image, pornography depicts itself as a glimpse of the 'hard-core' sleaze behind the air-brushed products of mainstream studio publicity, doing nothing to disguise the bruises on the legs of its hairsprayed starlets, nor the rather obvious signs that the beds on which all this sex is taking place aren't on studio sets, but in Los Angeles motel rooms. An industry which grosses approximately three billion dollars a year, pornography independently produces, markets and distributes its products entirely outside of the dominant Hollywood system.

It is for this reason that, contrary to its traditional classification as a film genre, I prefer to categorise pornography as a discrete system of representation itself internally comprised of a variety of genres, depending on the ostensible viewer to whom it is marketed: gay, straight, bisexual, bi-curious, transvestite, transsexual, lesbian, 'couples'; those desiring scenarios featuring all black, Asian or Latino actors; S&M, fist-fucking, and bondage enthusiasts; even the contested ghost-genre of child pornography. These genres themselves further divide into a series of sub-genres that increasingly narrow the sexual focus according to whatever the viewer allegedly wants to see.

All of Ron Jeremy's films fall under the rubric of 'straight' pornography, but his uncredited performance in a video entitled *Never Say Good-Bi* (1987) will be the subject of this essay's close reading, which takes aim at the presumption that mainstream 'straight' pornography fundamentally caters to an unconflicted heterosexual desire. What is Jeremy doing in this film? What kind of audience did the producers have in mind when they made it? While he grounds himself firmly in the realm of the 'straight' genre (unlike crossover porn actors such as Randy West or Jeff Stryker who perform in both gay and straight films), Jeremy's filmography exhibits his unparalleled ability to traverse the range of 'straight' sexual particularities. After all, in pornography, preference *is* genre; not even heterosexuality gets figured as monolithic, and in porn, genre is both obsessively circumscribed and confoundingly elided. A cursory glance at Jeremy's list of credits – *and* the porn section of any video store – reveals a striking number of films with anally-fixated themes (*Mistress Hiney: The Beverly Hills Butt Broker* (1993); *My Anal Valentine* (August West, 1992)), 'gang bangs' (in one annual series, *The World's Biggest Gang Bang* (John T. Bone, 1995) Jeremy appears as the Master of Ceremonies and traditionally 'closes' the event by being the last man to have intercourse with the woman), and also with fat fetishism (*Let Me Tell Ya 'Bout Fat Chicks* (Guillermo Brown, 1987); *Fatliners* (Joe W. Brown, 1990)). While these films appear to address their viewers' specific predilections with un-ambivalent directness, most adult video stores tend to lump all of their 'straight' titles together in no discernible order, not even alphabetical.

Although it is impossible to say for sure at this point, I am inclined to believe that *Never Say Good-Bi* was originally located on a shelf amongst a number of 'straight' videos, and that its titular promise was not intended to appeal to a 'bisexual' or even a 'gay' viewer, though I am sure it also found its fair share of those. Instead, I contend that *Never Say Good-Bi*, while perhaps more articulate about the inner workings of pornography than many other texts of its kind, is exceedingly typical of the 'straight' film's synthesis of the confirmed heterosexuality of its presumed male viewer *and* the ineloquent homoerotic curiosity that invisibly sutures him to the text.

Ron Jeremy most frequently appears in, and is most generally associated with, a genre which I will call the 'pornedy': a hybrid mode that signifies the pornographic lampoon of a cultural staple such as a popular film, television show or media event. Examples include the notorious Jeremy-directed *John Wayne Bobbitt Uncut* (1994) featuring the famous amputee's surgically-reconstructed and obstinately flaccid penis, and *Divine and Sunset* (1996), a parodic self-billed 'doc-Hugh-drama' dramatising the 1995 Hugh Grant/Divine Brown prostitution scandal. A flamboyant interpenetration of the class-coded dialectic of high culture and mass culture, flawlessly illustrating Bakhtin's theory of carnivalesque politics in the Rabelaisian inversion of popular forms, the 'pornedy' enters the sacrosanct space of the popular narrative and re-tells it uncensored.[7] What the original version was compelled to sublimate, the pornedy renders explicit; whereas the much-beloved television show *The Honeymooners* could only 'speak sex' through clever innuendo, *The Horneymooners* (Irving Weiss, 1988) (in which Jeremy portrays Ralph Kramden, wearing his bus-driver's hat even during sex – 'I'm a bus driver *first*', he tells one of his partners when she asks why he doesn't take it off) literalises the erotic subtext. More cartoon than critique, the pornedy is an animated pun, an extended raunchy sight gag, and the joke is always on heterosexuality, its mating rituals and romantic myths, its hypocritical reticence to show what it tells so relentlessly. The punning of the porn film title has become almost mandatory by now, and if titles are meant to advertise the product on display, it often presents a rather different picture of what the viewer may desire from it than has been traditionally painted: a regressive strain of infantile, anal-stage humour inextricable from lawful carnal desire, the mischevious pleasures of being 'in' on the vaguely nostalgic cultural reference, the slyly beckoning finger of the hermeneutic key of the naughty joke. A sampling of Jeremy's pornedy titles make clear this fusion of the frisky and the farcical: *Desperately Sleazy Susan* (1985), *The Raunchy Porno Picture Show* (Walt Jizzney, 1992), *Generally Horny Hospital* (Jean Pierre Ferrand, 1995) and *Terms of Endowment* (A. C. Simpson, 1986) to name just a few.

CARNAL AND CARNIVALESQUE: RETHINKING THE MALE PORNO BODY

The issue of pornography's carnivalesque political engagement with hypocritical morés has been wonderfully argued by Laura Kipnis and Constance Penley, who in their respective works contend that pornography subversively de-bunks and degrades bourgeois mythologies of sexual hierarchy, and exists as a site of turbulent cultural contention that interrogates rather than affirms dominant ideology.[8] On the other end of these arguments, critics from Andrea Dworkin to Nancy Armstrong to Susan Gubar – their assaults on the genre, admittedly, pitched at varying degrees of polemical and emotional intensity – insist that pornography represents patriarchal dominance more explicitly than any other cultural form, and affirms in relentless repetition the symbolic violence of heterosexual subjugation.[9] Due to the work of a number of scholars such as Kipnis, Penley, Linda Williams, Susan Stewart, Thomas Waugh and others, it is now possible to enter into the critical discourse of pornography without being required to address the now rather overdetermined question of 'value'.[10] The conversation has finally shifted to issues of the potentially subversive – or, at least, potentially complex – semiotics of visual porn, and is now more attentive to the cryptic opacity of pornographic iconography rather than its previously presumed transparency.[11] It is in this vein that I suggest we take the critical discourse on pornography a bit further, and pressure this issue of iconography as a means of exploring that liminal territory between more familiar 'for' and 'against' arguments.

While I agree that porn undeniably contains subversive content, I also believe that it depends for its very existence upon a deep and silently confirmed sexual conservatism. The graphic display of the hard-core spectacle codes more than it de-codes, and my purpose in isolating the mode of comedy is to ask how comedy *mystifies*, and not how it illuminates the specular sexual 'fact'. Because this mystification ends up producing those very images of super-banalised heterosexuality that appear so generically self-evident on-screen, we might ask ourselves just what, in fact, we are 'really' looking at, what pleasures pornography 'really' promises, and what it actually delivers. Pornography, like any other mode of entertainment, asks us to measure it not so much against an aesthetic of verisimilitude but in terms of fantasy, as an elaborate *anti-realism*.

My greatest difficulty with criticism that defends pornography is that by privileging the hard-core spectacle as a site of compulsive Foucauldian truth-telling – as signified by the mandatory narrative closure of the 'money shot' – such theory figures the pornographic image as transparent and unmediated, a fantasy of pure cinema that delivers the 'Real' free of aesthetic or ideological contamination. Why should we assume that pornography, more than any other cinematic mode, tells the truth? Obviously I do not deny that porn compulsively translates everything, no matter how mundane, into 'sexual' (i.e. visual and corporeal) terms – an operation which Ron Jeremy himself embodies in his overstuffed, over-determined form – but to me the more pressing question is, what does it *not* show? For what un-representable content does the pornographic image so obsessively overcompensate? As it stands now, porn is theorised as that cinematic genre that exists purely to arouse the viewer, and which in its most mainstream form relies upon the objectification of the woman's body and the privileging of male orgasm as an inscription of 'truth' and the linchpin of visual pleasure. If pornography exists purely to arouse, why then the imperative of laughter? Most critical writing on porn highlights the visual primacy of the woman's body and imagines the male sex performer as somehow invisible, incidental to the scene, while paradoxically insisting upon the visual revelation of male orgasm as *the* compulsory display in the entire scenario. If the porn film by its very nature directs the male viewer's gaze inexorably to the female body, then how do we account for Ron Jeremy's stardom? For the presumed male viewer to 'see' Jeremy in a porn film at all contradicts the terms the discourse on porn has in play right now.

Another problematic assumption in the writing on pornography is that of the *privacy* of viewing. Admittedly, pornographic film left the movie theatres of the 1970s and colonised the home-video market in the 1980s, but this shift of venue does not represent a privatisation of pornographic consumption, but in fact merely enables its publicity in and under the cover of a mainstreamed and safely domesticated pseudo-private sphere. In order to fully come to terms with the means by which this is achieved, we must consider the impact of the home-viewing market's expansion on the production of pornographic film, and undertake an analysis of porn in terms of its *televisual* as well as its cinematic aspects. In doing so, we can begin to form a new understanding of the conditions of reception for the pornographic film and the crucial importance of the 'scene'' of spectatorship. As Cindy Patton explains:

The structure of erotic experience now enmeshed with rather than opposed to routine consumer activities and domestic rituals; a couch potato do-me ethos replaced the nomadic activity that once characterized the XXX cinema … People consumed pornography in the same space, on the same machines, where they had watched the news, their favorite TV series, or the Weather Channel only hours before.[12]

Patton's analysis adroitly illustrates how pornography's colonisation of the home-video market signifies both a cultural transgression of symbolic/spatial boundaries and a normalising and domesticating of the 'genital show' on the TV screen. In this vein, I am interested in examining how the transfer of the pornographic film from the public space of the theatre to the private realm of the home assists in privatising what I consider to be a pleasure essentially public in nature. From its earliest beginnings, pornographic films were watched socially: at stag parties, frat houses, masonic lodges, or in the back rooms of bars or taverns, gradually moving on to big-screen exhibition. While now the masturbatory potential of porn seems to have been fully realised with the advent of video, it is my argument that porn has not changed from something watched in groups to something now watched alone, but that it has internalised in its very structure what I will call the 'compulsory homosociality' of its viewer address. One of its most important strategies is the omnipresence of porn legend Ron Jeremy, who, with his raunchy comedic style and parodic body, seals the social contact between the viewer and the movie by reassuring him that he is, in fact, not alone. Doesn't comedy always presume a group reception? And does it not feel much stranger to *laugh* alone than to, well, do other things? As Jeremy himself has said, 'People can't laugh and get a bone on at the same time. That's what they say.'[13]

In order to further investigate pornography's roots in a distinctly social mode of exhibition, one important direction for porn studies to take would be to go back to the very beginning, to the earliest days of photographic and cinematic media. The most relevant starting point, I believe, would be Tom Gunning's exegesis of the early 'cinema of attractions', his provocative counter-theory to the hegemony of narrative cinema, outlining a film genus characterised by a specific mode of address that differs from the primary spectator relations set up by classical cinema: monstration, not narration. A plotless series of displays or transformations rather than a progressive sketch of narrative continuity, whatever story exists at all acts merely as a pretext for effects, just as the narrative in porn is commonly understood as merely establishing a time and a place for the sex to take place. This early 'cinema of attractions', Gunning argues, does not vanish with the advent of narrative film but rather 'goes underground', into avant-garde practices and in genres of spectacle, such as the musical. Gunning does not mention pornography, but I think it certainly belongs in his analysis, particularly as additional evidence against the archaic developmental model of cinema. Gunning wants to consider the 'cinema of attractions' as a mode in its own right rather than a primitive phase or precursor of the more sophisticated machinery of classical narrative.[14] Another crucial aspect of looking at such early films is the element of the non-integrity of the diegesis; as a number of scholars such as Linda Williams, Miriam Hansen and Noël Burch have argued, such films do not elaborate a hermetic diegesis precisely because they want their viewers to remain firmly oriented in the social scene of exhibition. Rather than addressing the shifting points of internal identification that operate in cinematic narration, the 'primitive' film confronts its audience directly rather than abstractly introducing it into the space of the film.[15]

I would like to take a brief anecdotal digression here, as a way of providing some evidence that I cannot just footnote. A male friend of mine who identifies himself as bisexual often frequents adult movie theatres that feature 'straight' films. He never goes near the gay movie houses, he says. 'What's the point?' Inside the theatre, where there is never a woman to be seen except on the screen, men cruise from aisle to aisle, stopping to masturbate each other or engage in oral sex. My friend told me a story about a man who once got up from his seat during the film, walked down the aisle towards the front of the theatre, faced the screen and ejaculated in time with the money shot. My friend has been to these 'straight' theatres all over the country, and he invariably witnesses and participates in scenes nearly identical to this one. Tales like these beg a series of questions, not the least of which concerns what the pornographic viewer is really watching – the film or the audience? And who is he most interested in looking at – the woman or the man? And if pornography is indeed transgressive, as we are so invested in claiming, then what prohibited content does it *really* represent? While researching this essay, I spent a lot of time trying to track down a copy of *Never Say Good-Bi*, which I had seen in college when a friend rented it as research for a paper he was writing on porn and Jean Genet. 'Who the hell is that guy?' I asked when Ron Jeremy came on the screen; it seemed so absurd that someone of his 'type' had been cast in a movie like this. My friend told me he had been in just about every porno movie he had ever seen. Years later I had a lot of difficulty finding *Never Say Good-Bi* to review for this essay. In one adult video store I mentioned to the manager that Ron Jeremy had appeared in it, hoping that this would help to focus the search. He rolled his eyes. 'Are you kidding me?' he said. 'Ron Jeremy's in *everything!*'

With his anti-aesthetic physique and tasteless hilarity, Jeremy's simultaneously incongruous and ubiquitous presence in the porn film serves, quite like the woman's body, as the alibi for the male viewer, who, through his engagement with Jeremy's comedic antics and derision of his generically-inappropriate body, can both indulge and disavow his desire to view the male body, and to view it in a social rather than anti-social context. Jeremy's intertextuality and cultural diffusion, symbolically coded by his physical largesse and the corresponding rude extroversion of his performance style, disclaims for the male viewer the solitary 'queerness' of the scene of spectatorship. He may appear to be the visible exception to the rule, the adipose anomaly among a series of tight muscular male bodies, his formidable prevalence revealing him to be a virtual manifestation of pornography's inner censor. Pornography, in effect, *dreamed* Ron Jeremy, providing through the operations of condensation and displacement what Kaja Silverman describes, in her explication of the secondary processes of repression, as 'acceptable representations for unacceptable wishes'.[16]

HUMOUR AND 'HETEROSEXUALITY': WHY RON NEVER SAID GOOD-BI

Ron Jeremy is a main character in the mass-marketed porn video *Never Say Good-Bi*, but his name does not appear on the videocassette case, nor in the film's credits. It begins, as do many porn films, with a kind of preview of coming attractions: a series of brief clips from the forthcoming sex scenes over which the minimal opening credits are superimposed. An incongruous 'Duelling Banjos'-esque theme song accompanies a montage of men having sex on a sofa and a woman penetrating a man with a strap-on dildo. Immediately the juxtaposition of soundtrack and image sets up the film's heavily ironic and self-subverting *modus operandi*: it establishes a systematic cooperation of the comic and the sexual. The narrative begins with a medium shot of two young men sitting on a couch eating chips, dressed in vaguely athletic garb: one with a towel around his waist, the other in a tank top, shorts and tennis shoes. Their conversation reveals their names to be, respectively, Tony and Neil. Tony is detailing for Neil a recent sexual encounter with his friends TJ and Samantha. 'How did it all start?' Neil inquires with interest.

The film then cuts to a close-up of Tony's face, and as he begins to tell the story the image slowly goes out of focus, signifying the change of scene from the *mise-en-scène* of the present to the setting of fantasy. Then the film jump-cuts to an outdoor swimming-pool. Tony (still wearing only a towel) and TJ are depicted sitting on the diving-board, debating in numbingly repetitive dialogue whether or not Samantha will 'show up'. ('I don't think she's going to show up'; 'How much do you want to bet, man?'; 'I don't know, man, I don't think she's going to show up'). Finally, late-1980s porn star Samantha Strong materialises: a buxom blonde in a bikini, deeply-tanned and sporting a mane of stiff blonde curls. A brief conversation devolves into an interminable *ménage-à-trois* which finally concludes with Tony and TJ simultaneously masturbating themselves to orgasm as Samantha impassively watches.

Though Ron Jeremy doesn't appear in this scene, I discuss it for several reasons: its explicit employment of the woman as a pretext for the erotic encounter between two men, an encounter which systematically writes her out of the scene; the double nature of the money shot which, it could be argued, directly mirrors the masturbatory homosocial union of the extra-diegetic viewers, either literally sharing the viewing space (as do Neil and Tony) or in an unavowed fantasy relation; the way the film edits Samantha Strong's performance ('Oh, it's *so* hot out here, one could just die', she intones archly during the small-talk preceding the sex) to highlight her utterances of sarcasm and irony, boredom and impatience. This clever codification of Strong's performance rhymes with the traditional comic framing of Ron Jeremy, quite economically distracting and unpleasurable, and provides a tantalising view into the crucial importance of the disruptively-reflexive moment to pornography, of the rapidly accumulating instants when the viewer is made aware of that genital event as staged and the actors as 'faking'. ('Tony, I *asked* you if you liked my cock', Samantha – who is penetrating Tony with a strap-on dildo – later demands in a deadpan tone we can now interpret as subtly sardonic; 'maybe if you took his dick out of your mouth you could answer me.') Within this spectacle of three-way sex, the presence of Samantha Strong enables the fiction of derisive non-(homo)arousal, not only functioning as an erotic distraction, but as a frankly comic object.

For the first several minutes of the scenario, Tony and Samantha take turns fellating TJ, who remains conspicuously non-erect; the shots of his flaccid penis are intercut with one recurring shot of TJ crooning, 'Oh, yeah, nice.' The persistent repetition of TJ's face 'speaking' pleasure and its juxtaposition with shots of his non-erect penis perform a crucial dialectic: between a language of pleasure and a spectacle of impotence that contradicts the presumption of porn's valorisation of male sexual potency, an image of *dis*pleasure that disavows its corresponding shadow of homoerotic gratification. Additionally, the repetition of this particular shot and the way the scene doubles back on itself in other ways – its compulsive return, for example, to a moment when Samantha hands TJ's limp penis to Tony and says, 'Tony, why don't *you* suck his cock?' and then sighs, almost imperceptibly rolling her eyes, effects a temporal slippage which marks the scene as *nothing* but scene or setting, as pure fantasy: removed from real time, constructed, designed, and not for real. And this isn't an entirely pleasurable fantasy, either, but a fantasy about a man who won't get hard, no matter what, who is half in and half out of the scene, only partially participating.

The film also makes what appear to be senseless editing choices that seemingly break the erotic spell. After the long fellatio sequence, the film abruptly cuts to a long shot of Tony bending over the diving-board as Samantha stands behind him wearing a strap-on dildo, lubricating him with baby oil. TJ sits idly at the other end of the diving-board, rubbing what appears to be suntan lotion on his thighs. Tony, eagerly stroking his penis, issues some audible sexual command to Samantha, who replies, 'Hey, I'm getting a hard-on over here, will you chill out?' Instantly the three of them dissolves into giggles. Then she inadvertently drops the bottle of baby oil, which prompts more laughter. After picking it up Samantha pushes gently on the small of Tony's back and says, 'Get down farther, babe; I gotta get a good angle with my cock.' At this point the actors start laughing again, even harder this time, looking just beyond the camera, presumably at the also-laughing crew. As Samantha sticks the tip of the dildo between Tony's buttocks, Tony turns his face toward the camera, screws up his face in exaggerated ecstasy and exclaims, 'Oh!' Samantha stops and looks down at him. 'Did you say 'ow'?' Tony turns around and replies calmly, 'No, I said, 'Oh.' And the actors fall to laughing once again, this time for several moments as Samantha jumps around and claps her hands to her knees in delight.

Conceivably, this entire sequence could have been edited out, and the scene could have just started at the moment when Samantha penetrates Tony with the dildo. While we might just write this off as a further sign of the filmmakers' ineptitude, I still think it constitutes a *choice*, and therefore something that is meaningful. Additionally, the *choice* of including a single male/female encounter, the participants of which never engage in 'bi' sex later in the film, seems equally important; every other character in the film has at least one sex scene with another character of the same sex.

The entire film seems to set up Ron Jeremy's character for a sexual 'fall': he spectates at a series of male/male encounters, in which the film intercuts shots of the sex with shots of Jeremy standing in the doorway watching, rolling his eyes in disbelief and craning his neck to get a better look. 'Is everyone gay but me?' he reflects to himself as he eats pizza in the kitchen. 'Maybe I'm missing out on something.' From his first scene, it is clear that Ron Jeremy literally polices the ambi-sexual activity in the film, patrolling the tenuous boundary between straight and queer sex. At the conclusion of the swimming pool three-way fantasy, the film returns to Neil and Tony sitting on the couch; Neil is rubbing his crotch and saying, 'Man, this is turning me on big time.' Suddenly, a loud off-screen voice announces jovially, 'Hey, guys, I'm here!' Neil quickly removes his hand from between his legs as Ron Jeremy appears in the frame, wearing a pair of shorts and a t-shirt that reads, incredibly, *SECURITY*. (In their conversation he tells friends that he works as a security guard at 'the Bonanza'.) Apparently they all went to junior college together, and are meeting up for a class reunion. The men slap hands and Jeremy helps himself to the bowl of chips on the table before looking at his two friends and remarking, 'Hey, you guys are sitting awfully close there, aren't ya?'

At this point Tony asks Jeremy if he's had any 'wild fantasies' lately. Jeremy nods and replies, 'Yeah – Bobby.' Neil and Tony look at each other, raising their eyebrows, and eagerly encourage Jeremy to tell them about it. As Jeremy begins to describe the memory, the camera moves in on his reflective face and loses focus, abruptly cutting to a shot of a pair of legs. The camera travels upwards in what is a hilariously straightforward Freudian play-by-play of fetishism, slowly revealing that the legs belong to a woman. The long scene depicts Jeremy and 'Bobby' having both oral and vaginal sex in a variety of positions, alternately in 'real time' and slow motion, before returning to the college reunion. At the conclusion of his story Jeremy finally says, 'Man, *she* was *hot*', and Tony and Neil look at each other in surprise and disappointment, finally dispelling the fantasy for them that Jeremy was describing a male/male scenario. This is the only scene in the film in which Jeremy's character actually has sex, though he appears in nearly every scene. This in and of itself is not exactly remarkable: he is rarely the sole 'lead' of his films and generally plays featured 'character' parts in some kind of ensemble. Unlike younger 'straight' (and more conventionally attractive) stars such as T. T. Boy or Peter North, Jeremy is also rarely shown on the cover of his films' videocassette cases, though his name almost always appears above the title. It is almost as if he is there, but is not quite there, just as the viewer vascillates inside and out of his spectatorial situation. Bounding on and off the screen with Benny Hill-like fleshly mischievousness, Jeremy is the star behind the scenes, serving a purpose not entirely (or merely) sexual in nature, but palliative and conservative.

By appearing on the scene of his male friends' fantasy, Jeremy both interrupts and enables the homoerotic encounter. In furnishing his two male friends with a new fantasy, he unwittingly provides himself as the necessary third term to the triangle that completes the porno-specular arrangement, just as TJ and Tony could not fool around until Samantha Strong 'showed up'. In her intensely Lacanian analysis of the semiotics of pornographic magazine photographs, Berkeley Kaite describes this triangulation of desire as a necessary inference, that 'men in these images never touch or penetrate each other, except in a signifying chain: i.e. "A" (male) touches "B" (female) who touches "C" (male)'.[17] And in so doing, *Never Say Good-Bi* reveals the seemingly straightforward male/female sex scene to possess a queer dimension, and reveals the graphic display of sexual fantasy to be coded, not natural. As a fantasy diegetically directed to a homosocial audience, the Jeremy/Bobby sequence exists in an implicit relation to the 'original' queer scene – especially considering its placement in the identical setting of the swimming pool and its employment of the same synthesiser soundtrack – and by erasing the second male from the erotic figuration, translates the homoerotic spectacle into a hermetic, quintessential pornographic fantasy of heterosex. Additionally, Jeremy's more general narrative function as the repressive suturing thread among the tableaux of sexual variety, his positioning as the incredulous spectator who remains uncontaminated by the queer sex he watches with such avid interest, allows the 'straight' viewer to watch in equal safety, to feel comfortable and 'at home', pacified by the snack-like empty calories of Jeremy's comic intercessions.

Never Say Good-Bi is both an anomolous and typical text in the Ron Jeremy filmography. Considering the vast number of films he has made, I have seen only a relatively small number of his films, and among those and the others of which I am aware there is not another one explicitly 'bi-sexual' in nature, except, of course, for the rampant 'lesbian' scenes ubiquitous in adult 'hetero' cinema. It is structurally impossible to read the female-on-female scenario within the schema of homosociality – not to mention untenable in nearly every other respect – but I would venture to suggest that its semiotics are, in fact, not so different from the ones I have been describing in this essay. The scene of two women having sex in the straight porn film could not have less to do with 'lesbian' sexuality, or even *female* sexuality for that matter; the electric charge of the scenario is in its consolatory sublimation of the homosocial element to an image of homosexual (and, perhaps even more importantly, deliciously prohibited) sex. The man's elimination from the scene is not threatening, as 'real' lesbian sex would be, but in fact rather reassuring: he is watching from a safe distance a scene of same-sex sex in which there is nary a man to be seen. To me this further supports my impression of pornography's true perverseness: not that it represents sex, but that in pornography sex represents something even more disorderly, chaotic and potentially threatening to the order of things. Ron Jeremy, whether he be portraying a Jerry Falwell-esque televangelist in *Deep Throat 2* (Larry Revene, 1987) (who is one minute preaching to the cameras about the sins of pornography and the next minute having sex with two women at once on the very same stage), or randy incarnations of a host of lovable buffoons like Fred Flintstone or Al Kramden or Mario from *Super Mario Brothers* illustrates pornography's canny ability to dilate the form of the icon to its furthest limit. In pornography, the sign of sex is nothing but just that, a sign that constantly plays with its own subversion, exploiting its innate realism to produce a realm of remorseless fantasy.[18]

In her book *Bound and Gagged: Pornography and the Politics of Fantasy in America*, Laura Kipnis uses the example of the porn genre of fat fetishism to illustrate her thesis that pornography compulsively exposes for political and sexual effect those culturally abject bodies and practices which have been banished from the mainstream. 'Isn't fat always sort of pornographic anyway?' Kipnis inquires, pointing out that a magazine like *Dimensions*, which

153

features soft-core photographs of overweight women in lingerie, can only be purchased in adult stores, thus suggesting that the visual disclosure of the fat body enacts a form of corporeal truth-telling similar to pornography.[19] In Ron Jeremy's case, the overweight body does not provoke the erotic anxiety of a transgressive pleasure so much as it soothes and normalises a less conspicuous disquiet. The visual investment in Jeremy's body fills a symbolic gap in the scene of spectatorship – even, in a sense, the space between the viewers on the couch – and assuages in its embodiment of surfeit a tension that mimics hunger, providing a pleasure that can be experienced in the body, but safely: that of laughter, which manages the threat of contact while providing a less dangerous social response. As Lauren Berlant describes it, 'as a thing that denotes an unquantified substance, fat's very fixity accrues to itself an unshakable stability of identity'.[20] The 'fat' body in this case has an anchoring effect in the pornographic arrangement, not so much because Jeremy is an unthreatening, perhaps even especially *realistic* male subject with whom the viewers can easily identify (and therefore more successfully enter the heterosexual fantasy), but because he embodies the very operation of displacement upon which the entire formula depends.

With every year, Ron Jeremy's popularity grows along with his steadily thickening cult of personality. The more he infiltrates the mainstream, the more efficiently he functions as an alibi for the male porn viewer, who, in recognising Jeremy in both the public sphere *and* the private publicity of the scene of porn spectatorship, can avow knowledge of him as culturally legitimate while possessing an 'other' knowledge of him in excess of his mainstream representation. He bears the burden of a pornographic representation that can only make sex visible by obfuscation, by bloating the image into a manifest hyperreality that disguises its 'Real' with layers of flesh. Pornography exaggerates itself so much as representational – with its obsessive allusionism, highly self-conscious 'acting', and confounding insistence on narrative – to conceal the fact that what preoccupies it so much cannot be visually avowed. To gorge oneself on porn's significatory excesses is to ingest it like junk food, is to internalise the degraded spectacle under the cover of displacing it, just as Ron Jeremy immediately turns from spectating at a male/male sexual encounter in *Never Say Good-Bi* to stuff himself with pizza. 'Watching all that sex', he says thoughtfully, before slapping his hands together and turning towards the refrigerator, 'makes me feel … hungry.'

CHAPTER 12
'I GUESS THEY GOT PAST THEIR FEAR OF PORN': WOMEN VIEWING PORN FILMS

Clarissa Smith

> Do you have a reptile brain? Or an angel brain? That's how I describe what determines
> your enjoyment of pornography.[1]

Popular discourse on pornography and its viewing often stresses the need for limits on its
consumption: like junk food, pornography is, at best, okay in moderation but too much is bad
for one's health. This being the case, it can be very difficult to find willing participants for a
research project which seeks to go beyond general questions about occasional use to ask more
searching questions about the place of pornography in an individual's life – no one wants to be
identified as the possessor of a reptile brain.

In this chapter I briefly examine women's use of pornographic films, using interviews
with six women aged 25–48, in relationships of various kinds: two in long-term heterosexual
partnerships (more than 15 years and with children); two in heterosexual relationships of

three or more years (no children); one in what she described as a fairly casual heterosexual relationship (not living together) and one woman who identified as bi-sexual and was currently in an exclusive relationship with a woman. Each described themselves as 'open-minded' about sexual issues and keen on representations of sexual activity. All identified themselves as regular viewers of pornographic films, though the term pornography had a very flexible border – for one, Diane, pornography meant films with significant sexual themes such as *In the Cut* (Jane Campion, 2003) and *Eyes Wide Shut* (Stanley Kubrick, 1999). None had seen films viewed by the others – reception research can usually rely on naturally-occurring audiences who have a *shared* interest in a particular film, TV programme or the coherence of a media genre but when it comes to pornography, the term encompasses thousands of titles with sometimes very little similarities of form, style or substance. Hence the interviews threw up a range of very general points of similarity (in particular, histories of viewing) and then widely different experiences and tastes in viewing, which does not, of course, make for easy assimilation into a short chapter.

TALKING SEX

It is important that we 'allow them [consumers of pornography] to speak'[2] but if we are to fully understand the use of pornography in everyday life and its significance as a form of representation their words will require critical scrutiny. Not that users of porn are to be understood as particularly 'unreliable' – I absolutely reject Michael Gilding's comment that 'just because a self-selecting group of pornography consumers say that pornography is good for their mental health and marriages does not make it so'.[3] That observation reduces the importance of audience research to simple assertion of 'benefits' in particular media usages and fundamentally misunderstands the nature of the descriptions and feelings consumers offer researchers. As Alan McKee has argued, 'there is a systematic "othering" of pornography consumers in academic research and in public debate about the genre. They cannot know themselves; they cannot speak for themselves; they must be represented'.[4]

Given the continuing suspicion of those who indulge in pornographic viewing, it is not surprising that counter-discourses focus on the potential therapeutic, recreational or oppositional usages of pornography and strive to ensure that an 'ethics of pleasure' is established in relation to hard-core. For instance, in his recent discussion of the aesthetics of pornography, McKee notes that

> There was absolute agreement that these users of pornography wanted to see actors genuinely enjoying themselves. There was no discourse available for celebrating pornography which was non-consensual. There was no suggestion that 'anything goes'. Some interviewees went further and noted that financial inducements or drugs might place limits on genuine consent – and they had little interest in watching such material.[5]

While understandable, this defensiveness condenses the sense-making involved in viewing porn to simple alternatives – for example, judging 'genuine' and 'non-consensual' porn. Moreover, it presupposes that the fundamental purpose of researching pornographic consumption is to find 'acceptable' usages. The ambivalences expressed by many viewers in watching a porn movie – number one being 'is she actually enjoying this?' – are taken as evidence of viewers' 'better' judgements in relation to their viewing. Thus, it seems to me that much audience research has looked to find evidence in consumers' talk of measuring pornography for its 'quality' and 'egalitarianism', not to question how and why consumers might feel the need to offer those explanations but in order to construct a case redeeming pornography from the arguments of 'harm'.

Academic discussions construct enjoying or not enjoying a film or story as linked to a notion of 'good' (consensual, authentic, free of coercive elements or ambivalence) or 'bad' (problematic, psychologically complex, difficult to gauge the nature of participants' pleasure) pornography. Seemingly, academics are afraid of arguing for the possibility of finding 'bad' porn exciting or interesting.

This defensiveness may well be an indication of the continuing influence of anti-pornography feminism which constructed pornography as a special category of representation, particularly for women. Simply put, anti-porn feminism and, specifically, Andrea Dworkin's arguments about pornography revolve around the belief that heterosexuality is predicated on women's subordination and status as chattel. Thus sexually explicit representations are part of an armoury (also including rape and domestic violence) to eroticise men's power over women and their bodies. Her most familiar publication, *Pornography: Men Possessing Women* (1981), described porn as systematically dehumanising women by characterising them as dirty, masochistic and desirous of sexual pain. Thus, for Dworkin, heterosexual intercourse is a form of occupation, something *done* to women and, moreover, done to them without their consent.

I have argued elsewhere that Dworkin's arguments are a part of the fabric of meaning-making for pornography's consumers and commentators alike.[6] Hence, the 'good' porn consumer demonstrates that s/he assesses their pornography for signs that the actresses act of their own volition and free will, as Parvez Z. Fareen's research demonstrates that it is seemingly impossible for women to engage with pornography without thinking about their responsibilities *qua* women to other women.[7] As Maggie, an interviewee for this chapter said,

> I think I ought to say something about the actresses – see this is where it gets difficult 'cos within the film you can sort of say 'oh yes, the story they're telling is this one and that's fine' but then sometimes I think about what happened later and I think but can those women then decide 'well I've done something once but that's it, I don't want to do it again'? I mean can they make that choice and that worries me. 'Cos its like you know that if they've done a two guy one girl scene that its difficult to say no to doing three guys and then four and so on. And if they've done anal then why not DP and then TP and then who knows?[8]

Maggie's worries came towards the end of an interview in which she had been enthusiastic about various forms of pornographic representation and practices including BDSM and group sex which she thought would probably upset most 'ordinary people'. I *could* use this quotation as an indication of 'a conscience'; however, that does not adequately reflect her discussion of pornography as a whole. The comment doesn't start from a questioning of harm within the image (is this woman having an authentically good time?) and she is not worried about the effects of the image on either herself or other viewers; instead her quandaries revolve around questions of agency for the actress. To make any claim of 'conscience' for this woman is to perpetuate the picture of the pornography consumer as a special case divided into 'good' consumers and 'bad'.

Public talk about women using porn often emphasises a level of coming to terms with sexually explicit materials, a sense that women have had to 'desensitise' themselves or practice some form of 'aversion therapy' in order to enjoy porn and sexual pleasure (as advocated by Germaine Greer in the 1970s[9]); even as the numbers suggest a rise in women's consumption of pornographic representations, they are often dismissed as a coarsening of a natural and properly feminine sensibility towards the sexually explicit, something which is evident in women's own ambivalences in discussions about watching pornography:

> I wasn't sure that I would like it, or that, or that, I could like it. I mean … I was always told that it was dirty and that it was … well brutal and that women just had things done to them. Y'know that men do and women are done to and that they don't really want to be there… So when I watched … not the first time, but later I was kinda surprised to find I was enjoying it and it was like my dirty little secret at first … and sometimes, well it still is… I mean, I'm still not sure it's okay to do it … I couldn't say [anything] about it at work or to my neighbours or anything.[10]

There is a constant 'self-surveillance' in relation to the arguments about harm which are both about the viewers own reactions – are these signs of corruption, the unruly nature of desire in the face of 'bad' sexual practices? – and acknowledgements of being judged by others as someone who is doing something dirty or, as Judith suggested, 'doesn't care about women'. So what motivates women to watch pornography, what do they get out of it, what emotional investments are made in their viewing?

MOTIVATIONS

Often accounts of 'pornographication' and sexualisation have emphasised the ease with which people can now access pornography;[11] indeed, in the critical accounts it is asserted that it is difficult to *avoid* porn – it appears to be everywhere, bursting upon us when we least wish it.[12] However, even as sexualised imagery crops up in mainstream media, porn viewing, like most interests, is one that needs to be pursued. DVDs or downloads have to be chosen and purchased, sometimes at considerable expense. Time needs to be set aside to watch them – and often viewers have to ensure that there will be no interruptions to get the best out of their film. Unless the film is being screened in company, viewers try to avoid the need to explain why they are watching: 'God, I'd just die if he knew I was watching it on my own!'[13] Consuming porn requires space to engage one's imagination: this may be to separate the body from what it was doing earlier – domestic chores in the case of some of my interviewees – to engage with it as a feeling and possibly aroused body. This setting aside of time is a symptom of our cultural shame around viewing pornography but is also a requisite of engaging properly with the material.

So why do women watch pornography? For Chris its importance in her life is very complex:

> I like to watch porn because it reminds me that I'm not just this part-time worker and full-time mum and a long-term partner and stuff, but that I have a body which feels sensational sometimes, does that make sense? It's like it's possible to be me in my everyday life but at the same time feeling like I used to before kids and everything… I have friends who complain … that it all used to be different when they first got together – well of course it did, you didn't have kids, probably didn't have a job you really cared about or needed or whatever … you go from feeling kind of loved up, really interested in each other's bodies and stuff to just a quick peck and roll over … everything else is in the way. And that's really what I get out of watching porn is that you can sort of gear yourself up … get yourself feeling excited again … I feel more laid back and stuff if I've watched a film (and not just if I've actually come when I watch it) I mean sometimes I just watch them like I would some daytime TV programme and it just lifts my spirits and gives me a kind of high all day and I really like that and … later I'll be really touchy feely with Paul and I just enjoy that, I just enjoy that sensation of being relaxed and not cross with the world and just able to sit stroking his hair or letting him do that to me while we watch the telly and we go to bed and maybe we have sex but not always and that's great too. Its just I feel more open rather than my usual tense and kind of resentful self if I've had a bad day – some people probably go to the gym for that or have some wine or something but I do like reading or watching or just thinking about sex to make me feel less tense.[14]

This fits with the idea of pornography as an outlet for feelings not met elsewhere – the therapeutic model of consumption. However, there is something more offered here – a sense of preparing and planning for being part of a couple. A way of reinvigorating not just sexual feelings towards a partner but of preparing oneself for interactions which are not fraught with the domestic problems of the everyday and of reconnecting with one's own body. The offered motives also deflect any likely criticisms – within the context of her loving and monogamous relationship, pornography is a means to ensure that she's not tense and irritable when the children and her husband come home; orgasms, feeling sexy are not necessarily experienced as spontaneous, they are part of family life and need to be planned for.

Yet Chris doesn't use the vocabulary of performance enhancement – learning techniques, for example. Instead, she talks of pornography's place in her personal history. Her sex life (articulated at various points in the interview in terms of not having time or energy for sex) has seemingly fallen out of alignment with her self-image; Chris described her life in ways that showed she valued her former, sexy, spontaneous, responsive self and was unhappy to find these qualities disappeared with the advent of children, marriage and career. Her viewing of pornography stemmed from this disappointment. Anthony Giddens' concept of the project of the self could be used to explain her desire to retain some element of that former sexy self but as Nick Crossley suggests in his discussion of gym-going,

> *Contra* Giddens, these agents were not setting out, pro-actively, to construct a particular body or narrative. They were seeking to recover something they had lost, to return to former glory. For the same reason, talk of social norms and ideals is not quite right either. Their concern was more focused upon the contrast between past and present selves and was framed as a personal preference, even if preferences tended to coincide with social norms and ideals. The reference point of the agent was not a social standard, accessed through advertisements, celebrities or some other conduit of common culture, but rather their own past self, as revealed by experiences that effected a contrast.[15]

So, drawing on this, I suggest that for Chris a reason which explains her viewing also justifies her further use of pornography: it is her personal response to the problems of long-term monogamous relationships – the comfort and domesticity, the mundaneity that goes to destroy passion – but it is also one which contributes to the smooth maintenance of her marriage and, by extension, her family.

However, I do not suggest that her sexual-consciousness or motivations for watching porn are simply an appropriation or effect of discourses of 'keeping her man'. Her porn viewing is a response to particular circumstances and a particular reflexive understanding of herself and her body. Chris's motivations could be understood as doubled: watching porn keeps alive her sense of sexual feeling for herself *and* provides a sense of excitement in the midst of the domestic – she uses porn precisely because it fractures the notion of the mundane, the routine, even though her use of it could be understood as routine, watched as if it is daytime TV:

> I like the feeling of being turned on, of feeling sexy, of just… Of having my body feel kind of tingly all day and then there might be sex or not but it doesn't matter whether I … masturbate or if when Paul comes home – I mean when we go to bed, whether we have sex or not because its just a nice feeling, feeling my body.[16]

This seems to me to seriously complicate the claims that porn viewing is entirely tied up in the structural inequalities of heteronormative, patriarchal society. It is important to recognise the very individual personal histories that are intertwined with the sense-making and pleasures of pornography. Pornography may involve processes of learning but why should we believe these are limited to compliance with instructions? Fantasy and imaginative-play clearly have a role to play. Moreover, the motivations Chris outlines make clear that fantasy is not a separate sphere from her 'real' life: it has an organic role, it doesn't dominate her life or skew her perception of 'normal' sex as anti-porn theorising might suggest.

Fantasy offers rich kinaesthetic pleasures firmly allied to Chris's sense of her own body. Chris declared that masturbation was not the key imperative of her porn viewing, rather her interest often lay in *feeling* aroused and the pleasures of a heightened perception of her body throughout the day. This may well be an example of transforming one's 'being in the world', one's sense of embodied self. For Chris, watching porn brings the body back into focus in ways that are positively felt: emotionally, psychically and physically. Her newly re-embodied self moves alongside her motherly, wifely and employee self. In some ways of course, through her discussion of her earlier history as a sexually active woman, she may be suggesting that this embodied self is closer to her 'true' self.[17] These pleasures or possible uses of porn are available to Chris because she puts in the time and effort to view porn, she can discriminate between different forms, she knows what she wants in a film and what films will suit her on a particular day.

161

FIGURE 12.1 Fantasy spaces and everyday actions: active female gratifications in the films of Anna Span

AUTHENTICITY AND THE PROBLEMS OF PORNOGRAPHIC PERFORMANCE

What does it mean to think about porn viewers as discriminating consumers and how do they discriminate between films? Even those commentators who investigate pornography as more than sets of images invading softened minds have a tendency to generalise about individual films, claiming that sex scenes and the sex acts encountered therein are interchangeable. It is simplistic in the extreme, to claim that all porn is the same; for regular viewers there are clearly means by which one chooses between titles, although these are unlikely to be easily accessible to market research! As Angela told me,

> Oh … I do like some of the celebrity stuff – I like the fact I can do two things at once, get the gossip as it were and get turned on! I like the Pammy and Tommy vid, probably for all the same reasons everyone ever says – that it looks like they're in love and all that but it does some really … it's authentic, that's how they were feeling so that's really good. I saw the Paris Hilton thing too but I can't stand how she looks so apart from the interest in seeing what she does in the nude and when she's getting rude, I didn't enjoy that much. Oh god … I watched the Lea one – from *Big Brother* – YUK! That's one thing I don't like is the fake tits – I understand why women might want to do enlargements or whatever but in a movie they just look hideous, when a guy is groping them or whatever, they just move like balloons and the nipples are so stretched you can't believe they have much sensation so I hate that… I do quite like that amateur stuff though, the audition tape stuff and Ben Dover although I get really bored with all the anal – I don't mind watching that but sometimes films just have too much of it and its like … enough already with the arseholes! Do something else![18]

This account is contradictory – the means by which *Pam and Tommy Lee: Stolen Honeymoon* (1998) is judged is only partially applied to the Paris Hilton tape: both are celebrity videos and score on that count, but Hilton's is judged by how she looks and Pam by the 'authenticity' of the performance. The Lea video is found wanting because of her breasts but this is not applied to Pam (also a possessor of enhanced breasts). Anal sex is okay but too much ruins the film.

How then might we assess films for their possible pleasures? For some, the notion of authenticity has been an important device for understanding viewers' pleasures; the claim is that viewers obtain satisfaction from judging whether or not the pleasure they are viewing on screen is *real*. This presents a very interesting problematic – pornography is a form of representation purporting to show real people having real sex but viewers' relations to this element of the real is not straightforward. Viewers clearly understand 'real' sex in multifaceted ways: for example, a number of levels of distinction are employed in Maggie's talk of authenticity.

> I'm not on the scene [BDSM] or anything, no way … I couldn't … I couldn't now – I wish I had before… So really its now just watching and reading about it. I love the

whole play thing, the fact that two people have decided to work together to see how far they can go, just … to go further into your fantasies … An' what I like, what I love to watch is the real … the way people's muscles move, when they're being bound or something an' their eyes close and … the muscles tighten everywhere – in the face, their neck and no-one's saying anything (I like that best) – them just concentrating and you can feel the anticipation … and the tension…[19]

Maggie's relationship with BDSM is vicarious; as a wife and mother she feels she has no way of accessing the lifestyle or scene for herself except through pornography. Her interest in BDSM films was particularly focused on the possibilities of play and of agreeing to explore fantasy. While aware of the very scripted nature of the scenarios she watches on screen, the quotation above demonstrates she also sees these as revealing something 'real' to her. In the theatricality of BDSM – the costumes, the tying up, the silences and slow pacing, the scenarios reveal a truth to her in the unconscious responses of the muscles, the closing eyes and silences as evidence of the surrender of control, the giving up to pleasure. In witnessing this transformation from contract to unconscious response, Maggie can feel the anticipation, the tension and the intimacy of the moment that is being shared on screen – it is real to her.

This pleasure in authenticity was something other women talked about, sometimes in relation to the ways in which pornography can fail to deliver the 'truthful' performance. For example, Judith talked about girl/girl scenes:

I'm not a big fan of girl-on-girl action not 'cos I'm anti lesbian-sex but 'cos the scene just doesn't seem to come from them … the angles are wrong, they kind of do that stretching their bodies up against each other and kissing with lots of tongues but so that you get to see everything, not 'cos they're feeling really passionate. And I think the really made up girls, lots of big hair, red lips all that stuff, they're male fantasies rather than their own, d'y'know what I mean? I suppose I like the actors who are not so fake-looking … and whose performances are not so fake…[20]

While Judith knows that these are *performances* of sexual interaction there is a level of sincerity about the performance she requires for it to 'work'. It may be that what is lacking for her in such scenes is a sense of intimacy in the interaction but its signal failure lies in the bodily performance which is too aware of its audience. Her measure here is of two performance styles – one, the stylised porno girl-on-girl routine and the other, an imagined ideal where women are more interested in each other than in the camera. Chris also talked about the failure in genuine sexual connection:

One thing I wish is that they'd follow the line of sex through – y'know they're showing really hot sex and it seems like its all really them … them losing all their inhibitions and stuff but then it never really goes the whole way. Like in orgy scenes you have a few guys and girls getting it on and of course there's always the girl/girl scene but you never get a boy/boy scene except y'know the double penetration or double anal but y'know if they were really turned on then I think the guys'd start blowing each other or touching each other, even fucking each other and I'd really like to see that. I think it'd be sooo hot...[21]

Thus, the self-claimed excess of pornography – the multiple couplings and the supposed abandon of the orgy scene – can work against viewer pleasure in that it demonstrates pornography's own boundaries and taboos. While what is being performed is 'real' – couples are engaged in sexual interactions – the emotional and sensual real is thwarted by the actors' adherence to the taboo on male/male intercourse. The actors don't test enough boundaries, the film disappoints because it doesn't deliver what it promises. This was something Samantha complained of:

But why I didn't like some of the films was the soft focus stuff, I really don't, where they're pretending it's something more than it really [is]. Where they pretended it wasn't really porn ... more classy than that and I know a lot of that was just to get around the censors but in a way if you're going to go in for watching other people having sex you might as well make it dirty sex that the people on screen are really enjoying...[22]

So authenticity, as required by Samantha and others, is a sense of the performance exceeding its own scripting where the performers appear to go beyond the call of duty (to present 'real' sex) to a spontaneous loss of their professional control in unguarded pleasure. And, in addition, a filmic experience true to the form of pornographic representation, that is not afraid to say this is sex for the pleasure of watching sex. Angela described this ideal:

I like Anna Span films [...] Actually this is going to sound ridiculous but .... I LIKE their clothes! I mean I like their style ... quite funky, nice jewellery and stuff ... and they look like normal everyday people.

The guys are nice looking in a kind of ordinary way ... what's really nice is that the guys smile a lot ... they do lots of eye contact and flirting and stuff and you really feel like they're into each other ... like they're really pleased they've struck lucky with each other... The one I really like has this girl going to the country with her friends and them driving around in a fire engine and then her and this one guy get it on while their friends go for beers or something. I like that one a lot 'cos he smiles ALL the time, its like he can't believe his luck and the other thing is that when he's doing oral on her he keeps looking up at her like he actually wants her to enjoy what he's doing... There's another scene on that vid I like too – where the guy is doing oral and he's pushing his fingers in and out of her too and I dunno... the angle you see from is just good ... that bit always turns me on because he's obviously enjoying what *he's* doing to her and so is she...[23]

FIGURE 12.2 The pleasures of porn performance: authenticity as audience satisfaction in *Anna's Mates*

165

Angela enjoys what might be termed the 'ordinariness' of certain genres of pornography – at one level the pleasure of this film lies in its story, the outline of an emerging relationship that justifies the sexual interaction and the seeming genuineness of the various performances.

But also there's a mundaneity to the storyline that suggests a particular kind of recognition for her: the realness of the sex is allied to a recognition of 'ordinariness' (the jewellery, the clothes, the men are all familiar). Chris appreciated a more overtly 'professional' performance:

> This guy runs flames over the woman's body – fast, mind – and touches … like they do with waxing to calm the nerves … and I think that looks incredibly hot … ha ha… sorry!… um I mean it looks like a really sexy thing to happen but y'know I think about how that might feel; but also know it'll never happen because if I suggested it to Paul and he said yes and we tried it I'd be scared stiff he'd do it wrong and like the guy in the film obviously knows what he's doing – its like watching people in the circus … ha … yeah that's what its like … like its really exciting to watch because it is dangerous because only some people have the nerve for it and the skill to do it… So in a way what I'm saying is that some stuff, that I know other people find disgusting, I can find it fascinating or horny or whatever because they're skilled at it.[24]

Even as they are aware they are watching an 'artificial' performance of sex, viewers can appreciate the performance on a number of levels – if the performers demonstrate a sense of spontaneity, a skilfulness or playfulness, the opportunity of sharing an intimate moment, there is the possibility of the film revealing a genuinely real moment – a truth about the transformative potential of sexual abandon and sensual enjoyment: a sensual enjoyment which is seen on the bodies of the performers and felt in the bodies of the viewers. This pleasure does not have to be straightforwardly transparent to Chris:

> Sometimes though I don't think it has to be about having a good time; I also like stuff where people look a bit trepidatious, like they're worried about what's going on – I think that's why I like *The New Devil in Miss Jones* even though it's a bit cheesy … she's acting all that shyness and stuff but she does it well and then when she has the sex of all kinds you have the feeling that it is a revelation, that she's learning about her body and finding out that she can really feel things. And the fact she's been scared is good for that.[25]

Thus interviewees talked of more complex pleasures coming from particular moments in films which could be 'difficult' to watch, as Samantha explained:

> Y'know there's such a lot of spitting in films now and I can't get my head round why… I mean I know its good to have lots of lubrication when you're having sex and being really wet can feel amazing but … um … um spitting is a horrible habit and sometimes they do it in the films with this real sense that they think its disgusting too and that what they're spitting on is disgusting. And, I don't know how to react to it 'cos sometimes it's just part of a great oral scene and its good and then other times … just makes me want to gag or even worse … I just feel … I feel like … it's kind of degrading … and then I can feel real bad that I was enjoying this 'cos I think that guy hates women … he … uuuugh! And I think who's it for? Is it for lube or is it 'cos everything is dirty … Am I supposed to know she's a … a … slut?
>   *CS: And does that ruin the film for you? That it's horrible to women?*
>   Not always, no … 'Cos lots of women do it too to the guys … it's the spitting that's really horrible … sometimes the way women spit on the guy's dick is just … uuuugh.[26]

For this woman, spitting might be what Martin Barker and Melanie Selfe have called a challenge moment – 'moments of abrasion between points in the film, and cultural and ethical presumptions in viewers'.[27] Challenge moments appear to need reconciliation in terms of plausibility or meaning both within and outside the film. Pleasure in the film seems to be dependent on whether such reconciliation is possible, although Samantha questioned the necessity for this.

> But its interesting, isn't it, that its only in porn where we expect everyone to make clear that they're enjoying it? 'Cos in other kinds of films we can watch people crying

and think yeah this is part of the story, and yes I feel bad for you and stuff, but that it doesn't then ruin the story, it's a part of it. But here in porn, its like you can't have any complications and that you're a bad person if you're watching someone, man or woman, looking like they're having a bit of a hard time. And also, if there's like a kid in an ordinary film, crying 'cos their mum's died or whatever, we don't immediately think that's terrible how could the producers treat that little girl like that, we don't immediately think that distress is for real, but we do in porno.[28]

My own research, and that of others in the field, shows that female consumers of pornography are constantly dogged by questions of harm, subordination, objectification and authenticity and the need to consider women's well-being before their own pleasures in watching or reading pornography – but this may be as much to do with the questions and approaches researchers take. Do researchers construct and determine the socially acceptable or naturally feminine response to pornography? What experiences are we sidelining in our attempts to ensure that the porn consumers we interview are the 'good' ones?

CHAPTER 13

'IF YOU ACHE BENEATH YOUR INTESTINES OR SCREAM SILENTLY IN THE CAVITIES OF YOUR CHEST, THEN THIS PICTURE IS FOR YOU': CURT MCDOWELL'S *THUNDERCRACK!*

Kevin Heffernan

In 1976, over two thousand midnight moviegoers at the Los Angeles International Film Exposition (FILMEX) were treated to a film which a local journalist later described as 'a raunchy, campy epic modelled on early Warhol efforts, those outrageous films starring Divine, the most static passages in *Night of the Living Dead*, and some of James Whale's *The Old Dark House* with a little Tennessee Williams thrown in for leavening'.[1] This 150-minute black-and-white epic, *Thundercrack!* (1975), contained non-simulated hard-core sex, and was written by noted underground filmmaker George Kuchar. The film was directed, photographed and edited by Kuchar's former student, longtime artistic collaborator and lover, the thirty-year-old Curt McDowell. At the film's intermission, half of the audience walked out of the auditorium.

Like the early films of John Waters, *Thundercrack!* is both an eccentric hybrid of several styles and genres of filmmaking and a highly illustrative case study of the rapidly-changing modes of film financing, distribution and exhibition in the mid-1970s. Also, all of these films were conceived by their makers as serious, if highly distinctive, moneymaking entries in the world of commercially-distributed feature filmmaking. But Waters' *Pink Flamingos* (1972) slowly built a word-of-mouth cult following during its long midnight run at the Elgin Theater in New York, while *Thundercrack!* was turned down by Waters' distributor, New Line Cinema, and was to enjoy only sporadic success at midnight screenings at the Roxie in San Francisco and at film festivals. Where the success of *Pink Flamingos* and Waters' subsequent films are a testament to their maker's almost Olympian insights into the relationship between transgression, sentiment and popular taste, the key to both the extraordinary artistic success and notable commercial failure of *Thundercrack!* is found in its dogged refusal to adhere to any coherent set of aesthetic categories or models of spectator engagement and pleasure. Also, the curious tale of *Thundercrack!* is as much a story of changes in the way independent and 'cult' movies were being financed, made and distributed as it is of the eccentricities of McDowell, Kuchar and company, which were considerable.

THE CULT OF CURT

Curt McDowell was born in 1945 in Lafayette, Indiana to 'middle-class teetotalers named Donald and Harriet,' he told *The Advocate* in 1977:

> They were the perfect example of good Christian people with the perfect marriage and three perfect children, and I'm not sure to this day but what they are still the perfect family (sic.). My father always said, 'Son, when you meet the girl that you can't stand to live without, then that's the girl you should marry.' Well, I met him, and moved in with him in the winter of '61, when I was 16. I told my family right away, as I have a passion for honesty, and good Christians that they were, they accepted it.[2]

The young Curt inherited from his mother a passion for family photography and intricately pasted and annotated scrapbooks. He also spent his time singing, writing music and drawing, first designing costumes for his little sister Melinda's dolls, then eventually designing and sewing dresses for Melinda herself, endlessly drawing, painting and photographing the person to whom his diaries repeatedly refer as 'the most beautiful girl in the world'.

Curt enrolled at the San Francisco Art Institute in 1968 on a scholarship in painting and studio art, 'but by the following semester,' he later recalled,

> I was a confirmed filmmaker, stud[ying] with several influential filmmakers there, among them George Kuchar, James Broughton, Gunvor Nelson, Larry Jordan, and Robert Nelson. I was perhaps more prolific than careful and turned out fifteen or more films by the time I received my Master of Fine Arts degree in 1973.[3]

McDowell's early films include *A Visit to Indiana* (1970), *Confessions* (1972) and *Nudes: A*

Sketchbook (1974). Each in its own way documents their maker's yearnings for family, friendship and erotic adventure, and many explicitly acknowledge the contributions of his mentor and lover, George Kuchar.

Kuchar, along with his twin brother Mike, had been one of the most important filmmakers in the 1960s New York underground movie scene. His short films were delirious, overheated parodies of Hollywood melodramas. *Corruption of the Damned* (1965), *Hold Me While I'm Naked* (1966), *Color Me Shameless* (1967) and *House of the White People* (1968) revelled in characters' emotional breakdowns acted out by self-consciously 'bad' actors and helped to define an entire era's Pop Art sensibility and ironic attachment to its cinematic past. Ensconced on the film faculty at the San Francisco Art Institute, George became a tireless and generous catalyst to generations of talented and iconoclastic filmmakers, none more iconoclastic than the satiric and satirical McDowell, whose Rabelaisian celebration of the carnal clashed head-on with the dour and paranoid artistic sensibilities of Kuchar.

Curt's diaries from this period (and later) are filled with detailed accounts of his cruising adventures and amorous exploits, which fuelled his never-ending curiosity and creativity. In alimentary imagery cut from the same cloth as *Thundercrack!*'s screenplay, Kuchar later recalled that McDowell

> was generous enough to share those memories with his audience, giving them what they secretly craved. The beefcake and cheesecake he dished out pumped blood into flaccid extremities, oozing life onto raincoat hidden laps. He believed in sex as a thing of celebration and many of his parties took on a wild flavor as he licked the candy canes of the revellers, lapping up cream-filled Ding Dongs while all the time guiding his own sensing organs into areas of dark delight and fudge encrusted wonders.[4]

In 1972, a year in which McDowell would complete no fewer than eight short personal films, he and his friend and collaborator, Mark Ellinger, formed Liberty 5 Productions to produce the sixty-minute commercial pornographic feature *Lunch* for a budget of $36,000, most of which was deferred and eventually covered by the film's distributor, Unique Films. McDowell's only feature film shot in colour, *Lunch* recounts the sexual goings-on in a San Francisco apartment complex and centres on the character of Gloria, played by the gloriously-named Velvet Busch, who is almost obsessively focused on the pleasures of fellatio. Ellinger contributed the musical score and a notable cum shot in his role as 'Dave Powers', and the movie played 16mm storefront porno houses for three years, yielding Ellinger and McDowell total producers' shares of almost $10,000 apiece. The cheques arriving from Unique over this period enabled McDowell to cover some of his living expenses through the period of *Thundercrack!*'s writing and preproduction.[5]

The idea for *Thundercrack!*'s story came from discussions between Mark and Curt, who imagined a horror-porno-comedy which could be both a moneymaking proposition and a transitional work from the purely commercial *Lunch* to more eccentric and personal projects.

In April 1974, the two sat on the steps of a park on Hyde Street and 'worked out the general plot: one night in a thunderstorm, eight people thrown together by fate'.[6] Kuchar acknowledged that the script he gave to Curt in early June had taken the movie in a completely new direction, recalling years later that Curt 'thought of sex as sort of celebration or joyful union of things, and I always looked at it as a horror in people's lives full of obsessions and stuff that they can't control, and therefore the script was sort of colored in that direction'.[7] This was to be the glorious alchemy at the heart of *Thundercrack!*: Kuchar's anxieties and phobias would push classical horror movie conventions to the fore, while McDowell's love of pansexual carnivalesque celebrate the very transgressions from which the classical horror film recoiled in revolted fascination.

(THUNDER)CRACKING THE CINEMATIC CODE

Thundercrack!'s convoluted and overwrought narrative concerns eight people who seek shelter from a thunderstorm in an isolated Nebraska farmhouse owned by the insane and alcoholic widow Mrs. Gert Hammond. The tweedy, pipe-smoking Chandler has picked up a hitchhiker, Bond, a working-class stud who senses both attraction and hostility from his host. Meanwhile, lesbian couple Roo and Sash pick up hitchhiker Toydy and his crate of stolen bananas. When Roo reaches into the back seat and grabs Toydy's crotch, a jealous Sash grabs the wheel and the

FIGURE 13.1 *Thundercrack!*(ing) cult cinema: McDowell creating the controversial classic

car crashes off the road. In the other car, Chandler grabs Bond's crotch just as Wilene Cassidy knocks on the window to offer them autographed pictures of her husband, country singer Simon Cassidy. While Chandler and Bond go to investigate the explosion from the other car, Wilene walks to Gert's foreboding mansion, Prairie Blossom, to ask to use the phone. Chandler and Bond arrive with the three survivors of the crash, and Gert invites them all to change clothes and stay for supper.

In the night which follows, all of the guests change clothes in what the script calls the 'lewd bedroom', the room which had belonged to Gert's son Gerald, who 'no longer exists'. While they change (and play with the many sex toys which litter the room, along with walls covered with porn), Gert watches them from a peephole and masturbates with a peeled cucumber. Sash and Chandler go down to the basement to get a bottle of wine for dinner and act out a cross-dressed male hustler scenario set in a bus depot which ends with Chandler making love with Sash nude in the missionary position and achieving orgasm all over her to their shared delight. Toydy comes on to Gert in the kitchen and is ready to sodomise her using bacon grease as lube when his cruel insults send her into a rage and she nearly castrates him with a meat cleaver. The virile Bond easily seduces the naïve Wilene, and the two fall in love. Soon afterward, Toydy takes Bond aside and offers to exchange his hidden crate of bananas for Bond's ass.

As the story progresses, each character reveals a hidden trauma or shameful secret. Gert's husband had been devoured by locusts and is pickled in a jar in the basement. Chandler's wife,

FIGURE 13.2 Cast and crew discuss sexually subversive strategies on the set of *Thundercrack!*

lingerie heiress Sarah Lou Phillips, had died when her girdle caught fire, and the trauma has left him impotent. Finally, the deranged circus driver Bing arrives after crashing his animal truck in a suicide attempt. He reveals that he is hopelessly in love with the female circus gorilla Medusa and that the two are sexually involved. The escaped gorilla is crazed with lust and rage. And Gerald is not dead, but hidden behind a locked door, an insatiable monster with enormous distended testicles which hang to the floor. Medusa breaks through the front door, and Bing leads her to the back bedroom, dressed in Gert's wedding dress, while everyone makes their escape. When Roo and Toydy open the locked door hoping to find a family fortune, a hideously disfigured Gerald staggers out of the darkness, and Gert pushes the two interlopers into Gerald's cell and locks the door. The movie's dénouement signals a deeply ironic 'return to normality' featuring three heterosexual couples. Bond and Wilene drive off together, Chandler and Sash turn their car away from Waco, Texas and Chandler's plan of setting fire to the girdle factory, and Gert opens the jar containing Charlie's remains, pours a glass of whisky into it, and invites him to join her in a toast.

FUNDING FLESH: THE PRODUCTION CONTEXTS OF *THUNDERCRACK!*

Who could McDowell and Kuchar persuade to invest in such an idea? How about the same people who devised the fast-food 'value combo' of flame-broiled hamburger, fries and a coke for 40 cents in Indiana in the 1950s? San Francisco residents John and Charles Thomas were sons of Burger Chef chain founder Frank Thomas, who had sold the company to General Foods in 1969, placing the young Thomas brothers in a position to serve as patrons of the arts. Furthermore, tax shelter laws in 1974 enabled investors to put up as little as 25% of a film's budget in cash and take an investment credit on the full 100% of that movie's total cost. This enabled an investor in a modest feature film to wipe out taxes on tens, perhaps hundreds of thousands of dollars of non-movie income.

The Thomas brothers, present on the fringes of the San Francisco bohemian community, knew Curt McDowell through mutual friends at the Art Institute and were excited to invest in an iconoclastic underground horror-comedy-porno film and to use the commercial potential of distributing such a film under the banner of their newly-formed Thomas Brothers Studio as a springboard for other projects. In 1975, John and Charles Thomas put up $4,500 apiece for 50% ownership of Thundercrack Ltd., a California limited partnership of which they each owned 25%. The other 25% interests were owned by Kuchar and McDowell.[8] Then, in late September, two of the most crucial pieces of the *Thundercrack!* puzzle fell into place: Curt went on unemployment, and Melinda permanently moved to San Francisco from Indiana.

The relationship between Curt McDowell and his sister Melinda is one of the most distinctive artistic collaborations in all of independent cinema. Since his earliest creative expressions drawing cartoons and writing songs, his baby sister had been his constant muse and closest confidante. It was Melinda to whom a tearful-eyed Curt came out as 'queer' at age 16 when Melinda was nine years old, and Curt's scrapbooks are full of photographs he took

173

of Melinda looking up from children's books, standing in Yosemite with flowers in her hair, or glowing in high-contrast black and white photographs emphasising her wide, round eyes. To Curt, this idealised and protective view of his little sister Melinda was reinforced rather than compromised by his celebration of her adult sexuality in both his films and their adventures together in the clubs and bath houses of San Francisco. It was in the person of his beloved sister that the two worlds of Curt McDowell, the security of his Indiana home and the sexual freedom of San Francisco, found their deeply longed-for unity.

With George's *Thundercrack!* script in hand, Curt and assistant director Margo O'Connor began scouting locations, scouring the city for props and casting the film. The role of the gentle and childlike Sash immediately went to Melinda. The professional porn actor Ken Scudder, who was dating Melinda at the time, auditioned for the role of Toydy, but that role eventually went to a local portrait artist, Rick Johnson, who Curt was excited to find was 'a true bisexual' and capable of performing passionately and uninhibitedly with both male and female cast members. Ken was then assigned the role of the rough-trade hitchhiker Bond, and Maggie Pyle won the role of the initially-naïve Wilene. The foul-mouthed and constantly scowling Roo was played by local actress Moira Benson, and George Kuchar (who applied the actresses' makeup up under the *nom d'ecran* 'Mr. Dominic'), agreed to play the role of the demented circus driver Bing. Curt himself played the sexual monster Gerald, the source of his mother's shame and possessed of insatiable appetite and balls which hang to the floor.

Another young actor answering the casting call was Phil Heffernan, who had just finished producing a 16mm character-driven porn feature entitled *Sip the Wine* (Dan Caldwell, 1976). His audition and screen test landed him the role of the conflicted and neurotic Chandler (he was billed in the film's credits as 'Mookie Blodgett', originally a screen name devised by Curt and George for Moira Benson). Heffernan's other contribution to *Thundercrack!* was bringing the casting call to the attention of his leading lady in *Sip the Wine*, Marion Eaton, who read for the role of Mrs. Gert Hammond. Before performing in *Sip the Wine*, the 45-year-old Eaton was an actress with a long list of roles in community theatre and independent drama productions including Desdemona in *Othello* and, importantly for her role as Gert, Maggie in Tennessee Williams' *Cat on a Hot Tin Roof.*

Although no fan of conventional porn films, Eaton was outspoken in her defence of on-camera sex as a legitimate part of the actor's craft, likening scenes of explicit sexuality to 'emotional arias' which can grow out of an actor's embodiment of the character.[9] In Marion Eaton, Curt had found an actress able to anchor the film's wildly divergent narrative lines and emotional registers with a performance wholly consonant with prevailing norms of virtuosity and professionalism. Gert's fragile façade of gentility set gingerly atop a boiling cauldron of loneliness and rage both elicits genuine audience sympathy and sets the movie in the tradition of 'menopausal horror' exemplified by *What Ever Happened to Baby Jane* (Robert Aldrich, 1962) and *Hush... Hush Sweet Charlotte* (Robert Aldrich, 1964). In short, the casting of Marion Eaton in *Thundercrack!* would be McDowell's big score. The movie would ultimately belong to her.

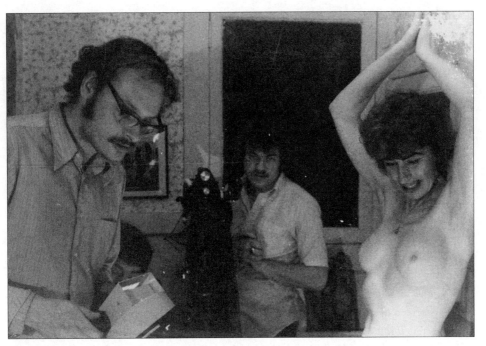

FIGURE 13.3 Eaton's ecstasy: Marion on the set of *Thundercrack!* with George Kuchar and Curt McDowell

SHOOTING SEX: THE CULT SKIN FLICK TAKES SHAPE

Shooting for *Thundercrack!* began in early March in Charles Thomas's house, which doubled for the Prairie Blossom farmhouse. The first scenes McDowell shot were the crucial explicit sex scenes which punctuate the story: on the first day, Melinda and Phil enacted Sash's basement seduction of Chandler. For the remainder of the week, the cast and crew worked on the explicit scenes, including the 'lewd bedroom' scenes of masturbation, Bond's hallway encounter with Roo, and Bond's deflowering of Wilene. The following week, Curt shot most of the living room scenes and the volcanic sex scene between Toydy and Bond with Chandler seated at bedside.[10] A major asset to the production was the speed, style and efficiency of Kuchar's lighting design and execution. The living room scenes feature bold, expressionist striated patterns of light, and the high-key lighting of the sex between Bond and Toydy emphasises the finely-toned muscles on the actors' bodies and the glistening and dripping sweat which convey the heat and passion of Bond's first receptive anal experience.

By the end of the second week, the shoot was picking up speed, and the actors, particularly Marion, were nailing their lines and hitting their marks on the first take. One exception was Maggie Pyle, who was showing up drunk to the shoot every day, blowing her lines, and spending her down time passed out in an upstairs bedroom 'just like Hollywood', an angry McDowell notes in his diary.[11] Fed up with her unprofessionalism, Curt and Marion exacted revenge: 'Returned to do the Wilene eats the cucumber scene,' he notes on March 14. 'I laughed so hard

I actually wasn't looking through the camera. Wilene, unknowingly, ate the very cucumber Gert had up her coozie two days ago. Everyone kept a straight face but me.'[12]

For the next six months, McDowell worked on post-production. A rough cut was ready by May,[13] and filming of the flashbacks began in July.[14] In August, George consented 'to show his pecker in the flashback,'[15] and the following week, Margo O'Connor set aside the gorilla costume (she had played Medusa in many scenes under the name 'Pamela Primate') so Curt could don the fur, turn the camera over to Mark, and 'shoot a scene that ought to go down in history: George (as "Bing") being masturbated to climax by the Gorilla! (an all-time first!)'.[16] Ellinger provided the needed music cues as the final cut took shape, and Curt sent the elements to Leo Diners film lab to make the answer print just in time for George, Curt and Melinda to take a happy Christmas vacation to Indiana.

The film that emerged from Leo Diners in the last days of 1975 contains almost every imaginable element of sensational spectacle while self-consciously subverting any coherent framework needed for these elements to appeal to either a genre audience or the various sub-cultures which constituted the mid-1970s audience for the cult film. The first twenty minutes of the movie is a high-camp parody of the 'old dark house' horror thriller, complete with a thunderstorm, a diverse group of stranded travellers, and an isolated house hiding a shameful family secret. *The Old Dark House* (1932), directed by James Whale and featuring Boris Karloff and a colourful gallery of Hollywood's closeted (and not so closeted) gay, lesbian and bisexual character actors, provides the most obvious source, complete with its bolted inner sanctum containing the insane and pyromaniacal Saul Femm, the progenitor of *Thundercrack!*'s Gerald Hammond. The assembled travellers bare their neuroses, some coming to horrible ends, until the family evil is vanquished and the new heterosexual couple of Roger Penderel (Melvyn Douglas) and Margaret Waverton (Gloria Stuart) leave the following sun-drenched morning, signalling the movie's return to 'normality'. *Thundercrack!* extends its parallels to *The Old Dark House* in the retribution meted out to Toydy and Roo, who use their sexuality to manipulate others and gain money, power or access to the hidden secrets of Prairie Blossom and are punished by their perpetual imprisonment with the deformed and insatiable Gerald.

And then there's the porn. The use of explicit sex in *Thundercrack!* is suffused with McDowell's characteristic combination of knowing irony and rapt erotic fascination. First, the porn elements in the movie are constantly colliding head-on with the basic opposition between the Normal and the Monstrous which is at the heart of the classical horror film. In films such as *Dracula* (Tod Browning, 1931), *Dr. Jekyll and Mr. Hyde* (Rouben Mamoulian, 1932) and *The Old Dark House*, monsters are the figures which threaten the stable, safe world of monogamous heterosexual desire. It is the eruption of a transgressive sexuality, usually an inverted mirror image of the world of white Christian monogamous heterosexuality, which is at the heart of the classical horror film's phobic imaginings, and it is the defeat of the monster and the return to a heteronormative sexual economy which resolves the film's narrative. Porn, on the other hand, imagines the normal world as oppressive, exhausting, and numbing, and the release of the characters into an experimental 'pornotopia' of abundance, energy and pleasure enables

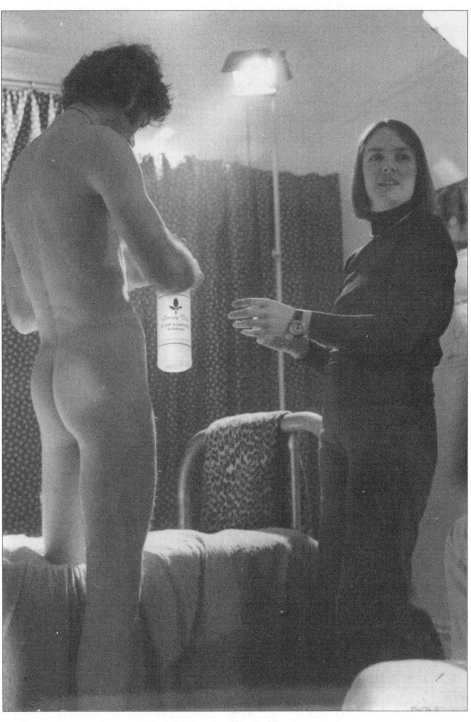

FIGURE 13.4 Porno productions: Melinda McDowell and Ken Sudder rehearse on the set

them, in the classical 1970s phase of the porn narrative anyway, to return to the normal world transformed and regenerated.[17]

But it is not merely in the deep structures of the horror and porn genres that *Thundercrack!* exhibits its delirious incoherence. The movie's classical horror elements are also its most deliberately anachronistic, from the black-and-white cinematography to the special effects, musical score and dialogue. It is difficult to reconcile the swaying twigs standing in for trees in a thunderstorm, the milk poured into an aquarium to signal roiling clouds, and swarms of murderous locusts played by coffee beans thrown onto the actors with the obviously unfaked close-ups of bodies and organs grinding together, eventually displaying their unruly physicality as sweat, saliva, semen and K-Y jelly glisten under George Kuchar's Colortran lights. Also, Mark Ellinger's musical score studiously avoids the 'wakka chikka wakka chikka' pelvic rhythms of most (library) porn scores and instead substitutes horror film cues and other jarring themes to the scenes of sexual union. Some of the masturbation scenes in the lewd bedroom are scored to a sprightly boogie woogie theme, changing to a waltz with each cut-in to the voyeuristic Gert. Roo's masturbation with the enormous dildo is scored to a fairground calliope waltz, and Sash's appearance in the lewd bedroom (she does not play with the sex toys, but instead makes childlike faces at a wooden handpuppet while making it dance) and her sex scene with Chandler are scored with a lyrical love theme so melodic that the first time Mark played it for Curt in post-production, he 'almost cried, it was so beautiful'.[18] The only scene in *Thundercrack!* scored in traditional 'porn' style is the topping of Bond by Toydy, which is accompanied by pounding drums and searing guitar licks.

But it is in its dialogue that *Thundercrack!* most humorously (and subversively) undercuts the aesthetic norms of the porn genre. Film pornography's florid erolalia, or sex talk, is one of its most immediately recognised and frequently parodied features. *Thundercrack!*, on the other hand, extends the Production Code-era indirect and metaphorical descriptions of sexuality characteristic of the classical horror film into the explicit scenes and allows the characters to declaim long speeches while engaged in every imaginable sexual act.

Although the sex dialogue in *Thundercrack!* makes use of many hilarious metaphors, it is in the obsession with food that Kuchar's screenplay provides its most sustained and hilarious parody of Production Code discretion in the discussion of sexual matters. The mostly-consumed remains of Charlie Hammond, pickled in a jar, find their correlative in the unpickled cucumbers with which Gert relieves her loneliness. The frustrated Gert is paralleled by the rage-filled Medusa, who craves similarly phallic-shaped bananas to assuage her angry guts. At times, the Production Code seems to have taken a detour through a seventh-grade boys' locker room. In the lewd bedroom, Toydy grabs Sash's breasts from behind while announcing, 'I heard this was melon season, and now I believe it,' and he later bends Gert over the kitchen counter to sodomise her because she reminds him of 'something Greek, like a nice piece of shish kebab meat'. Roo's later hallway fellating of Bond is described in terms of frankfurters, mustard and ketchup, and, getting Toydy in the identical situation, she sneeringly demands his 'cream gravy' to go on her 'boiled tongue' and 'baked potatoes … with the jackets on 'em.'

Pangs of hunger, shudders of fear and spasms of pleasure are locked in a titanic struggle for 150 minutes. *Thundercrack!* careens so wildly between these different registers of ecstasy that the ultimate audience reaction is another bodily convulsion; raucous laughter. Kuchar's tongue-in-cheek allusion to the bodily immediacy of genre cinema in the movie's trailer could very well state the irreducible nature of *Thundercrack!*'s appeal as horror, porn, melodrama and comedy: 'If you ache beneath your intestines, or scream silently in the cavities of your chest, then this picture is for you!'

ROGUE RECEPTIONS

So who *was* this picture for? On 29 December, the film had its world premiere at Anthology Film Archives in New York. Anthology, conceived, built and run by Lithuanian-born Jonas Mekas, tireless connoisseur, promoter and impresario of experimental cinema, was the ideal venue for introducing the movie to the New York experimental film community, of which George Kuchar was an emeritus member. McDowell notes in his diary that 'It was sold out even though it wasn't advertised… The film looked great to me and went over so well, that I was ecstatic (all sorts of stick-in-the-muds who normally would walk out stayed for the whole thing).'[19] Then, in January, Charles Thomas screened the movie for Mel Novikoff, an important San Francisco exhibitor and film festival organiser whose West Coast Surf Theater Chain would later form the basis for the national Landmark circuit of art theatres. Unlike New York's Ben Barenholz, who had responded favourably to Waters' *Pink Flamingos* and booked it into his Elgin Theater for weekly midnight screenings and allowed it to slowly build a reputation, Novikoff walked out of the screening of *Thundercrack!* before it even got warmed up with its lewd bedroom scenes.[20]

Later that month, the Thundercrack Ltd partners were delighted to learn that the movie had been accepted at FILMEX. Not only would this be a prestigious high-profile event, it could also lead to a distribution deal if the screening went well, much as later independent filmmakers hoped that acceptance into Sundance would bring their movies into contact with willing distributors. According to Kuchar, the pre-screening committee at FILMEX had wanted to reject the movie out of hand before they had even watchedit. But one of the jurors, screenwriter and actor Buck Henry, told them that without *Thundercrack!* on the 1976 FILMEX programme, he would not participate in the event.[21] McDowell's diary reports that

> the show was like a dream, and the response was so overwhelming that I couldn't have asked for more… At the end, [festival hosts] invited me to get up and talk, and I felt the orgasm of applause… I was thrilled to death that Marion received a standing ovation (I know she was ecstatic).[22]

Unfortunately, McDowell did not leave FILMEX with any offers to distribute the film, but *Thundercrack!* did receive its first round of critical notices soon after its FILMEX premiere.

The reviewer for *Daily Variety* lambasted the movie's 'poor sound quality, amateurish acting, and interminable gab between the sex scenes [which] make the 150-minute running time an ordeal' and noted that 'Curt McDowell takes blame for direction, lensing, and editing' but praised Kuchar's lighting and Ellinger's score.[23] Other reviewers found the movie's pansexual subtext fascinating, troubling or both. Todd McCarthy, writing for *The Hollywood Reporter*, noted that 'masturbation and heterosexuality dominate up to a certain point, until finally the homosexual streak running through the picture resolves itself in a genuinely effective gay hard-core scene which is carefully photographed and effectively scored'.[24] Over a year later, Joseph Michaels, writing in *The Advocate*, would opine, 'gay this film ain't, and hardly erotic … by the end of the film, all the characters have realigned themselves into male/female couples'; for Michaels, the hetero porn elements cancelled out the horror motifs, making the movie's ironic ending a cop-out rather than a send-up.[25] Just a couple of months before Michaels' review appeared in *The Advocate*, Curt used that magazine's pages to note with some irritation:

> As far as the gay culture's attitude towards me: I think they're confused. They like my humor and vision of men, but they only like my women if they're all made up and caricatures… But I hate classes and categories, except as interesting subjects for film. It's far too limiting to latch onto a single group and dedicate yourself to a community that might as well as have walls around it. How can you possibly grow if you do that.[26]

Attempting to book *Thundercrack!* into commercial hard-core theatres was a fool's errand. With a black-and-white movie which dispenses of its sex scenes with maximum efficiency in order to get to its next long character monologue, which is too gay to be straight porn and too hetero to be gay porn, *Thundercrack!*'s only market niche appeared to be the midnight cult circuit which had been so kind to John Waters' *Pink Flamingos* and *Female Trouble* (1974). But here the movie's length hamstrung exhibitors: even a stoned youthful audience of urban ne'-er-do-wells would face exhaustion at the end of a 150-minute movie, and that's not counting trailers for coming attractions and the inevitable cartoon. Still, stimulated by the notoriety of its Anthology and FILMEX coastal premieres and buoyed by its success at the Seattle Film Festival, a positive review in *Sight and Sound*, and a run at San Francisco's Roxie Cinema, *Thundercrack!* brought in $5,000 in rentals in 1976.[27] The word-of-mouth increase in interest which had accrued to *Pink Flamingos* never attached itself to *Thundercrack!*, however. The following year only brought $3,200 in rentals for the film.[28]

Since *Thundercrack*'s two-and-a-half-hour running time was becoming a liability in securing midnight bookings for the film, the situation which all agreed was ideal to allow word of the movie to spread to an audience; in early 1977 Curt prepared a shorter 110-minute version to submit to New Line Cinema. John Thomas had written to McDowell six weeks earlier stating that Waters had told the Thomas Brothers that 'New Line was really the only company and/or the best company to handle' the movie and that he had been treated fairly and paid well by New Line.[29] But the 70/30 deal proposed by New Line in 1978 never came to pass, and dealings between Curt and John and Charles became increasingly strained. Even before the New Line deal soured, George Kuchar became disillusioned with the in-fighting between the general partners and the artistic compromises represented by the shortened version of the movie and withdrew himself from the partnership, seemingly on the eve of a potentially lucrative deal with New Line. In a letter to Curt's legal advisor Robert Brandes, Kuchar asks that publicity and advertising for the film list him only as an actor in the film 'since the picture makes less sense that it originally did [and] I don't want the fact that I wrote it played up big in their advertising'.[30]

Since the partnership had withdrawn the film from circulation for much of 1978 in anticipation of the New Line deal, that year's film rentals amounted to a paltry $800.[31] By 1980, McDowell had enlisted the services of veteran film booker Anita Monga to distribute the short version of *Thundercrack!* under the rubric of Taboo Films, but this was largely a shell company to hide the fact that Curt was essentially self-distributing the film with Monga serving as booking agent. The one-off Taboo engagements of the movie over the next two years would bear a greater resemblance to the non-theatrical bookings of Curt's short films through Canyon Cinema Cooperative than to the commercial distribution of a feature film.

THUNDERCRACK! AND BEYOND

The devolution of *Thundercrack*'s commercial prospects, depressing enough in itself, was particularly painful to McDowell since the entire enterprise had been conceived to make money to finance more personal projects. Shortly after completing editing on *Thundercrack!*, Curt began a project which would eventually be his ultimate love letter to Melinda, *Sparkle's Tavern* (1985),[32] but in early 1976, John Thomas told Curt that the money for the new project was not forthcoming.[33] The reason for this would become apparent later in the year, when revisions to the Internal Revenue Code limited tax deductions to motion picture investors to the amount at risk.[34] Despite these setbacks, McDowell shot *Sparkle's Tavern* throughout late 1976, deferring huge parts of the budget to keep the project going. McDowell was indefatigable in his efforts to secure completion financing for the project, applying for an American Film Institute Independent Filmmaker Program grant in 1978 as well as a National Endowment for the Arts grant to finance the post-production and release prints of *Sparkle's Tavern*, but his applications were denied. It was not until late 1984 that Curt would finish post-production on *Sparkle's Tavern* courtesy of a loan of more than $10,000 from Marion Eaton and her spouse Bill Feeney. Curt was diagnosed with AIDS just two years later, and he passed away the following year, on 3 June 1987.

In one of the bitterest ironies in this tale of McDowell's cursed and brilliant film, Curt died at precisely the moment that many eccentric filmmakers found an entirely new source of financing and distribution for their work in the expanding market of home video. Companies such as Island Records, Vestron Video and RCA Columbia Home Entertainment began to finance first dozens, then hundreds of feature films, and holy fools of filmmaking silent for years such as Ken Russell, Nicholas Roeg and John Waters found themselves back in the director's chair with multi-picture deals. Also, a New Queer Cinema emerged as home video cultivated profitable niche markets with carefully calculated production budgets and videocassette price points. Filmmakers such as Todd Haynes, Gus Van Sant, Greg Araki and Rose Troche used the money from video presales to finance a queer cinema in a queer voice. Canada's Bruce La Bruce, whose highly idiosyncratic films such as *No Skin Off My Ass* (1991) and *Super 8½* (1993) integrated hard-core sex scenes with trenchant observations on the foibles of queer culture, followed in the footsteps of McDowell. These and other descendants of Curt McDowell would soldier on in the absence of their advance scout, and every salvo of explicit sexuality they discharged could not help but invite comparison to *Thundercrack!*, which in the words of the movie's original FILMEX programme notes, had 'created a new motion picture genre, a transcendent, meta-porno flick which elevates the viewer to hitherto undreamed of heights of salacious consciousness'.[35]

Author's note

Since the financial collapse of the Curt McDowell Foundation in the late 1990s, Melinda McDowell has been the sole custodian of all of Curt's papers, diaries, films, and financial records. Unless otherwise noted, all of the citations given are taken from Curt McDowell's diaries and scrapbooks. For this reason, some bibliographic details such as dates and page numbers from long-discontinued local and countercultural newspapers and non-indexed newspapers and trade journals have been impossible to recover.

CHAPTER 14
'LET'S DO SOMETHING YOU WON'T ENJOY': DOMINATRIX PORN, PERFORMANCE AND SUBJECTIVITY

Jenny Barrett

The concern of this chapter is to analyse the representation of the dominatrix in sadomasochistic pornography from Britain and America, identifying a complex interplay of performances by the dominatrix and the implications for female subjectivity. British S/M porn frequently falls into the 'amateur sadomasochism' category as described by Linda Williams which owns a stronger sense of the 'real' than the 'aesthetic sadomasochism' of films such as *The Punishment of Anne* (aka *The Image*, Radley Metzger, 1979).[1] Stylistically, it tends towards a documentary-look owing to its often low production values. Its performers are varied in age and looks, and have an overwhelming sense of the boy-, girl- or dominatrix-next-door, in contrast to the apparent glamour of American S/M porn. Stylistically, American S/M on video often has relatively high production values, dedicated 'film sets' and props, and frequently stars female porn performers who are youthful, attractive, with perfectly applied make-up, coiffed hair, false nails and false breasts.

The profusion of movies coming from one particular production venture in Britain,

DOM Promotions, accounts for a particular style and cueing of expectations that places this dominatrix porn aesthetically somewhere between American S/M and European S/M (often hailing from Germany or Holland and typically more hard-core). British dominatrix porn plays towards the glamour of the dominatrix on one hand and the spectacle of the activity on the other, whilst signalling that this woman might have time for 'you' in her diary, placing the British dominatrix, perhaps more than any other, at a border that is becoming increasingly central to debates on representations of tough and violent women in popular culture: on the border between subject and object.

A LABYRINTH OF PERFORMANCES

The overwhelming mode and essence of dominatrix porn, possibly more than any other pornography, is performance. This works at many levels and it would be useful to explore some of these to demonstrate how multi-faceted the performance truly is and how the dominatrix features within it. Arguably the most obvious is the narrative of the pornographic episode, the scenario, in which are found the dominant woman and the submissive, possibly also other actants such as a second submissive who may be permitted to aid the dominatrix in her work (contrary to some writing on S/M porn there is a fairly strong female submissive presence in many of these movies).[2] Toughness, a trait that we might attribute to the dominatrix and which has been discussed in relation to tough female characters in films and TV by Sherrie A. Inness, can be regarded as a performance. Inness implies the performative nature of toughness when she writes that 'clothing is an important element in the performance of toughness because it serves as a visual reminder that a woman has distanced herself from femininity'.[3] Costume is discussed below, but the key point to take from this is that the tough woman is understood here as a performing woman. Furthermore, sadomasochistic behaviour is often regarded as performative, even theatrical, with its conventionalised characters, scenarios, props and so on. Valerie Steele in her study of fetish costuming describes the sadomasochistic scenario as 'an elaborate erotic drama' containing 'ritualized sexual performances'.[4] Connie Shortes similarly describes S/M as 'a fantastic, erotically charged tableau in which the dynamics of dominance and submission are performed'.[5] Linda Williams draws attention to the complexity of sadomasochistic porn when she argues that S/M behaviour is made up of 'acts' that in reality affect the submissive's body, 'yet they can also be acts in the theatrical sense of shows performed for oneself or others'.[6] In dominatrix porn this is certainly the case with the added likelihood of some hard-core sexual activity as part of the dramatic performance. Frequently the scene will be set instantly through *mise-en-scène*, physical relations on-screen and dialogue. Punishment may proceed immediately, then reasons for the punishment are raised, the punishment proceeds, sometimes in several episodes, and the scenario eventually ends, frequently punctuated with the departure of the dominatrix from the room leaving the submissive alone to contemplate the events that have just taken place.

This simple narrative trajectory tends to omit the action that led to the submissive's punishment; the crime is not important to see since the purpose of the scenario is the acting out of punishment, but it can be virtually anything from playing with Mistress's doll (*Busty Bondage Lesbians*, Sunset Media, 2004), enjoying a punishment too much ('You're enjoying that too much! Let's do something you won't enjoy' – *Mistress Smoke*, DOM Promotions, 2008), failing in a duty ('You know why I'm spanking you? Because you didn't put enough sugar in my tea this morning' – *Mistress Smoke*), or even betraying the Mistress by visiting another dominatrix across town (*Asphyxiation 69: Desires of a Dominatrix 5*, Bizarre Video, 2006). Generally speaking the crimes are trivial and not in keeping with the severity of the punishment, which introduces a sense of the absurd and vaguely humourous into the narrative. How, for example, does a female submissive whose crime is being a 'whore' learn her lesson by performing fellatio on the Mistress's strap-on, then being penetrated after her vaginal lips have been clamped with plastic pegs? As incongruous as the link between crime and punishment may be, it is often referred to by the dominatrix throughout the punishment by way of consistently justifying her actions. She will also consistently apply a label or name that seems spontaneously chosen at the beginning of the scenario, one that reinforces her dominant relation to her submissive through humiliating insinuations: cockroach, little piggy, doggy, little boy, little girl, little dolly, Barbie, bitch, whore, slave, subby girl.

The implicit narrative that lies behind the scenario performed on-screen is that this woman lives her life fulfilling her responsibility to teach naughty people a lesson. She labours constantly to show them the error of their ways. This is, as much as is the enacted scenario, a central dynamic of the dominatrix's performance: to labour in her necessary role. It is, of course, all a game, a masquerade, one that is perfectly understood by those involved, since what she truly serves is a range of physical and psychological desires in the submissive and the viewer (and arguably in herself also), and it is in this that she labours on-screen throughout the length of the performance. Not only does she work to make sure that the camera is able to capture the most desirable view of the action (in common with pornography and most mainstream narrative media), but she also demonstrates a great deal of effort to enact a range of physical and mental punishments. The dominatrix of *Mistress Gemma's London Dungeon* (DOM Promotions, 2008), like many others, moves from one activity to the next, from the application of restraints, to a period of partial asphyxiation, to the insertion of an electric butt-plug, pegs on the testicles, flogging the genitals and blowing smoke into the tube attached to the submissive's gimp mask, regularly engaging him in dialogue concerning his crimes, his pain and the condition of his genitals. She is rarely ever stationary, she is almost constantly in motion, often off-screen selecting a new implement from her array of sadistic paraphernalia. She works hard to maintain and gradually amplify the level of torture to a climax of multiple, simultaneous punishments across the submissive's body. She is, thus, a working girl, a woman whose work is never complete because people just keep on being naughty.

This level of performance, of the woman on-screen performing as a dominatrix, is further complicated when she is a professional dominatrix in her actual career. DOM Promotions' 'Live from the Mistress' Dungeon' series goes to great lengths on the DVD boxes and at the

185

beginning of the movies to alert the customer/viewer to the 'genuine' nature of the material and its participants. 'Warning!' the DVD box proclaims. 'This movie was filmed in a real Dungeon. *Not* to be confused with inferior quality productions!' – the allegation clearly being that 'staged' S/M movies featuring porn performers are not the real thing. The movies begin with a notice stating that 'all participants were given a safe-word or signal which they could exercise at any point to halt the proceedings'. The message is that this is real sadomasochism, the dominatrix is a professional, she really knows what she is doing, and for the British viewer at least she is attainable, reachable, being in London, or as with Mistress Smoke, easy to contact because her mobile number is provided inside the DVD box together with her opening hours at her dungeon in Swindon. So the labyrinth of performances evolves. Not only is a scenario and a stereotypical role performed, but a real dominatrix performs her job in a space that itself performs as a 'dungeon', which is not a real dungeon at all, simply a space that is given that name in the enactment of rule-based sadomasochistic games.

With so many of the activities having an overt sexual aspect to them, such as the insertion of a butt-plug, fisting, penetration with a strap-on, nipple torture and so forth, not to mention the sexual nature of the dominant/submissive scenario, the sexual performance of the dominatrix is important to consider. Moving image pornography, by Williams' definition, is distinguished by its 'element of performance contained in the term *sexual act*'.[7] Albeit non-simulated sex, it is still performed by actors serving a pre-established scenario. The dominatrix herself never submits sexually to her submissive, but often engages in sexual behaviour. Mistress Beverley, for example, in *Yes Mistress* (DOM Promotions, 2007), enters a small dungeon space where two white males kneel on all fours, their heads down. She loudly proclaims 'Now then, you two. Today, I am in the mood for a little bit of amusement. One of you is gonna get shagged and the other one is going to watch.' The unlucky/lucky submissive who receives this treatment is next seen lying prone on a padded bed, his legs supported in gynae-style leg rests waiting to receive a 'really good bitch-fucking' from a topless Mistress Beverley. The sex act is certainly not simulated (penetration shots are provided in extreme close-up), so as in mainstream hard-core pornography what is witnessed is 'real'. In all other ways, however, this is a sexual performance complete with gasps from both participants, including Mistress Beverley using a strap-on, the display of her bare breasts (artificially enhanced) and an eventual 'money-shot' in which the submissive is ordered to ejaculate on a count of ten (he makes it at eleven) and is congratulated as a 'good boy'. Throughout, as in all of her activities, the dominatrix repeatedly alternates between blandishment and encouragement, from 'dirty boy' to 'good boy' and back again, facilitating the submissive's pleasure. Again, she is working – working to facilitate the satisfaction of the client and working to perform her own satisfaction to make the scenario complete, the irony of which is summed up in Mistress Beverley's statement: 'Suffering for you, pleasure for me' when it appears more to be 'Pleasure for you, work for me.'

So the dominatrix is involved, one might say, in women's work which is a labour and which is never finished. Before investigating the relationship that this has to the role of mother and the performance of motherliness, the most basic and essential of her performances should be inspected, that of 'woman'. Principally in her costume and her body the dominatrix exemplifies the performance of exaggerated femininity encountered in much mainstream pornography. As explored by Valerie Steele, 'the costume of the dominatrix has remained amazingly unchanged for decades'[8] and includes rubber, leather, PVC, high heels, corsets and uniforms of various kinds. Making the most of a woman's shape, often emphasising her breasts and curves, these outfits have come to connote sexuality, danger, the erotic and a pleasurable sinfulness that is celebrated by a number of sub-cultures. The majority of representations of the dominatrix in the popular media follow this look, the 'dominatrix-look'. It is present in a covert form in many a female super-hero or villain, and seems rather like a rite of passage as a look for popular musicians in their music videos and live performances (exemplified, of course, by Madonna, the domina-diva herself). This look is also present across the mainstream pornographic product as a signifier, one could argue, of both sexually aggressive and sexually accommodating females. Reading these costumes in dominatrix porn, however, must take place in the context of *mise-en-scène* (the almost ubiquitous red and black dungeon, the black padded furniture, the sadistic props carefully arranged around the room) and the performance of the dominatrix herself. All contribute to the construction of a violent yet self-controlled womanhood that exists within the walls of the dungeon (she does not and cannot exist outside of the dungeon, a problem encountered in mainstream cinema's representations of the dominatrix who is not accepted by civilised society).

It is with this construction of a violent woman that a study of dominatrix porn begins to contribute to a contemporary discourse on the presence of tough women in popular culture. Debates revolve around considerations of gender performance and mythologies of gender, often with recourse to Judith Butler's position on the performativity of gender and on the concept of 'masquerade' from feminist criticism.[9] The usefulness of a critical awareness of masquerade, whether as a performance of gender or of any socially sanctioned role, is that once it is noticed it reveals identity as a construction. The broadly accepted position now is that gender is made up of a series of learned behaviours, performances or masks, reaffirmed by popular culture, fashion, social interactions, language and so on. From these emerge (often unconscious) expectations of men to perform masculinity and women to perform femininity. The woman who performs masculine signifiers or traits – violence, anger, dominant or aggressive sexuality – may be regarded socially as sacrificing part of her femininity and thus is 'less feminine', or could equally be understood as exposing gender as a construction.

Critics such as Sherrie A. Inness, Yvonne Tasker[10] and Jeffrey A. Brown[11] have analysed representations of tough women in film and TV who, ostensibly, conduct a masculine performance as they karate-chop, kick and shoot their way through narratives, and they have arrived at some very interesting conclusions. Brown, for instance remarks upon the affinity that tough, heroic female characters in movies have to the dominatrix figure, writing that 'rather than masculiniz[ing] women, the action heroine often functions within the symbolic realm of the dominatrix by both breaking down and exploiting the boundaries between the sexes'.[12] What he rejects is the perception that tough women 'swap' one gender performance for another, and rather personify and exaggerate both masculine and feminine roles, thus contesting the social acceptance of gender roles. For this reason the tough heroine is a transgressive character who 'straddles both sides of the psychoanalytic gender divide'.[13]

Brown's observation that this inevitably associates the tough heroine with the dominatrix is telling. The dominatrix straddles this same gender divide and not least when represented in pornography. Here is a woman whose breasts, hair, nails, make-up, costume and voice all scream out exaggerated femininity, whilst her manner, her range of sadistic behaviours, her language, her constant action, even her tattoos, contribute towards a performance of masculinity, exemplified in the action of penetrating a submissive with a strap-on. As her title implies, the dominatrix performs dominance, and traditionally that is the domain of men. But, as Brown argues with reference to Thais E. Morgan's excellent article on dominatrix pornography, the action heroine like the dominatrix 'mocks masculinity as she enacts it',[14] creating an oddly ambiguous performance. One should add that even if her submissive is female the dominatrix's performance is a mockery of masculinity, a kind of reversal of the pantomime dame, perhaps even more scornful since it declares that man need not even be present for the joke to work. When the male submissive *is* present, it should be noted, he is frequently emasculated by punishments enacted upon the penis, such as pegging, bondage or kicking, and also through language concerning the genitals or anus. An anus may be referred to as a 'pussy' or a 'box' whilst some form of penetration proceeds, further feminising the male sub. Others have their genitals referred to as 'two little squashed tomatoes', 'a little hedgehog', and 'a shriveled up prune', Mistress Beverley, for instance, announces loudly to one male sub, 'That's not a cock, that's a clit!', then bursts out laughing at her own joke.

The range of insults employed by these mistresses is impressive and often humourous which serves to remind us that these performances are forms of entertainment that the mistresses themselves cheekily play up to. A notable scenario has Mistress Smoke applying pegs to a submissive's scrotum, then beginning to play 'he loves me, he loves me not' ('And you'd better not love me,' she warns), and one cannot help but count the number of pegs left before he inevitably suffers for loving the mistress after she exclaims, 'Uh oh. He loves me.' Finding humour in pornography is not necessarily unusual. Constance Penley argues that attitudes to pornography as 'something *done* to women' have obscured the fact that it contains a bawdy, self-conscious humour, 'closer to *Hee Haw* than Nazi Death Camp fantasies' she writes, which often places the male as the butt of the joke.[15] Dominatrix pornography having such a propensity for verbal communication, principally from the mistress herself, allows such mocking bawdiness a liberty possibly lacking in other pornographies.

MOTHERLINESS AND MONSTROSITY

As implied by the kind of language used in dominatrix porn, 'little girl,' 'bad boy,' and so on, the power relationship that is performed is close to that of mother and child. The dominatrix does not literally play the character of a mother (at least not in any of the pornography that

FIGURE 14.1 Mistresses and the maternal: the older female dominatrix as a controlling mother figure

I have seen), but she does play the role of mother as archaic figure. Similarly, the submissive is not literally acting the character of a child, but frequently emulates signs of childlikeness and childishness, such as thumb-sucking, playing with a doll, and sticking out a tongue at the dominatrix. The act of spanking over the mistress's lap is a typical enactment of the mother/child relationship, and in a sense all of the activities fulfill the dominatrix's role as punishing mother.

This is not the place to enter an extended psychoanalytic account of the dominatrix and what she represents, but a typical reading would place the dominatrix as phallic woman who threatens castration (quite literally in some cases) and the submissive as pre-Oedipal child desiring complete fulfillment from the mother. She could equally represent a physical manifestation of the super-ego who rebukes the submissive for pursuing the urges of the id. These are all important concerns. However, my concern here is with the pornographic text and its immediate significations. Foremost in the construction of motherliness are the tones of voice adopted by the dominatrix when addressing the submissive. One moment she will speak slowly, in a slightly raised register, as if to be heard clearly and understood, and in simple phrases that are frequently posed as questions: 'Are you very sore? Are you going to cry?' (*Mistress Gemma's London Dungeon*), or 'Pretty little dolly' (*Desires of a Dominatrix 5*), the tone and meaning of the utterance strongly suggesting motherliness. This tone may switch without warning to something altogether more threatening and harsh, such as 'Head. Down!' from Mistress Gemma or 'Give me a smile, bitch!' from Nicole Sheridan (an American porn actress) in *Desires of a Dominatrix 5*, who has been 'sexually assaulting' then tickling her female submissive. It is part of the alternating structure of the dominatrix's performance and perfectly matches her gender-straddling transgression: gentle mummy then cruel matriarch. This all takes place in the black and red dungeon, reminiscent of the comforting womb one moment and of fascist imagery the next. It is both a welcoming and brutal place which overwhelms the client into submission where he returns to a foetus, inactive, helpless. He or she may even return to the foetal position as does 'Cockroach', the male submissive repeatedly kicked on the floor with gusto by Mistress Smoke.

The parallel to Barbara Creed's concept of the monstrous-feminine[16] is unavoidable, that of the maternal figure who represents a threat to the symbolic order and who is, in herself, abject because she sits on the border between 'proper' gender roles. Such a construction becomes even more noticeable in dominatrix porn when one takes account of punishments such as licking mud from boots, dog training by urinating on newspaper, and anal penetration with a boot heel. These activities constitute abject behaviour that, as the implicit narrative goes, teaches the submissive his or her proper place in the transgressive symbolic order in which father is absent and mother is in charge. The irony of dominatrix pornography is that the submissive (and most likely the viewer also) adores the monstrous-feminine and wants her to stay that way. Consequently, in dominatrix porn the monstrous mother is never punished.

THE CAMP AND THE MUNDANE

In keeping with the alternating modes of performance, feminine/masculine, gentle/cruel, there is also in dominatrix pornography an alternation of the spectacular and the everyday. The various dungeon activities that take place on-screen are by their very nature extraordinary. It is not the everyday experience of most people to be encased in a rubber body bag, or to be told by a glamourous woman to sit on a leather studded chair that has a dildo fixed upright on the seat. Certain punishments are more spectacular than others, such as Nicole Sheridan completely covering a male sub's tongue in hot green wax (*Desires of a Dominatrix 5*) or Mistress Smoke putting out a cigarette in her sub's mouth (*Mistress Smoke*). Typically, these moments are represented in close-up allowing a non-interrupted gaze at the effects of the violation as the camera consistently seeks out the spectacular. These are the 'money shots' of dominatrix porn, occasionally accompanied by the more conventional money shot of male ejaculation by a submissive or a Master.

Similarly, there will almost always be a moment when the effects on the submissive's body become evident; the welts raise up, the skin reddens and bruises may even emerge, all occurring in real time (accentuated in the cheaper porn which is produced with a hand-held camera and thus reduces editing to a minimum). Despite the spectacular nature of the performance at moments such as these, it is ironically a sense of the real that is constructed: real time, real violent behaviour, real physical responses, none of which can be expected in mainstream cinema's representations of the dominatrix which are far more concerned with gazing at her than at the

FIGURE 14.2 Spectacular punishments as a source of sexual climax in *Mistress Smoke*

191

effects of her work. Strangely then, spectacle gives rise to the reality of sadomasochism and equally the reality of sadomasochism is spectacular, a fantasy performance with very real effects on the body. The spectacular nature of the videos, together with the exaggerated gendered performances and the performance of a scenario, contributes to a deliberate camp sensibility and effect, consciously excessive in style and content and all the more charming for it.

However, there are various ways in which the deliberate camp nature of dominatrix porn is overwhelmed. Certainly the general predictability of the *mise-en-scène*, the activities and the language may threaten the spectacle of dominatrix porn, but there are surprisingly regular instances in which the performance is overtly exposed. A Brechtian moment occurs in *Mistress Gemma's London Dungeon* when the leather paddle hits the too-close camera and the Mistress whispers 'Sorry' to the male camera-operator. Instantly, the illusion is destroyed. The woman on-screen not only does something accidental and thus loses her control over the scenario, but she also reveals her performance by apologising and, effectively, submitting. Although the scenarios of dominatrix porn are blatantly performative, these accidental moments upset faith in the fantasy of the dominatrix figure despite being somehow touchingly authentic admissions to the 'real' woman underneath, the one who makes mistakes and says sorry for them. When a transvestite maid drops his feminine tone of voice to his everyday deep register to ask Mistress Gemma to leave longer gaps between strokes of the cane, the dominatrix has failed in everything that she represents and thus reveals a failed seriousness, a naïve camp, as Susan Sontag might have claimed.[17]

The illusion can be broken in a variety of ways: the dominatrix glances at the camera, she absent-mindedly chews gum every few seconds, she sighs in boredom, or coughs, or cannot get the suction pump to attach to the nipple. Such apparent lack of professionalism can equally be found in the acting abilities of those on-screen. The beginning of a scenario with Miss Chambers in *Yes Mistress*, for example, is strongly reminiscent of Victoria Wood's and Julie Walters' comedy sketch 'Acorn Antiques' as the performers wait frozen for the camera to tilt up to their faces before they launch into their dialogue. The cheaper videos may have such poor sound quality that the dialogue cannot be distinguished or the director may be heard to say 'Hold on. Stills,' halting the action in order to take photographs for the DVD cover or website. A consequence of these accidents and inadequacies is the introduction of the everyday, the mundane, into the performance. Suddenly, the woman on-screen is a real person earning money by spanking bottoms. She is being told what to do by a director who, usually, is male. She might even show a kindness not expected of the dominatrix, as when the Mistress of *S for Slavegirl* (DOM Promotions, 2008) warns the female submissive not to open her eyes once her Master has ejaculated on her face. She smiles and glances at the camera, a knowing look which says 'We all know it burns when it gets in the eyes.' She is made real, possibly even vulnerable, laughable and exposed, but it is only momentary. Within seconds she has returned to her self-controlled, efficient performance and the power dynamic is re-established.

CONCLUSION: OBJECT OR SUBJECT?

It is the claim of Thais E. Morgan that dominatrix pornography has a critical and political consequence since it

> moves towards a critical reinscription of both genders by parodically re-marking femininity in the masculine and masculinity in the feminine. The dominatrix thus figures a post-modern (female) subjectivity in the process – a subjectivity which interrogates the very ground of sexual difference from which it takes off.[18]

Put in the terms of my own perspective, the dominatrix performs/parodies masculinity and thus, with the performance of the (male) submissive, she embodies a critical subjectivity which casts doubt on traditional expectations of gender and encourages the viewer to play with gender performance too. Although 'woman' does not traditionally signify active subjectivity, Morgan's argument goes, the pornographic dominatrix inscribes a new femininity, one that allows 'woman' to signify 'subject'. It must be said that one of the reasons that dominatrix porn 'works' is that the women are not behaving like ordinary women, but then neither does the average woman work as an assassin, a bounty hunter, or a stripper with a vendetta, nor does she have a bionic body. Perhaps they are all sexual objects of the heterosexual male gaze, but they are equally women in action. Jeffrey A. Brown asks the question: 'When women are portrayed as tough in contemporary film, are they being allowed access to a position of empowerment, or are they merely being further fetishized as dangerous sex objects?' The answer, for the pornographic dominatrix, is 'yes' and 'yes'. Or perhaps she is fetishised as a dangerous sex subject, and thus remains on that border between subject and object. Surely, this is the paradox described by Judith Butler (from Michel Foucault) as 'subjectivation', when one becomes both subject and subjected.[19] This state is nowhere more evident than in the recognition of the real dominatrix on the screen. Her presence in the DVD operates as an advertisement for her wares, she is publicising herself and her business by performing her skills on camera. The viewer, potentially, could become one of her clients and she thus becomes something to be desired in a whole new manner of consumption, a commodity that can be bought. So which is she, business woman or working girl? Desiring woman or desired woman? Role model or sex object? Free agent or slave to patriarchal lusts? Whatever the answer, if one exists, it is difficult to deny the mischievousness and self-conscious artificiality of the pornographic dominatrix who at the very least exposes sex and gender as dramas and comedies that we perform.

CHAPTER 15

NEO-LIBERAL AVANT-GARDE SEXPLOITATION IN JAPAN: THE INTERPLAY OF COLLABORATION AND REVOLUTION IN THE PINK FILM

Alex Zahlten

'Already a development is beginning in the film world that is exactly like the Soviet invasion of Czechoslovakia.'

– From the introduction to a 1968 *zadankai* (round table) discussion featuring the six most prominent film directors of the time, regarding the majors' entry into 'Pink' territory by producing 'Pink' lines.[1]

The above quotes encapsulate the feeling of antagonism towards the major studios that the protagonists of the Pink film industry formulated again and again in the 1960s and early 1970s. The allusion to the suppression of the Prague Spring also speaks of the surplus value consistently attached to the genre: political anti-authoritarianism and the smell of revolution. This sweeping trope of resistance – against the economic authority of the major studios, the political authority of the state, the moral authority of the established media and various public institutions – has been attached to Pink film repeatedly over the decades since it first appeared in the early 1960s and became the biggest cinematic success story of the decade, indeed one of the biggest in the entire history of film in Japan. In the three years from 1962 to 1965, what would later be called Pink film went from non-existence to over 200 films and 44 per cent of total feature film production. And unlike most of the cinemas of sexploitation reviewed in this volume, Pink film is still alive and active, if ailing, producing around seventy 35mm films a year.

Yet how accurate is such a claim of resistance as a generic trait? It has, with slightly different nuances, migrated across various parties over time: the Pink film industry itself in the 1960s, the student movement in the late 1960s, Japanese film critics of the late 1970s and early 1980s, and, more recently, American and European academics and curators involved in the revival of interest in the genre. It is no coincidence that in 2007 Meike Mitsuru's, Nakano Takao-scripted *The Glamorous Life of Sachiko Hanai* (*Hanai Sachiko no Karei na Shôgai*, 2004) became an international festival success and the first Pink film in decades to be released theatrically in the United States. The considerable publicity the film received focused on its absurdist-framed criticism of the Iraq War: the protagonist, a sex worker specialising in role-play, becomes entangled in the international hunt for a replica of George W. Bush's finger, endowed both with the ability to trigger the apocalypse and a lusty life of its own. In September 2007, the French Federation of Film Critics (SFCC) officially protested the rating of the re-release of Wakamatsu Kôji's *The Embryo Hunts in Secret* aka *When the Embryo goes Poaching* (*Taiji ga Mitsuryô suru Toki*, 1966) as restricted to audiences below 18 years of age. The aura of Pink resistance politics is not only still glowing even in Europe and the US, it also obviously influences the kinds of films that are selected for release. A similar paradox occurs in Japan, where the histories of Japanese film – such as those by Satô Tadao or Yomota Inuhiko – tend to only slightly touch upon Pink film.[2] When they do, however, they focus on the exception to the exclusion of virtually all else. Wakamatsu Kôji, the first (though by far not the only) brand name in Pink film, and, in the 1960s, the Pink director and producer most prone to explicit political expression and formal experimentation, becomes a *pars pro toto* of the entire genre. This kind of strategic spotlighting simultaneously hides a vast part of the genre from view while enabling a kind of legitimatisation of a disreputable section of cinema history.

PINK FANTASIES

The marginal role of Pink film in the US, and increasingly in Japan, may further support this tendency, enabling reflexes of projection and nostalgia. In its formative period, however, Pink film was anything but marginal. In 1962, three of what would later be defined as Pink films were released in Japan. In 1963, 24, in 1964, 65, and by 1965, an astounding 213 Pink films were released, a number that would decline only slightly for many years (although the definition of a Pink film is usually vague enough to allow for slight variations in numbers, depending on who's counting). How involved in actual 'resistance' can a genre as a whole be, when it at one (later) point provides more than half of the entire feature film output? Pink film certainly participated in complex social, political, aesthetic, even literary discourses. This essay will not dispute the discursive space that Pink film opened for film practitioners and audiences, nor their *potential* for strategic political interventions. It will, however, focus on the mechanisms of collaboration that made the opening of such discursive spaces possible in the first place. It will trace the specific historical circumstances of an industrial pragmatism that was not at all anathema to the narrative of resistance, even on the side of the major studios. And it will examine how Pink film influenced the restructuring of the Japanese film industry to enable its very survival, initially playing the role of an economic and political avant-garde but soon becoming a time-lagged storage room of traditions.

There is no question that Pink film latched onto a number of discourses that were of considerable significance and heightened salience especially in the 1960s. The Pink film industry stood for a return to independent production and, more importantly, distribution after a decade of near total major studio monopoly. Independent production was still heavily associated with the concretely leftist positions of the by-then extinct independents of the early 1950s, which were often linked to unions or political organisations. The emphasis on the body was connected to immediate post-war discourses as formulated by the 'literature of the flesh', which used the body as a starting point for re-establishing a sense of personal subjectivity. The opposition towards official definitions of obscenity were part of the larger package of discontents with a state that was perceived as authoritarian and under Western influence. On-location realism in aesthetics and storylines clashed with the stylishness of the major studios. Class was being problematised in the relationship of the small independent sexploiters and the majors, spanning from the ideas about Pink film audiences and the directors' pedigrees: only those with elite educational records could even hope to enter the studios, and Pink directors habitually portrayed themselves as a much more blue-collar lot. All of this of course carried implications for the construction of nation.

The two scandals of 1965 that heaved Pink film into the public limelight in Japan both carried deep national implications: Wakamatsu Kôji's film *Affairs Within Walls* (*Kabe no Naka no Himegoto*, 1965), highly critical of the social order accompanying the boom economy, screened at the Berlin International Film Festival and was dubbed a 'national disgrace film' in the press. The highly publicised obscenity trial against *Black Snow* (*Kuroi Yuki*, Takechi Tetsuji, 1965) concerned itself with a film that polemically criticised the American military presence in Japan. In the late 1960s the student movement was quick to pick up on these undercurrents, and Pink films played regularly at university gatherings. Adachi Masao, one of the most experimental, intellectual and political figures from the Pink film industry eventually left Japan to join the Japanese Red Army

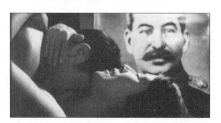

FIGURE 15.1 Desire under the eye of a dictator: Wakamatsu Kôji's scandalous *Affairs Within Walls*

in Lebanon. All of this played into the larger image of Pink film as a genre, and all of this contributed to the considerable power of attraction it held for a certain period of time.

Yet unsurprisingly the point of departure for what was to be called Pink film was economic reasoning, the unfailing ability of sexually-charged films to attract an audience. While the idea of Pink film as resistance was real (at least for certain groups at certain times), the question remains how structurally founded it was. At the root of Pink film's identity lie the supposed dichotomy of Pink film and the major studios, and it merits closer inspection. At the beginning of the 1960s the six Japanese studios Daiei, Tôhô, Shôchiku, Shintôhô, Tôei and Nikkatsu were all in dire straits. The booming economy brought on not only by television but by a whole host of new and newly affordable leisure activities, all in direct competition to the film industry. The majors devised several coping strategies, one of which was the focus on specific segments of the general audience. Eventually, all but Tôhô proceeded to focus increasingly on the preferences of the male spectator, abandoning the female audience to foreign films and the new medium of television. Yakuza films, action films and increasingly explicit sexual content soon dominated the screens. Pink film was, at this time, often portrayed as a threat to the majors' hegemony and very survival, an unwanted invader in an already troubled market. This characterisation of Pink film was summed up in typical headlines such as 'The 3 Million Yen Films that are Threatening the 5 (Major) Companies' or 'To What Degree are They Eating the Majors' Market?'[3] However, this is not the whole truth. In fact, several of the majors' strategies not only created a virtually ideal environment for the meteoric rise of Pink film, they even relied heavily on Pink film to sustain the exhibition industry. At some point every single one of the majors inserted Pink films into their programmes and theatres, and most even dabbled in Pink film production, though often surreptitiously, something we will touch upon later.

From 1959 on, the financially imperilled studios starkly reduced production and resorted to 'setting free' the creative and technical staff, previously strictly bound by studio-exclusive contracts, and at the same time curtailed their production activities. The resultant reduction in films created immense problems especially for the second- and third-tier theatres which depended almost solely on studio production to fill their weekly changing double- and triple-bills. In 1956/57, the distribution income of independently-produced feature films comprised a miniscule 0.34 per cent of the total gross, so initially there simply was no alternative. Yet because audience turnout declined rapidly after the first week of screening, weekly programme changes were an absolute necessity. Pink films closed this cinematic gap perfectly. Low production budgets of under 3 million Yen (a little more than $8,000 in 1965) and a legion of now underemployed film industry workers provided an ideal environment for Pink film production. Takahashi Eiichi calculated the following statistics in 1968: in 1958 the major studios released 503 films; by 1965, this number was down to 277, which was supplemented by 225 Pink films (by his count) – which amounts to the previous total of 503 films.[4]

Pink production was highly flexible, and in comparison to the studio system a vanguard of liberalised labour relations. The director simultaneously functioned as the producer, setting up a pro forma production company; upon making a deal with a distributor about the script, he would receive a part of the budget for actual production, and the rest for the completed film. This provided the director with a significant amount of influence over the finished product, and often the distributors didn't care about the aesthetic or political specifics as long as the required amount of 'sexiness' was supplied. Staff was assembled for each separate production, not continually employed. The studios' new policies left some highly-skilled practitioners out of work, and they found ready (and often anonymous) employment in the Pink film industry: for his 1965 debut feature *Hussy* (*Abazure*), the young Watanabe Mamoru was able to use a cameraman that had worked with Mizoguchi Kenji and a lighting chief that had worked for Kurosawa Akira. Motogi Sôjirô, a prominent Pink film director, had originally worked as a producer for Tôhô, producing among others Kurosawa's *Rashomon* (1950) and *The Seven Samurai* (*Shichinin no Samurai*, 1954).

However, Pink films were embraced by exhibitors for more reasons than simply stuffing the gaping hole the studios had left. They attracted audiences with a welcome predictability, and the distributors charged much lower fees for the films than the majors did. By 1965 over seventy small companies were involved in the production of Pink film, and they either self-distributed their films or sold them to the regional distributors that were popping up by the dozen. The pressure of overproduction and inexperience in distribution quickly led to dumping prices for Pink films. At the most, exhibitors were charged 20 per cent of the box office for Pink film screenings, while major productions commanded 50 per cent. And, at least in the early phase of Pink film, audience turnout was often better than that achieved by studio films.

As so few Pink films from this period survive or are available for viewing, it is difficult to explore their aesthetics and narratives. In terms of storylines, the mid-1960s were far less standardised than the genre would eventually become. One of the pioneering successes was the female Tarzan film *The Valley of Desire* (*Jôyoku no Tanima*, 1962) by, appropriately, animal documentary specialist and later prominent Pink film director Seki Kôji. Another was *Lara of the Wild* (*Yasei no Rârâ*, 1962) by strip-show owner Kitasato Toshio, advertised as the story of a 'vampire fly from the Soviet Union [that] provided a woman with an ecstatic death while sucking her blood'.[5] A very large portion of the films feature storylines about the fate of innocent girls violated by malevolent men, but also stories about honeymoons gone bad, action films, period films and even Pink ghost films (*pinku kaidan*) such as Ogawa Kinya's *Supernatural Tale [of the] Dismembered Ghost* (*Kaidan Bara Bara Yûrei*, 1968).

Pink film has always been characterised by an uneven spread of ambition: some directors attempt to make the most of the low budgets and the often astonishing freedom for narrative and formal experimentation, while others simply go through the motions. However, themes and stories would generally become much more formulaic and immediately sex-centred in the early 1970s, with subgenres such as the *mibôjin* (widow) films, *danchi dzuma* (suburban wife) films, *joyû* (woman's bath house) films, or the infamous *chikan densha* (train molester) films. This standardisation is rooted in several factors, but two seem most important: the attempts by powerbroker Ôkura Mitsugi to craft a Pink film industry on the model of the studio system, and the major studios' increased involvement in and encroachment on the Pink film industry.

PINK PIONEERS

Ôkura Mitsugi has variously been stylised as a visionary businessman, a box-office record breaking producer, a pusher of *ero-guro* (erotic-grotesque) films, an egomaniacal one-man show and the father of Pink films. The legends woven around him have as much to do with his flamboyant and provocative self-promotion as with his radical business methods. Ôkura first gained a hold in the film business as a *katsuben* or *benshi*, the narrators who accompanied silent film (and, for a short time, sound film) with their explanations and theatrics. Ôkura was very popular in this line of work and accumulated some wealth, eventually entering the film exhibition business by building a chain of 36 theatres. On 29 December 1955, Ôkura entered a more public position by becoming head of the smallest of the major studios, Shintôhô. Ôkura immediately restructured the company, cutting budgets and shooting days, limiting the maximum length of a film, and exchanging veterans for younger, less experienced (i.e. cheaper) and supposedly fresher staff. This included directors, actors, cameramen and set designers, and was a radical move in a working environment dominated by the traditional seniority system. He also reasoned that stars were expensive, and that it was better to rely on genres to sell a film, a stance he would later take with regard to Pink films as well. With his assumed expertise gained from his experience of exhibition, he adjusted the company's genre palette to the low-brow audience of the second- and third-run theatres that Shintôhô had by now ended up supplying. Ôkura strategically split up production between big-budget extravaganzas and much cheaper genre fare. On the lower-budget end of the spectrum was *The Revenge of the Pearl Diving Queen* (*Onna Shinju Ô no Fukushû*, Shimura Toshio, 1956), with Maeda Michiko as a scantily-clad pearl diver (or *ama* in Japanese). The very successful film featured the first nude scene in a film from Japan, although all audiences saw was a very short glance of a backside. As a grand spectacle he produced the first film featuring the Tennô as a character, *Emperor Meiji and the Great Russo-Japanese War* (*Meiji Tennô to Nichiro Dai Senso*, Watanabe Kunio, 1957), which generated fever-pitch publicity and became the most successful Japanese film of all time.

However, towards the end of the 1950s audiences began to drop off, and Shintôhô felt it most severely. Ôkura eventually abandoned the risk of big-budget projects and focused on films spiced heavily (for the time) with horror, violence and eroticism. As the studio's fortunes declined, so did the patience of his scandalised studio employees. Never a stranger to controversy (when once asked at a press conference if the rumour he had made actress Takakura Miyuki, star of several Shintôhô films, his mistress were true, Ôkura responded that he hadn't made an actress his mistress, he had made his mistress an actress), he was eventually forced to resign due to an in-house money scandal related to the sale of the studio lot. In consequence, Ôkura initially focused on his exhibition chain, showing a mix of second-run films from Japan and imported films, among them so-called *shô eiga* (show films, usually fake documentaries of strip shows) and Roger Corman films. He also re-entered production with another 70mm spectacle and several smaller films, but the results were disappointing apart from one low-budget film called *Flesh Market* (*Nikutai no Ichiba*, Kobayashi Satoru, 1962), that would later be called the very first Pink film. The film was based on a serial in the magazine *Bessatsu Naigai Jitsuwa* which in turn was based on an incident that supposedly actually occurred in October 1961 in the Roppongi section of Tokyo, at the time a central hangout for American GIs and seen as a hothouse of hedonistic Westernised culture. In the story, Harue and her fiancée Kinoshita visit a club in Roppongi. She is raped in the toilet, and Kinoshita consequently breaks off the engagement. When Harue commits suicide by jumping from the roof of a building, her little sister Tamaki enters the Roppongi club scene to investigate, looking for revenge. The film ran into legal problems when the police confiscated all prints on suspicion of dissemination of obscenity, despite having been passed by the Administration Commision for the Motion Picture Code of Ethics (Eirin). The film was released again after several cuts were made, and became a considerable success due to the publicity. Ôkura then refrained from further sex-heavy productions for a while, but his films met with very limited success. Two years later he apparently realised that the proliferating business of low-budget erotic productions promised much wider profit margins than horror films and risky big-budget war films. Ôkura had Ogawa Kinya, an assistant director from his earlier productions that had shot some Pink films for the production company Kokuei in the meantime, shoot the very successful *Female Animal, Female Animal, Female Animal* (*Mesu, mesu, mesu*) in 1964, and this was the start of Ôkura's enduring and exclusive focus on Pink films for the rest of his career and life.

Ôkura went to work immediately, merging with several Pink production/distribution companies and forging the first national distribution and exhibition circuit for Pink films, the OP (Ôkura Pictures) Chain, in 1965. OP was vertically structured, much like the major studios themselves: it possessed theatres, a distribution arm and even a small studio lot. This gave it an immense advantage over the majority of the more improvised Pink production outfits, which often had only two or three employees and a ramshackle office. Ôkura's dominance eventually forced a trend for consolidation among Pink film companies, a number of which banded together to form the loosely structured Dokuritsu (Independent) Chain, which included Tôkyô Kikaku, Century Eiga, and the still active Kokuei and Shintôhô (the latter being a different company from the major studio of the same name, which had filed for bankruptcy in 1961). OP launched with ten theatres specialising solely in Pink film exhibition and a host of theatres which used Pink films as programme supplements. Although evidence is sketchy, it is probable that these were the first theatres specialising in the exclusive exhibition of Pink films in triple bills, and Ôkura was certainly the first to systematically work on standardising Pink film production, distribution and exhibition. It is Ôkura's model that Pink film would eventually sink into in the early 1970s. Pink films would standardise to a length of sixty minutes to play in triple bills, their budgets would become basically fixed at around three million Yen, with much less variation than in the 1960s, and distribution was not free but attached to large distribution circuits. Ôkura's business strategy was heavily influenced by his time as the head of a major studio, and the Fordist model of film production he instituted adhered to the methods of the 1950s. At the same time the studios themselves were already moving out of this business mode, which they regarded as outdated and inefficient. Their trend was towards the casualisation of labour and attracting audiences via sexually and violently charged spectacle, for both of which they borrowed liberally from Pink film. While Ôkura was attempting to build a Pink studio system, the majors were heavily restructuring and trying to shed the vertical organisation that OP was aspiring to.

The majors themselves had been part of the early pioneering for more sex-themes in feature films. Ôkura had prepared some of the way during his time at Shintôhô in the late 1950s. In 1963, seven of the 37 films classified as *seijin eiga* (adult films) by Eirin were made by the majors, among them *Lies* (*Uso*) by Masumura Yasuzô at Daiei, Imamura Shôhei's *Insect Woman* (*Nippon Konchû–ki*) at Nikkatsu and Narusawa Masahige's *Naked Body* (*Ratai*), distributed by Shôchiku. 1964 then saw the majors more than quadruple their adult film output to 31, with Nikkatsu producing Nakahira Kô's *Monday Girl* (*Getsuyôbi no Yuka*) and Suzuki Seijun's scandal-invoking *Gate of Flesh* (*Nikutai no mon*), based on the classic story by Tamura Tajirô of the postwar 'literature of flesh', and the first film from Japan to feature full-frontal upper-body nudity. Tôei produced Watanabe Yûsuke's *Two Female Dogs* (*Nihiki no Mesu-inu*) and *Evil Woman* (*Akujo*) for their new line of sex films. Shôchiku had experimented with its brand of Shôchiku *nouvelle vague* films for similar reasons. Now it turned to an outside *seijin eiga* production, Takechi Tetsuji's *Daydream* (*Hakujitsumu*). Tôhô likewise bought and distributed an independent production, Teshigahara Hiroshi's *Woman in the Dunes* (*Suna no Onna*). The distribution of films the majors had not produced themselves had become virtually extinct in the 'golden age' of the late 1950s. However, Tôhô had extensive experience with the efficiency of subcontracting production in the late 1940s, and was now leading the way in reviving a practice that would eventually become the industry standard – and had been the mainstay of Pink film production from the beginning. In 1970 Tôhô took a historic step when it outsourced its recording, art direction, technical and special effects divisions to affiliate companies it established, and the entire production division itself followed in the same year. The other majors followed suit.

Following the *Black Snow* trial in 1965, the majors cut back on potentially controversial material; in 1966 Shôchiku even pulled out of a distribution deal for the Wakamatsu Kôji film *Phone, Please* (*O-Denwa Chôdai*). But by the late 1960s the situation was desperate, and this time the mining of Pink film began in earnest. Nikkatsu began distribution of Pink films in 1968, as well as producing sex-themed films such as *The House of Strange Loves* (*Onna Ukiyo Buro*, Ida Motomu, 1968). Tôei was continuing its highly successful erotic lines with films like *Genealogy of Tokugawa Women* (*Tokugawa Onna Keizu*, 1968), *The Joy of Torture* (*Tokugawa Onna Keibatsu-shi*, 1968) and *Hot Spring Massage Geisha* (*Onsen Anma Geisha*, 1968), all helmed by Ishii Teruo, the *wunderkind* director of lurid material from the original Shintôhô. Much to the chagrin of the Pink film industry, the latter film employed eleven of the biggest star actresses from Pink film. Essentially, Pink film was being used as an experimentation ground, to see what could be repackaged by the majors.

Nihon Shinema had produced the 3D Pink film *Pervert Freak* (*Hentaima*, Seki Kôji, 1967),

FIGURE 15.2 Erotic narrative and 3D thrills: Seki Kôji's *Pervert Freak*

and used Tôei's developing lab for the complicated technical side. In 1969, Tôei proceeded to release the animated film *Red Shadow* (*Tobidasu bôken eiga-Akakage*, Kurata Junji) as Japan's first 3D film, for which they were forced to apologise. Tôei set up its Pinky Violence line in the early 1970s, transposing the Pink recipe to a genre where Pink budgets were increasingly unable to follow: action films. Nikkatsu stuck closer to the Pink formula when, cornered by extreme financial straits, it switched its entire production to (technically highly accomplished) sexploitation films and created the label Roman Porno. This move from the oldest existing major studio in Japan was a severe shock for the film world at the time, and led to an initial exodus of Nikkatsu employees and stars unwilling to make the transition; consequently, the first stars of Roman Porno such as Shirakawa Kazuko or Tani Naomi were all recruited from Pink film. Likewise, many of the subgenres Nikkatsu embraced had been developed by Pink film: widow films and train molester films became standard fare. Tôei founded Tôei Central Films for the production and distribution of Pink films in 1976, relying heavily on Pink director and producer powerhouse Mukai Kan. Even Shôchiku, the company that was successfully churning out the family-friendly *Tora-san* series, founded Tôkatsu as a Pink production and distribution outfit. This relied mostly on Pink director Kobayashi Satoru, who by the end of the 1970s was shooting an unbelievable 36 feature films a year for the company. Slyly, the name Tôkatsu is written with Chinese characters that can be found in Tôei and Nikkatsu, but not in Shôchiku.

While all of this may have looked dangerous for Pink film, it ultimately transformed the Pink industry more than it threatened it. Nikkatsu Roman Porno actually brought some stability to the business: Nikkatsu theatres showed triple bills, consisting of two Nikkatsu Roman Porno films and one Pink film. For this, Nikkatsu subcontracted to Pink film companies such as Prima Kikaku or Watanabe Production, which both relied heavily on director Yoyogi Tadashi (who for this reason found himself ensnared in the 1972 obscenity trial against Nikkatsu). In terms of actresses, genres, themes, the aesthetics of rough realism, and even production practice, most of the majors were heavily borrowing from and participating in Pink film; indeed, this partially ensured their further survival. In 1972, an astonishing 196 of the 395 Japanese films released that year were designated as *seijin eiga*, and the proportion would further rise until the early 1980s.

EROTIC LEGACIES

In response to the major studios' strategies, the Pink industry, with Ôkura at the helm, increased its drive for consolidation. In 1968 the OP chain assembled eleven of the main Pink production/distribution companies to form a single large distribution network for the Kantô region (Tokyo and surroundings). After only three months, Kokuei, Tôkyô Kôgyô and Nichiei left the agreement, and continued loosely linked but independent distribution. While the OP chain was now geared towards releasing around ten films a month, the three independents together supplied around three films a month. After Roman Porno appeared in 1972, however, the Pink industry was forced to stabilise and standardise even more. The industry settled into the basic structure it would preserve for the next thirty or so years; even the freewheeling Kokuei joined the Shintôhô distribution circuit for good in 1975. While exceptional and ambitious films continued to be produced throughout the genres existence, the idea that Pink film was structurally connected to resistance was rapidly fading. The dichotomy of Pink film and major studios was less and less difficult to uphold in view of the complex web of interdependencies that had developed, and politics, while often still visible, increasingly submerged into abstract storylines or atmospherics. One of the last cases of using Pink film as direct political commentary on current affairs was Yamamoto Shinya's *Molester 365* (*Chikan 365*, 1972). This film responded to an official warning issued by the metropolitan police that sexploitation films were becoming too daring. Yamamoto's film features a mysterious case of serial molestation, and the culprit turns out to be a perverted policeman.

Pink film budgets have nominally stayed fixed at around three million Yen since that time, while the value of the money has of course changed considerably. The rise of hard-core pornography available for home video affected the more cinematic Pink film with its simulated sex theatrics much as it did 35mm sexploitation in other countries, but perhaps unusually the Pink film business has managed to hang on until today. In fact, by the 1980s it had become one of the last ports of entry for young directors into a moribund film industry, and today it almost seems difficult to find an established Japanese director that was not at some point connected to Pink film or Roman Porno. The much larger shock for Pink film was the revision of the Law Regarding Businesses Affecting Public Morals in 1984, which put heavy restrictions on posters, themes and film titles. In the latter half of the decade, the majors retreated from the Pink business, and when Nikkatsu pulled out of Roman Porno in 1988, Pink film almost completely came to rely on the specialised Pink exhibition circuit. It is only since the early 1990s that the indomitable Kokuei has attempted to break out of the Pink screening space and tailor its often quite ambitious and experimental films for consumption on video, satellite TV, and in arthouse theatres. It is also Kokuei that has made the biggest mark on international film festivals and markets with the 'Four Devils of Pink' (Zeze Takahisa, Satô Hisayasu, Sano Kazuhiro and Satô Toshiki) and the newer generation of the 'Seven Gods of Luck', to which the aforementioned Meike Mitsuru belongs.

So where does this leave the overall role of Pink film? Undoubtedly the genre went through various shades of relevance that were often mediated and always historically specific. The mid-1960s presented a time of experimentation and atomised industrial activity. Small companies proliferated wildly and created a great diversity in themes, narrative patterns and styles; this diversity found unity mainly in its common independent production and distribution methods as opposed to the major studios. Pink film's economically and thematically anarchic character and its affinity to a number of long-standing discourses of anti-authoritarianism supported its explosive rise in a decade of social upheaval and political discontent. The studios in turn found that the very disorganisation and variety of the Pink industry made it an ideal testing ground for not only styles and themes, but also for liberalised labour relations and, eventually, young talents. The studios eventually participated in the Pink industry through distribution and even production, and in turn exerted pressure and influence on the Pink industry to organise and standardise. This process was cemented by Roman Porno's triumph and the appearance of an exclusive Pink film distribution/exhibition circuit. Ironically, Nikkatsu used its Roman Porno success to remain the only one of the surviving majors to maintain a vertically organised studio system, while the other majors became distributors/exhibitors that coordinated a highly liberalised production sector. Just as ironically, the Pink film industry is presently the only section of the Japanese film industry to still employ a strict seniority system in training and production. Directors are, in practice if not in a contractually formalised way, bound to certain producer/distributors. Once a radical reservoir for stories characterised by ambivalence and sexual violence, and economic strategies that threatened the film world's status quo, Pink film has largely become an archive for remnants of the world it once seemed to oppose. This is not to say that there are not still ambitious and challenging Pink films being produced. But it increasingly seems that further survival will entail breaking out of the Pink screening spaces that once preserved it and increasingly isolate it. What will then be found on DVD racks, in art-house theatres and on the Internet will conceivably not be Pink film any more.

CHAPTER 16
'HOW FAR WILL A GIRL GO TO SATISFY HER NEEDS?': FROM DYKESPLOITATION TO LESBIAN HARD-CORE

Claire Hines

Lesbian exploitation, also known as 'dykesploitation', is a category of exploitation cinema that has been rediscovered and reclaimed by queer video producers, distributors and audiences. Most recently, in July 2007, Wolfe Video (the 'oldest and largest exclusive distributor of gay and lesbian feature films') released two classic dykesploitation films from the 1960s and 1970s on DVD as part of its expanding Vintage Collection, *That Tender Touch* (Russel Vincent, 1969) and *Just the Two of Us* (aka *Sexual Desire* (Barbara Peeters and Jaque Beerson, 1975)).[1] Before the rise of hard-core pornography in the mid-1970s, low-budget dykesploitation films like *That Tender Touch, Just the Two of Us, The Fourth Sex* (*La Quatrième Sexe*, Michele Wichard, 1961), *Chained Girls* (Joseph P. Mawra, 1965) and *Fanny Hill Meets Lady Chatterley* (Barry Mahon, 1967) were originally aimed at a heterosexual male audience, who were lured into the cinema by the promise of provocative themes, mild nudity and scenes of soft-core girl-on-girl sex. However, as Wolfe Video's recent showcasing of *That Tender Touch* and *Just the Two of Us* proves, in a cultural climate that is generally more receptive to queer-positive imagery, and with the aid of historical distance, dykesploitation can provide contemporary queer audiences with a glimpse of a less than positive past that still offers plenty of camp entertainment.

Consequently, while dykesploitation was originally marketed to and consumed by men, it has since been re-appropriated, marketed to and consumed by lesbians. It is this contemporary phenomenon – what could be described as the 'queering' of dykesploitation – that this chapter sets out to investigate. Using *Chained Girls*, *That Tender Touch* and *Just the Two of Us*, I will first explore classic dykesploitation themes, and then move on to examine the pleasures that these films might hold for a contemporary lesbian audience. Lastly, I shall consider that not only has there been a revival of the soft-core lesbian-themed exploitation films of the 1960s and 1970s but they have also influenced SIR (Sex, Indulgence and Rock n' Roll) Video Production's hard-core lesbian porn. Made for and by lesbians, SIR's *Sugar High Glitter City* (Jackie Strano and Shar Rednour, 2001) finally puts the dyke into dykesploitation, recoding the films' original form to include real lesbians having real sex.

UNNATURAL LOVE OF WOMEN FOR WOMEN!

Of the three classic dykesploitation films focused on in this chapter, *Chained Girls* is undoubtedly the most damning in the treatment of its subject. The film begins with the voice of a male narrator (Joel Holt) asking a series of questions – 'Who and what is a lesbian? Is lesbianism a disease or a natural occurrence? Is lesbianism reserved for only a few people, or is it a common happening? How do lesbians live? Are they happy with their lives?' It is noted that although these are *not* questions that *Chained Girls* will attempt to answer, the film's purpose *is* to discuss them for its audience, purportedly as a form of 'preventative education'. After all, as an intertitle later informs us, 'only through understanding the facts can we keep lesbianism from becoming a serious social problem'. The use of an authoritative male voiceover, black and white photography and the spurious treatment of 'fact' all afford *Chained Girls* a documentary-style realism that is typical of educational exploitation films. On the surface, the film takes a pseudoscientific approach to female homosexuality, bombarding the viewer with statistics that reveal the frightening extent to which lesbianism is endemic throughout Western culture – 'among teenage girls 40 per cent have lesbian desires … and experiences'; '25 per cent of college girls have had a lesbian experience' – and the psychological conditions that are its root cause – an 'unfounded hatred of all men' and the 'neurotic fear of marriage'. As with most dykesploitation films, the tone and message of *Chained Girls* is above all cautionary, as lesbianism is treated as a social and psychological disease to be observed, documented and, ideally, cured.

At the same time, *Chained Girls* intends to titillate its audience. Significantly, both the film's writer/director, Joseph P. Mawra (who had also directed the *Olga* series (1964–66)), and its producer, George Weiss (who worked with Mawra on the *Olga* series and with Ed Wood on *Glen or Glenda* (1953)), were filmmakers already experienced at exploiting taboo subject matter for the screen. As an example of the way that dykesploitation films were marketed to straight male audiences, *Chained Girls*'s publicity promised 'Shackled Women in Unashamed

207

Lovemaking!' in 'A Film So Daring … So Hush-Hush…' that such sentences could only end with either an exclamation mark or an ellipsis.[2] In reality, though, the film's soft-core scenes are scarce. Between the many medical studies and statistics quoted, the camera prowls the streets of New York after dark to expose the 'twilight world' of urban lesbians, who are glimpsed kissing and fondling one another in public telephone boxes, apartment block doorways and on the backseats of parked cars.

The sex scenes in *Chained Girls* are shot voyeuristically, and represent varying (low) levels of female nudity and explictness. For example, the audience watches as one lesbian seduces another in a one-night stand. The camera lingers on the couple as they lie on a bed and begin slowly kissing and caressing each other. The relatively butch seductress expertly removes her companion's bra, swiftly followed by her own. But as their bodies meet in a topless embrace, the point-of-view abruptly shifts to the bedroom floor and the scene ends. Similar staging is employed a number of times in *Chained Girls*. Later on in the film, during another lesbian sex scene, both women remain fully clothed, yet the camerawork is again suggestive of more explicit events. As one of the women lies back on the bed, the other woman moves down her body and leans forwards, out of the frame. Oral sex is clearly implied. The camera continues to cut between shots which register pleasure on the face of the first woman, and shots of the second woman licking her lips.

FIGURE 16.1 No smoke without sexploitation: the pipe-wielding dykes of *Chained Girls*

FIGURE 16.2 Female desires and male constructions: lesbian lip-licking in *Chained Girls*

The camera then coyly shifts its gaze to a discarded pair of ladies shoes by the bed. For the duration of these soft-core scenes the *Chained Girls* narrator suspends his stern commentary, highlighting the important role that visual pleasure, or at least the anticipation of the potential for visual pleasure, played in the dykesploitation film.

This tension between lesbianism as social problem and lesbianism as visual pleasure is also evident in *That Tender Touch* and *Just the Two of Us*. Made by Russel Vincent and starring *Playboy* centrefold Sue Bernard (also co-star of exploitation director Russ Meyer's cult classic *Faster Pussycat! Kill! Kill!* (1965)) as a young woman who has left her lesbian lover for a man, *That Tender Touch* uses flashbacks to recall the story of their past love affair. At the beginning of the film, Marsha's (Bee Tompkins) arrival at the home of newly-wed couple Terry (Sue Bernard) and Ken (Rick Cooper) symbolises both the threat and the thrill that lesbianism represents. If, as Michel Foucault states, marriage is the cornerstone of society, then lesbians threaten to undermine this basic structure, infecting wives with the temptations of unnatural sexual desire.[3] In *That Tender Touch*, it seems that Marsha's mere presence is enough to ignite the secret sex cravings of almost every female in Terry's new suburban neighbourhood: one after the other, Dodie the British maid (Margaret Read), lonely housewife Jane (Victoria Hale) and troubled teen Wendy (Phae Dera) all try unsuccessfully to seduce Marsha. Tormented by her love for Terry yet unable to win her back, Marsha vows that 'it is better to have felt the crudeness of a man, than the tenderness of a woman'. Even more than *Chained Girls*, *That Tender Touch* is a moral tale, warning against the evils of homosexuality. As Jenni Olson, one of the few critics to have written on dykesploitation, notes 'just like most Hollywood films of old, the exploitation genre tended to kill off its queer protagonists'.[4] Following this convention, at the end of *That Tender Touch*, Marsha's lifeless body is found floating in the pool – finally she has 'submitted, suffered and died for that tender touch'.[5]

Chained Girls's diagnoses that lesbians are women who are either sexually immature, insecure, or have in some way been mistreated by men are then borne out in *That Tender Touch* and *Just the Two of Us*. In the latter, Denise (Elizabeth Plumb) and Adria (Alisa Courtney) embark upon their affair when they are left home alone for long periods by their husbands. Because mutual boredom, loneliness and curiosity become catalysts for the exploration of their 'deep sexual desires', *Just the Two of Us* was marketed as 'An Explicit Picture Every Husband and Wife Should See!'[6] Similar to Marsha and Terry in *That Tender Touch*, it appears that Denise and Adria's relationship is doomed since whereas Denise (like Marsha) decides that she is a 'real' lesbian, Adria (like Terry) seems only to be experimenting and she soon tires of their affair, swapping Denise for a young actor, Jim (John Aprea). Given the tradition of killing off the queer protagonist during a film's final moments, it is therefore surprising that *Just the Two of Us* ends with Denise and Adria reunited. Having lost both her husband and her male lover, a dejected Adria returns to Denise. Though the film's ending could hardly be described as conventionally 'happy', the two women are at least alive and together.

AN EXPLICIT PICTURE THAT EVERY HUSBAND AND WIFE LESBIAN SHOULD SEE!

It is significant that this uncharacteristically upbeat ending is found in a dykesploitation film made by a woman. *Just the Two of Us* was written and co-directed by Barbara Peeters (with Jaque Beerson), a filmmaker who has been labelled a feminist exploitation pioneer.[7] Much like Stephanie Rothman, during the 1970s Peeters worked within the exploitation genre and directed a number of films (including *Bury Me An Angel* (1971), *Summer School Teachers* (1975) and *Humanoids from the Deep* (aka *Monster*, 1980)) for Roger Corman's independent production/ distribution company, New World Pictures. Writing about the films Rothman made for New World, Pam Cook has argued that they can be seen as 'a prime example of feminist subversion from within, using the generic formulae of exploitation cinema in the interest of her own agenda as a woman director'.[8] So, in *Student Nurses* (1971) and *The Velvet Vampire* (aka *The Waking Hour*, 1971) Rothman plays with and encourages an awareness of popular exploitation stereotypes, parodying the genre's basic principles, codes and conventions. A similar argument can be made for Peeters' work, and Cook cites *Humanoids from the Deep* as a film that both conforms to and questions the exploitation genre's standard form and appeal.[9]

Released at the end of the cycle of 1960s and 1970s dykesploitation films, *Just the Two of Us* likewise demonstrates Peeters' awareness of the requirement to exploit lesbian sexuality, but at the same time it undermines expectations that pathologically queer characters must be

★VINTAGE COLLECTION★

Living next door to each other
they could only dream—
until their husbands left . . .

JUST THE
TWO OF
US

THE TRAGEDY OF TODAY'S
LONELY HOUSEWIFE

Wolfe
DVD

FIGURE 16.3 Dyksploitation as feminist text: Barbara Peeter's subversive *Just the Two of Us*

killed off, with its final, subversive act of bringing the lesbian couple back together just before the credits roll.

If *Just the Two of Us* is, then, an example of what Cook refers to as 'subversion from within', the recent DVD release of Peeters' film by Wolfe Video suggests that dykesploitation may also be subverted from without.[10] For, whereas straight males were dykesploitation's original target audience, Wolfe's identity as an exclusive distributor of lesbian and gay feature films suggests that *That Tender Touch* and *Just the Two of Us* have been reappropriated by a queer-owned company. Seeking to reach a lesbian market, Wolfe's press release describes these films as 'push[ing] the boundaries depicting lesbians in cinema'.[11]

To support this claim for dykesploitation's historical significance, each film comes with a colour mini-reproduction of its original press book. For a contemporary lesbian audience, this glimpse into the films' previous advertising campaigns serves a dual purpose. Firstly, the press book is an all-important reminder of the cultural and industrial context in which these films were first made and received. The viewer is at once reassured by her historical distance from the images and attitudes represented on screen, and made aware that, however problematic, dykesploitation should form part of a lesbian film canon. In the same way that Cook reassesses low-budget exploitation cinema, and Rothman's work in particular, to argue for their historical significance to feminist film culture, dykesploitation can thus be thought to make a comparable contribution to lesbian film culture.

Secondly, the sensational claims made in the press books call attention to the ironic gaps that exist between the dykesploitation films, their original promotional material, and a contemporary lesbian audience. For example, the press book for *That Tender Touch* includes various posters designed for lobby displays to accompany the film's release. The provocative taglines ask 'How far will a girl go to satisfy her needs?' and 'The Wall Between Two kinds of Love …Which Will She Choose?', advertising a cast of characters that fits somewhere between melodrama and male fantasy: 'The Maid: Cute … Ready to Serve!' and 'The Teenager: Young … Which Way Will She Go?' *That Tender Touch* was publicised using images that captured some of the film's most titillating moments as 'A Woman's Picture every Man must SEE!'[12] Typical of the dykesploitation film, it's promotional material teased its audience with suggestions of much more sexually explicit content than are actually delivered. Although the film does not really deliver the lesbian sex it promises, it does deliver lesbian melodrama, in excess.

The use of flashbacks, the triangular set-up which in this case sees the still bi-curious Terry tempted away from her husband and all that is 'good' by 'evil' lesbian Marsha, and the recourse to psychological discourses in order to explain transgressive female desire, are all common melodramatic tropes. Melodrama is also known to employ highly stylised *mise-en-scene* as an outer symbol of inner emotions.[13] Because it is a low-budget exploitation film, *That Tender Touch* does not have the conditions to reproduce mainstream production values, but it does exude a kind of over-exaggerated artificiality that makes it well suited for camp appreciation.

Like queer reading practices in general, Harry Benshoff and Sean Griffin note that, historically, camp created a subject position from which the reader 'could revise a text's original meanings, and thus it strongly figured in the creation of a shared community'.[14] They go on to say that 'bad' acting, cheap sets and histrionic narratives 'make B and exploitation films especially fertile ground for camp viewing'.[15] Camp readings of the 1960s and 1970s dykesploitation films certainly do appear popular with today's lesbian media and audiences. For example, in a review that celebrates 'Lesbian Grindhouse' and the DVD release of *Just the Two of Us* and *That Tender Touch*, writing for *The Advocate* (a magazine aimed at a queer readership), Michelle Kort observes that both films 'are hilariously bad, but in a good way – perfect for watching with a group of hooting camp-loving friends'.[16] Here, Kort confirms that lesbian viewers can deliberately take pleasure in dykesploitation's sensationalised treatment of lesbian sex and narratives focused on relationships between two women, and that these films are best enjoyed as part of a collective viewing experience.

This form of nostalgic camp appreciation is also expressed by Tracy Gilchrist in her review of the films for the lesbian community website, LesbianNation.com. She states that dykesploitation should be reclaimed as 'delicious campy fun', and not as demoralising to a lesbian audience. For her, it is the extensive use of 'gauzy lighting, over-the-top ballads, flashbacks and superimpositions' that make episodes like the highly-strung emotional scenes that dwell on the dyke drama of Marsha's desperate longing for Terry in *That Tender Touch*, 'endlessly entertaining'.[17] Indeed, it is this mixture of melodrama and sex that has made the contemporary TV series *The L Word* (2004–2009) so popular with lesbian viewers. Together, the camp pleasures offered by these cult texts mean that watching them is widely understood as an amusing and engaging, rather than alienating, experience.

Considered retrospectively, dykesploitation is becoming increasingly acknowledged, and even enjoyed, as part of lesbian film history. The LGBT historian, critic, collector and curator, Jenni Olson has championed the category, stressing that while 'We [the queer community] wouldn't exactly embrace these films as positive portrayals of lesbian or bi life', at the time of their release dykesploitation films did at least make lesbianism visible, and 'from our current historical distance [they can] offer loads of campy entertainment value.'[18] As already discussed, the contemporary marketing and reception of dykesploitation is aware of and plays on a number of ironic gaps that exist between the films' original audience, their new audience, their sensational promotional materials, and their camp content. It seems that it is precisely these disparities between intention, expectation and fulfilment that make the classic dykesploitation films so appealing to present-day lesbian audiences. However, the legacy of dykesploitation does not end with a reclamation of the cycle of 1960s and 1970s films, since it can also be argued that many of the category's traditions are continued and developed by contemporary hard-core lesbian-made pornography.

VERY EXXXPLICIT: 100% DYKE PRODUCED

Sugar High Glitter City is a clear example of how contemporary lesbian porn might be related to dykesploitation. Significantly, it begins with a female voiceover, which introduces the fantasy that the film's narrative is based around:

> It's the future … sugar is outlawed. The power mongers of the earth control the flow of the beautiful white gold through their sticky fingers. Kickbacks and payoffs are the name of the game. No place knew the score more than Glitter City … caneville … sweet town … an underworld of sugar pimps and candy 'hos filled with cane-addicted dykes peddling their own flesh to keep the sweet trip going.

Like *Chained Girls*, *Sugar High Glitter City* uses its narrator to provide motivation for and contextualise the characters and plot that, in this case, link a series of hard-core sexual scenarios together. But while the role of the narrator remains largely unchanged, the shift from an authoritative male voiceover to an authoritative female voiceover, points to one of the key differences between dykesploitation in its original formula, and the queer version that continues in lesbian porn. Opening *Sugar High Glitter City* with a female narrator immediately helps signal a change of address from a straight male to a lesbian audience. Moreover, the fact that this voice is later identified in the credits as belonging to San Francisco-based lesbian photographer, artist and activist Honey Lee Cottrell further adds to the film's aura of active appropriation; her queer authority overrides the patriarchal voice and instead asserts lesbian sexual agency in a very real sense.[19]

From Cottrell's voiceover we learn that Glitter City's futuristic lesbian underworld is a subculture based entirely on and around exploitation. In Glitter City, sugar is a drug that has now been outlawed, but sugar-hungry lesbians will stop at nothing, even selling themselves, to feed their addiction. Sugar is then explicitly connected with other illegal substances and with promiscuous sexual activity in *Sugar High Glitter City*, causing all manner of sinful behaviour – corruption, cravings, habituation and dependency.

These vices are in turn associated with lesbian culture, as the city's inhabitants all share an irrepressible desire for that 'sweet dyke currency' of sugar/sex. This is clearly reminiscent of the 1960s and 1970s dykesploitation films, which had also exploited lesbian sexuality and sex in order to attract audiences even as they portrayed lesbianism as both a deviant behaviour and a serious social problem. *Sugar High Glitter City*'s playful conflation of lesbian sex and sugar implies that in the future both are regarded as illicit, guilty pleasures that mainstream society has (once more) declared immoral and legislated against. It is interesting to note therefore that the societal structures, such as the secular state and the Church, who denounce deviant sexuality, are critiqued in the film via the character of the Reverend Dew (Shar Rednour).

The Reverend Dew is first seen dressed in army camouflage and employed in folding pamphlets entitled 'Say No to the Sugar Life'. She preaches redemption on the streets of Glitter City, urging those she comes across to 'keep away from the sugar life… The sweet life leads to soul decay.' Due to the links made between sugar and sex, the Reverend Dew's virulent condemnation of 'the sweet life' is, by association, also a denunciation of lesbian sexuality. But all is not as it seems. For, while we watch the Reverend Dew lecturing on the 'evil ways of sugar'

FIGURE 16.4 Dykesploitation imagery in contemporary lesbian porn: cover art for *Sugar High Glitter City*

to a small group of lesbian hustlers, her sermon is interrupted by the narrator who informs us of the Reverend's past: 'she used to be Honey Dew, one of the best candy 'hos ever to strut the streets… Glitter City's not been the same since she became sugar free.' This is followed by a flashback to Honey Dew's last experience of sugar-fuelled lesbian sex before she converted. In the flashback, Honey Dew uses her fingers to penetrate Cherry Glaze (Josephine X) and bring her to orgasm, as they each suck hungrily on the same lollipop.

FIGURE 16.5 Lips like sugar: sex and saccharin addiction in *Sugar High Glitter City*

Having set up the Reverend Dew as a former addict/lesbian and born-again preacher, the film later goes on to show her re-conversion back to sugar and the joys of lesbian sex. The Reverend Dew's return to her old lifestyle is prompted when she comes across Cherry Glaze and another of her ex-lovers – the corrupt cop Blue (Jackie Strano) – dealing sugar in a doorway. The Reverend's attempt to reform Cherry Glaze fails, and instead Blue seduces Reverend Dew by reminding her of how much she misses sugar/ lesbian sex. The Reverend Dew is finally converted back to Honey Dew as she, Blue and Cherry Glaze enjoy a femme-butch-femme lesbian threesome and

some contraband confectionary together. Reverend/Honey Dew can be read as a metaphor for the way that *Sugar High Glitter City* turns dykesploitation around – in the same way that she has been reabsorbed into the lesbian underworld, the dykesploitation form has been reappropriated by these lesbian filmmakers.

Made by the independent lesbian production company SIR, *Sugar High Glitter City* is, as the DVD cover states, '100% dyke produced'.[20] SIR's films (other titles include *Hard Love* (2000) and *How to Fuck in High Heels* (2000)) are all written, produced and directed by 'real life' lesbian couple Shar Rednour and Jackie Strano. Rednour and Strano also star in their porn films, alongside a diverse cast drawn from the local lesbian community. SIR's claim to authenticity – real lesbians having real sex for a real lesbian audience by the company's close links to the San Francisco lesbian community where SIR is based, is particularly important to its status as specifically 'dyke porn'. In her historical account of the development of lesbian pornography since the 1960s, Heather Butler views dyke porn as the most recent stage in the representation of lesbian sexuality and sex. According to Butler, what distinguishes this form of lesbian pornography from what came before it is that

> Dyke porn is safe-sex savvy and not afraid to appropriate sex acts once considered definitive of heterosexual and gay male pornography, such as penetration, dirty talk, rough sex, and role-playing, to name a few. Anything once considered off-limits, perverted or inappropriate (for either political or personal reasons) is now up for grabs – literally.[21]

So, dyke porn is described as inclusive, as it assimilates and makes acceptable a wide range of sexual practices. As a result, films like *Sugar High Glitter City* can be seen to challenge the notion that certain sex acts do not or cannot belong in the representation of lesbian sex by co-opting dykesploitation's heterosexual configurations to create an authentic 'utopian' lesbian fantasy space.[22]

Crucially then, *Sugar High Glitter City* has put the dyke into dykesploitation. Butch characters were originally very few and far between in this exploitation sub-genre. Out of the three classic dykesploitation films discussed above, only *Chained Girls* actually features any butches. *Chained Girls* establishes the stereotypical butch/femme relationship – the butch not only assumes the traditionally masculine role, she is also masculine in her appearance.

In contrast to the film's narcissistic and sexually immature femme characters, the butch characters are represented as violent, predatory and controlling. For example, one scene in *Chained Girls* depicts a young femme's forced initiation into the 'love cult of lesbianism' by a pipe-smoking butch who is encouraged by a flesh-hungry group of her 'bull dyke' friends.

Again, the fact that these dykesploitation films were mainly produced by and aimed at men in the audience means that, on the few occasions she did appear, the 'mannish' butch lesbian was not eroticised in the same way as her glamorous femme counterpart. In fact, it has been noted that erotic representations of the butch body still remain problematic, even in 'real' lesbian porn that routinely focuses on butch/femme dynamics.[23] Michelle Tea suggests that this is because 'Butches are supposed to be the silent, non-glamorous types... The reality of womanly curves and soft flesh can feel like betrayals to dykes cultivating a tough machismo.'[24]

FIGURE 16.6 The butch is back: contemporary dykesploitation imagery in *Sugar High Glitter City*

217

However, *Sugar High Glitter City* does address this dilemma. Alongside the many episodes of butch/femme and femme/femme sex, the film also features a rare butch/butch sex scene. Both Blow Pop (Chester Drawers) and Gooden Plenty (Rocko Capital) are marked as butch 'sugar bois' (for lesbians, a boi is a dyke with a boyish presentation) and both wear strap-on dildos. As the scene between them progresses, their butch bodies are increasingly exposed; as Gooden Plenty penetrates Blow Pop from behind both of them are topless (Blow Pop is bottomless too, apart from her harness) and Gooden Plenty expresses her pleasure by fondling her own breasts. With scenes like this, SIR's dyke porn has sought to challenge any deep-seated reluctance to bare all, and a desire to sexualise butch women has been central to the filmmakers' pro-feminist, pro-sex agenda.[25]

In *Sugar High Glitter City* we see all kinds of lesbians engaging in all kinds of lesbian sex that includes multiracial butch/femme role-play, sex toys and female ejaculation. So, for example, in another scene from the film, the Asian butch hustler Rock Candy (Charlie Skye) and her rich client, black femme Goldie Icing (Aimee Pearl) enact a lesbian 'Daddy girl' fantasy in which the strap-on dildo also figures prominently. The role-play begins with Goldie Icing begging Rock Candy to let her touch and lick that 'special package … Daddy's cock', and climaxes with her orgasm after she is finally penetrated by Rock Candy's dildo (like Gooden Plenty and Blow Pop, Rock Candy also uncovers her butch body during sex). In the context of dyke porn, the dildo is seen as an important, if contested, accessory of lesbian sex that was previously absent from classic dykesploitation.[26]

Like the reappropriation of dykesploitation, the reappropriation of the phallus, role-play and use of the word 'cock' points to contemporary lesbian politics and the representation of active female sexuality. *Sugar High Glitter City* uses scenes like this to realise a camp *mise-en-scène* of lesbian desire; for instance, all of the props, costumes and make-up used, glitter and sparkle under the studio lights. This extends from the silver metallic dress, earrings and eye shadow worn by Goldie Icing in the scene described above, to all the women's glitter-sprinkled bodies, and even the brightly coloured dildos. In addition to *mise-en-scène*, the parodic dialogue and style of fantasy role-play in this scene, and indeed the whole of the film, are intentionally camp, suggesting what Judith Butler has termed the performative nature of gender and sexuality.[27] Here, as elsewhere in contemporary lesbian porn, the butch/top-femme/bottom couple perform their representation of sexual desire and pleasure calculatedly, deploying the dildo and the conventions of mainstream porn in a way that, Ragan Rhyne says, has enabled SIR to 'recode them' in the context of lesbian sexuality.[28] Therefore, it seems that whereas the earlier dykesploitation films, whose address is clearly towards heterosexual males, may be thought of as (unintentionally) camp through the lens of historical distance, *Sugar High Glitter City* is an example of a (deliberate) camp fantasy made unequivocally for an informed lesbian audience.

CONCLUSION

Although *Sugar High Glitter City* is not the only contemporary lesbian porn film in which a dialogue with dykesploitation can be detected, it is noteworthy that the blurb on the DVD cover explicitly connects the two, stating that this film 'slams the dykesploitation genre into fast-forward'.[29] Beyond SIR's influential work, other recent examples of lesbian-made porn associated with dykesploitation might include, in the US, those films written and directed by Shine Louise Houston, such as *The Crash Pad* (2006), *Superfreak* (2006) and *Wild Kingdom* (2006), and in the UK, Angie Dowling's *Tick Tock* (2001) and *Madam and Eve* (2003). Not only has dykesploitation inspired a creative re-vision in the form of contemporary lesbian porn, but films like *Sugar High Glitter City* can prompt a rereading of the original, exploitative approach to lesbian-themed narratives, which is now, in its turn, being exploited.

CHAPTER 17
FLESH (FUR) AND FURY:
AN INTERVIEW WITH CHRISTINA LINDBERG

Xavier Mendik

Over the last decade, critics and theorists have made a number of advances in reclaiming those genres and cycles of European cult film previously dismissed as examples of 'trash' or bad cinema. A central emphasis of these attempts to drag Europe's darkest pleasures into the academy has been the critical reconsiderations of leading performers/icons within the previously marginal cult film text. This has resulted in a variety of innovative approaches being adopted to explore a range of issues such as the sexually menacing persona of Eurotrash female stars,[1] as well as disquieting representations of race and ethnicity that their representations often evoke.[2] While female sexual identity/racial affiliation have often been central to these various approaches, recent accounts have also dissected male constructions of suffering and masochism using a range of approaches derived from differing philosophical currents.[3]

Although Italy has proven to be the dominant paradigm for recent considerations of the Euro-cult performer, other continental regions such as Sweden also display long traditions of promoting stars who embody both the titillating and traumatic potential which encapsulates the cine-erotic. Arguably, the most influential and infamous performer to emerge from Sweden's golden era of eroticism remains Christina Lindberg. The actress was born in 1950 in Gothenburg and raised in a female-headed, working-class family. Having read Latin at school, Lindberg developed interests in aesthetics, leading to plans to train as an architect. However, these ideals were sidelined by her incorporation into Sweden's 'sexual revolution' of the late 1960s, which saw her elevated from a photographic 'glamour' model to one of the leading erotic soft-core performers of the decade. Between 1970 and 1974, Lindberg made 18 films which confirmed her as a smouldering sexploitation icon, in a range of productions which often fused sex with social commentary on the changing Swedish society of the period.

FIGURE 17.1 A sexploitation signifier: Lindberg's films as reference to wider social change in 1970s Sweden

Building on her international status as leading erotic pin-up, it is noticeable that many of these films were German productions, often completed by Walter Boos. For instance, Lindberg's contributions to *Teil-Was Eltern oft verzweifeln lässt* and *Mädchen, die nach München kommen* (both 1972), remain among some of the more memorable *Schulmädchen-Report* films, which used erotic tropes and spicy vignettes to expose restrictive national ideologies of gender and the body.[4] Not only did Lindberg feature significantly in a range of such Eurotrash productions during this era, but she also travelled to Japan to work with significant 'Pink' directors such as Norifumi Suzuki and Sadao Nakajima. Here, she completed two significant feature films: *Furyô anego den: Inoshika Ochô* (*Sex and Fury*) and *Poruno no joô: Nippon sex ryokô* (*Pornstar Travels Around Japan* (both 1973)), whose extreme images of sexy, sword-wielding female avengers are often cited as influences on contemporary directors such as Quentin Tarantino.

Although often dubbed as the leading sex icon of the Swedish porn industry of the 1970s, Lindberg's films often reveal more complex and contradictory representations of sex and social mores than their salacious titles would suggest. For instance, *Exponerad* (*Exposed*, 1971), lifts the lid on the male-dominated discourses of the 1960s counterculture, by ranging the heroine between an number of male suitors who attempt to control her desires through either direct threat or manipulative mind control. The later film *Anita – ur en tonårsflickas dagbok* (*Anita: Swedish Nymphet*, 1973), functions more like a Swedish social problem film than a sexploitation potboiler, depicting how a young woman's uncontrollable sex drive leads to her gradual isolation from the more conformist domestic surroundings that the narrative depicts.

Anita revealed that Lindberg was more than able to handle more demanding acting roles, in a narrative that saw her ranged against more established, art-focused performers (including a young Stellan Skarsgård).

Arguably, it was Lindberg's willingness to push the parameters of what was expected from the porno performance that led to her accepting the most controversial cult role of the period: as the lethal female vigilante Madeleine in Bo Arne Vibenius's shocker *Thriller* (aka *They Call Her One Eye*, 1974).

The film (which was instantly banned in Sweden due to its excessive depictions of sexual violence), casts Lindberg as a mute girl who is ensnared into a brutal world of enforced prostitution, drug addiction

FIGURE 17.2 Iconic avenger: Lindberg's infamous role as the one-eyed female killer in *Thriller*

and violence at the hands of the suave but psychotic pimp Tony (played to chilling effect by Heinz Hopf). When Madeline attacks one of her clients in an early act of defiance, Tony brutally blinds the heroine by stabbing a scalpel into her eye. This scene (which reportedly featured a close-up of a human eye secured from a local morgue), gave *Thriller* its instant notoriety. Equally, subsequent images of Lindberg toting a shotgun whilst wearing a single black eye-patch also gave *Thriller* an enduring cult iconography, that in part explain the genesis of the similarly disabled but potent female character of Ellie Driver in Tarantino's *Kill Bill: Vol. 1* (2003).

Even more than 35 years after its controversial release, *Thriller* remains unconventional and uncomfortable viewing, not least because of Vibenius's insistence of splicing hard-core footage (derived from a Swedish sex club) into the frequent scenes of Madeleine's abuse. As startling as these jarring shock inserts is Lindberg's towering performance in the film. Denied access to any dialogue, she evokes the heroine's predicament and eventual empowerment through a wide range of carefully orchestrated body gestures that give genuine conviction to an otherwise difficult role. This performance is in part assisted by the unconventional film style with which Vibenius shoots his heroine in *Thriller*. Whilst the final scenes of Madeline taking revenge on her (male and female) oppressors are shot in extended slow-motion scenes which betray a clear debt to Sam Peckinpah and genre cinema, the colour codings, camera movement and use of naturalistic sound reveal a more distinct, more legitimate basis derived from European art cinema (doubtlessly inspired by the director's training with Ingmar Bergman). The end result is a movie that is both shocking and thought-provoking, ultimately revealing an image of potent female vengeance rarely equalled in mainstream film. As Michael Mackenzie noted in his *DVD Times* review of the film, *Thriller* remains 'an engaging and at times touching piece of work: a rare exploitation movie that actually comes close to being an art film'.[5]

Whilst the release of *Thriller* remains Lindberg's most prominent feature to date, it also marked her gradual withdrawal from a 1970s European erotic industry increasingly dominated by hard-core, conventional narrative features. In more recent years Christina Lindberg retrained as a journalist before becoming one of Sweden's most high-profile environmental and animal rights activists. In the following interview, the actress reflects on the continued influence and infamy of some of her 1970s erotic roles, whilst also commenting on how her new passion as an animal rights spokesperson allows her to combine flesh, fur and fury.

Xavier Mendik: *Sweden became synonymous with sexploitation during the 1970s: was this purely to do with titillation or a more serious portrayal of the country and culture during this period?*

Christina Lindberg: Well, I think it was a mixture of the two. Many of the films were an excuse for nakedness, but some of the directors working in this area wanted to display a kind of social pathos in the situation. In particular Torgny Wickman, whose films had a dark side to them. I worked with him on *Anita – ur en tonårsflickas dagbok*. If that film is showing the Sweden of the 1970s, it was not in a very nice way as it was kind of a little bit dark movie.

Yes, absolutely. Was there as much soul searching as sexploitation in these movies then?

(Laughs.) In a way, yes. But these were not necessarily films for the home market. Often when producers wanted to sell the movie they picked me because then they knew that they could sell it to a lot of other countries apart from Sweden, because I had a pin-up profile. So Sweden wasn't the main market for doing those movies.

But the thing that was interesting with those movies is that I was cast against big actors from Sweden at the time. It was always those actors from so-called serious films and, you know, they were very poorly paid at the time. So they had to have some money, which is why they ended up doing sexy movies. And when I took off my clothes I felt they were good to me, those guys. You know, it would always be the same people running the technical aspects, cameras, directing, writing the songs and writing the scripts. These were all well known and respected Swedish artists, actors and filmmakers.

This sweeps away one myth about 1970s Swedish sexploitation cinema: that it was a backstreet industry with no links to the cinematic mainstream.

Yes. These films were anything but dark, dirty, small works.

One film about which there is a whole cult mythology is Thriller. *What attracted you to the movie?*

The chance not to play myself!

What an intriguing comment! What do you mean by this?

I was no actress, so I had to place all my own feelings and expressions into these films: I was Christina Lindberg in those movies. And when Vibenius came and asked me to do *Thriller*, I thought, well this is something! Now I can show people that I can actually act. And then he also told me that I was going to be mute and I also thought that was a good thing because then I could concentrate on my body acting; which is a language also.

The most difficult form of acting is body acting, and you did an incredible job in Thriller. *I mean, do you feel you really managed to portray everything you wanted totally through gesture?*

Mmm, yes. But this was achieved by very small gestures, because that's the problem with theatre actors: they are big behavers! But I wasn't used to acting, so I was very faint in my acting and that suits the tone of the movie and the role very well.

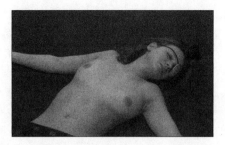

FIGURE 17.3 Grindhouse gestures: Lindberg's use of body, movement and expression in *Thriller*

A lot of people have said Vibenius is a difficult guy to work with. How did you find your relationship with him?

Well, I didn't have so much of a relationship with him, to be honest. This is because while he is a very special guy, he can also be a little bit cold in some ways. He didn't care about me too much, you know. So I don't know him very well, to be honest.

But in a way it's quite liberating as an actor because it seems as though that gave you more freedom. You had an unrestricted space through which to develop the character of Madeleine.

Yes, that's true. He wasn't on my back all the time, he only told me what to do when strictly necessary. What also made it a pleasure for me was that I played against a very good actor, Heinz Hopf. I also acted with him in *Exposed*, and we were very good friends.

223

You didn't find it a challenge in any way, moving from Exposed *into a much more character-driven movie?*

I found it a challenge, yes. But then *Thriller* was a film full of challenges! I had to go to training school for karate, for example, and I also had to get trained for hand-to-hand combat, weapons with live ammunition and so on. So it was tough! And because I was aware that I didn't have a background in acting, I wanted to make the action in my scenes as believable as possible. Like when the girl hits me and so on, and I would say 'We will film the scene only once, so hit me, so I can feel that you are doing it!' I didn't want the actress to hit me too hard you know, but I wanted her to make contact. That was my way of performing in that movie. The purely physical became my mechanism for reacting without having acting experience.

Talking of the purely physical, Thriller *became notorious for Vibenius's insertion of hard-core inserts into the already distressing rape scenes. What were your thoughts on those porno inserts?*

Not good, only because I didn't know about them. They were put into the movie and no one thinks they were necessary. And these scenes were made by a couple that were very well-known during the 1970s. They're called Romeo and Julia [Swedish for Juliet]. Romeo and Julia were stars at the porno clubs in Sweden, because at that time in Sweden you used to have porno clubs where people were on stage, you know, having intercourse in front of people.

I'm not a defending those scenes, but I have a comment linked to them, which is that some people have argued that rather than glamourise rape, those scenes make porn look ugly.

To be honest, I haven't seen them, but I have heard that they are not attractive at all.

I mean they're so unappealing that they push the film into the realms of the anti-pornographic. Do you think this was what Vibenius intended?

At a wider level, I think so. Yes, that's correct. It's in his personality. This is a film that confronts and questions desire, so I think you're right.

From the anti-pornographic to the apparently un-feminist, Thriller *was released at the height of the whole 1970s feminists against porn movement. Do you think the film actually got caught up in those wider political debates at all?*

Oh yes, but only because it appeared to be a separate world to what we were doing with the film and what I was intending to do as a performer. I am not sure what it was like in the rest of Europe, but in Sweden, political feminism of the 1970s was dominated by women from the upper class. You were never quite sure if they intended to rescue or police working-class women. My parents were very hardworking, ordinary people. I grew up with only my mother because my parents divorced when I was very small. But no one from my class was connected with those political movements. And when I started school, I went to read Latin and languages and there were not too many lower-class children who did that, but I was one of them! We were never too enthusiastic about this political talk, it was always people with the money and power that seemed to engage in these conversations on our behalf … whether we wanted them too or not!

I can imagine your movies were pretty popular with them … not!

(Laughs.) Yes. A colleague once did tell me that the Swedish feminists of the 1970s did have a picture of me, which they would throw darts at! I guess to them they I symbolised all that was bad with Swedish sexploitation cinema of the period, which is quite funny.

The irony being that a movie like Thriller *is all about confronting, rather than gratifying, male desire, particularly through the theme of the vengeful woman.*

Exactly. But you know, at that time they thought I was a victim. It's so funny because today it's so different with *Kill Bill* and so on; there is now a new generation of strong woman who are clearly modelled on 1970s sexploitation films such as mine. And the funny thing is that I have always felt very strong when I was performing in these films. People would often ask me, 'Don't you feel like a victim?' No, I took care of myself; I've always taken care of myself and I felt respected. And in a way a film like *Thriller* is all about what happens when a woman is not respected in that way.

Do you feel you really set the trend with Thriller?

Yes, both in later American films, but also here in Sweden. Recently, on television, we had a series which featured a black singer who loses an eye and then goes out for revenge. As with *Thriller* she has an eye patch, and as with *Thriller* she is also very strong. But this is very amusing because although the film was so influential, in Sweden they never, ever mention *Thriller*. They destroyed it and never mentioned the name. The film has been totally ignored as a key part of Swedish movie culture. I talked with a journalist yesterday and now they are beginning to write about this. And you know, she is about 23 or 24. When I meet young people and particularly girls, they always say 'Oh, how interesting, I didn't know anything about this. Could you send me a movie? I would like to see this.'

Perhaps the film's exclusion is also down to the difficultly in pinning it down: some people see Thriller *as a thriller; other people have seen it as an art movie.*

Yes, I know. In Sweden particularly, they want to classify it as one thing or the other. They are very anxious: they want to see the film as either this or that, when it in fact it is a perfect combination. They got very confused, you know. But when you asked about the art angle: it's true, because Vibenius worked together with Ingmar Bergman, and he was acclaimed for his technical skills. And I definitely think that his work with Bergman certainly influenced the look and style of *Thriller*; it's dark and rhapsodic. As with Bergman's movies, *Thriller* tells the story in a very articulate and artistic way.

225

Moving from visual styles to violence. Thriller *remains an extreme movie. How did you cope with those images?*

Rather well I guess! But, you know, a lot of strange things happened when we were shooting that film. For example, the scene in Drottningholm, when I got out of the police car and start shooting, the locals had no idea it was a movie scene, so the people in front of me were terrified! They saw this girl with a black eye patch and a rifle pointed at them and then start shooting at the police car. It was absurd, but they saw me with that gun and ran for their lives!

So they actually thought it was for real?

Yes, because Bo Arne never told anyone he was going to do a scene, he just went and did it! The police car we were using was chased by the Swedish police all the time, because it was against the law to paint an ordinary car like a police car. He never told the police that he was going to do it. After some days the police called me and said that local people have reported me for threatening them with a shotgun! So I had to go the police station and try to explain! I was there, 21 years old, sitting there terrified, and Bo Arne didn't help me at all. I was used to taking care of myself so I was all right, you know. But there were a lot of those things happening all the time during the shoot, so it was rather tough at a number of levels!

I can imagine. Although the movie was banned in Sweden, have you been surprised how internationally it's gained this massive cult reputation?

FIGURE 17.4 A female icon for the Tarantino generation: Lindberg's influence on *Kill Bill*

Yes, but I must say I'm flattered and it feels rather good, but still in Sweden they don't want to admit that *Thriller* has something to tell Swedes.

Yes, that is incredible. Obviously you're aware of the Tarantino endorsement and the influence your character had on Kill Bill. *What are your views on this?*

I am delighted, of course. I mean, he's one of the very best. I can tell you that such an endorsement is also a great compliment to the director of *Thriller*. Bo Arne Vibenius, always had the dream to make a second *Thriller* film. It was a pity he couldn't do that, because he spent too long chasing money to try and make it, but he talked with me about making the second *Thriller* and I think it was a real shame that it was never made.

Is there any chance he would resurrect the idea because of the Tarantino endorsement? I mean, if it were to happen, would you do it?

No, no, I'm too old today… I wouldn't want to drive around in that police car again!

After Thriller, *you went on to do a lot of interesting projects such as the two movies you made in Japan,* Sex and Fury *and* Pornstar Travels Around Japan. *What are your memories of those two projects?*

Well, I only have some good memories of Japan, because, at that time, I was a little bit shy, in fact, I was extremely shy! You may not believe that considering the films I made, but it is true. Therefore, the Japanese people really suit me: they are also very reserved and shy and I have their manners, you know, so we all got along very, very well. After I made those two movies they asked me to stay. They wanted me to sign a long-term contract with one of the companies there, to do multiple movies. But at the time, they worked day and night, twenty-four hours. I made those movies and I did calendar and fold-out work there, as well as television programmes. After three months of that, I was so tired, so I said, 'I have to go home, I think!' I then said, 'In Sweden we have eight-hour working days!' But they didn't believe me, I think. So then I went home to make *Anita*, and I didn't go back.

Since Thriller *and your Japanese period, you've diversified into a number of different roles, even campaigning for environmental issues in Sweden. I mean, I'd be really interested just to hear briefly why you've moved in that direction.*

To be honest, I haven't moved into it, because I have always been fond of nature and animals. When I was small I was always taking care of cats and dogs and even used to pick worms when they were on the pavement to put them back in the grass. I was very sorry to have had to live in a city when I was small. I have always felt like that I didn't belong there. For over ten years I have lived in the countryside and it suits me perfectly. I love all animals but specifically, I had written a lot of debate articles in the national daily newspapers about predators: the wolf, lynx and bears. Because we have these hunters in Sweden, you know, and they are very powerful, so there's a lot of hunting in Sweden.

That really surprises me. I would have thought Sweden would have a really good reputation.

For human rights yes, not for animal rights. When I see television from places like the UK, I see how they save animals and so on. We have nothing like that in Sweden. You are free to donate your money to saving-homes for cats and dogs, but no money comes from the Swedish Government is contributed. And because the Government has not allowed any wolves in the whole of northern Sweden, we only have a small population living in the middle of Sweden, where the hunters are chasing them all the time and because of that, they are going to disappear. We now have only around a thousand wild cats in Sweden and the Government still allows the hunters to shoot them. It's incredible. We have so much land, so we have a responsibility to keep those animals for the future, to give the children the chance to see them.

FIGURE 17.5 Porn survivor: Lindberg as a symbol of the empowered sexploitation heroine

One final question. Many porn actresses feel a lot of social pressure to renounce their former roles in the sex industry, most famously Linda Lovelace.

Yes.

227

Are you ashamed of your porno past or do you feel that films like Thriller *did make a legitimate contribution to cinema culture?*

Not ashamed at all. As you say *Thriller* did make an impact, and in a very good way. I hope that I have given people something positive to consider in my films. Certainly, I never sought to portray women as victims or weak in any of my films. Instead they are a warning to men who do not realise the potential power women have.

I want to offer my sincere thanks to Christina Lindberg for agreeing to this interview. My thanks also to Eve Bennett for transcribing the interview material.

CHAPTER 18

BLACK & WHITE FRILLS/SILENT THRILLS: A CASE STUDY IN PROGRAMMING AND EXHIBITION FROM 'THE SMOKING CABINET: A FESTIVAL OF BURLESQUE AND CABARET CINEMA 1895–1933'

Simone Pyne

Since its inception in 2006, 'The Smoking Cabinet: A Festival of Burlesque and Cabaret Cinema 1895–1933' has run highly-successful micro film festivals, it has occupied a residency in one of the UK's leading independent cinemas, the Curzon Soho, and also gone on tour at music and film festivals throughout the UK.

The festival was born, and has continued to grow, during a period that has seen a clear renaissance in social, cultural and critical interest in cabaret and burlesque. Opportunities to both watch and actively participate in this renaissance have opened up in social clubs, music venues, dance schools and nightclubs across the UK, specifically in London.

Despite this resurgence of interest in burlesque, cabaret and vaudeville, the fact that all of these forms found a natural home in early cinema, and were often also the focus of early experiments in filmmaking, is often overlooked. It's ironic, therefore, that the relationship between dance, the body and the moving image has been explored extensively and is clearly established within cinema history in other contexts. Distinguished by tableaux and static shots, early cinema emphasised performance within the frame and basked in the novelty of filmed movement, both as spectacle and also as a form of entertainment in its own right. The fit then between film, dance and performance was explicit in cinema's nascent years, simply due to the limited technical sophistication of filmmaking at this time. In acknowledging and exploring these issues, the festival offers a unique opportunity to better understand and experience the intersection between burlesque, cabaret culture and the medium of film.

Many of the films screened by The Smoking Cabinet have been either largely forgotten or have simply been inaccessible to the majority of cinema-goers, film fans and arts lovers for decades. The Smoking Cabinet offers a rare chance to see an eclectic range of films with occasionally risqué and suggestive burlesque and cabaret content within a festival that strives to position these films within a specific context. It is arguably contradictory: a specialist film festival aimed at a potentially wide-ranging audience. However, as will be discussed in more detail below, there is in fact a large and diverse audience for a festival that exhibits the alliances that silent and early cinema had with variety, burlesque and cabaret performance.

Thus, many of the films programmed by The Smoking Cabinet represent examples of the most significant films in the history of sexuality and sex on screen from this period, whilst others offer a similar insight into the history of dance in film. Although considered somewhat tame by today's audiences, these influential films and their memorable erotic scenes were both groundbreaking and controversial at the time they were produced. A look at some of the films programmed reveals the extent to which many challenge sexual politics of the time and highlight the representation of sexuality during this period.

WOMEN WHO DANCE, GIRLS WHO GAZE

The earliest known pornographic films began to appear in France in the early 1920s and were known as 'risque' films, sold on the black market and viewed mostly in private settings. Lesbianism and heterosexual intercourse were the most common subjects of these films, whilst depictions of male homosexuality were extremely rare. To date, The Smoking Cabinet has not programmed a compilation of 'early pornography'. However, in the process of researching countless explicit films that would certainly be considered graphic, even by today's standards, were identified.

Whilst explicit feature-length 'pornographic' films are not considered to have emerged widely until the 1920s, there was nonetheless a tradition of representing titillating or suggestive material on film even from the very first years of cinema's invention. For instance, the festival has focused on films such as *Fatima's Coochie-Coochie Dance* (Edison Manufacturing Co. 1896), a short nickelodeon film of a gyrating belly dancer named Fatima. Fatima became well-known following her dancing shows at the World's Exhibition in Chicago, USA, in 1893.

Fatima's Coochie-Coochie Dance is notable for being the first film to be subjected to censorship. It was specifically the sexually suggestive nature of Fatima's gyrating that was objected to and this was covered up, albeit slightly ineffectively, with a grid-like pattern of white lines. Fatima and her dance is an superb example of the numerous risque films that featured exotic dancers during this period.

Other films, such as a *Trapeze Disrobing Act* (George S. Fleming, Edwin S. Porter, 1902), in which American vaudeville trapeze artist and strongwoman 'Charmion' strips from full Victorian *outré* wear to her knickers in less than one minute, whilst still swinging on her trapeze, are a triumph of early cinema. They present erotically-charged examples of female sexuality speaking predominantly to male audiences. This has lead some theorists to argue that these films can be understood as representing one very specific perspective in terms of the act of spectatorship, namely 'the gaze'. Whilst it is true that the image and eroticisation of the female form was crucial to the success, and immense popularity, of these early forms of entertainment, there are examples of films featured in the festival that do still recognise women as agents of change, in dominant roles, and negotiating situations on their own terms. This can be said of not only the characters they played but also of their position as 'celebrities' in the real world.

The dancing vaudeville performer Annabelle Whitford Moore was also featured in many of the earliest nickelodeon films. Known popularly as 'Peerless Annabelle' her routines were famously captured by the film pioneer Thomas Edison. *Annabelle Butterfly Dance* (William K. L. Dickson, 1894) was one of her most well-known performances, but her output was exhaustive and she also featured in *Annabelle Sun Dance* (Edison Manufacturing Co., 1894), *Annabelle Serpentine Dance* (Edison Manufacturing Co., 1895), *Serpentine Dance by Annabelle* (William K. L. Dickson, 1896), *Annabelle in Flag Dance* (American Mutoscope Co., 1896), *Skirt Dance by Annabelle* (American Mutoscope Co., 1896), *Tambourine Dance by Annabelle* (American Mutoscope Co., 1896) and *Sun Dance – Annabelle* (Edison Manufacturing Co., 1897). Male audiences were enthralled watching these early depictions of a loosely-clothed female dancer through a kinetoscope, the ever-popular peep show device often used to view short films in this period. These devices operated conveniently in terms of spectatorship allowing the audience to view risqué dances or suggestive films discreetly, and certainly helped fuel perceptions of the eroticism of star performers such as Annabelle Whitford Moore.

The Smoking Cabinet has also screened the Ernst Lubitsch's extravagant spectacle *So this is Paris!* (1926). The film features a cast of hundreds of performers dancing the Charleston beneath a pair of giant plastic legs. The avant-garde film *Oramunde* (Emlen Etting, 1933) features a mysterious nude-in-nature and Jean Renoir's controversial *Charleston Parade* (1927) stars African-American vaudeville performer Johnny Hudgins and Catherine Hessling (in a fur bikini) engaging in an early form of 'dance-off', a celebration of the 1920's most popular dance craze the Charleston.

As well as classic shorts, The Smoking Cabinet programmes feature films, most notably *Piccadilly* (1929) and *Der blaue Engel* (1930), director Josef von Sternberg's first collaboration with the legendary Marlene Dietrich. This was also accompanied by a panel discussion

'Women in Burlesque & Cabaret: Empowerment vs. Titillation' which addressed how and why a seemingly male-focused art-form has become a popular form of expression for so many women. The panel considered whether these forms offer a political platform for female performers to explore issues of gender and sexuality or whether they simply reinforce traditional notions of female sexuality. With this in mind, the film, appropriately, tells the story of a meek and repressed teacher, Professor Immanuel Rath (Emil Jannings), who is seduced and destroyed by a sensual and predatory top-hatted entertainer named Lola at the Blue Angel nightclub. The recent restoration of E. A. Dupont's *Piccadilly* has also been timely, given the current burgeoning of the New Burlesque movement. *Piccadilly* explores the dividing line between empowerment and exploitation. It boldly challenges 1920s taboos in its celebration of feminine wiles, and exotic Anna May Wong's transformation from scullery girl to burlesque diva and dancer *par excellence* enthralls the audience.

CABARET CULTURES AND CULTURED CINEASTES

The principal aim of The Smoking Cabinet is to investigate the legacy of early cabaret, vaudeville and burlesque forms in cinema between 1895–1933. Starting with the birth of film in 1895 and closing with the end of the Weimar Republic in Germany in 1933, four years after the coming of sound to cinema, it encompasses a period of considerable innovation in art and technology throughout Europe and America. During this period the 'modern world' emerged. It was a time of phenomenal developments in all aspects of modern life, including major socio-political changes. Set against this backdrop the style and technique of filmmaking also rapidly evolved. Filmmaking was transformed from being tableaux in composition, with static shots and long unedited takes, to continuity editing, synchronised sound and the emergence of the studio system whose model of producing, distributing and exhibiting film we still broadly recognise today. Early cinema, which by virtue of its 'newness' was both experimental and seminal, offered its audience a glimpse into the unknown and brave new world of mass visual entertainment. Cabaret, burlesque and film all emerged to become major forms of popular entertainment. During this period, the alliances between these forms were often explicit, with early film shows essentially taking the form of variety programmes interspersed with short films. In watching examples of these films The Smoking Cabinet festival's audience are able to imagine what it must have felt like to be positioned on the brink of modernism; expectant and excited about the rapidly changing world evolving in front of their eyes.

Cabaret reached its peak during the Weimar Republic of the late 1920s and early 1930s, although it has always been an art form that has fascinated its public. In this respect The Smoking Cabinet aims to do something that cabaret as an art-form does; to present a mixed bill of exotic and eclectic acts and entertainment. The Smoking Cabinet programming is, therefore, by definition eclectic. The selection of films poses a question: it does not aim to dictate what can be understood by the idea of cabaret and burlesque film, but asks 'what *can* be understood by the term cabaret and burlesque cinema?' Programmed material includes the work of leading and revered filmmakers such as Georges Méliès, Man Ray, highly influential work by the Dadaists, Percy Smith, Fred Evans and Adrian Brunel. Exceedingly rare footage such as *Moody's Club Follies* (Castle Films, 1923) was also featured at the festival with original footage from a 1923 revue performed in London along with content featuring music hall stars such as Elsa Lanchester and lesser-known curiosities including late-nineteenth-century erotica, trick films and novelty shorts.

Some of the material programmed could certainly be classified as documentary or reportage in a broader sense and several of the featured films were initially intended to be light-hearted news items. One of our headline features of the 2008 festival which included several examples of this type of film was our Coney Island programme. This also included Fatty Arbuckle and Buster Keaton in the 1917 classic *Coney Island* (Fatty Arbuckle, 1917). The Coney Island programme offered a wonderfully eclectic mix of curiosities, with the *King of Coins* (Alf Collins, 1903) sharing the bill with both 'boxing cats' and the muscle man Eugene Sandow, one of the first entertainers in America to have their reputation enhanced by the moving image.

As well as recording the performances and culture of cabaret and burlesque during this period the films programmed for the festival also reflect the art-forms that influenced society at large. One could argue that Percy Smith's classic film *Birth of a Flower* (1910), featuring blossoming flora, has little to do with cabaret or burlesque. However, bursting with suggestive sexual allure, it is a subtle tease in cinematic form. Films such as this encourage the audience to consider just how far burlesque and cabaret cinema extend, and thus engage more wholeheartedly with what they are viewing. Whilst some of the films selected for the festival are more subtle and allegorical in their relationship to cabaret and burlesque performance, others are most certainly not. For instance, the burlesque qualities of a title like *Disrobing Trapeze Act* require little interpretation. The point here then is that the content programmed for the festival is at times as disparate and diverse as the cabaret and burlesque scene itself. And, of course, this is what gives the festival its edge and excitement. The festival is a showcase for potent, stunning and previously unavailable films that have inspired artists, filmmakers, performers and dancers of the past. It is hoped that all the films programmed encourage a deeper understanding of the relationship between cabaret, burlesque and the evolution of early cinema.

STAGE-MANAGING THE SEDUCTIVE

Not surprisingly, agreeing on the content for the festival was a subject of keen debate amongst the four producers who as a team also had responsibility for fundraising and sponsorship, PR and Press, copy-writing, design, event running and production. A large part of the material programmed hails from the British Film Institute and the National Film and Television Archive. Journalists often have a nostalgic view of what archive film programming entails; imagining the programmers brushing off dusty film tins and 're-discovering' long-lost classics. In actual fact it involves endless research on databases, dead-ends, and the relentless pursuit of individuals and companies for rights clearances. We have searched thousands of database entries and titles in order to find content for the festival, and this is an on-going process.

Our searches began initially with research into 'the smoking concert' films – a collection of mild erotica made for male audiences around the turn of the last century. As it transpired, many of these films were either inappropriate, unimaginative or incomplete. Our research has also focused on circuses, trapeze artists, striptease, magicians, burlesque acts, comedy duos, stage shows and music hall stars. We embraced search terms and subjects that reflected the diversity of cabaret, burlesque, vaudeville and music hall entertainment and this in its self required extensive research on these subjects in order to learn more about the star performers of the time. Lisa Appignanesi, the patron of the Smoking Cabinet and author of *The Cabaret* (Yale University Press, 2004) was a huge help here. Her book features extensive accounts of the origins of these forms, from 1880s politically motivated *chanson* singers and literary cafés in Paris, through to the Weimar period and beyond. Research for festival content is always followed by lengthy viewing sessions – often operating Steenbecks for the screening of short-listed 16mm and 35mm film in the depths of the National Film & Television Archive. This in itself raises an important question of how The Smoking Cabinet producers choose to define cabaret and burlesque cinema. The answer is to avoid any approach that may put a limit on what it has, can or may mean. We chose to consider it as an attitude as much as an act – a projection of spirit as much as literal performance. This wide embrace is best captured by the magazine *Dazed & Confused*'s description of the festival as 'deliciously eclectic; the ultimate tease in film festivals'.

The Smoking Cabinet offers not only screenings, but also the opportunity to see live performances, music, discussions and workshops. Debate and audience participation is evident at any Smoking Cabinet event, whether in the form of traditional panel discussions, Q&As following screenings, detailed introductions or informal group discussions. The festival generates a significant amount of debate between professional performers, film historians, archivists and the general public, and this is key to both its vitality and the atmosphere generated during the festival. This interest in discourse has also been encouraged through podcasts conducted by The Smoking Cabinet. These podcasts, which feature interviews with leading figures in the contemporary cabaret and burlesque movement, are available on The Smoking Cabinet website (www.thesmokingcabinet.com). The festival offers a platform for observation, understanding and debate, as arts practitioners, performers and entertainers who use cabaret or burlesque in their work take part in a series of post-screening discussions. The topics covered include issues such as representation, the body, women and the role of migration in early cinema, as well as inevitable debates around sexuality, form, Otherness, aesthetics and the growth and future of cabaret and burlesque itself.

The Smoking Cabinet is, however, still modest in size, attracting approximately a thousand guests each year over a three-day period, with on average six or seven screenings and events. The major challenge in our first year was funding. This did not come as a great surprise in a climate of increasingly curtailed funding for the arts, but the obvious effect of this was simply that in our first year we had to scale back both our budget and our ambitions for the festival. Practically speaking, this meant cutting workshops, ensuring that all screenings were at one venue and reducing the number of screenings. In our second year we were able to introduce workshops and expand on our efforts due to the fact that we secured sponsorship from a boutique lingerie company, Playful Promises. We have developed other partnerships which have allowed the festival to grow, receiving support from Westminster Arts, 10th Planet Digital Media and importantly the British Film Institute and the National Film and Television Archive.

The festival has consistently made efforts to go one step further and ensure that we host 'events' and not just 'screenings', with the aim of providing real value for our audiences. The cinema exhibition model is changing rapidly. Developments in technology and the growth of the DVD markets and downloads are affecting how and when we watch films and this has often meant that cinema audiences can, at times, be elusive. In many cases it is no longer possible to simply programme a film and anticipate that this in itself will be enough to woo an audience. This is specifically true of attendances for repertory screenings, which have dropped dramatically in recent years. It is this fact, coupled with a desire to offer screenings and events that are genuinely unique and exciting, that has guided the festival. The Smoking Cabinet regularly transform and extravagantly decorate the venues used for the festival and guests have also embraced the spirit of the festival by donning vintage and burlesque clothes. We have hosted DJs and numerous live burlesque performances, staged musical cabaret acts and preceded film screenings with specially commissioned and bespoke burlesque performances. We also produce extensive programme notes for all screenings in order to contextualise the films screened. We have recreated the seaside fun of Coney Island with typical seaside amusements and ice lollies, and have also re-created the feel of a 1920s gin palace for our opening night in 2008. We have had DJs play from vintage gramophones, and have hosted free education events and dance workshops.

Enhanced financial support in 2008 enabled us to introduce both the education dance workshops that we had hoped to offer in our first year. The education workshop was hosted by our sister organisation Mirror Mirror. This was established early in 2008 to enable us to offer educational events centered around early cinema; naturally risqué content could not be featured in these workshops which directly led to the formation of a sister company in order to keep this project separate from The Smoking Cabinet. The workshop was focused on one film, a short comedy made in 1910 called *Vice Versa* (David Aylott). A young boy steals a magician's wand which miraculously upsets the social order to funny but culturally poignant effect. The education event was used to investigate the types of characters and situations presented in the film, leading to further investigation into genre, social structure and stereotypes. Comparing and contrasting the screening with life today illustrated how things have changed in a hundred years. The education event was hosted with Film Education and proved extremely popular, with full attendance. Mirror Mirror is a strong example of how fluid events and film programming can be and as an initiative has continued to grow at an impressive rate. Mirror Mirror offers school children an opportunity to see rare examples of early cinema and contextualises them with the same energy and enthusiasm harnessed by The Smoking Cabinet, using the history of entertainment and the moving image to investigate the past and present in a fun and atmospheric way. Mirror Mirror has now extensively toured schools and organisations across the UK (see http://mirrormirroreducation.wordpress.com).

The dance workshop, enabled by additional funding, was hosted as part of The Smoking Cabinet by a group called The Bees Knees and focused on basic moves used in the Charleston. The session commenced with a very gentle warm-up routine and participants were then introduced to simple steps, followed by a routine – to which they were encouraged to add their own variations during a collective dance party at the end. The dance workshops took place on the same day as The Smoking Cabinet's *On With The Dance* programme and proved a great opportunity to get moving, explore dance and celebrate physicality in film. We hosted two workshops, both of which were free to those who wished to take part. Such workshops add not only to the sense of occasion, but have developed and encouraged greater audience engagement with the festival.

FUNDING THE FLIRTATIOUS

Organising a public festival with funding and support requires reporting and analysis of the festival and its operation. We evaluated the festival by encouraging all ticket holders to complete surveys in order that we could get direct feedback. We made sure our audiences were aware that we wanted to hear their opinion not only on what they thought we did well, but also on the things we could improve on. To our delight, feedback forms from the festival have showed a positive response of 95–98 per cent of audience members. In producing funding applications and in asking organisations to support us we have also had to be extremely aware of who our audience would be and in this we found ourselves lucky – during this process we discovered our audience had the potential to include a wide range of people and it is this fact that has helped us generate strong ticket sales and sell-out screenings.

The festival speaks to all people interested in the moving image and those film fans who want to access rarely-screened cinema. As well as being a centrally located art cinema that draws people from across London, the Curzon Soho is also a local cinema catering to the needs of the local community. Soho supports many of the performers and artists who continue to develop and nurture the tradition of cabaret and burlesque in London's West End. The gay community also comprised a notable part of our audience demographic, having traditionally embraced cabaret and burlesque. The festival also drew an audience of fans of dance and performance, those with an interest in social histories and representation, as well as those working in the performing arts community.

We broke down our target audience principally, though not exclusively, into the following groups:

1. Crossover neo-burlesque fans; young people (19+) seeking something unique and culturally fresh.

2. Early cinema fans; cinephiles, historians and academics (of film, of London, of music hall and cabaret) and teachers.
3. Locals from Soho's diverse communities.
4. Westminster and wider London's gay community
5. The avant-garde, burlesque performers, retro-obsessives, fashionistas.
6. Independent cinema fans, interested in discussion-based events and the chance to see early cinema.
7. Students of film and media studies.

Knowing your audience is key to good marketing and of course marketing is also key to ensuring that your festival has an audience. As well as targeting the groups identified above, The Smoking Cabinet was fortunate to be featured in a wide range of publications, from *The Guardian* to *Dazed & Confused*, and *The Metro* to Radio 4's *Woman's Hour*. We also consciously sought coverage in London's weekly free website and email listings, from LeCool and Urban Junkies, to Kulture Klash and Daily Candy. These mailing lists go out to recipients in their hundreds of thousands. The news media were drawn to the novel nature of The Smoking Cabinet festival and, as a result, we found we had a proposition that people were very eager to

236

FIGURE 18.1 Our main poster from the first year of The Smoking Cabinet

FIGURE 18.2 Our main poster from the second year of The Smoking Cabinet

feature, whether it be online, in print or on the radio.

Our marketing would not have been half as successful were it not for the fantastic design work of Kate Grove, a graphic designer and also one of the producers of The Smoking Cabinet. The design work for The Smoking Cabinet has developed over time allowing the development of a distinctive and unique feel each year. The design work, however, maintains a level of continuity in the key themes and focuses of the festival. The image of the butterfly with eyes ensures continuity between the designs for the two festivals, and has been something we have continued to deploy, whether on promotional badges, in flyers for the festival, or one-off follow-up events.

The festival comes together over the course of the year, and during that year we also work on The Smoking Cabinet's guest appearances at other festivals and events. In essence the year breaks down into two parts: planning and research, lasting eight months; and production lasting four months. In the former we ask: What will we host – in terms of scale and style? What will we programme? Who are our target audience? What will we charge? How will we fund it? How do we market the festival? How will it stand out/why is it unique? Answering these questions allows us to formulate a clear strategy around marketing, programming, rights clearances and fees, design, funding applications, press and PR. With all these bases covered it is onto production and actually hosting the festival. In the four months before the festival we focus on sponsorship, audience development, press releases, additional marketing, finalising the programme, festival logistics and event running, decorating venues, and booking DJs, cabaret performers, acrobats and live musicians.

The Smoking Cabinet offers a model of how to produce a distinctive and unique festival within a film exhibition culture where, if anything, there are perhaps too many festivals. It's a model of how, with passion, dedication and a lot of commitment, something unique can be created on a shoe-string, generating momentum and excitement not only for its audience but also those people producing it. Perhaps one of the enduring triumphs of The Smoking Cabinet is that each year the festival is produced for less than £2,000.

One of the highlights of the festival has certainly been hearing the audience's reaction to rediscovering those films which have been locked away from public viewing for years. The spontaneous laughter, clapping and even cheering was truly heart-warming, and vindicated our belief that the concept for the festival could be successfully realised. This was matched by the amazing live performances and music, and the quality of speakers the festival offered. In terms of attendances, the festival has exceeded expectations, with our opening nights and performances repeatedly selling out. With an eclectic mix of forgotten cabaret classics, rare burlesque cinema, stimulating discussion and naughty-but-nice live performances.

The Smoking Cabinet is produced by Aymie Backler, Claire Cooke, Kate Grove and Simone Pyne
www.thesmokingcabinet.com

CHAPTER 19
THE ADVENTURES OF BUCK NAKED:
THE THRILL OF THE TRANSGENDERED PEEP SHOW

Marcelle Perks

Debates about transexualism have been predominantly concerned with some form of feminised masculinity. It seems to be more natural and less threatening when men want to become women and thus adopt an inferior social position. The story of FTM (female to male) transsexualism is less well known, although Christie Milliken in the article 'Unheimlich Maneuvers: The Genres and Genders of Transsexual Documentary'[1] details recent documentary films on the topic, as does publications like Leslie Feinberg's *Stone Butch Blues* (1993)[2] and Loren Cameron's photo-book *Body Alchemy Transsexual Portraits* (1996).[3] However, a relatively new American porn performer, Buck Angel, has been championing the FTM transsexual cause through his groundbreaking work which challenges the whole notion of a gender binary system and makes us question our own narratives of sexual identity. On film, the literal body of the transsexual becomes marked as a sign of their inner conflict. Documentaries that feature the transgendered subject, such as *Sex Change Hospital* (Chris McKin, 2007), often show very masculine women and unusual-looking men who do not quite look the part of their desired gender. Part of the pleasure for the spectator is identifying those foibles which 'give the game away' because even post-surgery a transgendered identity can remain an ambiguous one. As Milliken writes, 'in other words, while a transsexual might become an effective representative of the other sex, an opposition between physical and sexual signifiers remains as a reminder of his/her crossing over'.[4] Significantly, most MTF (male to female) transsexual porn narratives reinforce a world view that is rigidly gender binary. The transgendered porn subject is typically presented as someone abnormal who fails to pass successfully as male or female, and thus becomes reduced to being only a sexual curiosity or a joke. One of Angel's stated aims in making porn in the first place is to work against presenting the sexualised MTF as something freakish.

TRAVERSING THE TRANSSEXUAL

In a non-pornographic context (where genitals do not have to be revealed), the irony is that Buck Angel looks so completely masculine there remain no female signifiers to indicate his former gender. His body (especially his upper torso) is heavily muscled and his face looks suitably macho and so in his porn work we have not been cued by errant female signifiers to anticipate a set of female genitalia between his legs (Angel chose not to have the phalloplasty procedure and describes himself as 'the dude with the pussy'.) In addition, Angel refuses to portray his sexuality as 'Other', even in his most obviously gay film *Buckback Mountain* (Lawrence Roberts, 2007). Here, his male co-stars make no comment on his prosthetic penis or on what is between his legs, and thus he challenges the viewer to accept his transgendered sexual identity as a natural one.

Angel claims to be the world's first FTM transsexual porn star and significantly his films are not made specifically for transgendered interests, he describes his audience as being primarily gay. In other words, his target audience finds him attractive *in spite of* his female genitalia (and how bizarre that they would be the group least likely to find images of his vagina sexually stimulating, a fact which is capitalised on ironically in Richard Kimmel's *Schwarzwald* (2007)). These ironies form part of the contradictory persona that is Buck Angel, a man who wills you not be interested in his sexual differences, even as he capitalises on making films which feature his unique biological characteristics.

Through his films Angel seems to want to go beyond sexual difference. Not having a biologically functioning penis does not seem to have created phallic envy in him, as seen by his unselfconscious use of a plastic dildo as a substitute penis. Sexually he seems happy to play out a variety of roles and scenarios, at times his vagina is penetrated or he uses his prosthetic penis to penetrate others, or even to masturbate with his own dildo. In a typical Buck Angel film, every performer displays the right of sexual gratification regardless of how this is achieved, how they look, and what props they need to use. And if they are happier not reaching orgasm, that is acceptable too. In focusing on pleasure, rather than mainstream porn's formulaic necessity and obsession in depicting the 'cum shot', Angel's films offer a sex positive model of sexuality that is all-embracing.

FIGURE 19.1 Capitalising on the uncategorised: Angel's films and the marketing of sexual ambivalence

CONSUMING BUCK ANGEL

For instance, let us take his directorial debut, *The Adventures of Buck Naked* (2004), which offers a variety of scenarios designed to stimulate. The style is gonzo with limited camera angles that are often crudely framed. It opens with Angel undoing his fly to reveal a large plastic dildo in his pants. A series of extreme close-ups photograph this rubber member as if to signify its virility, but there is no attempt to disguise the fact that it is a toy or to conceal where it joins on to Angel's skin. It is treated exactly as if it were a real penis, and performer Kitty even puts a condom over it before performing fellatio in close-up. It is a classical porn shot with a twist, because we know that it's a fake penis but our eyes make us believe momentarily that a real blow-job is taking place. Indeed the point of the Angel film is to privilege the fake, to endow it with a hyperrealism so that Angel's artificial penis becomes better than a biologically functioning one.

Cut to a long shot that reveals female performer Kitty's rather impressive tattoos and piercings which signify her as 'alternative' in her own way as Angel. When she walks over to a blanket, the camera follows Angel's bobbing dildo obsessively before she sits astride it. Angel's penetrative shots obsessively focus on vagina/dildo activity without the standard cut-away shots that would normally locate the performers in situ. In fact, it is impossible for the viewer to work out exactly how Kitty is lying in order to achieve the shot. Even though objectively we know that Angel can feel almost nothing penetrating Kitty with the dildo, the repeated inter-cutting showing images of his flushed face privileges his pleasure and allows us to suspend belief and feel his sexual mastery of the situation. It also allows female spectators the opportunity to imagine what it might be like to adopt the traditional male role of penetration.

At some point Kitty just seems to disappear out of the frame and we get more close-ups of Angel's erect and bobbing dildo which we note is held firmly in place by his tight pants. Seemingly satisfied with his penetrative display, Angel immediately throws the dildo down and begins to masturbate, and extreme close-up shots display his testosterone-enlarged clitoris. (In the FTM porn film we learn that transmen prefer to handle their clitoris differently, they 'jill off' exactly as if they were handling a miniature penis.) This contrasts with mainstream porn, where performers do what *looks good* rather than what feels pleasing.

In the next scene, a fellow transman, Bear Bud, performs a long masturbation scene. Because he is not as masculine and macho as Angel, despite the fact that he sports a moustache and a beard, he does not pass for male quite as successfully. Nonetheless, he is given a large amount of screen time and we note how he masturbates a dildo even though we know that he can get no direct stimulation from it. After making his point, he pushes the dildo aside to reveal his clitoris underneath and then a series of extensive close-up shots detail his masturbation efforts. Kitty appears and puts his dildo back into place and performs fellatio on him. The power of this scene lies in Bear Bud's ability to mimic the imagined effect of being the recipient of fellatio and the practised mannerisms in which he handles his dildo. The film blurs the boundaries of real and imagined pleasure and asserts his right to feel comfortable performing both with a dildo and as a 'dude with a pussy'. The viewer is left unable to identify which signifiers are significant and which are empty.

This scene of ambiguity is replaced by a sexual sketch in which Angel is penetrated by 'Dykeboy', which offers an opportunity to depict the effect on Angel's already enlarged clitoris. Dykeboy dons black rubber gloves and helps him to masturbate by teasing Angel's clitoris to full size through his fingers. The skin is framed by the black gloves, emphasising Angel's assets and again it is treated like a small penis rather than a part of female genitalia. The irony is that although Dykeboy is a biological male, for most of the scene his penis hangs down limp and he fails to get an erection, demonstrating again that Angel's dildo cock is superior to Dykeboy's real one. (Not that a failure to 'get wood' is a problem in an Angel film, male performers slap erotically with their penises if they are unable to penetrate.)

In scene four, Angel is depicted masturbating in an open air scene. In contrast to Bear Bud's performance jacking off a dildo, Angel uses a dildo only for penetrative masturbation. It's part of the elasticity of his sexual identity that in one scene a transman can insist that a dildo must stand in for his penis, and then in another it is just a sex aid for better masturbation. Much of the scene is filmed in long shot and Angel often covers up much of his genitalia with his hands, a feature that would be avoided in mainstream porn. As viewers we are encouraged to identify with the primacy of the performer's need to experience orgasm rather than expecting camera angles that would cater better for our scophilic pleasure.

The film ends with a number of bonus features which serves to demonstrate Angel's sexual prowess in a variety of situations. There is a frenetic double dildo scene with Lina Ramone. Another scene offers extreme close-up shots of Angel's vagina when Kitty is depicted giving cunnilingus. Not only does it emphasise the length of his clitoris, but at one point Kitty actually gives performs fellatio on it exactly as if it were a penis. There's also some S/M role play in a scene with Bridget where Angel initially penetrates her using his dildo, then takes it off and masturbates her with it manually. Finally, Angel is depicted in long shot dressed in leather and masturbating with a Hitachi magic wand.

Throughout the film, the viewer is offered a wide range of scenes involving Buck Angel as penetrator, and penetrated, and a dildo that we are encouraged to identify with as a substitute penis can in the next moment be thrown down and discarded or used as a sex toy. It makes it impossible to for the viewer to identify the source of Angel's sexual obsessions because he uses what Louise Kaplan describes as 'perverse strategies' to deflect his true intent.[5]

243

BLACK QUEENS AND PHALLIC FEARS

Through the extra-sexual functions of Buck Angel the viewer is free to identify sexually with whichever role they choose. Recent psychoanalytical theory has finally acknowledged audiences ability to identify across a much wider range of positions than previously thought. As Laura Kipnis asserts:

A psychoanalytically-inflected theory of fantasy suggests the mobilities and complexities of identification and proposes that pornography viewers can imaginatively identify with any aspect of the pornographic fantasy scenario or all of them: with any characters, action, detail, or even with the form or sequence of the fantasy.[6]

A film that very knowingly uses Buck Angel's porn persona is the gay avant-garde music spectacular *Schwarzwald*, directed by Richard Kimmel. Apart from being a part celebration/documentation of the NYC gay event known as The Black Party, a framing story set in the Black Forest uses mythological characters to represent archetypes which are largely oedipal in nature. Ironically, Buck Angel plays a biologically-born male, The Black Prince, who is castrated and raped at the command of his mother, thus becoming a 'woman' who is forced to go around in a blue velvet dress and is initiated into perverse rites by a number of animal men to be reborn as a sexual being. It is a reversal of Buck Angel's real-life quest for transgendered transformation, and fully makes use of the intertextuality of Angel's ambiguous sexuality.

The film has no dialogue and makes use of old-fashioned screen cards and some borrowed clips from silent movies to convey information. The fantastic environment of the Black Forest with its animal men, is contrasted with the equally bizarre environment of the club and its pulsing soundtrack and floor shows. Significantly when Angel behaves sexually with the Wolf-Man he meets in the woods, his mother punishes him for his transgressions by instantly castrating him. This act is symbolic of one of the earliest sexual dilemmas to be experienced by young boys (fear of the phallic mother) and significantly the Black Queen is shown as the aggressor with black phallic stripes across her face. Barbara Creed re-read Freud's case-notes on the famous case of Little Hans whose sexual curiosity (especially about his mother's genitals) led him to experience neurosis. Creed defines the 'phallic mother' as a source of terror; 'it is more likely that the boy endows the mother with a penis retrospectively, after he becomes consciously aware for the first time that she might castrate'.[7] It is interesting that through the fairy tale allegory (albeit with adult themes) *Schwarzwald* consciously grapples with these deep-seated childhood fears. Fortunately, Kimmel provides a cathartic sexual display and a happy ending to dispel any neurosis invoked. It is only after Angel survives a man's worst fears (castration) that he effectively becomes free and is able to tear himself away from the Black Queen.

The film reveals a lot of different manifestations of male lust, although there is no standard porn cum shot. Rather, it revels in the idea of sexuality, and shows that someone's gratification can come in many different ways – from being covered in hot candle wax, being beaten, or being forced to receive a large dildo. Some of the hard-core scenes are softened by frenetic editing using images from German expressionist cinema and Disney pop pastiche. For instance, a fisting scene is inter-cut with images of flowers and mythological figures on horseback to help legitimise this quest for pleasure. In this sense, the film can be considered what Richard Dyer calls a 'gay heritage film' in that it uses historical persons (like Merlin) to insist that homosexuality has existed in some form for centuries (the film titles state that men have always

FIGURE 19.2 Transgendered and transgeneric excess: sexual and stylistic experimentation in *Schwarzwald*

danced the naked tribal ritual). Dyer has described how such films serve to rewrite history to encompass the queer spectator; 'in this perspective homosexual heritage cinema is about envisaging homosexual men among the attractions of pastness'.[8] *Schwarzwald* goes further by allowing for various forms of sexual pleasure to be seen as legitimate ones and part of the 'sacred ritual'.

Kimmel uses the motif of the burning forest fire (the sacred circle) to symbolise burning passion that also redeems. In the club the fire is made analogous to the burning candles that sit on the bare stomach of a bound man, who becomes a willing sacrificial victim (molten candle wax is poured all over his body). Although *Schwarzwald* contains a few hard-core scenes of sexual activities such as fisting, the camera angles privilege scenes that focus on S/M activity or full-length shots of scantily-clad muscular bodies. Indeed, the men are so masculine that they effectively practise homovestism to become a caricature of maleness. And the film, with its parade of various personalities and animal-men reminds us of the many varieties of homosexual men – from queens, leather men and flaggers, and, of course, the ambiguous figure of Buck Angel himself.

After some transgressive sexual acts are seen in the club, Angel beats a man as he is given fellatio by another man, and after he has shown his capacity for violence, he regains his masculinity and becomes crowned and hailed as the Black Prince. It's a reminder that part and parcel of masculinity is bound up with violence and aggression, and even the sexually ambiguous like Angel can be a man if they are prepared to be aggressive enough.

CARNAL CONCLUSIONS

It is telling that the main character in this gay promotional film is a transgendered man, and that the transgressions are staged so the emphasis is on theatricality rather than sexuality. Laura Kipnis reminds us how often porn (contrary to expectation) does use such theatrics to impart its message; 'pornography holds us in the thrall of its theatrics of transgression, its dedication to crossing boundaries and violating social strictures'.[9] Buck Angel quite literally crosses all kinds of psychoanalytical and gender boundaries in this role, and it is all in the name of entertainment. *Schwarzwald* is so frenetic and full of meaning, it leaves us quite literally dizzy.

The fact that Buck Angel is a porn star must mean that there is something stimulating and reassuring in the porn narratives he creates that are relevant to us. Perhaps the male porn viewer (most of Angel's fans are men) is tired of being expected to identify with the standard same-sex porn star and wants a creative sexual space and permission to be different. Angel's films certainly provide a lot of safe- and better-sex instruction, and Angel's strong personality encourages the viewer to feel it is possible to revise sexual strategies. Angel is very much a pioneer at the cutting edge of porn, and it's important to remember that his sexual transgressions are our gain; he kindly consented to the interview which follows…

THE BUCK ANGEL INTERVIEW

Marcelle Perks: *What kind of fans do your films attract?*

   Buck Angel: My fan-base, surprisingly, is around 80 per cent gay men, although over the last year there's been a large influx of females becoming interested in my porn who can be bi-sexual, gay, straight whatever.

Is that surprising for you?

   No, because I think it's not so much about my genitals, it's about me as a man and I'm macho. Gay men are attracted to that and so I attract more the leather/fetish men. I do have another kind of fan-base, people who love what I'm doing and think it's great, but they're not really into pornography so I have fans who actually don't watch my films.

You're one of the first FTM transsexuals making porn; what do you want to achieve?

   One of the reasons why I started my porn is that I didn't want somebody to make the kind of 'freak porn' they do a lot with transsexual females. I wanted to start a movement in a positive way and show that guys like me are not just freaks, and to represent something different, to show a positive outlook on sex, sexuality and gender.

Was it a difficult decision to opt for a sex change?

   For most of the transsexuals I know – whether it's female-to-male or male-to-female – we all basically feel not quite right. It was very difficult for me throughout my life to understand that I felt like a guy but nobody could explain to me that I was really a man. It got to be a life-threatening situation for me literally, I tried to kill myself; I was homeless on the streets as a drug addict, constantly trying to sabotage my life until I realised I could literally physically change my gender. I still get quite emotional thinking about it, even though I've had sixteen years since my sex change. It's hard to explain that to people who've never had to live in that situation, but when you finally get the opportunity to fix this kind of birth defect, the whole world opens up. I can still remember my first hormone shot.

Why did you opt not to have the phalloplasty operation to turn your vagina into a penis?

   I always wanted to have a penis because I thought that's what I needed to complete my surgery. Then I did research and talked to guys who had had the penis surgery and opted not to. If they could make me a penis that is going to be able to get a hard-on and that I can pee through, then I probably would have opted to do it, but they can't make a functioning penis like a biological man. The world makes everybody believe that it's what's between your legs that defines you, and my message to the world is that it's just not true.

I can imagine some transsexual men might feel embarrassed about their vagina, but you almost seem to have embraced your vagina in your films.

247

Prior to me coming to terms with my vagina I was very embarrassed about my body and would have to get drunk and stoned to have sex with women (before I only had sex with women). I was very stone butch and wouldn't let girls go down on me. I wouldn't be penetrated and would orgasm by rubbing against a lover. But I had this kind of epiphany when I just thought my genitals are always going to be here, so I had to change my attitude towards myself and my body. My porn work has helped me tremendously to become comfortable with my sexuality.

In your films I was expecting your sexuality to be portrayed as something freakish, but it wasn't like that at all. In The Adventures of Buck Naked, *you present the dildo in your pants exactly as if it was a penis. It's obviously fake but you don't hide that.*

Yeah, I do because I see it as an extension of me. My strap-on is part of me, it's just not attached to me. When I put it in my pants it feels very natural. I'm a really lucky person because I can have a penis if I want, or a vagina and my penis can stay hard all the time! I can also still have an orgasm. That was one of the other reasons why I opted not to have the phalloplasty surgery because you have a fifty per cent chance of losing your orgasm capability. I'm a very sexual person and I could not even imagine not having an orgasm.

In the films, as soon as you take your trousers down, no one comments on the fact that you don't have a penis.

That was the whole point of the movie, for it to be as natural as possible. Going back to the commenting thing again, which I've done in some of my movies, it does sort of add to that freakish element which is what I'm trying to stay away from. I want to show that men with pussies are no big deal.

On film, your clitoris seems to be very large.

That's definitely from the hormones. I remember being very self conscious of my vagina when I was younger. It was already a little larger than the average clit, but with the testosterone hormones it grew to the size of my thumb – which is pretty big!

It looks like a small penis.

Yeah, well the clitoris and the penis are made from the same material in the womb. It just grew larger after the testosterone injections and it continues to grow. My hormone treatment is for the rest of my life and I have to have injections every two weeks. I see changes in my body even now after doing it for fifteen years.

Transmen seem to masturbate completely differently. You play with your clitoris as if jacking off a penis. Is this deliberate?

I think it's deliberate and a lot of transmen feel their clitoris is a small penis to them. That's how they get off on it. It makes them feel more masculine as opposed to masturbating more like a female (however that is – I don't really know). More than fondling it, they rub it up and down the shaft just as if it was a penis and it makes them feel comfortable about what they have there.

In The Adventures of Buck Naked, *your clitoris was filmed exactly as if it were a penis – I'm thinking of the shot when Kitty is sucking it.*

It's deliberate because it is sucked and played with that way. Sometimes in my head it feels like a penis and sometimes it feels like a vagina, I guess it just depends on the mood I'm in. When we're turned on and I want to talk nasty, sometimes I say – 'Now suck my cock!' Kitty sucked me and it turned her on too.

From your chest upwards you are completely male and so are your legs, but there's this inverted V from your vagina to your stomach that on film always seems completely female.

I'm just trying to change the way the whole world thinks about masculine/feminine. Even though you think of me as male, the minute it goes to the one shot between my legs the mind just shifts back to female. Many people have said to me that that part of my body is very female.

Previously you've described your film style as gonzo. If I was there behind the scenes, watching the film, what would I see?

A very natural environment, first of all we always sit down and talk a little bit and make everybody comfortable on my set. There's no attitude or making fun of somebody if they're not getting a hard on, it's always very natural and as fluid as possible. If I don't have a good rapport with somebody and feel sexual energy we pretty much won't shoot because I really think you have to have that sexual interaction with each other for that to come off on film.

In regular hetero porn it's all about the men having a long, hard dick but in real life a lot of men watching it don't have this, and could feel threatened. In your films there are always lots of different sexual possibilities…

My movies aren't made specifically for transgendered people; what I'm trying to do is show is that we all have different sexual fantasies and ways of feeling turned on. People need to understand that whatever turns you on, as long as it's safe and consensual, you should just go ahead and do it and not worry about what other people think about you. You'd be amazed at how your sex life could blossom into something that you could never even imagine.

In The Adventures of Buck Naked, *Dykeboy plays with a floppy penis. I found it liberating that your performers didn't have to have a completely hard penis in the standard porn style.*

If you look at most porn, guys have rock hard hard-on's the whole time and that's not natural, they're all on Viagra or some type of drug. No man holds a hard-on like that. They do go on and off and that's a natural thing. I did make that a deliberate thing, to show, you know what, we're still having a good time. I got a lot of complaints about that, but I don't really care, I just wanted to show a more natural, sexual environment.

And also it didn't really matter how you got off, whether you used a sex toy or masturbated or had sex with someone else, everything was possible, that was the feeling your films left me with.

That's really what I wanted to show. I know lots of people in the porn business who work for these multi-million-dollar porn companies and they have a formula they do. I just go in with my camera and I want everyone to actually really have an orgasm on film, whatever it takes to do that, and to show that there's so many different ways.

Buckback Mountain *is beautifully filmed, especially the nature shots and your co-star Enis is very good looking.*

He's a really great guy; he's very bisexual and we were totally into it. We had a great sexual experience. I'm very proud of that film.

Buckback Mountain *is a real feel-good gay cowboy film. What's been the reaction so far?*

It's a film that has never been done in porn. Whether it's gay, straight or whatever, it's a very unique film that's getting great reviews. That was the whole point, I wanted it to be feel-good porn. I just wanted it to be a natural kind of thing happening between two guys and one just happens to have a vagina (laughs); no big deal!

When you have sex with the boss, he seems to have a problem coming and I liked the fact that it was just about him getting off.

He was camera shy, to be honest with you. It's interesting how men and women want different things from porn films. Men want to get off and they don't like to wait too long for that for that situation to happen, whereas women like to drag it out a little more, with more foreplay, and more things going on.

What I liked about Buckback Mountain *that it was possible to achieve orgasm through any means. When you have sex with your male lover you do completely different things and most of the time he hits you with his penis.*

Exactly, there's a basic script there but it's all filmed naturally and that's why I like to have guys who are genuinely turned on by each other. We try not to be conscious of the camera being there. It was hot that day and it's harder when you're a man to perform.

You give a very animalistic performance as a porn performer. How do you portray that?

Most of the time I'm pretty horny on the set! When we start filming I'm ready to go. I pump myself up for that. I like wild, nasty sex and I think especially gay guys like to hear that whole bbrrr grunting! Being verbal that way adds to that nastiness and more male way of raw sex.

CHAPTER 20

PUNISHING THE PEEPSHOW: CARNALITY AND THE DANGEROUS IMAGES ACTS

Julian Petley

Question: what do *Lady Chatterley's Lover* (1928), *Last Exit to Brooklyn* (1964) and *Inside Linda Lovelace* (1974) have in common? Answer: they were all subject to failed prosecutions under the Obscene Publications Act 1964 (OPA). Next question: what do the Protection of Children Act 1978, the Video Recordings Act 1984, the Criminal Justice Act 1988 and the Criminal Justice and Immigration Act 2008 have in common? Answer: they are all attempts to circumvent the OPA, whose provisions the illiberal and censorious have long agitated against as overly liberal and 'permissive'. Thanks to the last of these measures, those suspected of possessing the 'wrong' kind of pornography can now look forward to having their homes and offices trashed by the police and their reputations publicly dragged through the mud; if convicted, they could languish for up to three years in prison. So how did we arrive at this extraordinary state of affairs?

Under the OPA it is an offence to publish (but not merely to possess) an obscene article, or to have such an article for publication for gain. For the purposes of the Act, an article is deemed obscene 'if its effect ... is, taken as a whole, such as to tend to deprave and corrupt persons who are likely, in all circumstances, to read, see or hear the matter contained or embodied in it'. Thus to be obscene, an article must be more than simply sexually explicit and must have considerably more serious effects than merely shocking or disgusting certain people. These effects have to be considered in respect of those likely to seek it out as opposed to the 'average' or 'reasonable' person, or those deemed 'vulnerable'. Works have to be judged by their 'dominant effect', that is, taken as a whole and not simply on the basis of their more lurid passages, and the Act also contains a 'public good' defence, by which those accused of publishing obscene material can argue that publication is in the interests of science, literature, art or learning. And although the Act makes no overt reference to current standards of acceptability in the area of explicit imagery, one of the great virtues of the 'deprave and corrupt' test is that it does, inevitably, move with the times in this respect. As Geoffrey Robertson and Andrew Nicol put it in *Media Law*, in an obscenity trial 'the collective experience of 12 arbitrarily chosen people is assumed to provide a degree of familiarity with popular reading trends, with what is deemed acceptable on television and at cinemas and on the Internet and with the degree of explicitness that can be found in publications on sale at local newsagents'.[1]

A VAGUE AND ILL-DEFINED LAW

Thus in obscenity cases the bar for the prosecution is set high – far too high for certain sections of opinion. The first serious attempt to circumvent the OPA was the Protection of Children Act 1978, which, like so many examples of bad legislation in this field, came into being on the back of a moral panic spearheaded by Mary Whitehouse and the press. This made it an offence to take, make or distribute images of young people under sixteen which were deemed merely indecent, a concept which the courts have proved worryingly unable to define except in the broadest terms such as 'offending against recognised standards of propriety' or 'shocking, disgusting and revolting ordinary people'.[2] Furthermore, the simple act of showing such an image to another person, even without any money changing hands, counts as 'distribution'. And merely accessing such an image on the Internet without actually downloading it can constitute an offence, as it would be stored in the browser's cache. Moreover, most of the defences available under the OPA are absent. The Criminal Justice and Immigration Act 2008 defined indecent photographs of a child so as to include: (a) a tracing or other image, whether made by electronic or other means, which is derived from a photograph or pseudo-photograph; and (b) data stored on a computer disc which is capable of conversion into an image of a kind which falls within the ambit of the Act. And in 2009 the Coroners and Justice Act made it illegal to possess drawings and computer-generated images of young people engaged in sexual activity; this is now known colloquially as the Dangerous Cartoons Act. For the purposes of this battery of child protection legislation, a young person is defined as someone under eighteen, or if the 'predominant impression conveyed' is that they are under eighteen.

Not content with this, however, the Criminal Justice Act 1988 then made it illegal even to *possess* an indecent image of a child, as well as increasing the maximum penalty for the offence to five years imprisonment and/or an unlimited fine. And in May 2008 the Ministry of Justice announced new proposals to make it illegal to possess drawings and computer-generated images of under-aged children engaged in sexual activity.

In the years since the original legislation was passed, case law has developed which suggests, according to Robertson and Nicol, that only 'pictures with some element of lewdness or sexual provocation' are covered by the Act.[3] However, this has not prevented the police from seizing, or threatening to seize, material which does not remotely fit this description, and they have done so with a frequency and a determination which suggests a concerted effort to deter the collection, publication or exhibition of images which the law, vague and ill-defined though it is, was surely never intended to catch. For example…

In 1991 the businessman Lawrence Chard was arrested and charged for taking around thirty pictures of his wife and children in the back garden of their home. The children, who had been swimming, were naked. The film processors tipped off the police, who arrested Chard in front of his children, who were then quizzed by social workers. When the case came to court fourteen months later he was unanimously acquitted, but by now the family's life had been comprehensively wrecked; they were forced to change their name and move to a different part of the country. As a result, the magazine *Amateur Photographer* launched a Campaign for Common Sense, aimed at photographic processors, following which a whole string of similar cases came to light.

Ron Oliver is a renowned photographer specialising in family portraits, a selection of whose works is held by the Bibliothèque Nationale. Some of his clients ask him to photograph their children naked. In January 1993 police raided his studios and seized his entire body of work – more than 20,000 prints. Two months later, he was arrested again, this time along with Graham Ovenden, an internationally respected artist, art critic and photographer who specialises in pictures of children, sometimes naked. Many of the 2,500 works seized were part of Ovenden's extensive collection of Victorian photographs, including works by George Bernard Shaw and Lewis Carroll. According to the *Daily Mail*, 13 March 1993, in an article entitled 'The porn victims from high society': 'up to 100 children – many from upper-class families – are thought to have been victims of a porn ring which could have been operating for 15 to 20 years'. In reality, the 'porn ring' was simply a loose association of artists which included Peter Blake, Graham Arnold and David Inshaw, all of whom had previously been members of the Pre-Raphaelite-inspired Brotherhood of Ruralists. After a campaign by Sir Hugh Casson, David Hockney and Laurie Lee among others, and after what the *Daily Mail*, 7 July 1995, called 'months of often heated talks with detectives' the charges against Ovenden were dropped and his property returned, although no apology was made. The *Daily Mail* helpfully noted that Oliver's studio is 'next door to a playschool'. Unwilling to put up with this kind of harassment by the police and press, Oliver left the country.

In November 1995 the newsreader Julia Somerville and her partner Jeremy Dixon were questioned into the early hours by police about photographs of their seven-year-old daughter naked in the bath. They had taken these to Boots to be processed, and the processing staff called the police. One or other of these two parties then gave, or sold, the story to the press, with entirely predictable results. After four weeks the Crown Prosecution Service (CPS) announced that it was letting the matter drop.

Robert Mapplethorpe's photograph of a three-year-old girl, *Rosie*, was removed from an exhibition of the artist's work at the Hayward Gallery in September 1996 after the gallery took advice from the Clubs and Vice Squad of the Metropolitan Police. The picture's subject, Rosie Bowdrey, now 22, was quoted in the *Independent*, 15 September, as saying that: 'I think this is all so stupid, everyone should see the picture.' She also described it as 'a very, very sweet picture, it captures childhood innocence'.

In March 2001 the Saatchi Gallery mounted an exhibition entitled *I am a Camera*. Prompted by journalists from the *News of the World* (which fulminated against 'a revolting exhibition of perversion masquerading as art' and a 'degrading exploitation of child nudity for commercial gain'), the police insisted on the removal of two pictures which Tierney Gieron had taken of her children. They also threatened to prosecute the publisher of the exhibition catalogue, Edward Booth-Cliborn, unless he removed it from distribution, and voiced concerns about a picture by Nan Goldin. However, both the gallery and the publisher made it abundantly clear that they would robustly defend any action taken against them. Furthermore, without commenting on the case directly, the culture secretary Chris Smith was quoted in the *Guardian*, 12 March, to the effect that: 'I am much more worried about paedophile material that's available on the Internet than about an art gallery somewhere in the middle of London', and warned that: 'we must be very careful in this country before we start censoring things that are happening, either in newspapers or in art galleries'. Shortly thereafter the CPS instructed the police to drop the case as there was insufficient evidence to provide a realistic prospect of conviction. According to the *Daily Mail*, 16 March 2001, the decision was made 'despite strong protests from the police', who feared that a 'dangerous precedent has been set which will help lawyers representing sex offenders'.

The Saatchi row resurfaced in October 2007 when the Nan Goldin photo about which the police had expressed concerns in 2001, *Klara and Edda Belly-Dancing*, was seized from an exhibition of her work at the Baltic gallery in Gateshead. No further action followed, since the CPS made it clear that it had already declared this picture not to be indecent at the time of the Saatchi furore. In which case, one wonders why on earth the police seized it and threatened the gallery in the first place. Taken in conjunction with the other cases noted here, it is hard to avoid the conclusion that legislation designed to protect children has actually unleashed a good deal of zealotry and moral entrepreneurship aimed at adults, and at artists in particular – albeit constrained, much to the irritation of the police, by the calmer counsels of the CPS.

A MASSIVE AND DRACONIAN APPARATUS OF STATE VIDEO CENSORSHIP

When in 1979 the arrival of home video made it possible for people to see films which the then British Board of Film Censors, now the British Board of Film Classification (BBFC), would have either cut or banned outright had they been submitted to them for cinema exhibition, there was of course an outcry from the censorious and illiberal. As is by now well known, in July 1982 the Director of Public Prosecutions (DPP) mounted a test case against *S.S. Experiment Camp* (Sergio Garrone, 1976), *I Spit on Your Grave* (Meir Zarchi, 1978) and *Driller Killer* (Abel Ferrara, 1979) in order to test whether the Obscene Publications Act, which had hitherto been used to prosecute only material deemed pornographic, could also be employed successfully against material whose problem, from the authorities' point of view, was violence. They succeeded, and further prosecutions under the Act followed. The problem was, however, that films which were found guilty in certain courts were equally found not guilty in others – *The Evil Dead* (Sam Raimi, 1981) having a particularly chequered history in this respect, its 47 appearances in different courts resulting at least in part from the fact that the video's distributor, Palace, outraged the police and the DPP by having the temerity to defend it in court and to encourage video dealers to do likewise. This unpleasantly vindictive campaign led to Judge Owen Stableford, at Snaresbrook Crown Court in July 1985, criticising the DPP for bringing the administration of justice into disrepute and ordering it to pay Palace's costs of over £20,000.

Nonetheless, those for whom the arrival of home video spelled nothing less than the end of civilisation as we know it were determined to fashion a law which would regulate the new medium far more effectively than the OPA had done thus far.

It is all too often forgotten that the first attempt to introduce video censorship in the UK was actually undertaken by a Labour backbencher. This was Gareth Wardell, the MP for Gower, who in December 1982 introduced a ten-minute-rule bill 'to prohibit the rental of video cassettes of adult category to children and young persons'. In the event, it failed to get government approval and was dropped. However, after the Tory election victory in June 1983, amidst an ever-swelling torrent of 'video nasty' scare stories in the press, Wardell proposed a Commons motion to the effect that 'this House urges Her Majesty's government to introduce forthwith legislation to control access by children to video nasties, thus honouring its election pledge'. And when the Video Recordings Bill duly appeared the following month it was supported as eagerly by Labour as by the Tories, partly out of genuine conviction (greatly strengthened, of course, by woeful ignorance of the actual contents of any contemporary horror films) and partly out of determination not to be portrayed as 'soft' on morality by the Tories and the client press.

But although the Video Recordings Act (VRA) was originally represented simply as a means of ridding the country of a few 'video nasties', what it in fact created was a massive and draconian apparatus of state video censorship whereby any feature film sold or rented in Britain on video had to be classified by the BBFC. Titles of which the Board disapproved were cut, and not infrequently banned outright. But the beauty of this scheme, from the authorities' point of view, was its sheer simplicity and the way in which it by-passed the OPA: from now on it would simply be illegal to supply a feature film on video (and now DVD) without a BBFC certificate. And the penalties for breaking the law are remarkably severe, including an unlimited fine or imprisonment for up to two years; indeed, even supplying a classified DVD or video in breach of its age restriction (for example selling an '18' rated video to a 15-year-old) can result in a fine of £5,000 and up to six months in prison.

Inevitably, of course, the VRA created a considerable underground market for the original versions of videos cut or banned by the BBFC. Denied legal access to vast swathes of horror cinema in particular, fans began trading unclassified videos at collectors' fairs and through the advertising sections of magazines such as *The Dark Side* and *Samhain*. However, as I have pointed out in some detail elsewhere,[4] it was not long before this amateur and extremely low-level activity came to the attention of the police and trading standards officers, who were clearly determined to enforce the VRA to the last dot and comma. For it is important to understand that Clause 1 (5) of the Act states that 'supply of a video recording' means 'supply in any manner, whether or not for reward, and, therefore, includes supply by way of sale, letting on hire, exchange or loan'. Thus in May 1992, police and trading standards officers, both of which groups one would have thought had better use for taxpayers' money, launched the first of a whole series of raids on the homes of video collectors across Britain. During the course of the following years, terrified teenagers were repeatedly to find themselves the victims of oppressive and threatening behaviour from these officials, who also ensured the maximum negative publicity for their victims at both local and national levels by assiduously briefing the ever-credulous and sensation-hungry media against them, resulting in screaming headlines such as 'Snuffed out: cops swoop to seize 3000 sick killer videos' (*Daily Star*, 8 May 1992) and thoroughly misleading statements such as 'a nationwide network selling snuff videos of torture, mutilation and cannibalism has been smashed in a massive undercover operation' (*Daily Express*, 8 May 1992).

What such hyperbolic nonsense concealed, of course, was what many would consider a grotesque waste of public funds, a serious abuse of legal process, and a considerable infringement of human rights. People had their lives turned upside down (in many cases, for example, having their savings accounts books taken and photocopied, and their bank accounts investigated), were publicly dragged through the mire, had their right to a fair trial prejudiced, and, on several occasions, were dealt with by police officers whose utter ignorance of the kind of material with which they were dealing should have instantly precluded them from working on cases of this kind. Thus, for example, the victim of a police raid told me that 'after long arguments with a vice squad officer about myths concerning "video nasties" and "snuff" movies he went on to say that if he hadn't caught me in time I would have moved on to child porn', whilst another related how, during a raid, the police had found a pair of child's mittens and seemed distinctly unwilling to believe that these were a memento of the collector's childhood. Whilst being driven to the police station an officer asked him if he had ever been sexually abused, and 'seemed genuinely to think that these films, in his words, "lead on" to child pornography'.[5]

THE DANGEROUS IMAGES ACT

In May 2008, a new measure to circumvent the Obscene Publications Act came into being. This was the Criminal Justice and Immigration Act, now known colloquially as the Dangerous Images Act, which makes it an offence even to *possess*, let alone to distribute, an 'extreme pornographic image'. The Act defines an image as pornographic if 'it is of such a nature that it must reasonably be assumed to have been produced solely or principally for the purpose of sexual arousal' and as extreme if it is 'grossly offensive, disgusting or otherwise of an obscene character' and 'if it portrays, in an explicit and realistic way, any of the following':

(a) an act which threatens a person's life,
(b) an act which results, or is likely to result, in serious injury to a person's anus, breasts or genitals,
(c) an act which involves sexual interference with a human corpse, or
(d) a person performing an act of intercourse or oral sex with an animal (whether dead or alive), and a reasonable person looking at the image would think that any such person or animal was real.

Those found guilty of possessing such images can be imprisoned for up to three years. This draconian piece of legislation has its origins in the simple fact that, thanks to the increasingly global nature of communications, and not least the development of the Internet, British subjects are now able to access material which the OPA would have made it extremely difficult to distribute in former times. As the Parliamentary Under-Secretary of State at the Ministry of Justice, Lord Hunt, put it in a Lords debate on the Bill:

> This legislation has been proposed because the controls in the Obscene Publications Act are much more easily evaded these days by the use of modern technology, namely the Internet, which makes it much easier to use and distribute and therefore easier to possess. As most such extreme material is hosted abroad, controls on publication and distribution are no longer sufficient.[6]

Obviously the new communications media do pose a challenge to all national systems of media regulation, but they pose a particularly acute one to the British authorities, habituated as they are in matters pertaining to sexual imagery to exercising a degree of control which citizens of other democracies would regard as simply intolerable and enforcing 'official' standards of taste and decency which they would (and indeed do) find utterly ludicrous. Naturally, the British government finds it quite incomprehensible that Johnny Foreigner does not adopt its standards in this matter (as opposed to regarding them as a bizarre anachronism) but even it realises that it is so out of line with other countries that arriving at any kind of transnational standards of acceptability is a complete impossibility. However, rather than sensibly leaving well alone, they decided that, as they could not criminalise the distribution of material emanating from abroad of which they disapprove, they would simply criminalise its possession instead.

This alone constitutes an extraordinary abridgement of individual liberty which may well fall foul of the European Convention on Human Rights. Indeed, in its pre-legislative scrutiny of the Bill, the Joint Committee on Human Rights noted that the government had already indicated that it felt that the seriousness of the proposed offences justified interference with Articles 8 and 10 of the Convention, which concern, respectively, an individual's right to private life and their right freely to receive and impart information (including information which is offensive or unpalatable). However, the Committee was concerned whether 'the definition of the new offence is sufficiently precise and foreseeable to satisfy the requirement' that interferences with these rights must in accordance with the law.[7] In particular it wondered whether an individual user of pornography would be able to know whether their possession of a particular image would constitute a criminal offence, and noted that 'an assessment of whether an image is or is not "extreme" is inherently subjective'.[8] However, highly subjective, not to say deeply moralistic, factors lie at the very heart of the Act's definitions of 'extreme pornography', and played a major role in every stage of its gestation. Thus in the consultation document which sparked off the whole process in August 2005, the material which the government wished to make it illegal to possess was described variously as 'abhorrent',[9] 'degrading'[10] and 'repugnant'.[11] And, announcing the consultation, Home Office Minister Paul Goggins, stated that 'this is material which is extremely offensive to the vast majority of people, and it should have no place in our society'. Indeed, as I pointed out in my response to the consultation, the government's mind was clearly so firmly made up on this matter that the whole exercise was a complete sham. And when in August 2006 the Home Office issued a press release announcing that it was indeed going to take action against 'extreme pornography', Home Office Minister Vernon Coaker was at pains to point out that it was doing so because 'such material has no place in our society' and because it wished to send out 'a strong message – that it is totally unacceptable and those who access it will be held to account'.[12] Entirely unsurprisingly, then, vague and loaded words such as 'grossly offensive' and 'disgusting' have found their way into the Act itself, even though subjective language such as this should have no place in legislation. However, barely had the Second Reading of the Bill commenced in the Commons than the Secretary of State for Justice and Lord Chancellor, Jack Straw, was denouncing this 'vile material' as 'deeply offensive'.[13] But as the Labour MP Ian Mikardo put it in a Commons debate prompted by one of the ill-fated Tory attempts in the 1980s to tighten up the OPA, the test of gross offensiveness

focuses upon the instant response of shock or disgust to particular pictures, either visual or conjured up in words. The party to the action is described as a reasonable person, but that is merely a code for a tribunal that will decide the issue. A reasonable person will not decide; the magistrate or jury – if there is a jury trial – will decide, and the term 'reasonable person' is really a code name for them. As judges and juries will, of course, always regard themselves as reasonable, they will test the material according to their own personal, subjective and immediate responses.[14]

Subjective and moralistic responses were again very much to the fore in the government's attempts to defend the measure in the Lords against a rising tide of concerted Liberal Democrat opposition led by Baroness Miller of Chilthorne Domer. Thus in response to a point raised by her, Lord Hunt stated that

> the noble Baroness asked whether, having viewed these images at Charing Cross police station a couple of weeks ago, I then felt violent or that I would indulge in some offence. I actually felt very sick, because they were pretty disgusting images, and I frankly find it horrific that they are available and that people can see them. I am sorry, but I do not take this very liberal approach of 'If it does no harm to the people taking part, why should we worry about it?' I do worry about it, and about the access that people have to that kind of disgusting material. I am afraid that is my position… We are targeting that material not on account of offences which may or may not have been committed in the production of the material, but because the material itself, which depicts extreme violence and often appears to be non-consensual, is to be deplored… It is appalling that this material is available and we have to do something about it.[15]

Nor does the Act's invocation of the 'reasonable person' let it off the subjective hook. The 'reasonable person' (who is quite distinct from the 'average person') is a useful legal fiction which denotes a reasoned and informed outlook on a legal question and is well known in areas such as negligence and contract law. For example, a negligence case might well turn on whether the defendant's conduct was culpable because it fell short of what a reasonable person would do to protect another individual from the foreseeable risks of harm. However, there is a very considerable difference between a jury being asked to decide how a reasonable person would act in such circumstances and how a reasonable person would judge an image – in particular, whether or not they would judge it 'to have been produced solely or principally for the purpose of sexual arousal'. To quote again from Ian Mikardo in the 1987 OPA debate: 'there is a difference between reasonableness in respect of a fact, such as negligence, and reasonableness in respect of perception. The Bill is about perception. Nothing is more indeterminate, vague and subjective than a perception.'[16]

But a juror in an 'extreme pornography' case would also be required to determine whether the material in question portrays certain acts in an 'explicit and realistic way' and whether a reasonable person looking at the images of those acts would think that the persons or animals depicted therein were 'real'. Again, this is a vain attempt to put a gloss of objectivity on what are bound to be subjective judgements, but in order to understand how on earth any government could think it necessary – and indeed possible – to legislate in matters pertaining to realism and verisimilitude, we need briefly to explore the genesis of this measure.

In 2003 Jane Longhurst was asphyxiated by Graham Coutts, who visited Internet sites which contained pornography involving violence. He was subsequently found guilty of her murder. As a result, her mother Liz organised a 35,000-strong petition calling for the banning of such sites, in which she was vociferously supported by the moral watchdog mediawatch-uk, her MP Martin Salter and her daughter's MP David Lepper. Inevitably the *Daily Mail* became a cheerleader for the cause, on 30 September 2004 running an article headed 'My sister was murdered by a man obsessed with violent Internet porn. So why won't anyone help me to close these websites down?', which argued that the murder was 'unequally disturbing in that it could have happened only in this high-tech age, committed by someone whose murderous fantasies were fuelled by appalling images freely available on the Internet'. That the court case produced no evidence whatsoever of a direct causal connection did not stop Salter and Lepper agitating remorselessly until they bounced this measure onto the statute book.

In other words, the government, terrified as always of being painted as 'soft' on such matters, produced a completely unnecessary, woefully ill thought out and thoroughly oppressive measure in response to a single incident – invariably the worst possible basis for legislation of any kind, as evidenced by the Dangerous Dogs Act 1991. Of course, it goes without saying that forcing adults to take part in sexual activity against their will is quite rightly a crime, and any measure which helps the police to track down the perpetrators of such acts deserves support. But this most emphatically is not such a measure; it is aimed not at the perpetrators of such acts but at those possessing what might be images of them – and of a very great deal else as well.

The main problem for the government in formulating this measure was that it wanted to avoid the situation in which, as Lord Hunt put it in the Lords, the prosecution would have

> to prove that the events being depicted had actually taken place – that a person's life had actually been taken or that a life-threatening injury had been inflicted; in short, that a very serious crime had taken place. That would place an insurmountable burden on the prosecution, particularly when so much material is produced abroad.[17]

One wonders if Lord Hunt has ever heard of Interpol, but, whatever, absolving the authorities of any need to prove that the images in question do indeed depict the commission of *actual* crimes widens the scope of the legislation to a truly alarming degree.

Thus, for example, a vast range of BDSM (bondage, domination, sado-masochism) material falls fairly and squarely within the ambit of the Act. Such material exists largely for the purposes of sexual arousal, may well be deemed grossly disgusting, offensive or obscene by the uninitiated, and may involve violence which certainly *appears* to be non-consensual, even though, in fact, the vast majority of it is merely role-playing by entirely consenting participants. As Susan Sontag put it:

> to be involved in sadomasochism is to take part in a sexual theatre, a staging of sexuality. Regulars of sadomasochistic sex are expert costumers and choreographers as well as

performers, in a drama that is all the more exciting because it is forbidden to ordinary people.[18]

Our legislators may not have read Sontag, but during the period of nearly three years in which the Act was in gestation they received literally hundreds of remarkably well-informed submissions making this point in one way or another – and entirely ignored them.

However, the net is cast even wider than this. Thanks to the government's mulish insistence – again, flying smack in the face of a great deal of expert opinion which it received – on including 'explicit and realistic' portrayals of certain acts within the remit of the legislation, the possession of certain entirely fictional feature films could well be a criminal offence. Films classified by the BBFC are exempt from the Act, but there is a huge range of unclassified material available from abroad on DVD at the click of a mouse. Particularly at risk, of course, are films which include both real sex and simulated violence. Examples which immediately spring to mind are Joe D'Amato's *Emanuelle Around the World* (1977) and Oswaldo de Oliveira's *Bare Behind Bars* (1980), many of the films of Jess Franco, and indeed whole swathes of European horror, crime and sex films which took advantage of relaxed censorship regimes in countries such as Italy and Spain from the late 1970s onwards. The fact that DVDs of these movies are easily available not simply from specialist dealers but from Amazon.com, hardly a sink of depravity, is the clearest possible indication that the standards of acceptability which this government is attempting to impose on British subjects are simply wildly out of kilter with those everywhere else in the democratic world.

Of course, it might be argued that as long as the police interpret this legislation sensibly, it will not capture the extremely wide range of material which I have suggested. However, the record of the police in the matter of allegedly indecent images of children hardly gives cause for optimism in this respect, as we have seen. Furthermore, the police were among the very few to respond positively to the consultation on this matter.[19] It is also important to realise that many of the police responses were also marked by bitter resentment that those arrested and charged under the OPA had dared to avail themselves of the defences available under it, demands for more resources so that the proposed new measure could be enforced effectively, and complaints that the proposed offences were too narrow and the proposed sentences too short. It's extremely hard to avoid the conclusion that many of the respondents regard those whom they are policing as, in the words of 'God's Cop' James Anderton, the former chief constable of Greater Manchester, 'swirling around in a human cesspit of their own making'.

The best example of this sort of attitude came not from the responses themselves but from an article by Detective Inspector Ian Winton of the Nottinghamshire police in the *Nottingham Post*, 31 August 2006, in which he threatened: 'We will not hesitate in using this new legislation. Those convicted of this new offence will have to sign the sex offenders' register which will affect not just their relationship with friends and family but also their careers. It will make many users of extreme pornography think again.' And in his actual response, Winton argued that any change in the law should be accompanied by a widespread publicity campaign which will 'inhibit people from "surfing" the Internet for pornography and accessing it'.

Meanwhile Detective Inspector Colin Gibson of the Economic Crime Unit, Durham Constabulary, was amongst the many arguing that the proposed measures did not go far enough. In his view:

> Whilst it is accepted that it is the intention to restrict any new offence to pornographic material many would argue that this is a conservative list and leaves room for development. Not all abhorrent images are produced for sexual gratification. Some are quite clearly just obscene and offensive and without a sexual connutation [sic] yet simple possession would still fall outside of current and proposed legislation.

Detective Sergeant Keith Wharton of the West Midlands Police wanted adding to the list 'the eating of faeces or urine', whilst Detective Inspector Winton stated that

> in our opinion acts of coprophilia (excrement, urination) within pornograph [sic] are examples of the total degradation of the person subject of such acts. It is our view that such acts are enjoyed by sadists. Likewise acts of belonephilia (needles fetish) agonophilia (pseudo rape) and other forms of extreme violence are also enjoyed by sadist [sic] and those persons with sadistic tendencies. Such tendencies would skew the mindset of the viewer of such material to believe that this is the norm. As such we feel it should not be tolerated.

Most worrying of all, however, was the response from John Francis, the General Secretary of the Police Federation of England and Wales, who argued that

> the circumstances in which the material is found is not, at the present time, considered when sentencing takes place, as only the image charged can be so considered. This applies when considering the sexual nature of an image. For example, so called 'snuff movies' whereby persons are actually killed on screen are currently not considered for a sexual motive. The circumstances in which the images are found should be considered. There is evidence of these movies being found with a great deal of pornography, which in itself is not illegal to possess. This also applies to mutilation images, scenes of crime images of murder victims, beheadings, etc. The question to be asked is why anyone would want these images in the first place. It is the circumstances in which they are found that implies a sexual motive. However, as legislation stands at present no account can be taken of them, as it is not illegal to possess these images.

Yes, you did read that right: it is being suggested in all seriousness that if you possess images of death and violence, and if you also possess pornographic images, then you possess the former for reasons of sexual gratification.

Such responses suggest all too strongly that the police simply cannot be trusted to act reasonably or intelligently in these matters. The fact that authoritarian zealots such as these have been handed yet another excuse to batter down people's doors in dawn raids, seize their computers, videos, DVDs, books and magazines, and ensure that their names are plastered across the local and, in the cases of the famous, national media, quite simply beggars belief. One's fears in this respect are only heightened by Lord Hunt's revelation that the police see this offence as 'a further means to take illegal material out of circulation and an additional tool to deal with individuals whose behaviour may be causing concern'.[20] In other words, having failed under existing laws successfully to prosecute people whom, for whatever reason, they want to see behind bars, the police have had this task greatly facilitated by conveniently catch-all legislation.

The anti-pornography clauses of the Criminal Justice and Immigration Act 2008 furnish a particularly striking example of how the government, having abandoned any pretence at regulating corporate behaviour, is ever more obsessively determined to micromanage people's personal behaviour. In this particular instance, not trusting British subjects to use the new communications technologies 'responsibly', it has opted to frighten them into doing so, so that every time they buy an unclassified DVD or visit a website with sexual content they will wonder if they are breaking the law and risking being sent to prison. In other words, the government is busily installing a police officer inside the head of each and every one of us. Truly we have entered the era of thought crime.

CHAPTER 21
SEMBLANCE AND THE SEXUAL REVOLUTION:
A CRITICAL REVIEW OF *VIVA*

Beth Johnson

As Eric Schaefer states in *Bold! Daring! Shocking! True!*, 'sexploitation films can best be described as exploitation movies that focus on nudity, sexual situations, and simulated (i.e., nonexplicit) sex acts, designed for titillation and entertainment'.[1] If Schaefer's definition is assumed to be absolute, then Anna Biller's film *Viva* (2007) is notably 'Other'. Biller's film, which tells the tale of a suburban 1970s housewife (Barbi) attempting to 'live' the sexual revolution, is filled with fun, frolics and fantasy vignettes. Additionally however, *Viva* is also a very serious, striking commentary which seeks not only to visually seduce the contemporary viewer, but significantly, to mentally stimulate them. While purposely spoofing the décor and cultural zeitgeist of the sexual revolution in America, *Viva* is consciously multi-layered. Despite frequent *au naturel* episodes, *Viva* is not a film designed only to sexually arouse or titillate (notably the action is cut before things get too hot), but can be understood as a text that focuses on nudity, sexual situations and sex acts in order to critically inform; to offer the viewer a different perspective, a different way of seeing sexploitation. Ultimately, Biller consciously plays with semblance, female servitude and shattered dreams. That is to say, her film sketches the solitude of the sexual revolution for both women and men.

Viva demystifies and makes visible the alienating and often ignored notion that sex in the 1970s was a sign or act of liberation. Via distinct narrative strands and clashing, multi-textured décor, Biller over-exposes the generic fantasy elements of s/exploitation cinema, screening and situating Barbi's journey amidst fashion photography, nudist camps, naughty neighbours and *Playboy*esque orgies. Barbi (notably played by Biller) is on a personal journey in *Viva* which can be seen as partially parodist, or more specifically, socially satirical. Often delivering her lines in a purposefully 'flat' way, Biller represents Barbi as naïve, narcissistic and initially nescient. While the purpose of this representation is always arguable, I suggest that Biller's representation of Barbi is politically informed. Unlike her female fun-loving neighbour in the film, Sheila, Barbi is a woman who desires something more (than preparing *Playboy*'s latest recipes for her handsome husband, Rick). Longing for the liberation that sex promises, Barbi is dissatisfied and forced to come to terms with both the myth of the sexual revolution as purely pleasurable and her status as the exotic other in suburbia. Biller's text then engages most pertinently with the themes of 'representation' and 'possibility' enabling political debate in the fields of gender, visceral desire, genre and spectatorship.

VIVA AND ITS REPRESENTATIONS

On a general level in the filmic medium, representation pertains to the construction and composition of aspects of 'reality'. *Viva*, existing as a period piece, realises, recreates and situates an authentic, effectual vision of exploitation movies from the 1970s. This is significant for several reasons. Firstly, filmic representation inherently involves a process of selection. Moreover, representation here stands in for and takes the place of what it represents. Biller, speaking of *Viva*, continuously notes the significance of her own experiences as a woman and relates these to the complexities of a 'gender problem that's universal and will always exist'.[2] While purposely recreating the pseudo-psychedelic vogue of the 1970s, Biller makes visible the episodic and excessive nature of the sexploitation film. That is to say that she represents the purposeful deformation of naturalness as a desired filmic style, and highlights the deformation of the traditional gender divide in relation to new desires (particularly female desire) for freedom; for something authentic; something more than domesticity. The authenticity of the text then is arguably attained through psychological realism. Barbi is represented as confused, bored, alienated and a little absurd, noting at a hippie nudist commune: 'I don't want to be a man's play-thing.' Barbi thus appears to search for an authentic experience associated with sex and perhaps, this is indeed, the greatest success of *Viva*. Notably, Barbi fails (of course) to find *jouissance*. In lieu of the Thing, she realises her own existential authenticity. As Tanya Krzywinska, author of *Sex and the Cinema* (2006) notes, sex and the representation of sex on-screen is often far from idealistic. Instead, sex and the complexities of sexual relations upon the individual are represented in order to highlight the thorny, unsettling effects of the social order:

A key motive behind the use of psychological realism, is to show that sex is a physical and problematic business. Realism is often used in films that focus on sex in the light of problems originating within the social order, and, in some cases, facilitate the demonstration of the effects of a hierarchical differentiation in the exercise of power.[3]

An additional motif of differential power positing can also be read into the continuous, obnoxious laughter of the diegetic characters. This dominant laughter can be decoded as a political comment on, and direct response to, some audience members who have one-dimensional expectation of *Viva*. In essence, the laughter could be understood to be directed at what Biller calls people's pre-conceived notions of the film as a 'bad' sexploitation movie. Commenting directly on this Biller asserts that

> This movie has been dismissed by many distributors ... because they see it as a trash film. The sexploitation genre is generally considered to be unsuitable for film festivals, and yet my film is not sexploitation, it's quoting sexploitation... I think a lot of them [distributors and audience members] can't understand where I'm coming from. A lot of them think, 'She's just doing an exact copy of a sexploitation movie. Those movies are so bad, why would anybody want to copy them?' They don't consider that the gesture of being a female making a sexploitation film and putting her in it makes it different. It's confusing because it looks and feels the same, yet it's completely different because of the context and point of view.[4]

The point of view Biller speaks of concerns representation. *Viva* is an indie film, directed by a woman. Continuously, it is the male rather than the female body that is situated and exhibited as the object of the gaze. Rick, Barbi's husband is the visible object of demand in the film. His shirtless torso so desired by Barbi operates in order to drive her desire for more. Yet, like the audience, Barbi is repeatedly disappointed. Reflecting the lengthy but non-explicit structure of the film, it can be supposed that on one level, Rick fails to live up to his reputed phallic potency. His sexual encounters with his wife are not enough to sustain her happiness or prevent her *ennui*. Barbi, we learn, wants more of Rick's time; Rick wants less of hers:

> Rick: I'm going to extend my business trip to a month ... This is important. If I don't ski now, I won't ski till next year.
> Barbi: Why don't you bring me along? I can learn to ski too.
> Rick: Oh no, it's not for you, you'd get bored.
> Barbi: I'm so disappointed... You're always working and I was looking forward to this vacation so that we could spend some time together.
> Rick: Why are you always on my back? Can't a guy just have some fun every once in a while? Look, Barbi, you're being a ball and chain. I need to go in the outdoors and express myself – it's who I am.

Barbi clearly finds the relationship inadequate. Rick fails to read her desire. Rick's reference to Barbi always being 'on his back' is also significant. Barbi's obvious sexual desire for Rick appears to be a discomforting experience for him. It can be inferred from Rick's comments that he views skiing as a male sport, an active expression of his lone phallic masculinity. Considering the significance of psychological realism in the text as noted above, the theories of psychoanalyst Jacques Lacan could arguably inform a reading of *Viva* here. Lacan notes in *Encore*: 'Phallic *jouissance* is the obstacle owing to which man does not come, I would say, to enjoy woman's body, precisely because what he enjoys is the *jouissance* of the organ.'[5]

Barbi's body and her *jouissance*, is represented as a complete mystery to Rick and moreover, to herself. Therefore, what is implied is some other knowledge, something that Rick is withholding from her. It is at this point that Barbi and her newly separated neighbour Sheila, decide to transform their own representations of self. Vocalising and then denying their self-blame, the women consciously dress in a sexy manner and set out on an episodic journey of self-discovery in the hope of discovering something more. The re-invention of their identities through alternate representations (as escorts) is again pertinent here. Barbi's clichéd journey of discovery is informed by hope for another era in which she understands herself and is understood. As Frantz Fanon argues:

> Representation is directed by a secret hope of discovering beyond the misery of today, beyond self-contempt, resignation and abjuration, some very beautiful and splendid era whose existence rehabilitates us both in regard to ourselves and in regard to others.[6]

This hope is undeniably embodied by Barbi's new alter-ego – Viva. While Barbi fails to fit in, Viva, scantily-clad and hopeful, is determined to 'live'.

MURKY MELODRAMA

The issue of generic and gendered belonging, or perhaps, more accurately, unbelonging is apt to discuss in relation to Biller's text. Discomfort is not only addressed in *Viva* through the experiences and desires of Barbi and Rick, but also through Biller's directorial style in relation to generic representations associated with gendered texts. As noted briefly above, *Viva* is absolutely episodic and as such can be understood on one level as a type of melodrama. Again here, realism is significant in a psychological rather than literal sense. The insights of Krzywinska are, as such, relative. Speaking of generic boundaries in relation to sex on-screen she notes that 'in some genres, such as melodrama, aspects of realism may be employed to highlight the difficult relationship between the ideals of romantic fantasy and the harsh realities of sex and sexual relationships'.[7] The formula that *Viva* follows (a formula of sexual discovery) can be contextualised via a soft-core aesthetic. That is to say, the soft focus employed by Biller, the stylised locations and rich over-exposed *mise-en-scènic* qualities of the text, function to legitimise and make visible the theme of negotiated, complex and conflicting sexual identities.

Barbi, unlike Viva, is positioned as the sexual subject rather than the sexual object of the film. Viva can be bought. Barbi cannot.

The formula of *Viva* is dominantly consumerist, presenting explicitly the power of buying into a specific representation of the 'American Dream'. Near the opening of the film, Rick and Sheila's husband, Mark, discuss the possibilities of new technology (colour television) in a leering manner. This desire for 'the good life' is made explicit by the lines: 'Live and love today and pay tomorrow – that's the American way!' The 'American way' is, of course, consumerist as referenced by Biller's constant ironic inclusion of product placement throughout the film. 'White Horse whisky' is given a full-frontal close-up and is symbolically reinforced through a Jacques Demy-style interlude involving Sheila, Barbi's white, bright neighbour, who utilises the spirit of the sexual revolution to dream-up her desires – a white horse, a rich sugar-daddy and a Cartier diamond bracelet.

The excessive nature of desire is arguably linked here to the notion of expenditure – an expenditure theorist Georges Bataille nominates as based upon a 'principle of loss'. Writing of the dream of jewels, a dream Sheila again reinforces by stating: 'I want to meet a rich man who'll buy me a fur coat and diamonds – not like my cheapskate husband', Sheila directly references the loss of her old self – Sheila the suburban settled wife. Interestingly, Bataille notes a connection between the dream of a diamond and personal loss or sacrifice. He notes: 'When in a dream a diamond signifies … a part of oneself destined for open sacrifice (they serve, in fact, as sumptuous gifts charged with sexual love).'[8] While Sheila is represented as

FIGURE 21.1 *Viva's* sexploitation aesthetic: attention to 1970s style

happily invoking the loss of her marital body, Barbi appears initially uncertain. Discussing a potential new adventure as call-girls, Barbi and Sheila respond distinctly. Sheila sees the role of a call-girl as 'romantic': 'I've always wanted to be a prostitute', she says dreamily. Barbi, a little more cautious, invokes ethical questions regarding this type of consumerism and the ethics of it: 'Isn't prostitution morally wrong?' she asks. 'No Barbi' Sheila replies, 'it's part of the sexual revolution – taking advantage of your new found sexual freedom.' While Sheila renames herself 'Candy' – an edible treat that can be bought, Barbi renames herself 'Viva' – Italian, she points out, for 'to live' – a desire that we may infer to be part sacrifice, part adventure, part reality, part fantasy.

The following journey of female sexual discovery is, as noted above, generically melodramatic. As Krzywinska notes however:

> The social and emotional consequences of obsessive romantic fantasy that have real effects on the protagonist's lives are primed to deliver a high-impact melodramatic experience. Through its focus on psychology and emotional effect … film is able to speak to audiences about the gulf between the reality and the ideal.[9]

While sexual discovery in film has long been associated with political change (in both negative and positive ways), *Viva* can be understood as a film that is distinct from the current sexual discovery oeuvre in several ways. Unlike films expressing the politics of sex such as *Belle de Jour* (Luis Buñuel, 1967), *Deep Throat* (Gerard Damiano, 1972), *The Story of O* (Just Jaeckin, 1975), *Romance* (Catherine Breillat, 1999) and *Baise-moi* (Virginie Despentes and Coralie Trinh Thi, 2000), *Viva* responds to and sits oddly between the pulp porn of Damiano and the avant-garde anger of Breillat. The film is neither solely a dreamy exploration of female sexuality nor a hard-core confrontation of sexual abuse. Instead, *Viva* is determinedly a text that refuses to 'fit' and this unbelonging has symbolic resonance. While disguised on one level as comedy, a quick scratch of the surface reveals its remarkable otherness. The thing that is distinctive and revolutionary about *Viva* is not the appropriation of gender politics and sexual inequalities in the 1970s, but rather, the fact that *Viva*, as a contemporary text, is informed by an understanding of identity as a historical transformation. As a period piece *Viva* juxtaposes irony and sincerity in order to simultaneously present, reminisce and reflect upon the romantisation of the sexual revolution.

WRITING THE ORGY

Libertine living in *Viva*'s orgy scene positions Viva spectacularly, on-display. Drugged, in gold baroque costume and dancing to the beat of bongo drums, Viva interpolates a bacchanal frenzy. She becomes another (we infer) through the mind-expanding influences of drugs; another who lives for pleasure without reason. Her costume is, as always, significant here making visible the transformative nature of play-acting, the power of disguise (the orgy is 'fancy dress') and the

269

sexual frisson of both voyeurism and scopophilia.

Through her costume, Viva becomes a spectacle; an object of desire that others are 'turned on' by yet, on the orders of the party organiser, Clyde, are prohibited from (fucking). The allure of transgression is associated with both Viva's pending adultery, and Clyde's regulation of the orgy here. As an object of fascination, Viva's dance/song transforms her into an agent of both the erotic and the exotic. Alienated by her 'otherness' – as the primary object of desire – Viva acts out both the pleasure and pain of her struggle to find an authentic experience. Viva's song nominates her 'throbbing' desires: 'Do with me what you will', she sings. The characters who surround her in this scene reiterate the visible exotic otherness of the orgy episode. Saturated with non-white characters dressed in loin cloths, the spell of otherness is only broken when Mark, Sheila's husband and her white male neighbour, kneels before her and calls her by her 'real' name: Barbi.

Indeed, Clyde at this point physically alienates Barbi, ordering her to be taken into another room, stripped and placed on a bed. The audience are here introduced to a new form of expenditure. Barbi's previous order for Clyde to 'do with her what [he] will' implies a turning over of rational control. Barbi's conduct is thus to be associated with erotic willing abandon. This type of abandon symbolised by her complete nakedness in the following scene can again be read in a Bataillean manner. That is to say, Barbi's naked abandon can be understood as a form of Bataillean eroticism: 'a state of communication revealing a quest for a possible

FIGURE 21.2 Song, dance and desire: *Viva*'s musical orgy number

FIGURE 21.3 Viva – spaced out and seduced after being drugged by Clyde at the orgy

continuance of being beyond the self'.[10] Again then, we see that Barbi, through Viva, is on a quest for an authentic erotic experience and this is, most poignantly, what the orgy episode exposes. Viva's lack of speech while Clyde removes her remaining clothing and disappears out of the camera's sight is also significant. In close-up we see Viva's face repetitively going out and coming back into focus. This is accompanied by her deep breathing suggesting an unknown pleasure that is perhaps experienced (for the first time) through being given pleasure rather than giving pleasure to others. This bestowed gift is, however, followed by a scene that suggests full penetrative engagement between Viva and Clyde shot from above.

Focusing upon a bowl containing three red apples next to the bed (one of which Clyde had already taken a large symbolic bite out of), Viva becomes transfixed. Her stare marks the beginning of an aesthetic and stylistic transformation. The apples become obviously animated, themselves growing mouths and teeth, one devouring the other two whole. The background, at this point a vivid pink/purple colour, then transforms into a psychedelic floral montage. The flowers then metamorphose again, become spinning tops before bursting (reminiscent of Linda Lovelace's orgasmic sequence in *Deep Throat*) at which point Viva and Clyde are once again made visible on-screen. Their bodies are overlaid, however, by bright red animated droplets that run down the screen like bloody tears. The connotations of both pleasure and pain here are obvious perhaps reminding the audience of the authenticity of 'real' eroticism as both a ruinous, irrational and painfully unknowable experience.

THE NARCISSISTIC DEMISE OF ROMANCE

According to Lynne Pearce, romantic love is also painful and unknowable and can best be understood as 'a heady cocktail of psychic drives, cultural discourses and social constraints … experienced by its subjects as a traumatic "impossibility" that is worse than irrational'.[11] The notions of im/possibility and/or ir/rationality are significant to discuss here due to the excessive nature of *Viva* discussed above. *Viva* functions as an episodic narrative saturated with romance, dismay and decay. Notably, however, *Viva* is also a text that is contradictory, combining sexploitation tropes with more conventional, heterosexual love narratives. Irrationality and impossibility are rendered significant in the film through a recognition that 'love does not live in the bedroom'. As Gilles Deleuze and Félix Guattari argue, desire is revolutionary; 'that does not at all mean that desire is something Other than sexuality, but that sexuality and love do not live in the bedroom … they dream instead of wide-open spaces, and cause strange flows to circulate that do not let themselves be stocked within an established order'.[12] The strange flows invoked in *Viva*, could be understood to function through the Barbi/Viva oscillation. Barbi/Viva is at once hopeful and disappointed, wife and adulterer, ordinary and extraordinary, rational and irrational. Happily liberated in one scene, Barbi/Viva is seemingly victimised in another. Barbi longs for romance, for sensitivity but, as Viva, seemingly enters into potentially violent or abusive scenarios repeatedly and to an extent, willingly. Romance or at the least Barbi's romantic desires, are, via these assaults on Viva, shown to be flawed. As Krzywinska points out, 'sex and romance is flawed because it resides mostly in fantasy and, despite the idealistic optimism … we never truly know the other'.[13] In terms of Barbi/Viva, her narcissism is both absent and present at differing times throughout the film. Pointedly however, Biller's own narcissism and naked voyeurism are unashamedly placed on display. Whether her fetishism is directed toward a by-gone era, a *Playboy* ideal, or a dream of revolution through new interpretations of the past, she undoubtedly produces a gaudy and pleasurable aesthetic. In terms of the audience, the pleasure of seeing a serious film director topless in her own film triangulates this already complex representation of negotiated identities and points to a desire of new, spectacular possibility.

Toward the close of *Viva*, Barbi and Sheila discuss their adventures, Barbi noting the darkness of her self-discovery. Some things are 'probably best hidden' she says. Referring to her/Viva's activities (particularly at the orgy) as excessive she notes that: 'It was too much … I became a female animal, made only for pleasure.' Such a comment implies of course a loss of human rationality. Barbi's dark reflection upon Viva's experiences relates to an excessive irrationality for pleasure alone which does not sit comfortably with Barbi's domestic role. It is at this point that a conscious distinction is again made visible between Barbi and Sheila. As a white woman, happy in and perhaps belonging to suburbia, Sheila exclaims that: 'I don't see what's so scary about living for pleasure. I've done it all my life!' Barbi, the exotic 'other' undoubtedly feels differently. Sheila then informs Barbi that she and Mark are pregnant. Barbi asks if she is sure that the baby is Marks. Again, Sheila's reply displays Barbi's otherness, her naivety perhaps: 'Oh Barbi, you don't really think I ever actually slept with any of the men at the agency do you?' In response, Barbi tells Sheila that she envies her.

In the next episode of the narrative, Mark, having previously arrived at Barbi's house intoxicated to find Rick still absent and Barbi alone, makes reference to the orgy at which they were both present. Exchanging views, Mark describes Viva as 'abnormal' and a 'filthy lesbian whore' – casting her as the perverse 'other'. When Mark then attempts to rape Barbi, she bites him and he apologises and leaves. It is moments after his departure that Rick returns 'home' – smells Mark's scent on his wife and storms out of the house again. While we, the audience see nothing apart from Barbi framed and dismayed in the open doorway of their home – we hear the screech of tyres indicating that Rick has been involved in a car crash. This detail is never explained; however, the next scene reveals Rick (with his leg in a medical cast), Mark, a pregnant Sheila and Barbi sat in the garden area – as they were at the opening of the film signalling a restoration of sorts.

The definitive idea of equilibrium as re-instated remains, however, questionable. Sheila, visibly pregnant, hands out *Playboy* canapés and Barbi notes that she must get the recipe so that she can make them for Rick (a domestic duty we saw Barbi undertaking at the opening of the film). While Mark and Rick discuss their new-found happiness (Rick declaring his enjoyment of his increased time at 'home' with Barbi, and Mark noting his impending fatherhood), Barbi, we infer has regressed back into the unfulfilling role in which the suburbia initially placed her. As such, the value of her journey – to 'live' the sexual revolution – is called into question by Biller.

This questioning of Barbi's journey is enhanced by strong references to other sexploitation films. The next episode sees Barbi and her pretty blonde friend (now having given birth to a baby boy) performing at the theatre. Adorned in red sequin dresses, diamante chokers and white feather boas, the 'girls' are told by a theatre director, Arthur (previously known to Viva) to 'give it everything'. Dancing and performing in unison, the girls tell the tale of their journeys – noting their 'normality': 'We're just two girls who have seen it all – things haven't always gone the way we planned. We've got into some serious trouble, but trouble be damned!' This musical number is both spectacular and fantastic. The girls sing of the significance of perspective noting that they can be 'lovers, mothers, singers, swingers and friends' depending on the 'point of view'. Again then, the issue of perspective is raised and addressed directly in association with spectatorship. Yet this performance also functions to highlight the issue of gendered spectatorship. In this scene the 'girls' are singing to and directly performing for Arthur and Rick – an exclusively male audience. Arguably, this could be assumed to be Biller's direct address to the (expected) male audience of *Viva*. The irony of the scene and the familiarity of it (as blatantly referenced through similarities to Jacques Demy's colourful musical *Les Parapluies de Cherbourg* (1964) as well as earlier references to Radley Metzger's musical scores and the episodic fantasy style invoked from *Belle de Jour* points to a political statement about the visibility and fetishistic status of women as performers in sexploitation films. As Biller's film is 'other', it could be suggested that she is indeed pointing out the perverse desire of male audiences here. As well as making a clear statement about its otherness, *Viva* is a female vision: sexploitation from the 'other' (the female directors' and female audiences') perspective.

The problematics concerning *Viva*'s acceptance at film festivals as mentioned above was perhaps then not surprising for Biller. Indeed, her indie film can be seen to recognise and predict this through Barbi's ultimate repositioning at the close of the film. While the musical sequence speaks of 'arriving', 'Viva la vita – we've arrived' Barbi and Sheila sing, the question that is left hanging is 'where?' Arguably, the point of Biller's film is to make visible the fact that each woman who experienced or lived through the 1970s sexual revolution had a different experience which can neither be represented nor understood as wholly bad or good. It would appear that Barbi is ultimately shown to have gained confidence through her episodic self-discovering journeys; however, perhaps most significantly, Barbi has learned to 'live' with her situation, her marriage, her unbelonging. Barbi and Sheila do not arrive at *jouissance*, but at self-recognition of the absurdity of living in what Mark brashly describes as 'a man's world'.

INTRODUCTION

1   L. Williams (2004) *Porn Studies*. Durham and London: Duke University Press, 1.

2   Ibid., 2.

3   A. Dworkin (1981) *Pornography: Men Possessing Women*. London: The Women's Press Ltd.

4   S. Griffin (1982) *Pornography and Silence*. London: The Women's Press Ltd.

5   A. Dworkin (1977) from *Letters From a War Zone*, reproduced in D. Cornell (ed.) (2000) *Feminism and Pornography*. Oxford: Oxford University Press, 27.

6   See L. Lovelace and M. McGrady (1980) *Ordeal*. New York: Berkeley.

7   E. H. D. Russell, in D. Cornell (ed.) (2000) *Feminism and Pornography*. Oxford: Oxford University Press, 55.

8   C. Mackinnon (1993) from *Only Words*, reproduced in D. Cornell (ed.) (2000) *Feminism and Pornography*. Oxford: Oxford University Press, 101.

9   Williams, L. (1989) *Hard Core: Power, Pleasure and the Frenzy of the Visible*. Berkeley: University of California Press, 203.

10   L. Segal and M. McIntosh (eds) (1992) *Sex Exposed: Sexuality and the Pornography Debate*. London: Virago Press.

11   K Mackinnon (1988) *Uneasy Pleasures: The Male as Erotic Object*. Madison, NJ: Fairleigh Dickinson University Press.

12   C. Penley (2004) 'Crackers and Whackers: The White Trashing of Porn', in L. Williams (ed.) *Porn Studies*. Durham: Duke University Press, 309–31.

13   R. Royce Mahawatte (2004) 'Loving the Asian: Race, Gay Pornography and the Essentials of Passion', in

P. Church Gibson (ed.) *More Dirty Looks: Gender, Pornography and Power*. London: British Film Institute. 127–37.

14   B. McNair (2002) *Striptease Culture*. London: Routledge; F. Attwood (2009) *Mainstreaming Sex: The Sexualisation of Western Culture*. London: I.B. Tauris.

15   See L. Sigel (2002) *Governing Pleasures: Pornography and Social Change in England*. Piscataway, NJ: Rutgers University Press.

16   E. Mathijs and X. Mendik (eds) (2004) *Alternative Europe: Eurotrash and Exploitation Cinema Since 1945*. London: Wallflower Press.

CHAPTER 1

1   J. Workman (1990) *Betty Being Bad*, Seattle: Eros Comix, 1.

2   Buszek, M. (2006) *Pin-Up Grrrls: Feminism, Sexuality, Popular Culture*, Durham: Duke University Press, 247.

3   See K. Essex and J. Swanson, J. (1996) *Bettie Page: The Life of a Pin-Up Legend*, Los Angeles: General Publishing, 49–57; and R. Foster (1997) *The Real Bettie Page: The Truth About the Queen of the Pinups*, Secaucus, NJ: Birch Lane Press, 32–9.

4   See M. Gabor (1995) *The Pin-Up: A Modest History*, Cologne: Evergreen, 77–8; and H. Merrill (1995) *Esky: The Early Years at Esquire*, New Brunswick, NJ: Rutgers University Press, 93.

5   S. Hall (1981) 'Notes on Deconstructing the Popular', in R. Samuel (ed.) *People's History and Socialist Theory*. London: Routledge, 228.

6   R. Allen (1991) *Horrible Prettiness: Burlesque and American Culture*, Chapel Hill, NC: University of North Carolina Press, 138.

7   Ibid., 125.

8   Ibid., 237.

9   *Wink*, October 1954, 22–3.

10   See K. Essex and J. Swanson (1996) *Bettie Page: The Life of a Pin-Up Legend*, Los Angeles: General Publishing, 143–4; and R. Foster (1997) *The Real Bettie Page: The Truth About the Queen of the Pinups*, Secaucus, NJ: Birch Lane Press, 55–7.

11   L. Mulvey (1975) 'Visual Pleasure and Narrative Cinema', *Screen*, 16 (3), 6–18.

12   E. Schaefer (1999) *'Bold! Daring! Shocking! True!': A History of Exploitation Films, 1919–1959*, Durham: Duke University Press, 311.

13   Ibid., 314.

14   A. Nadel (1995) *Containment Culture: American Narratives, Postmodernism, and the Atomic Age*, Durham: Duke University Press, 14.

15   E. T. May (1995) *Barren in the Promised Land: Childless Americans and the Pursuit of Happiness*, Cambridge: Harvard University Press, 127–34; and E. T. May (1999) *Homeward Bound: American Families in the Cold War Era*, second edn. New York: Basic Books, 82.

16   J. D'Emilio (1983) *Sexual Politics, Sexual Communities: The Making of a Homosexual Minority in the United States, 1940–1970*. Chicago: University of Chicago Press, 40–56; and J. D'Emilio (1989) 'The Homosexual Menace: The Politics of Sexuality in Cold War America', in K. Peiss and C. Simmons (eds) *Passion and Power: Sexuality in History*. Philadelphia: Temple University Press, 226–40.

17   Johnson, D. (2004) *The Lavender Scare: The Cold War Persecution of Gays and Lesbians in the Federal Government*, Chicago: University of Chicago Press.

18   See W. Kozol (1994) *Life's America: Family and Nation in Postwar Photojournalism*. Philadelphia: Temple University Press.

19   P. Biskind (1983) *Seeing is Believing: How Hollywood Taught Us To Stop Worrying and Love the Fifties*. New York: Pantheon, 4.

20 L. May (ed.) (1989) *Recasting America: Culture and Politics in the Age of the Cold War*. Chicago: Chicago University Press.

21 J. Foreman (1997) *The Other Fifties: Interrogating Midcentury American Icons*. Urbana: University of Illinois Press.

22 Ibid., 3–4.

23 B. Friedan (1963) *The Feminine Mystique*. New York: W. W. Norton.

24 J. Meyerowitz (1993) 'Beyond the Feminine Mystique: A Reassessment of Postwar Mass Culture, 1946–1958', *Journal of American History*, 79 (4), 1455–82.

25 See K. Essex and J. Swanson (1996) *Bettie Page: The Life of a Pin-Up Legend*. Los Angeles: General Publishing, 143–6; and R. Foster (1997) *The Real Bettie Page: The Truth About the Queen of the Pinups*. Secaucus, NJ: Birch Lane Press, 55–60.

26 B. Page (2000) *Betty Page: The Complete Interview* (CD). Bonn: QDK Records.

27 J. Butler (1990) *Gender Trouble: Feminism and the Subversion of Identity*. London: Routledge, 140.

28 J. Butler (1995) 'Melancholy Gender/Refused Identification', in M. Berger, B. Wallis and S. Watson (eds) *Constructing Masculinity*. London: Routledge, 31.

29 M. Buszek (2006) *Pin-Up Grrrls: Feminism, Sexuality, Popular Culture*. Durham: Duke University Press, 247.

30 See J. Slade (2001) *Pornography and Sexual Representation: A Reference Guide*, Vol. 1. Westport, CT: Greenwood Press, 203.

31 F. Jameson (1984) 'Postmodernism, or the Cultural Logic of Late Capitalism', *New Left Review*, 146, 65.

32 F. Jameson (1988) 'The Politics of Theory: Ideological Positions in the Postmodernism Debate', in F. Jameson, *The Ideologies of Theory Essays, Volume 2*. London: Routledge, 105.

33 J. Storey (2001) 'The Sixties in the Nineties: Pastiche or Hyperconsciousness?', in B. Osgerby and A. Gough-Yates (eds) *Action TV: Tough Guys, Smooth Operators and Foxy Chicks*. London: Routledge, 246.

34 F. Jameson (1984) 'Postmodernism, or the Cultural Logic of Late Capitalism', *New Left Review*, 146, 65.

CHAPTER 2

1   For examples of online reviews in this vein, see http://www.tranquility.net/~benedict/cafeflesh.html, or http://houseofselfindulgence.blogspot.com/2008/08/cafe-flesh-rinse-dream-1982.html.

2   S. Sayadian. Interview with the author, 21 August 2005.

3   Ibid.

4   S. Sayadian. Telephone interview, 8 November 2005.

5   L. Kipnis (1996) *Bound and Gagged*. New York: Grove Press, 153.

6   S. Sayadian. Telephone interview, 26 May 2005.

7   S. Sayadian. Telephone interview, 9 June 2005.

8   S. Sayadian. Interview with the author, 21 August 2005.

9   Ibid.

10 J. Hawkins (2003) 'Midnight Sex-Horror Movies and the Downtown Avant-Garde', in M. Jancovich, A. Lazaro Reboll, J. Stringer and A. Willis (eds) *Defining Cult Movies*. Manchester: Manchester University Press, 223.

11 Ibid.

12 Ibid., 224.

13 S. Sayadian. Telephone interview, 26 May 2005.

14 Ibid.

15 S. Sayadian. Interview with the author, 21 August 2005.

16 L. Williams (1989) *Hard Core*. Berkeley: University of California Press, 147–8.

17 J. Stahl. Email interview, 1 September 2005.

18 S. Sayadian. Interview with the author, 21 August 2005.

19 R. Cante and A. Restivo (2001) 'The Voice of Pornography', in M. Tinkcom and A. Villarejo (eds) *Keyframes*. New York: Routledge, 221.

20 L. Williams (1989) *Hard Core*. Berkeley: University of California Press, 124.

21 The term sonotope is a reference to Mikhail Bakhtin's concept of the chronotope, which he used to refer to 'the intrinsic connectedness' of temporal [chrono-] and spatial [tope] relationships that are artistically expressed in literature'; for Bakhtin, chronotopes such as 'the road' were a defining factor in the shaping of literary genres, functioning as 'organizing centers' for narrative events since they dictate settings, characters and types of interaction as well as a certain experience of time (M. M. Bakhtin (1981) *The Dialogic Imagination*. Austin: University of Texas Press, 84; 250).

22 See J. Laplanche and J.-B. Pontalis (1968) 'Fantasy and the Origins of Sexuality', in *The International Journal of Pyschoanalysis*, vol. 49, 17.

23 J. Hawkins (2003) 'Midnight Sex-Horror Movies and the Downtown Avant-Garde', in M. Jancovich, A. Lazaro Reboll, J. Stringer and A. Willis (eds) *Defining Cult Movies*. Manchester: Manchester University Press, 225.

24 S. Sayadian. Interview with the author, 21 August 2005.

25 J. Stahl (1985) '*Café Flesh* and Me: Confessions of a Cult Sex King', in *Playboy*, vol. 32, issue 4, 80.

26 Ibid.

27 S. Sayadian. Interview with the author, 21 August 2005.

28 J. Hawkins (2003) 'Midnight Sex-Horror Movies and the Downtown Avant-Garde', in M. Jancovich, A. Lazaro Reboll, J. Stringer and A. Willis (eds) *Defining Cult Movies*. Manchester: Manchester University Press, 229.

29 L. Williams (1989) *Hard Core*. Berkeley: University of California Press, 160.

30 S. Sayadian. Interview with the author, 21 August 2005.

31 J. Stahl (1985) '*Café Flesh* and Me: Confessions of a Cult Sex King', in *Playboy*, vol. 32, issue 4, 80.

32 S. Sayadian. Interview with the author, 21 August 2005.

33 J. Naremore (1988) *Acting in the Cinema*. Berkeley: University of California Press, 3

34 Ibid., 20.

35 See T. Castle (1986) *Masquerade and Civilization*. Stanford: Stanford University Press, 40.

36 J. Stahl. Email interview, 25 April 2005.

37 See P. Gilstrap 'Perv: A Success Story', http://www.sexwrecks.com. Accessed 25 April 2005.

38 S. Sayadian. Interview with the author, 21 August 2005.

39 Ibid.

40 J. Hoberman and J. Rosenbaum (1983) *Midnight Movies*. New York: Da Capo Press, 301.

41 S. Sayadian. Telephone interview, 8 November 2005.

42 S. Sayadian. Interview with the author, 21 August 2005.

43 J. Stahl (1985) '*Café Flesh* and Me: Confessions of a Cult Sex King', in *Playboy*, vol. 32, issue 4, 202.

44 J. Hoberman and J. Rosenbaum (1983) *Midnight Movies*. New York: Da Capo Press, 302.

45 Ibid., 328.

46 S. Sayadian. Interview with the author, 21 August 2005.

CHAPTER 3

1 K. Murphy (2004) 'Hells Angels: An Interview with Catherine Breillat', www.sensesofcinema.com. Accessed 21 April 2008.

2 A. Rich (1971) 'When We Dead Awaken: Writing as Re-Vision', in A. Rich (1979) *On Lies, Secrets and Silence – Selected Prose*. New York: W. W. Norton, 35.

3 C. Breillat (2004) 'The Opposite of Sex – *Anatomy of Hell*', *Reverse Shot Online*, http://www.reverseshot.

com/legacy/autumn04/anatomy.html. Accessed on 16 May 2008.

4   See A. Smith (2005) *French Cinema in the 1970s: The Echoes of May*. Manchester: Manchester University Press.

5   C. Darke (2008) 'French Cinema Now, Unbelievable But Real: The Legacy of '68', *Sight & Sound*, May, 30.

6   C. Breillat (2004) 'Interview with the Director', *Anatomy of Hell* DVD, Tartan.

7   See B. Price (2002) 'Catherine Breillat', www.sensesofcinema.com. Accessed 21 April 2008

8   Anton, S. (1999) 'Interview: Catherine Breillat Opens up About 'Romance,' Sex and Censorship', *IndieWIRE* http://www.indiewire.com/people/int_Breillat_Catheri_2A616.html viewed on 28 May 2008.

9   See C. Joyce (1999) 'Tainted Love', http://www.salon.com/ent/movies/int/1999/09/17/breillat/index. html. Accessed on 23 April 2008.

10 See S. Sherwin (2004) 'The Odd Couple – Interview with Catherine Breillat and Rocco Siffredi', *The Guardian* http://www.guardian.co.uk/film/2004/nov/19/2. Accessed on 30 May 2008.

11 G. MacNab (2004) 'Written on the Body: An Interview with Catherine Breillat', *Sight & Sound*, December, 20–2.

12 L. Williams (1999) *Hard Core: Power Pleasure and the Frenzy of the Visible*. Berkeley: University of California Press.

13 L. Williams (ed.) (2004) *Porn Studies*. Durham: Duke University Press, 1.

14 K. Boyle (2006) 'The Boundaries of Porn Studies: On Linda Williams' *Porn Studies*', *New Review of Film and Television Studies*, 4 (1), 1–16.

15 K. Boyle (2008) 'Courting Consumers and Legitimating Exploitation: The Representation of Commercial Sex in Television Documentaries', *Feminist Media Studies*, 8 (1), 35–50.

16 Ibid., 44.

17 Chris (2001) 'A Quick Chat with Catherine Breillat' at http://www.kamera.co.uk/interviews/catherinebreillat. html. Accessed on 23 April 2008.

18 C. Breillat (1999) *Romance – Press Kit*.

19 R. Sklar (with S. Gluck) (1999) 'A Woman's Vision of Shame and Desire: An Interview with Catherine Breillat', *Cineaste*, 25 (1), 31.

20 L. Downing (2004) 'French Cinema's New "Sexual Revolution": Postmodern Porn and Troubled Genre', *French Cultural Studies*, 15 (3), 269.

21 A. Gillain and M. Colvin (translator) (2003) 'Profile of a Filmmaker: Catherine Breillat' in R. Celestin, E. DalMolin and I. de Courtivron (eds) *Beyond French Feminisms: Debates on Women, Politics, and Culture in France, 1981–2001*. Basinstoke: Palgrave Macmillan, 204.

22 M. Beugnet (2007) *Cinema and Sensation: French Film and the Art of Transgression*. Edinburgh: Edinburgh University Press, 48.

23 V. Sélavy (2008) 'Interview with Catherine Breillat', *Electric Sheep*, 18, http://www.electricsheepmagazine. co.uk/features/2008/04/01/interview-with-catherine-breillat. Accessed on 28 May 2008.

24 M. Dargis (2004) 'Four Nights of Sex and Zero Nights of Fun', *The New York Times*, 15 October.

25 K. Murphy (2004) 'Hells Angels: An Interview with Catherine Breillat', www.sensesofcinema.com. Accessed on 21 April 2008.

26 A. Dworkin (1997) 'Pornography Happens', in A. Dworkin, *Life and Death: Unapologetic Writings on the Continuing War Against Women*. London: Virago Press, 126–7.

27 K. Boyle (2008) 'Courting Consumers and Legitimating Exploitation: The Representation of Commercial Sex in Television Documentaries', *Feminist Media Studies*, 8 (1), 45.

28 C. Breillat (2004) 'Interview with the Director', *Anatomy of Hell* DVD, Tartan.

29 A. Dworkin (1997) 'Pornography Happens', in A. Dworkin, *Life and Death: Unapologetic Writings on the Continuing War Against Women*. London: Virago Press, 99.

30 K. Boyle (2008) 'Courting Consumers and Legitimating Exploitation: The Representation of Commercial Sex in Television Documentaries', *Feminist Media Studies*, 8 (1), 46.

31 MacNab, G. (2004) 'Written on the Body: An Interview With Catherine Breillat' *Sight & Sound*, (December 2004).

32 B. Price (2002) 'Catherine Breillat', www.sensesofcinema.com. Accessed 21 April 2008.

33 L. Williams (2001) 'Cinema and the Sex Act', *Cineaste*, 27 (1), 20–5.

34 For example see L. Johnson (2004) 'Perverse Angle: Feminist Film, Queer Film, Shame', *Signs: Journal of Women in Culture and Society*, 30 (1), 1360–84; and K. Gorton (2007) 'The Point of View of Shame: Reviewing Female Desire in Catherine Breillat's *Romance* (1999) and *Anatomy of Hell* (2004)', *Studies in European Cinema*, 4 (2), 111–24.

35 L. Felperin and L. R. Williams (1999) 'The Edge of the Razor: Interview with Catherine Breillat', *Sight and Sound*, October, 13–14.

36 R. Sklar (with S. Gluck) (1999) 'A Woman's Vision of Shame and Desire: An Interview with Catherine Breillat', *Cineaste*, 25 (1), 31.

37 J. Hoyles (2002) 'Catherine Breillat: Taking Sex Seriously', http://www.moviemail-online.co.uk/scripts/media_view.pl?id=83&type=Articles. Accessed on 23 April 2008.

38 R. Sklar (with S. Gluck) (1999) 'A Woman's Vision of Shame and Desire: An Interview with Catherine Breillat', *Cineaste*, 25 (1), 31.

CHAPTER 4

1 For more information on the homophobic response to disco see W. Hughes (1994) 'In the Empire of the Beat: Discipline and Disco', in A. Ross and T. Rose (eds) *Microphone Fiends: Youth Music and Youth Culture*. London: Routledge; 147–58; and J. Kooijman (2005) 'Turn the Beat Around: Richard Dyer's "In Defence of Disco" Revisited', *European Journal of Cultural Studies*, 8 (2), 257–66. For a full account of the Disco Demolition Derby and a definitive account of dance music culture see T. Lawrence (2005) *Love Save's the Day: A History of American Dance Music Culture 1970–1979*. Durham: Duke University Press.

2 A. Goldman (1978) *Disco*. New York: Hawthorn Press, 117.

3 Ibid.

4 A. Kopkind (1979) 'The Dialectic of Disco: Gay Music Goes Straight', *The Village Voice*, 34 (7), 1–14.

5 Holleran, A. (2001 [1978]) *The Dancer From the Dance*. New York: HarperCollins.

6 A. Goldman (1978) *Disco*. New York: Hawthorn Press, 20.

7 Ibid., 22.

8 M. Cheren (2000) *Keep on Dancin': My Life and the Paradise Garage*. New York: 24 Hours for Life.

9 The bar is still open to this day on New York's Christopher Street.

10 R. Cante and A. Restivo (2004) 'The Cultural-Aesthetic Specificities of All-Male Moving-Image', in L. Williams (ed.) *Porn Studies*. Durham: Duke University Press, 147.

11 R. Dyer (1990) *Now You See It: Studies on Lesbian and Gay Film*. London: Routledge.

12 Quoted from the documentary *Gay Sex and the 1970s* (2005).

13 P. Moore (2004) *Beyond Shame: Reclaiming the Abandoned History of Radical Gay Sexuality*. Boston: Beacon Press.

14 R. Cante and A. Restivo (2004) 'The Cultural-Aesthetic Specificities of All-Male Moving-Image', in L. Williams (ed.) *Porn Studies*. Durham: Duke University Press, 143.

15 L. Williams (1999) *Hard Core: Power, Pleasure, and the 'Frenzy of the Visible'*. Berkeley: University of California Press, 122.

16 J. Gill (1995) *Queer Noises: Male and Female Homosexuality in Twentieth-Century Music*. New York: Continuum.

17 See R. Barthes (1975) *The Pleasure of the Text*. London: Hill and Wang.

18 A. Kopkind (1979) 'The Dialectic of Disco: Gay Music Goes Straight', *The Village Voice*, 34 (7), 11.
19 Ibid., 14.
20 R. Cante and A. Restivo (2004) 'The Cultural-Aesthetic Specificities of All-Male Moving-Image', in L. Williams (ed.) *Porn Studies*. Durham: Duke University Press, 143.
21 R. Dyer (1979) 'In Defence of Disco', *Gay Left*, 8, 20.
22 Ibid., 22.
23 P. Moore (2004) *Beyond Shame: Reclaiming the Abandoned History of Radical Gay Sexuality*. Boston: Beacon Press, xxv.

CHAPTER 5

1 Figure cited from the documentary *Desperately Seeking Seka* (Magnus Paulsson/Christian Hallman, 2002).

CHAPTER 6

1 J. Phillips (1993) *Sade: The Libertine Novels*. London: Pluto Press, 32.
2 M. Charney (1981) *Sexual Fiction*. London: Methuen, 35.
3 Ibid., 45.
4 Ibid., 34.
5 Ibid.
6 J. Phillips (1993) *Sade: The Libertine Novels*. London: Pluto Press, 43.
7 See D. A. F. Sade (1966) *The Marquis de Sade: The 120 Days of Sodom and Other Writings*. New York: Grove Press.
8 D. Badder (1977) 'Emanuelle and Françoise' (review), *Monthly Film Bulletin*,vol. 44, no. 526, 232.
9 Phillips. 54.
10 Ibid., 56.
11 M. Charney (1981) *Sexual Fiction*. London: Methuen, 33.
12 J. Phillips (1993) *Sade: The Libertine Novels*. London: Pluto Press, 43.
13 Ibid., 55.
14 M. Charney (1981) *Sexual Fiction*. London: Methuen, 38.
15 J. Phillips (1993) *Sade: The Libertine Novels*. London: Pluto Press, 51.
16 Ibid., 51–2.
17 See P. Lehman (1993) *Running Scared: Masculinity and Representations of the Male Body*. Philadelphia: Temple University Press.
18 Ibid., 173.
19 Ibid., 174.
20 J. Phillips (1993) *Sade: The Libertine Novels*. London: Pluto Press, 37.
21 P. Lehman (1993) *Running Scared: Masculinity and Representations of the Male Body*. Philadelphia: Temple University Press, 178–9.
22 J. Phillips (1993) *Sade: The Libertine Novels*. London: Pluto Press, 37.

CHAPTER 7

1 M. Raso. Interview with the author, June 2008.
2 E. Meehan (1991) 'Holy Commodity Fetish, Batman!: The Political Economy of a Commercial Intertext', in R. Pearson and W. Uricchio (eds) *The Many Lives of the Batman: Critical Approaches to a Superhero and his Media*. New York: Routledge, 49.
3 Note that ei Independent Cinema recently rebranded themselves as POP Cinema.

4   This is a quote from a Seduction Cinema press release, provided by Paige Kay Davis.

5   M. Raso. Interview with the author, June 2008.

6   From the author's email correspondence with P. K. Davis.

7   M. Raso. Publicity Glossy for *Kinky Kong* (2006).

8   D. Andrew (2006) *Soft in the Middle: The Contemporary Soft-core Feature in its Contexts*. Columbus, OH: Ohio State University Press, 232.

9   I. Q. Hunter (2006) 'Tolkien Dirty', in E. Mathijs (ed.) *The Lord of the Rings: Popular Culture in Global Context*. London: Wallflower Press, 321.

10 M. Raso, quoted in D. Andrew (2004) 'Just One of the Lesbian Vampire Guys: A Conversation with Seduction Cinema's Michael Raso', *Bridge*, 13, 33.

11 I. Q. Hunter (2006) 'Tolkien Dirty', in E. Mathijs (ed.) *The Lord of the Rings: Popular Culture in Global Context*. London: Wallflower Press, 319.

12 *Spiderbabe*. DVD back cover blurb.

13 C. Fischer (1992) 'Beyond the Valley of the Dolls and the Exploitation Genre', *The Velvet Light Trap*, 30, 20.

14 T. West, quoted in B. Hallenbeck (2003) 'Lord of the Muse', *Alternative Cinema*, 20, 42.

15 M. Raso. Interview with the author, June 2008.

16 P. Grainge (2007) *Brand Hollywood: Selling Entertainment in a Global Media Age*. London: Routledge, 12.

CHAPTER 9

1   See F. Attwood (2002) 'Reading Porn: The Paradigm Shift in Pornography Research', *Sexualities*, 5 (1), 91–105; C. Smith (2007) *One for the Girls!: The Pleasures and Practices of Reading Women's Porn*. Bristol: Intellect; L. Williams (1990) *Hard Core: Power, Pleasure, and the 'Frenzy of the Visible'*. London: Pandora.

2   Another pornographic take on *A Clockwork Orange*, discovered too late for inclusion in this essay, is *Avantgarde Extreme 53 Scatwork Orange* (Simon Thaur, 2007), a scatological fetish DVD directed by the owner of Berlin's KitKat Club.

3   R. Burt (1998) *Unspeakable ShaXXXspeares: Queer Theory and American Kiddie Culture*. New York: St. Martin's Press, 77–124. On exploitation cinema generally considered as a mode of adaptation, see I. Q. Hunter (2009) 'Exploitation as Adaptation', *Scope: An Online Journal of Film & TV Studies*, 15 (November) and Iain Robert Smith (ed.) (eBook) *Cultural Borrowings: Appropriation, Reworking, Transformation*, 8–33. On-line: http://www.scope.nottingham.ac.uk/cultborr/chapter.php?id=5. Accessed 27 May 2010.

4   See J. Staiger (2003) 'The Cultural Productions of *A Clockwork Orange*' in S. Y. McDougal (ed.) *Stanley Kubrick's A Clockwork Orange*. Cambridge: Cambridge University Press, 37–60; and M. DeRosia (2003) 'An Erotics of Violence: Masculinity and (Homo)sexuality in Stanley Kubrick's *A Clockwork Orange*', in S. Y. McDougal (ed.) *Stanley Kubrick's A Clockwork Orange*. Cambridge: Cambridge University Press, 61–84.

5   On porn versions of *The Lord of the Rings*, see I. Q. Hunter (2006) 'Tolkien Dirty', in E. Mathijs (ed.) *Lord of the Rings: Popular Culture in Global Context*. London: Wallflower Press, 317–33.

6   P. Kael (1972) 'Stanley Strangelove', *The New Yorker*, 48 (1 January), 50.

7   J. Staiger (2003) 'The Cultural Productions of *A Clockwork Orange*' in S. Y. McDougal (ed.) *Stanley Kubrick's A Clockwork Orange*. Cambridge: Cambridge University Press, 44.

8   On the relation between *A Clockwork Orange* and exploitation films, see I. Q. Hunter (2008) '*A Clockwork Orange*, Exploitation and the Art Film', in S. Martin (ed.) *Recycling Culture(s)*. Newcastle upon Tyne: Cambridge Scholars Publishing, 11–20.

9   L. R. Williams (2005) *The Erotic Thriller in Contemporary Cinema*. Edinburgh: Edinburgh University Press, 397.

10 R. P. Kolker (2003) '*A Clockwork Orange* … ticking', in S. Y. McDougal (ed.) *Stanley Kubrick's A Clockwork Orange*. Cambridge: Cambridge University Press, 32.

11 See S. Marcus (1966) *The Other Victorians: A Study of Sexuality and Pornography in Mid-Nineteenth Century England*. London: Weidenfeld & Nicholson.

12 J. W. Slade (2006) 'Margins to Mainstream: Pornography Refreshes American Culture', in R. Kick (ed.) *Everything You Know about Sex is Wrong: The Disinformation Guide to the Extremes of Human Sexuality (and Everything in Between)*. New York: The Disinformation Company, 143.

13 T. Krzywinska (1999 'Cicciolina and the Dynamics of Transgression and Abjection in Explicit Sex Films', in M. Aaron (ed.) *The Body's Perilous Pleasures: Dangerous Desires and Contemporary Culture*. Edinburgh: Edinburgh University Press, 188–209.

14 G. Genette (1997) *Palimpsests: Literature in the Second Degree*. Trans. C. Newman and C. Doubinsky. Lincoln, NE: University of Nebraska Press, 4.

15 See I. Q. Hunter (2006) 'Tolkien Dirty', in E. Mathijs (ed.) *Lord of the Rings: Popular Culture in Global Context*. London: Wallflower Press, 317–33.

16 L. Williams (1990) *Hard Core: Power, Pleasure, and the 'Frenzy of the Visible'*. London: Pandora, 48.

17 See A. Jukes (1993) *Why Men Hate Women*. London: Free Association Books, 208–22; L. Kipnis (1999) *Bound and Gagged: Pornography and the Politics of Fantasy in America*. Durham: Duke University Press, 179–88; and J. Stoltenberg (1989) *Refusing To Be a Man*. Portland, OR: Breitenbush Books, 44.

18 See L. Kipnis (1999) *Bound and Gagged: Pornography and the Politics of Fantasy in America*. Durham: Duke University Press, 185–6.

19 P. Bradshaw (2005) '*9 Songs*' (review), *Guardian*, March 11, http://film.guardian.co.uk/News_Story/Critic_Review/Guardian_Film_of_the_week/0,4267,1434764,00.html. Accessed 11 March 2005.

20 L. Williams (1991) 'Film Bodies: Gender, Genre, and Excess', *Film Quarterly*, 44 (4), 4.

21 M. Csikszentmihalyi (2002) *Flow: The Classic Work on How to Achieve Happiness*. London: Rider.

22 See M. E. P. Seligman (2002) *Authentic Happiness: Using the New Positive Psychology to Realize Your Potential for Lasting Fulfillment*. New York: Free Press, 118–19.

23 On masturbation and meditation, see M. Cornog (2003) *The Big Book of Masturbation: From Angst to Zeal*. San Francisco: Down There Press, 183–8.

24 The pioneering texts here are M. S. Davis (1983) *Smut: Erotic Reality/Obscene Reality*. Chicago: University of Chicago Press; D. Loftus (2002) *Watching Sex: How Men Really Respond to Pornography*. New York: Thunder's Mouth Press; S. MacDonald (1983) 'Confessions of a Feminist Porn Watcher', *Film Quarterly* 36 (3), 10–17; C. Nagel (2002) 'Pornographic Experience', *Journal of Mundane Behavior*, 3 (1), http://www.mundanebehavior.org/issues/v3n1/nagel3-1.htm. Accessed 21 December 2005); and P. Willemen (2004) 'For a Pornoscape', in P. Church Gibson (ed.) *More Dirty Looks: Gender, Pornography and Power*. London: British Film Institute, 9–26.

CHAPTER 11

1 Quoted in S. Faludi (1995) 'The Money Shot', *The New Yorker*, October 13, 70.

2 As William Ian Miller describes it, 'disgust is there to prevent the activation of unconscious desire, or, more precisely, disgust is part of the very process of repression that makes such desires unconscious'; in *The Anatomy of Disgust* (1997), Cambridge: Harvard University Press, 109.

3 On Arbuckle and comedy, see J. P. Telotte (1988) 'Arbuckle Escapes', *Journal of Popular Film and Television*, 15, 4, 172–9.

4 On the subject of these and other 'gross' film genres, see W. Paul (1994) *Laughing Screaming: Modern Hollywood Horror and Comedy*. New York: Columbia University Press. The most important piece of work on 'body-genres' remains L. Williams (1991) 'Film Bodies: Gender, Genre, and Excess', *Film Quarterly*, 44, 4, 141–59.

5 P. Mellencamp (1992) 'Jokes and Their Relation to TV', in *High Anxiety: Catastrophe, Scandal, Age, and Comedy*. Bloomington: Indiana University Press, 337.

6   A. Carter (1978) *The Sadeian Woman and the Ideology of Pornography*. New York: Harper & Row, 16.

7   See M. Bakhtin (1984) *Rabelais and His World*. Bloomington. Indiana University Press.

8   L. Kipnis (1993) '(Male) Desire and (Female) Disgust: Reading Hustler', in *Ecstasy Unlimited: On Sex, Capital, Gender, and Aesthetics*. Minneapolis: University of Minnesota Press, 219–42; L. Kipnis (1996) *Bound and Gagged: Pornography and the Politics of Fantasy in America*. New York. Grove Press; and C. Penley (1997) 'Crackers and Whackers: The White Trashing of Porn', in M. Wray and A. Newitz (eds) *White Trash: Race and Class in America*. New York: Routledge, 89–112.

9   See N. Armstrong (1990) 'The Pornographic Effect: A Response', *American Journal of Semiotics*, 7, 27–44; A. Dworkin (1989) *Pornography: Men Possessing Women*. New York: Plume; S. Gubar (1989) 'Representing Pornography: Feminism, Criticism, and Depictions of Female Violation', in S. Gubar and J. Hoff (eds) *For Adult Users Only: The Dilemma of Violent Pornography*. Bloomington: Indiana University Press, 47–67.

10   See L. Williams (1995) 'Corporealized Observers: Visual Pornographies and the "Carnal Density of Vision"', in P. Petro (ed.) *Fugitive Images: From Photography to Video*. Bloomington: Indiana University Press; and L. Williams (1989) *Hard Core: Power, Pleasure, and the 'Frenzy of the Visible'*. Berkeley: University of California Press.

11   See, for example, F. Ferguson (1995) 'Pornography: The Theory', in *Critical Inquiry*, 21, 670–95.

12   C. Patton (1996) 'Visualizing Safe Sex', in *Fatal Advice: How Safe-Sex Education Went Wrong*. Durham: Duke University Press, 128.

13   Quoted in 'The Money Shot: An Interview With Ron Jeremy' In: *The Onion*, September 1999. 3. Http:// avclub.theonion.com/avclub3119/avfeature3119.html.

14   See T. Gunning (1989) 'An Aesthetic of Astonishment: Early Film and the (In)Credulous Spectator', in *Art and Text*, 34, 818–32; T. Gunning (1996) 'The Cinema of Attractions: Early Film, Its Spectator, and the Avant-Garde', in *Wide Angle*, 8, 63–70; T. Gunning (1991) 'From Obscene Films to High-Class Drama', in *D. W. Griffith and the Origins of American Silent Film*, Illinois: University of Illinois Press, 43-67; T. Gunning (1996) '"Now You See It, Now You Don't": The Temporality of the Cinema of Attractions' in R. Abel (ed.) *Silent Film*. London: British Film Institute, 95–103; and T. Gunning (1996) and 'Primitive Cinema': A Frame-Up? Or, the Trick's On Us' in R. Abel (ed.) *Silent Film*. London: British Film Institute, 3–12.

15   See N. Burch (1990) *Life to Those Shadows*. Cambridge: Harvard University Press; M. Hansen (1991) *Babel and Babylon: Spectatorship in American Silent Film*. Cambridge: Harvard University Press; and L. Williams (1986) 'Film Body: An Implantation of Perversions', in P. Rosen (ed.) *Narrative, Apparatus, Ideology: A Film Theory Reader*. New York: Columbia University Press.

16   K. Silverman (1983) *The Subject of Semiotics*. New York: Oxford University Press, 61.

17   B. Kaite (1995) *Pornography and Difference*. Bloomington: Indiana University Press, 80.

18   See S. Stewart (1991) 'The Marquis de Meese', in *Crimes of Writing: Problems in the Containment of Representation*. Durham: Duke University Press, 235–72.

19   L. Kipnis (1996) *Bound and Gagged: Pornography and the Politics of Fantasy in America*. New York. Grove Press, 95.

20   See L. Berlant (1996) 'America, "Fat", the Fetus', in *The Queen of America Goes to Washington City*. Durham: Duke University Press, 83–144.

CHAPTER 12

1   S. Hampson (2007) 'Porn – the elephant in the bedroom', *Globe & Mail*, 12 July, available at http://www. theglobeandmail.com/servlet/story/RTGAM.20070712.wlgenex0712/BNStory/lifeFamily. Accessed 19 July 2007.

2   F. Attwood (2007) '"Other" or "One of Us"?: The Porn User in Public Academic Discourse', *Participations*, 4, (1), available at http://www.participations.org/Volume%204/Issue%201/4_01_attwood.htm. Accessed

1 June 2007.

3 M. Gilding (2004) 'Book Review: *Virtual Nation: The Internet in Australia*', *Australian Journal of Emerging Technologies and Society*, 2, (2), 153, available at http://www.swinburne.edu.au/sbs/ajets/journal/V2N2/V2N2-BR.htm. Accessed 26 March 2007.

4 A. McKee (2006) *The Aesthetics of Pornography: The Insights of Consumers, Journal of Media & Cultural Studies*, 20, (4), 524.

5 Ibid., 535.

6 C. Smith (2007) *One for the Girls!: The Pleasures and Practices of Reading Women's Porn*. Bristol: Intellect.

7 Z. F. Parvez (2006) 'The Labor of Pleasure: How Perceptions of Emotional Labor Impact Women's Enjoyment of Pornography', *Gender and Society*, 20 (5), 605–63.

8 'Maggie'; interview with the author, 22 March 2007. All interviewee names have been changed.

9 G. Greer (1971) *The Female Eunuch*. London: McGraw Hill.

10 'Judith'; interview with the author, 13 January 2007.

11 See B. McNair (2002), *Striptease Culture: Sex, Media and the Democratization of Desire*. London: Routledge.

12 See A. Levy (2005) *Female Chauvinist Pigs: Women and the Rise of Raunch Culture*. New York: Free Press; and P. Paul (2005) *Pornified: How Pornography is Transforming our Lives, Our Relationships and Our Families*. New York: Times Books.

13 'Angela'; interview with the author, 2 February 2007.

14 'Chris'; interview with the author, 20 February 2007.

15 N. Crossley (2006) 'In the Gym: Motives, Meaning and Moral Careers', in *Body and Society*, 12 (3), 31.

16 'Chris'; interview with the author, 20 February 2007.

17 N. Crossley (2006) 'In the Gym: Motives, Meaning and Moral Careers', in *Body and Society*, 12 (3), 32.

18 'Angela'; interview with the author, 2 February 2007. The films discussed here are *Pam and Tommy Lee: Stolen Honeymoon*, directed by Tommy Lee, Internet Entertainment Group, 1998; *1 Night in Paris*, directed by Rick Salomon, Red Light District, 2004; *Casting Cuties 4*, directed by Phil Barry, Pumpkin Films, 2006; Ben Dover is the nom de porn of Simon Lindsay Honey, British actor and director of the *Ben Dover* series of films made in the UK between 1996 and 2002.

19 'Maggie'; interview with the author, 22 March 2007.

20 'Judith'; interview with the author, 13 January 2007.

21 'Chris'; interview with the author, 20 February 2007.

22 'Samantha', interview with the author, 16 December 2006.

23 'Angela'; interview with the author, 2 February 2007. The film discussed here is *Anna's Mates*, produced and directed by Anna Span, Easy on the Eye Productions, 2002.

24 'Chris'; interview with the author, 20 February 2007. The film discussed here is *The New Devil in Miss Jones*, directed by Paul Thomas, Vivid Entertainment, 2005.

25 Ibid.

26 'Samantha', interview with the author, 16 December 2006.

27 M. Barker and M. Selfe (2007) *Audiences and Receptions of Sexual Violence in Contemporary Cinema: Report to the British Board of Film Classification: 66*, available at http://www.bbfc.co.uk/downloads/pub/Policy%20and%20Research/Audiences%20and%20Receptions%20of%20Sexual%20Violence%20in%20Contemporary%20Cinema.pdf. Accessed 21 October 2008.

28 'Samantha', interview with the author, 16 December 2006.

CHAPTER 13

1 Fairbanks, H. (1976) *NewsWest*, April 30–May 14.

2 P. G. Springer (1977) 'The World's No. 1 Voyeur', *The Advocate*, 9 March, 3.

285

3   Grant Application, 2.

4   G. Kuchar and M. Kuchar (1997) *Reflections From a Cinematic Cesspool*. Berkeley: Zanja Press, 57.

5   J. Ward, *Final Accounting – Lunch*, 1975.

6   C. McDowell (1974) Diaries, vol. 26, 17 April.

7   G. Kuchar. Video Interview (2004). Included as supplement on *Thundercrack*. Dir. Curt McDowell, 1976. DVD. Synapse Films, 2011.

8   Certificate, 1. Marion Eaton, promoting the film in 1977 when it screened at the Seattle Film Festival, used these identical figures when asked about the movie's budget. See J. Hartl (1977) 'Could it Happen Here?', *Seattle Times*, 31 May.

9   See J. Hartl (1977) 'Could It Happen Here?', *Seattle Times*, 31 May.

10   C. McDowell (1975) Diaries, vol. 27, 13 March.

11   Ibid., 15 March.

12   Ibid., 16 March.

13   Ibid., 20 May.

14   Ibid., 26 July.

15   Ibid., 7 August.

16   Ibid., 13 August.

17   For an analysis of the relationship between sexual acts and narrative in the porn feature of the 1970s and 1980s, see L. Williams (1990) *Hard Core: Power, Pleasure, and the 'Frenzy of the Visible'*. Berkeley: University of California Press.

18   C. McDowell (1975) Diaries, vol. 27, 24 March.

19   Ibid., 29 December.

20   C. McDowell (1976) Diaries, vol. 28, January 23.

21   G. Kuchar and M. Kuchar (1997) *Reflections From a Cinematic Cesspool*. Berkeley: Zanja Press, 39.

22   C. McDowell (1976) Diaries, vol. 28, 7 February.

23   Anon. (1976) '*Thundercrack!*', *Daily Variety*, 2 April.

24   T. McCarthy (1976) 'FILMEX Review: *Thundercrack!*', *The Hollywood Reporter*, April 2.

25   J. Michaels (1977) 'Cracking *Thundercrack!*', *The Advocate*, n.d.

26   Ibid.

27   *Income Statement*.

28   *Return of Income*, 1977.

29   *Letter*.

30   Kuchar *Letter*.

31   *Return of Income*, 1978.

32   C. McDowell (1976) Diaries, vol. 28, 18 February.

33   Ibid., 24 January.

34   The complete text of the revisions to the Internal Revenue Code contained in sub-subsection 465 is available online at http://www4.law.cornell.edu/uscode/html/uscode26/usc_sec_26_00000465----000-.html [Accessed January 6, 2009] These revisions drastically reduced financing available for independent filmmakers until the home video boom of the 1980s provided a new source of production money.

35   D. Edwards (1976) FILMEX Programme Notes, *Thundercrack!*

CHAPTER 14

1   L. Williams (1999) *Hard Core: Power, Pleasure, and the 'Frenzy of the Visible'*. Berkeley: University of California Press, 199.

2   See T. E. Morgan (1989) 'A Whip of One's Own: Dominatrix Pornography and the Construction of a Post-modern (Female) Subjectivity', *The American Journal of Semiotics*, 6 (4), 109–36.

3 S. A. Inness (1999) *Tough Girls: Women Warriors and Wonder Women in Popular Culture*. Philadelphia: University of Pennsylvania Press, 25.

4 V. Steele (2001) 'Fashion, Fetish, Fantasy', in E. Tseëlon (ed.) *Masquerade and Identities: Essays on Gender, Sexuality and Marginality*. London: Routledge, 74.

5 C. Shortes (1998) 'Cleaning Up a Sewer', *Journal of Popular Film and Television*, 26 (2), 72.

6 L. Williams (1999) *Hard Core: Power, Pleasure, and the 'Frenzy of the Visible'*. Berkeley: University of California Press, 195.

7 Ibid., 30.

8 V. Steele (2001) 'Fashion, Fetish, Fantasy', in E. Tseëlon (ed.) *Masquerade and Identities: Essays on Gender, Sexuality and Marginality*. London: Routledge, 76.

9 Butler, J. (1990) *Gender Trouble: Feminism and the Subversion of Identity*. New York: Routledge; see aso J. Riviere (1929) 'Womanliness as Masquerade', *International Journal of Psycho-analysis*, 10, 303–13.

10 Y. Tasker (1998) *Working Girls: Gender and Sexuality in Popular Culture*. London: Routledge.

11 J. A. Brown (2004) 'Gender, Sexuality and Toughness: The Bad Girls of Action Film and Comic Books', in S. A. Inness (ed.) *Action Chicks: New Images of Tough Women in Popular Culture*. Basingstoke: Palgrave Macmillan, 47–74.

12 Ibid., 50.

13 Ibid., 52.

14 Ibid., 69; see T. E. Morgan (1989) 'A Whip of One's Own: Dominatrix Pornography and the Construction of a Post-modern (Female) Subjectivity', *The American Journal of Semiotics*, 6 (4), 109–36.

15 C. Penley (2004) 'Crackers and Whackers: The White Trashing of Porn', in L. Williams (ed.) *Porn Studies*. Durham: Duke University Press, 314.

16 B. Creed (1986) 'Horror and the Monstrous-Feminine: An Imaginary Abjection', *Screen*, 27 (1), 44–54.

17 S. Sontag (1969 [1964]) 'Notes on Camp', in *Against Interpretation and Other Essays*. New York: Laurel. 277–93.

18 T. E. Morgan (1989) 'A Whip of One's Own: Dominatrix Pornography and the Construction of a Post-modern (Female) Subjectivity', *The American Journal of Semiotics*, 6 (4), 109.

19 J. Butler (1997) *The Psychic Life of Power: Theories in Subjection*. Stanford: Stanford University Press, 83.

CHAPTER 15

1 Anon. (1968) 'Go-sha no pinku kôgeki' kusokurae!' ('Five [major] companies Pink attack eat shit!'), *Seijin Eiga*, 33 (10), 4–9.

2 See I. Yomota (2000) *Nihon eiga shi 100 nen* (100 Years of Japanese Film History). Tokyo: Shûeisha; and T. Satô (2006) *Nihon eiga shi 3 (1960–2005)* (Japanese Film History 3 (1960–2005)). Tokyo: Iwanami Shoten.

3 See M. Murai (1964) '5-sha o Obiyakasu 300 Man Yen Eiga', *Eiga Geijutsu*, 12 (9), 93–5; and E. Takahashi (1969) 'Gosha no Shijô o Doko Made Kutte Iru Ka', in S. Takamaro (ed.) *Pinku Eiga Hakusho*. Tôkyô: Kinema Junpô-sha, 189–95.

4 E. Takahashi (1969) 'Gosha no Shijô o Doko Made Kutte Iru Ka', in S. Takamaro (ed.) *Pinku Eiga Hakusho*. Tôkyô: Kinema Junpô-sha, 189–95.

5 Author's translation.

CHAPTER 16

1 'About Wolfe', http://www.wolfevideo.com/about.asp. Accessed 20 November 2007.

2 See cover of DVD edition of *Chained Girls/Daughters of Lesbos*, released by Something Weird Video in 2003. Jenni Olson (2004) also comments on this use of punctuation in *The Queer Movie Poster Book*. San Francisco: Chronicle Books, 33.

3   See M. Foucault (1990) *The History of Sexuality: Volume One*. Trans. R. Hurley. London: Penguin.

4   J. Olson (2004) *The Queer Movie Poster Book*. San Francisco: Chronicle Books, 34.

5   See the press book that accompanies the Vintage Collection DVD edition of *That Tender Touch*, released by Wolfe Video in 2007.

6   Ibid.

7   See G. Morris (2000) 'Notes Toward a Lexicon of Roger Corman's New World Pictures', *Bright Lights Film Journal*, 27, http://www.brightlightsfilm.com/27/newworldpictures1.html. Accessed 20 November 2007.

8   P. Cook (2005) 'The Perils and Pleasures of Exploitation Films', in *Screening the Past: Memory and Nostalgia in Cinema*. London: Routledge, 55.

9   Ibid., 57.

10   Ibid., 55.

11   See https://www.wolfevideo.com/press_newreleases.asp#. Accessed 20 November 2007.

12   See press book, *That Tender Touch*.

13   See T. Elsaesser (1987) 'Tales of Sound and Fury: Observations on the Family Melodrama' in C. Gledhill (ed.) *Home Is Where the Heart Is: Studies in Melodrama and the Woman's Film*. London: British Film Institute, 43–69.

14   H. Benshoff and S. Griffin (2006) *Queer Images: A History of Gay and Lesbian Film in America*. Rowman & Littlefield, 69.

15   Ibid., 71.

16   M. Kort (2007) 'Lesbian Grindhouse', *The Advocate*, 22 May, 45.

17   T. Gilchrist (2007) 'So You Like To Watch?', 20 August, http://www.lesbianation.com/article.cfm?section=6&id=16079. Accessed 20 November 2007.

18   J. Olson (2004) *The Queer Movie Poster Book*. San Francisco: Chronicle Books, 33.

19   See S. Bright and J. Posener (1996) *Nothing But the Girl: The Blatant Lesbian Image*. London: Cassell. Cottrell's photography also appeared in the lesbian sex magazine, *On Our Backs*.

20   See cover of DVD edition of *Sugar High Glitter City*, released by SIR in 2001.

21   H. Butler (2004) 'What Do You Call a Lesbian With Long Fingers?: The Development of Lesbian and Dyke Pornography', in L. Williams (ed.) *Porn Studies*. Durham: Duke University Press, 181–2.

22   Ibid., 189.

23   See R. Rhyne (2007) 'Hard-Core Shopping: Educating Consumption in SIR Video Production's Lesbian Porn', *The Velvet Light Trap*, 59, 46.

24   M. Tea (2001) 'Boogie Dykes', http://www.languageisavirus.com/michelle-tea/modules/xfsection/article.php?articleid=449. Accessed 30 November 2007.

25   Ibid.

26   See C. Smyth (1990) 'The Pleasure Threshold: Looking at Lesbian Pornography on Film', *Feminist Review*, 34, 152–9; H. Butler (2004) 'What Do You Call a Lesbian With Long Fingers?: The Development of Lesbian and Dyke Pornography', in L. Williams (ed.) *Porn Studies*. Durham: Duke University Press, 167–97; and R. Rhyne (2007) 'Hard-Core Shopping: Educating Consumption in SIR Video Production's Lesbian Porn', *The Velvet Light Trap*, 59,42–50.

27   See J. Butler (1990) *Gender Trouble*. London: Routledge.

28   R. Rhyne (2007) 'Hard-Core Shopping: Educating Consumption in SIR Video Production's Lesbian Porn', *The Velvet Light Trap*, 59, 47.

29   Back cover DVD edition, *Sugar High Glitter City*.

CHAPTER 17

1   C. Jenks (1992) 'The Other Face of Death: Barbara Steele and La Maschera del demonio', in R. Dyer and J. Vicendeau (eds) *Popular European Cinema*. London: Routledge, 149–62.

2   See X. Mendik (2004) 'Black Sex, Bad Sex: Monstrous Ethnicity in the Black Emanuelle Films', in E. Mathijs and X. Mendik (eds) *Alternative Europe: Eurotrash and Exploitation Cinema Since 1945*. London: Wallflower Press, 146–59.

3   See P. MacCormack (2004) 'Masochistic Cine-Sexuality: The Many Deaths of Giovanni Lombardo Radice', in E. Mathijs and X. Mendik (eds) *Alternative Europe: Eurotrash and Exploitation Cinema Since 1945*. London: Wallflower Press, 106–16.

4   See J. Fay (2004) 'The School Girl Reports and the Guilty Pleasure of History', in E. Mathijs and X. Mendik (eds) *Alternative Europe: Eurotrash and Exploitation Cinema Since 1945*. London: Wallflower Press, 39–52.

5   M. Mackenzie (2004) *Thriller: A Cruel Picture Review* in *DVD Times*: http//www.dvdtimes.co.uk/content.php?content=12790. Accessed 6 October 2007.

CHAPTER 19

1   C. Milliken (1988) 'Unheimlich Manoeuvres: The Genres and Genders of Transsssexual Documentary', *Velvet Light Trap*, 41, 47–61.

2   L. Feinberg (1993) *Stone Butch Blues*. Ann Arbor: Firebrand Books.

3   L. Cameron (1996) *Body Alchemy Transsexual Portraits*. Berkeley: Cleis Press.

4   C. Milliken (1988) 'Unheimlich Manoeuvres: The Genres and Genders of Transsssexual Documentary', *Velvet Light Trap*, 41, 49.

5   L. Kaplan (1991) *Female Perversions*. New York: Doubleday, 9.

6   L. Kipnis (1999) *Bound and Gagged: Pornography and the Politics of Fantasy in America*. Durham: Duke University Press, 201.

7   B. Creed (1993) *The Monstrous Feminine: Film, Feminism, Psychoanalysis*. Routledge: London, 104.

8   R. Dyer (2002) *The Culture of Queers*. Routledge: New York, 206.

9   L. Kipnis (1999) *Bound and Gagged: Pornography and the Politics of Fantasy in America*. Durham: Duke University Press, 164.

CHAPTER 20

1   G. Robertson and A. Nicol (2008) *Media Law*. Fifth edition. London: Penguin, 206.

2   Ibid., 221.

3   Ibid.

4   J. Petley (2000) '"Snuffed out": Nightmares in a Trading Standards Officer's Brain', in X. Mendik and G. Harper (eds) *Unruly Pleasures: The Cult Film and its Critics*. Guildford: FAB Press, 203–19.

5   For further testimony by victims of these raids see G. D. (1994) 'Raided!', *Invasion of the Sad Man-Eating Mushrooms*, 33–5; D. Prothero (1994) 'Hell screen', *Shivers*, 10, January; D. Kerekes and D. Slater (2000) *See No Evil: Banned Films and Video Controversy*. Manchester: Headpress; and the letters columns of *The Dark Side*, nos. 31, 42, 44 and 72.

6   HL Debs, Vol. 701, Col. 269, 30 April 2008.

7   Joint Committee on Human Rights (2008) *Legislative Scrutiny: Criminal Justice and Immigration Bill*. London: The Stationery Office, 15.

8   Ibid., 16.

9   Home Office (2005) *Consultation: On the Possession of Extreme Pornographic Material*. London: Home Office Communication Directorate. This can also be viewed at http://www.homeoffice.gov.uk/documents/cons-extreme-porn-3008051/. Accessed 25 June 2008.

10   Ibid., 10.

11   Ibid., 11.

12 Home Office (2006) *New Offence to Crack Down on Violent and Extreme Pornography*. Press Release [online]. Available from http://press.homeoffice.gov.uk/press-releases/crack-down-on-pornography. Accessed 25 June 2008.

13 HC Debs, Vol. 464, Col. 60, 8 October 2007.

14 HC Debs, Vol. 113, Col. 1359, 3 April 1987.

15 HL Debs, Vol. 700, Cols. 1358–9, 21 April 2008.

16 HC Debs, Vol. 113, Col. 1355, 3 April 1987.

17 HL Debs, Vol. 699, Col. 895, 3 March 2008.

18 S. Sontag (1981) *Under the Sign of Saturn*. New York: Vintage Books, 103.

19 Responses to the consultation were initially available on the Home Office website. However, they are no longer there.

20 HL Debs, Vol. 701, Col. 271, 30 April 2008.

CHAPTER 21

1 E. Schaefer (2006) *Bold! Daring! Shocking! True!: A History of Exploitation Films, 1919–1959*. Durham: Duke University Press, 338.

2 '*Viva*: Q&A with Anna Biller', http://www.altfg.com/blog/hollywood/viva-qa-with-anna-biller. Accessed 3 March 2009.

3 T. Krzywinska (2006) *Sex and the Cinema*. London: Wallflower Press, 42.

4 '*Viva*: Q&A with Anna Biller', http://www.altfg.com/blog/hollywood/viva-qa-with-anna-biller. Accessed 3 March 2009.

5 J. Lacan, J. (1998) *Encore: The Seminar of Jacques Lacan Book XX*. Trans. B. Fink. New York: W. W.Norton, 7.

6 F. Fanon (1994) 'On National Culture', in P. Williams and L. Chrisman (eds) *Colonial Discourse and Post-colonial Theory*. New York: Columbia University Press, 37.

7 T. Krzywinska (2006) *Sex and the Cinema*. London: Wallflower Press, 42.

8 Bataille, G. (1985) *Visions of Excess: Selected Writings, 1927–1939*. Trans. A. Stoekl. Minneapolis: University of Minnesota Press, 119.

9 T. Krzywinska (2006) *Sex and the Cinema*. London: Wallflower Press, 43.

10 G. Bataille (2001) *Eroticism*. Trans. M. Dalwood. London: Penguin, 117–18.

11 L. Pearce (2007) *Romance Writing*. Cambridge: Polity Press, 2.

12 G. Deleuze and F. Guattari (1984) *Anti-Oedipus: Capitalism and Schizophrenia*. Trans. R. Hurley and H. Lane. London: Continuum, 127.

13 T. Krzywinska (2006) *Sex and the Cinema*. London: Wallflower Press, 45.